March 17–18, 2016
Santa Clara, California, USA

I0031388

**Association for
Computing Machinery**

Advancing Computing as a Science & Profession

ANCS'16

Proceedings of the 2016 Symposium on
**Architectures for Networking
and Communications Systems**

Sponsored by:

ACM SIGARCH, ACM SIGCOMM, & IEEE CS

Association for
Computing Machinery

The Association for Computing Machinery
2 Penn Plaza, Suite 701
New York, New York 10121-0701

Advancing Computing as a Science & Profession

Notice to Past Authors of ACM-Published Articles

ACM intends to create a complete electronic archive of all articles and/or other material previously published by ACM. If you have written a work that has been previously published by ACM in any journal or conference proceedings prior to 1978, or any SIG Newsletter at any time, and you do NOT want this work to appear in the ACM Digital Library, please inform permissions@acm.org, stating the title of the work, the author(s), and where and when published.

ISBN: 978-1-4503-4183-7

Additional copies may be ordered prepaid from:

ACM Order Department
PO Box 30777
New York, NY 10087-0777, USA

Phone: 1-800-342-6626 (USA and Canada)
+1-212-626-0500 (Global)
Fax: +1-212-944-1318
E-mail: acmhelp@acm.org
Hours of Operation: 8:30 am – 4:30 pm ET

Printed in the USA   .

ANCS'16 Organizer's Welcome Message

It is our great pleasure to welcome you to the Twelfth ACM/IEEE Symposium on Architectures for Networking and Communications Systems (ANCS 2016). ANCS is once again co-located with the USENIX Symposium on Networked Systems Design and Implementation (NSDI), providing an opportunity for participants from academia and industry to share cutting-edge, system-oriented research results at the intersection of computer and network systems architecture.

Out of 58 submissions, with a highly selective process with about 20% acceptance rate, we have selected 12 high quality papers from USA, Canada, Europe and Asia. This year we have introduced a short paper category to both help quick dissemination of preliminary results, and to support smaller contributions which do not require a full paper format. Each submission was reviewed by at least three PC members, over a very tight schedule; in fact, due to scheduling constraints, the TPC work efficiently and completed their work just before the end of the year. The final accept/reject decisions were made through an extensive online discussion.

The conference could not exist without the work of many people which we would like to thank. First of all authors, who chose to submit their work to our venue. TPC members did great work in providing timely and detailed reviews under deadlines shorter than usual, and near to major holidays. Finally, we are grateful to the members of the organizing committee who worked behind the scenes to make sure that the web site & communications (Haowei Yuan), publications (Norbert Egi), financial arrangements (Danai Chasaki), and poster session (Hyesook Lim), along with other organizational issues, were handled in a timely and effective fashion. We are also indebted to Eddie Kohler for producing HotCRP which greatly eases the entire review process.

We look forward to see you at ANCS'16!

Patrick Crowley, *General Chair*
Laurent Mathy, *TPC Co-Chair*
Luigi Rizzo, *TPC Co-Chair*

Table of Contents

Technical Session 1

Technical Session 2

Technical Session 3

Technical Session 4

Posters

12th 2016 ACM/IEEE Symposium on Architectures for Networking and Communications Systems (ANCS'16)

General Chair: Patrick Crowley *(Washington University in St. Louis, USA)*

Program Chairs: Luigi Rizzo *(Università di Pisa, Italy)*

Laurent Mathy *(Université de Liège, Belgium)*

Proceedings Chair: Norbert Egi *(Huawei, USA)*

Finance Chair: Danai Chasaki *(Villanova University, USA)*

Publicity/Web Chair: Haowei Yuan *(Washington University in St. Louis, USA)*

Poster Chair: Hyesook Lim *(Ewha Womans University, Korea)*

Travel Grants Chair: Ning Weng *(Southern Illinois University, USA)*

Steering Committee: Gordon Brebner *(Xilinx, USA)*
Chita Das *(Pennsylvania State University, USA)*
Bill Lin *(University of California, San Diego, USA)*
Andrew W. Moore *(University of Cambridge, UK)*
Walid Najjar *(University of California, Riverside, USA)*
Viktor Prasanna *(University of Southern California, USA)*
Scott Rixner *(Rice University, USA)*
Tilman Wolf *(University of Massachusetts Amherst, USA)*

Technical Program Committee: Theophilius Benson *(Duke University, USA)*
Gordon Brebner *(Xilinx, USA)*
Paolo Costa *(Microsoft Research Cambridge, UK)*
Patrick Crowley *(Washington University in St. Louis, USA)*
Luca Deri *(Università di Pisa, IT)*
Colin Dixon *(Brocade, USA)*
Lars Eggert *(NetApp, DE)*
Nate Foster *(Cornell University, USA)*
Dongsu Han *(KAIST, KR)*
Euan Harris *(Citrix, UK)*
Felipe Huici *(NEC Europe, DE)*
Layong Luo *(Microsoft Research Asia, CN)*
Richard Mortier *(University of Cambridge, UK)*
Rolf Neugebauer *(Netronome, UK)*
Craig Partridge *(BBN Technologies, USA)*

Sponsors:

O³FA: A Scalable Finite Automata-based Pattern-Matching Engine for Out-of-Order Deep Packet Inspection

Xiaodong Yu, Wu-chun Feng, Danfeng (Daphne) Yao
Department of Computer Science
Virginia Tech
Blacksburg, VA, USA
{xdyu, feng, danfeng}@cs.vt.edu

Michela Becchi
Dept. of Electrical and Computer Engineering
University of Missouri
Columbia, MO, USA
becchim@missouri.edu

ABSTRACT

To match the signatures of malicious traffic across packet boundaries, network-intrusion detection (and prevention) systems (NIDS) typically perform pattern matching after flow reassembly or packet reordering. However, this may lead to the need for large packet buffers, making detection vulnerable to denial-of-service (DoS) attacks, whereby attackers exhaust the buffer capacity by sending long sequences of out-of-order packets. While researchers have proposed solutions for exact-match patterns, regular-expression matching on out-of-order packets is still an open problem. Specifically, a key challenge is the matching of complex sub-patterns (such as repetitions of wildcards matched at the boundary between packets). Our proposed approach leverages the insight that various segments matching the same repetitive sub-pattern are logically equivalent to the regular-expression matching engine, and thus, interchanging them would not affect the final result.

In this paper, we present O³FA, a new finite automata-based, deep packet-inspection engine to perform regular-expression matching on out-of-order packets *without* requiring flow reassembly. O³FA consists of a deterministic finite automaton (FA) coupled with a set of prefix-/suffix-FA, which allows processing out-of-order packets on the fly. We present our design, optimization, and evaluation for the O³FA engine. Our experiments show that our design requires 20x-4000x less buffer space than conventional buffering-and-reassembling schemes on various datasets and that it can process packets in real-time, i.e., without reassembly.

1. INTRODUCTION

Regular-expression matching is a core task in deep packet inspection (DPI), which is a fundamental networking operation. A traditional form of DPI consists of searching the packet payload against a set of patterns. Network intrusion detection systems (NIDS) are an essential part of network security devices. A NIDS receives and processes packets, and then reports the possible intrusions. Some well-known open-source NIDS – such as Snort and Bro – employ DPI as their core; most major networking companies offer their own NIDS solutions (e.g., security appliances from Cisco and Juniper Networks). In NIDS, every pattern represents a signature of malicious traffic; thus, the DPI engine of a NIDS inspects the incoming packets payloads against all available signatures and triggers pre-defined actions if a match is detected. A regular expression can cover a wide variety of pattern signatures [1-3]. Because of their expressive power, regular expressions have been increasingly adopted to express pattern sets in both industry and academia. To allow multi-pattern search, current NIDS mostly represent the pattern-set through finite automata (FA) [4], either in their deterministic or in their non-deterministic form (DFA and NFA, respectively).

A large body of research has focused on developing efficient regular-expression matching engines. For memory-centric solutions, where the automaton is stored in memory, DFA-based approaches are more popular than NFA-based ones because of their predictable memory bandwidth requirements. Specifically, processing an input character involves only one DFA state traversal, which can be translated into a deterministic number of memory accesses. However, this attractive property comes at the cost of potentially large requirements for memory space. In fact, DFAs constructed from large and complex sets of regular expressions may suffer from the state explosion problem, making the storage requirements prohibitively large. State explosion can take place during DFA generation when the corresponding regular expressions have repetitions of wildcards and/or large character sets. Several variants of DFA [5-11] have been proposed to address this problem, and thus, limit the effects of state explosion with varying degree.

In real-world scenarios, a network data stream can span multiple packets. Those packets can arrive at network security devices out of order due to multiple routes, packet retransmission, or NIDS evasion. Thus, the packets must be re-ordered appropriately upon receipt. Previous work analyzing Internet traffic has reported that about 2%-5% of packets are affected by reordering [12-14]. However, these studies have focused on benign traffic; while attackers may intentionally mis-order legitimate traffic to trigger denial-of-service (DoS) attacks [14]. NIDS face challenges [15] when processing data streams that span across out-of-order packets, especially when performing regular-expression matching against traffic containing malicious content that is located *across* packets boundaries. In such cases, the malicious patterns are split and carried by multiple packets; and NIDS cannot detect them by processing those packets individually.

Several solutions have been proposed to address the problem of processing out-of-order packets in NIDS. One approach that is widely adopted in current network devices is *packet buffering* and *stream reassembling* [14, 16-18]. In this case, incoming packets are buffered and packet streams are reassembled based on the

ANCS '16, March 17-18, 2016, Santa Clara, CA, USA
© 2016 ACM. ISBN 978-1-4503-4183-7/16/03...$15.00
DOI: http://dx.doi.org/10.1145/2881025.2881034

information in the header fields. Regular-expression matching is then performed on the reassembled data stream. This approach is intuitive and easy to implement but can be very resource-intensive and vulnerable to DoS attacks, whereby attackers exhaust the packet buffer capacity by sending long sequences of out-of-order packets. Recently, researchers have proposed several new solutions [19-21] aimed to relieve packet-buffer pressure or even avoid packet buffering and reassembling. This is done by tracking all possible traversal paths or leveraging data structures such as suffix trees. While they alleviate the burden of handing out-of-order packets to some extent, these methods are either applicable only to simple patterns (exact-match strings or fixed-length patterns) or suffer from undesirable worst-case properties (and are therefore still vulnerable to DoS attacks).

In this work, we aim to provide a solution that (1) processes out-of-order packets without requiring packet buffering and stream reassembling, (2) relies only on finite automata, and (3) handles regular expressions with complex sub-patterns. One of the main challenges in our design comes from handling regular expressions that include unbounded repetitions of wildcards and large character sets. Why is this a challenge? These sub-patterns can represent unbounded sets of exact-match substrings that cannot be exhaustively enumerated. Our solution leverages the following observation: *all exact-match strings that match a repetition sub-pattern are functionally equivalent from the point of view of the regular-expression matching engine and interchanging them will not affect the final matching result.* Our proposed solution consists of regular DFAs coupled with a set of supporting FAs either in NFA or DFA form. The supporting FAs are used to detect and record – using only a few states (typically no more than five) – segments of packets that can potentially be part of a match across packet boundaries. While processing packets out-of-order, those segments can be dynamically retrieved from the recorded states and can be then used to resolve matches across packet boundaries.

To be efficient, any automata-based solution requires minimizing the number of automata, their size, and the number of states that can be active in parallel. Our approach includes optimizations aimed to achieve these goals. In summary, our contributions are as follows:

- O³FA, a new finite automata-based DPI engine to perform regular-expression matching on out-of-order packets in real time, i.e., without requiring flow reassembly.
- Several optimizations to improve the average- and worst-case behavior of the O³FA engine and an analysis of how packet ordering affects the buffer size.
- An evaluation our O³FA engine on various real-world and synthetic datasets, where our results show that the O³FA engine requires 20x-4000x less buffer space than conventional buffering and reassembling-based solutions but with only 0.0006%-5% traversal overhead.

2. BACKGROUND & RELATED WORK

Finite automata (FA) are widely used to perform regular-expression matching. In automata-based approaches, the matching operation is equivalent to a FA traversal that is guided by the content of the input stream. Worst-case guarantees on the input processing time can be met by bounding the amount of per-character processing. As the basic data structure in the regular-expression matching engine, the finite automaton must be deployable on a reasonably provisioned hardware platform. As the size of pattern-sets and the expressiveness of individual patterns in-

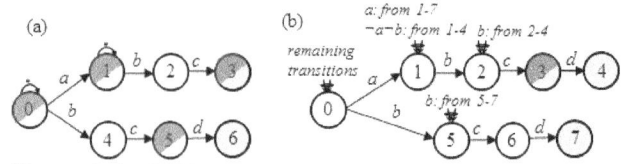

Figure 1. (a) NFA and (b) DFA accepting regular expressions a.*bc and bcd. Accepting states are colored gray. States active at the end of the processing of input acbc are highlighted with a diagonal filling. In the NFA, states 0 and 1 have a self-loop on any characters of the alphabet. In the DFA, state 1 has incoming transitions on character b from states 1 to 7, and incoming transitions from states 1 to 4 on any characters other than a and b (incoming transitions to states 0, 2 and 5 can be read in the same way).

crease, limiting the size of the automaton becomes challenging. The exploration space is characterized by a trade-off between the size of the automaton and the worst-case bound on the amount of per-character processing. Non-deterministic and deterministic finite automata (NFAs and DFAs, respectively) are at the two extremes of this exploration space. NFAs have a limited size but can require expensive per-character processing, whereas DFAs offer limited per-character processing but at the cost of a possibly large automaton. As an example, Figure 1 shows the NFA and DFA accepting regular expressions a.*bc and bcd (the dot-star sub-pattern ".*" represents any segment with any length). In the figure, the states active after processing input stream acbc are highlighted using diagonal filling. As can be seen, the NFA consists of fewer states, i.e., seven (7) versus eight (8), while the DFA leads to less per-character processing, i.e.,one (1) versus four (4) concurrently active states.

While offering this attractive traversal property, DFAs can suffer from the well-known state explosion problem. Each DFA state corresponds to a set of NFA states that can be simultaneously active [4]. Therefore, given an N-state NFA, the functionally equivalent DFA may potentially have up to 2^N states. This state explosion may limit the DFA's ability to handle large and complex sets of regular expressions (typically those that include bounded and unbounded repetitions of wildcards or large character sets). Existing proposals targeting DFA-based solutions have focused on two aspects: (i) designing compression schemes aimed at minimizing the DFA memory footprint; and (ii) devising new automata to alternate DFAs in case of state explosion. Alphabet reduction [5, 22-24], run-length encoding [5], default transition compression [22, 25], state merging [7] and delta-FAs [26] fall in the first category, while multiple-DFAs [5, 6], hybrid-FAs [7], history-based-FAs [8], XFAs [9], counting-FAs [10], and JFAs [11] fall in the second category. All of these solutions, however, have been designed to operate on reassembled packet streams.

The classic approach (to tackle the packet reordering problem) buffers the received data packets, reorders them, and finally reassembles the packet stream (or packet flow). Dharmapurikar et al. [14] propose a system to buffer and reorder packets. Their system consists of a packet analyzer, an out-of-order packet processing unit, and a buffer manager. It mitigates the risk of denial-of-service (DoS) attacks by forcing attackers to use multiple attacking hosts. However, the system is still vulnerable to attacks, exhausting the buffer capacity. Similar packet buffering and stream reassembly solutions have also been proposed and adopted in industry (e.g. Cisco [16], Nortel Networks [17], and Netrake [18]).

Despite its widespread adoption, this buffering and reassembling approach is vulnerable to DoS attacks whereby attackers exhaust the buffer capacity by sending long sequences of out-of-order packets. There have been a handful of proposals attempting to reduce these risks by avoiding packet buffering and stream reassembly.

For example, Varghese et al. [27] propose Split-Detect. This system splits the signatures of malicious traffic into pieces, performs deep packet inspection on these sub-signatures, and diverts the TCP packets for reassembly from the fast path to the slow path upon detection of any of these sub-signatures. Split-Detect can achieve up to 90% storage requirement reduction compared to conventional NIDS. However, rather than avoiding stream reassembly, it offloads it to the slow path. In addition, Split-Detect is restricted to exact-match signatures and patterns with a fixed length. In contrast, our approach works on arbitrarily-sized patterns.

Johnson et al. [21] propose a DFA-based solution that, for each packet, performs parallel traversals from each and all DFA states. Because the initial DFA state is unknown when processing an out-of-order packet, any DFA state must be considered a potential initial state. A post-processing step is then be performed to reconstruct valid traversals at packet boundaries. Although this scheme may be effective in the presence of non-malicious traffic (where the traversal is limited to a few DFA states), it does not provide a good worst-case bound, and it may involve a large amount of post-processing.

More recently, Chen et al. [20] propose AC-Suffix-Tree. This scheme avoids packet buffering and stream reassembly by combining an Aho-Corasick DFA with a suffix tree. Zhang et al. [19] propose On-Line Reassembly (OLR), a scheme that stores patterns in a directed acyclic word graph (DAWG). Both of these solutions, however, apply only to exact-match patterns and are unable to handle regular expressions, which are more common in real-world applications. Our approach does not suffer from this limitation.

3. O³FA DESIGN

In this section, we present our approach for performing regular-expression matching on out-of-order packets without requiring prior stream reassembly. The main challenge in this problem comes from *the handling of matches across packet boundaries*. At a high level, our proposed solution couples one or more DFAs with *supporting-FAs*. The DFAs find matches within a packet while the supporting-FAs detect and record segments of packets that can potentially be part of a match across packet boundaries. While processing out-of-order packets, these segments can be dynamically retrieved from the state information collected on the supporting-FAs, and they can subsequently be concatenated to the incoming packet in order to handle cross-packet matches.

To have an intuition of this idea, consider matching input stream *cabcdeab* against pattern *b.*cde*. Let us assume that this input stream spans across two packets: $P_1=cabc$ and $P_2=deab$. We can observe that pattern *b.*cde* is matched across packet boundaries (the match starts in P_1 and ends in P_2; the *segments* of P_1 and P_2 involved in the match are underlined). If we use a DFA, this match will be detected only if packets P_1 and P_2 are processed in order. If the packets are processed out of order, we will need a way to detect that segment *de* of P_2 and segment *bc* of P_1 are partial matches (specifically, they match the suffix and the prefix of the considered patterns, respectively). We will then use this information to reconstruct the match. Our proposed supporting-FA

serves this purpose. We note that, because *b.*cde* is neither an exact-match string nor a fixed-length pattern, it cannot be handled by previous approaches such as SplitDetect [27], AC-Suffix-Tree [20], and ORL [19].

Because we are concerned about patterns with variable length, we focus on regular expressions containing repetitions of characters (e.g., $c+$ and $c*$), character sets (e.g, $[c_i\text{-}c_j]*$), and wildcards (.*). We note that regular expressions without these features can be handled by traditional methods. For example, a regular expression containing a non-repeated character set $[c_i\text{-}c_j]$ can be transformed by exhaustive enumeration into a set of exact-match patterns. For readability and in the interest of space, the remaining description focuses on the more general case (wildcard repetitions); however, our solution applies to all kinds of repetitions.

A central question in the O³FA design is as follows: how can we identify the *minimal* packet segments that must be recorded in order to handle cross-packet matches? We note that excessively long segments would pose pressure on the required packet buffer and on the amount of processing involved in the matching operation, thus leading to inefficiencies. Our design leverages the following observations.

Observation 1: If a regular expression R is matched across a set of packets $P_1,..., P_N$, then the suffix of P_1 must match a prefix of R and the prefix of P^N must match a suffix of R.

Observation 2: Given a regular expression R in the form $sp_1.*sp_2$ and an input stream I containing a matching segment of the form M_1M*M_2, where M_1 matches sp_1 and M_2 matches sp_2, any modifications to I that substitutes $M*$ with a shorter segment will not affect the match outcome.

According to Observation 1, O³FA must detect segments of incoming packets that match any suffixes/prefixes of the considered regular expressions. These segments are recorded by storing the corresponding matching states information, and they can be dynamically retrieved and properly concatenated with later-arrival packets to detect cross-boundary matching. For example, while matching regular expression *b.*cde* on packets $P_1=caba$, $P_2=dcac$ and $P_3=dead$ that arrive in order $P_3 \rightarrow P_1 \rightarrow P_2$, we first detect that segment *de* in P_3 matches suffix *de*, and then that segment *ba* in P_1 matches prefix *b.*. When P_2 arrives, we retrieve those segments and concatenate them with P_2, then conduct regular expression matching on *badcacde* and detect the cross-boundary matching of *b.*cde*. In general, prefix *b.** can match arbitrarily long strings, which may span across any number of intermediate packets.

However, according to Observation 2, in order to reconstruct the match, it is sufficient to record the shortest segment of the input stream that matches the regular expression with the wildcard repetition. In the considered example, rather than recording segment *ba* of packet P_1, we can simply record segment *b*. In addition, if a regular expression *p.*s* is matched across a set of packets $P_1,..,P_N$ such that the suffix of P_1 matches p and the prefix of P_N matches s, recording the intermediate packets $P_2,..,P_{N-1}$ will not be necessary for matching purposes.

The design is complicated by the fact that multiple regular expressions would require recording multiple segments, possibly leading to inefficiencies. In section 4 we propose a mechanism (that we call Functionally Equivalent Packets) to combine segments related to different regular expressions. As we will discuss, this method leverages the overlap between different segments.

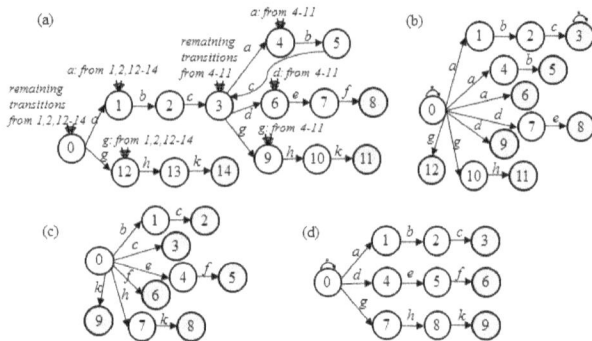

Figure 2. (a) DFA accepting pattern set {abc.*def, ghk}, (b) prefix-FA, (c) anchored suffix-FA and (d) unanchored suffix-FA built upon corresponding prefix set, anchored suffix set and unanchored suffix set. Accepting states are colored gray.

3.1 O³FA Data Structure

We now discuss the design of O³FA, a composite automata-based solution that implements the scheme described above. As mentioned, O³FA consists of two components:

- One or more "regular" **DFAs** used to perform regular expression matching and constructed based on the given regular expression set. Any automata optimization techniques [5-11, 22, 25, 26, 28] can be applied to these DFAs.
- **Supporting-FAs** used to detect and record significant segments of incoming packets. According to the above discussion, supporting-FAs should be constructed to detect segments matching regular expressions' prefixes and suffixes, and can therefore be of two kinds: *prefix-FAs* and *suffix-FAs*. These automata can be in either NFA or in DFA form.

In order to build the prefix- and suffix-FAs, we split the regular expressions at the positions of the repetition sub-patterns. For example, regular expression *abc.*def.*ghk* will be broken down into three sub-patterns: *.*abc.**, *.*def.** and *.*ghk* (the .* before *abc* is due to the fact that the original regular expression is unanchored, that is, it can be matched at any position of the input stream). This breakdown is possible because the supporting-FAs are used to record packet segments, and not to perform pattern matching; the short packet segments recorded by breaking down the regular expressions into sub-patterns will be concatenated into larger segments during processing. This breakdown allows significantly simplifying the supporting automata: by allowing dot-star terms to appear only at the beginning or at the end of each pattern, it will avoid state explosion when representing the supporting-FAs in DFA form. The full prefix and suffix sets corresponding to the given sub-patterns are: {.*abc.*, .*abc, .*ab, .*a, .*def.*, .*def, .*de, .*d, .*ghk, .*gh, .*g} and {.*abc.*, abc.*, bc.*, c.*, .*def.*, def.*, ef.*, f.*, .*ghk, ghk, hk, k}, respectively.

However, some simplifications are possible. First, since the suffixes must be matched at the beginning of packets (Observation 1) and can end anywhere within a packet, the ".*" at the end of each suffix is redundant. Second, patterns that are common to prefix and suffix sets (e.g. .*abc, .*def, .*ghk) can be removed from the prefix set (these patterns would lead to the detection of the same segments[1]). Third, sub-patterns that are covered by more general

patterns belonging to the same set (e.g. *abc* is a special case of .*abc) can also be eliminated. After these simplifications, the prefix and suffix sets used to build the prefix- and suffix-FA will be {.*abc.*, .*ab, .*a, .*def.*, .*de, .*d, .*gh, .*g} and {.*abc, bc, c, .*def, ef, f, .*ghk, hk, k}, respectively. Note that the suffix set contains both anchored and unanchored patterns (the latter start by ".*"). These two groups of patterns can be compiled in two different suffix-Fas (i.e., an *anchored* and an *unanchored suffix-FA*) to allow space optimizations when representing the automata in DFA form.

During processing, upon a match within a supporting-FA, the corresponding accepting state must be recorded, and it will then be used to retrieve the packet segments to be concatenated to the current input packet. This "extended" input packet will then be processed by the "regular" DFA. However, some matches that occur within the supporting-FAs can be discarded, thus diminishing the amount of information that must be recorded to reconstruct relevant packet segments. First, since prefixes need to be matched only at the end of packets (Observation 1), all prefix matches occurring in the middle of any packets can be discarded. Second, if multiple anchored suffixes of a regular expression are matched, only the longest one must be recorded (shorter suffixes will be subsumed by it).

Figure 2 shows an example on regular expression set {abc.*def, ghk}, both patterns are unanchored (that is, they can be matched at any position of the input stream). The prefix set, anchored suffix set and unanchored suffix set are {.*abc.*, .*ab, .*a, .*de, .*d, .*gh, .*g}, {bc, c, ef, f, hk, k} and {.*abc, .*def, .*ghk}, respectively. Figure 2 (a)-(d) show the resulting regular DFA, prefix-FA, anchored suffix-FA and unanchored suffix-FA; all supporting-FAs are left in NFA form. We assume three input packets: P_1=*bhab*, P_2=*cegh* and P_3=*adef*, with the arriving order being $P_3 \rightarrow P_1 \rightarrow P_2$. After P_3 is processed, the matching state sets of regular DFA and anchored suffix-FA are empty; the unanchored suffix-FA matching states is 6; the prefix-FA matching states are {8, 9}; since those matches do not happen at the tail of P_3, they will be discarded. Then, we process P_1; the matching state sets of regular DFA, anchored suffix-FA and unanchored suffix-FA are empty; the prefix-FA matching states are {5, 6}; since only matching state 5 is active at the end of P_1 processing, this sole prefix-FA state will be recorded. When P_2 arrives, we should first check the recorded information of its previously processed neighbor packets (i.e., predecessor P_1 and successor P_3): P_1 has a recorded prefix-FA state 5; the retrieved segment is *ab* and should be concatenated to P_2 as a prefix. P_3 has a recorded unanchored suffix-FA state 6; the retrieved segment is *def* and should be concatenated to P_2 as a suffix. Then, the modified P_2 is *abceghdef*; after it is processed with the regular DFA, the matching of the pattern *abc.*def* will be reported.

4. OPTIMIZATIONS

Our basic O³FA design has two limitations: it can lead to false positives (that is, it may report invalid matches) and it can suffer from inefficiencies during processing. In this section, we describe a mechanism – called Index Tags – to avoid false positives, and a suitable format for the supporting-FAs and two auxiliary data structures to improve the matching speed.

---

[1] The reason why these patterns are removed by the prefix set will become apparent later. Specifically, since all prefix matches in

the middle of packets can be discarded, keeping these patterns in the suffix set ensures that they will be detected by the suffix-FA.

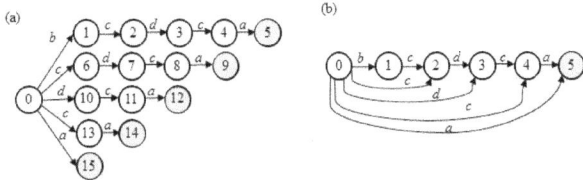

Figure 3. (a) Basic asNFA and (b) optimized csNFA built upon anchored suffix set {*bcdca, cdca, dca, ca, a*}. Accepting states are colored gray.

4.1 Index Tags

Our initial O^3FA engine design may report false positives in the presence of multiple regular expressions. For example, consider a dataset with two regular expressions: {*bc.*d, acd*}. Two input packets P_1:*caaba* and P_2:*cabdc* are received out of order ($P_2 \rightarrow P_1$). Obviously, no matches should be reported on the corresponding input stream *caabacabdc*. However, in our basic O^3FA design, the anchored suffix-FA will detect the segment *cabd* of P_2 that matches suffix *c.*d* of the first pattern; when P_1 arrives, segment *cd* will be retrieved and concatenated to P_1 as a suffix, leading to the extended packet *caabacd*. Processing this packet with the regular DFA will lead to the false match *acd* to be reported.

To understand the root cause of this problem, we make the following observation.

Observation 3: Let R be a set of regular expressions, R' a proper subset of R, and r a regular expression belonging to R but not to R'. Let S be the set of segments of the input packets that match any prefix or suffix of regular expressions in R'. If there exists at least a segment in S that also matches a prefix or suffix of regular expression r, then a false positive can be reported during processing.

In the example above, let R be {*bc.*d, acd*}, and R' be {*bc.*d*}. We observe that segment *cd* of P_2 matches pattern *bc.*d* in R as well as pattern *acd* that belongs to R but not to R'. This fact leads to the false positive indicated above.

Based on this observation, in order to eliminate false positives, we must correlate the matched suffixes and prefixes with the corresponding regular expressions. To this end, we assign an *index tag* to each regular expression, and associate these index tags to the corresponding accepting states within regular and supporting FAs. During processing, we store the index tags associated to all traversed supporting-FA accepting states in a *tag list*. When the regular DFA reports a match, if the index tag of the matched regular expression is in the tag list, then the match is valid; otherwise, it is a false positive. Consider the example above; let *tag1* and *tag2* be the index tags of patterns *bc.*d* and *acd*, correspondingly. When the prefix *cabd* of P_2 is detected to match suffix *c.*d* of the first pattern, *tag1* is pushed in the tag list. After the extended packet *caabacd* is processed against the regular DFA, the match of pattern *acd* will be discarded as false positive, since the index tag *tag2* is not in the tag list.

4.2 Compressed Suffix-NFA

As mentioned above, the supporting-FAs may be represented either in NFA or in DFA form. We recall that NFAs are compact but may suffer from multiple concurrent state activations, which may negatively affect the processing time. On the other hand, DFAs have the benefit of a single state activation for each input

character at the cost of a potentially large number of states, affecting the memory space required to encode the automaton. In this section, we point out the most effective representation for each of the supporting-FAs.

We recall that, in our O^3FA design, the anchored suffix set contains only exact-match patterns. An NFA containing only anchored exact-match patterns can have only one active state. Thus, the anchored suffix-FA can be left in NFA form without loss in processing efficiency. We denote this automaton as **anchored suffix-NFA (asNFA)**.

The anchored suffix set can have a large amount of redundancy due to the nature of suffixes. An n-character pattern can lead to n-1 suffixes, with every two adjacent suffixes differing in only one character. This creates compression opportunities for asNFA. We propose a **compressed suffix-NFA (csNFA)** representation, which reduces both the asNFA size and bandwidth requirements. Specifically, given the nature of the suffixes of any given pattern, we merge the asNFA states and transitions starting from the tail states. Figure 3 shows an example. Figure 3(a) is the asNFA built upon anchor suffix set {*bcdca, cdca, dca, ca, a*}; Figure 3(b) is the corresponding csNFA. In this example, the compression reduces the number of NFA states from sixteen to six and removes six transitions.

While being more compact, csNFA requires a more elaborate segments retrieval procedure. In an asNFA, segments retrieval can be done by simply tracking back from the recorded matching states to the entry state. However, in the optimized csNFA, this straightforward approach does not work since the backtracking may lead to ambiguity at some states. To address this problem, during csNFA traversal we identify all states that are active after the processing of the first input character and assign state pair <*start_state, end_state*> to each active state, where *start_states* are these active states and *end_states* are last states of the traversed paths originating from them. Only state pairs <*start_state, end_state*> such that *end_states* are accepting states are significant; moreover, as we discussed in Section 3, only the state pair representing the longest matching path needs to be recorded. The matched segment can then be retrieved by tracing the csNFA matching path using the recorded state pair. Since the anchored suffix set includes only exact-match patterns, the *start_states* set has a limited size and the active paths are expected to go dead after the processing of a small number of input characters, reducing the amount of processing. Our experiments in Section 6 confirm the efficiency of this proposed compression scheme.

As an example, we consider the csNFA of Figure 3(b) and input *cadc*. csNFA processes the first input as {0}—$c\rightarrow${2,4}; we assign state pairs to both active states and track the traversal: {2}—$a\rightarrow${∅}, {4}—$a\rightarrow${5}. Since the first path goes dead and the second path reaches the tail state of the csNFA, the traversal leads to two state pairs: <2,2> and <4,5>. Since only state 5 is an accepting state and <4,5> matches the longest segment, only state pair <4,5> needs to be recorded. State pair <4,5> should then be back-traced as 5—$a\rightarrow$4—$c\rightarrow$0, leading to the retrieval of segment *ca*.

4.3 Prefix- and Suffix-DFA with State Map

We recall that all patterns in the prefix set and unanchored suffix set are unanchored (that is, they may be matched at any position of the input stream). Since their entry state is always active (po-

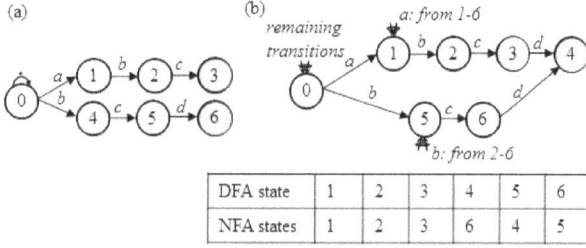

Figure 4. (a) NFA format and (b) equivalent sDFA format with states map for unanchored suffix set {.*abc, .*bcd}. Accepting states are colored gray.

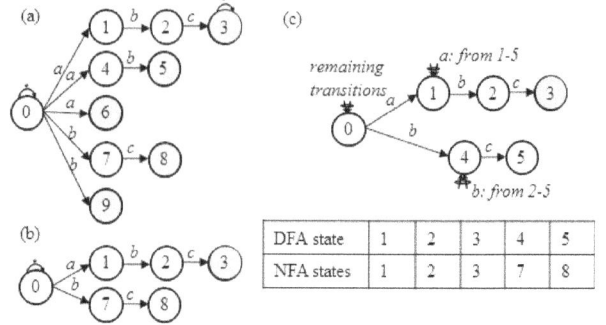

Figure 5. (a) original NFA format, (b) optimized NFA, (c) pDFA with states map for prefix set {.*abc.*, .*ab, .*a, .*bc, .*b}. Accepting states are colored gray.

tentially leading to the concurrent activation of multiple NFA branches), NFAs accepting unanchored patterns tend to have multiple concurrent active states, which negatively affect the processing time. By requiring a single state activation for each input character processed, a DFA representation guarantees minimal processing time, potentially at the cost of a larger memory requirement. However, we recall that patterns in the prefix and suffix sets do not have wildcard repetitions, and thus do not lead to significant state explosion. Thus, the DFA format is suitable for both prefix- and unanchored suffix-FAs; we denote these automata as **prefix-DFA (pDFA)** and **suffix-DFA (sDFA)**.

The number of states in a DFA can be minimized through a well-known procedure [4]. In addition, as discussed in Section 3, all prefix matches occurring in the middle of packets can be ignored. This allows further optimizations to the prefix-DFA. Specifically, all accepting states that do not present a self-loop can be made non-accepting, and all self-loops can be removed from the remaining accepting states. This simplification can both reduce the size of the prefix-DFA and simplify the processing (by making a filtering step to remove non-terminal matches unnecessary).

The use of a DFA representation for these automata, however, has a drawback: it complicates the retrieval of the matching input segments. Since there may be multiple paths leading to the same DFA state, it is not possible to retrieve the input segment solely based on the recorded DFA state. To tackle this problem, we propose using a *state map*, which maps the pDFA/sDFA states to the corresponding NFA states; segment retrieval can then be done by back-tracing NFA paths. Since pDFA and sDFA do not suffer from state explosion, the size of this state map is contained. One DFA state may map to multiple NFA states; in those cases, however, only the NFA state that leads to the longest retrieved segment needs to be included in the state map, allowing a one-to-one mapping.

We illustrate this design through an example. Let us consider pattern .*abc.*bcd. The corresponding unanchored suffix and prefix sets are {.*abc, .*bcd} and {.*abc.*, .*ab, .*a, .*bc, .*b}, respectively. The corresponding automata are shown in Figure 4

and 5. Specifically, Figure 4 (a) and (b) show the unanchored suffix-NFA and the sDFA and state map, respectively. Figure 5(a), (b) and (c) show the prefix-NFA, the reduced prefix-NFA obtained by applying the optimizations discussed above, and the resulting pDFA and state map, respectively. Suppose that the input packet is *bcdbabcdcb*. The traversal of pDFA in Figure 5(c) is: $0—b\rightarrow4—c\rightarrow5—d\rightarrow0—b\rightarrow4—a\rightarrow1—b\rightarrow2—c\rightarrow3—d\rightarrow0—c \rightarrow0—b\rightarrow4$. The traversed accepting state (state 3) and the final active state (state 4) must be recorded. To retrieve the input segments, we first map those states to NFA states 3 and 7 by looking up the state map, and then back-trace along the NFA. This operation leads to the retrieval of segments *abc* and *b*. Segment retrieval on the sDFA is performed using the same procedure.

4.4 Quick Retrieval Table

Retrieving input segments by back-tracing along NFA paths can be inefficient. To improve efficiency, we propose the use of a *quick retrieval table*, which maps the NFA states directly to portions of regular expressions. This table allows retrieving input segments without back-tracing. A quick retrieval table lookup returns an offset in the relevant regular expression; the input segment can then be extracted directly from the regular expression. This data structure is particularly beneficial in the case of long segments.

As an example, consider regular expression *abcdca*. The anchored suffix set and corresponding csNFA are the same as for the example in Section 4.2. Figure 6 (a) shows the csNFA and Figure 6(b) shows the quick retrieval table, which stores *<index_tag, offset>* pairs. We recall that index tags point to regular expressions. If the recorded state pair is <4, 5>, for example, a lookup in the quick retrieval table will return index tag *tag1* corresponding to pattern *abcdca*, and start- and end- offsets 5 and 6, respectively. This will result in retrieving segment *ca*.

4.5 Functionally Equivalent Packets

Any incoming packet may contain multiple segments that match a prefix or a suffix. For example, the sample packet in Section 4.3 contains two segments that match two different prefixes. All these segments should be recorded and retrieved properly, and all retrieved segments should be processed with the current input packet. A simple approach is to sequentially concatenate the segments retrieved to the current packet and process all modified current packets. For example, supposing that the current packet is *efgh*, using the same example of Section 4.3, then two retrieved seg-

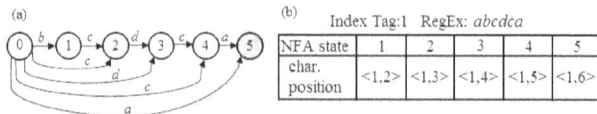

Figure 6. (a) csNFA and (b) quick retrieval table for anchored suffix set {bcdca, cdca, dca, ca, a}. Accepting states are colored gray. Each char. position is a pair of index tag and offset, i.e., <tag, offset>

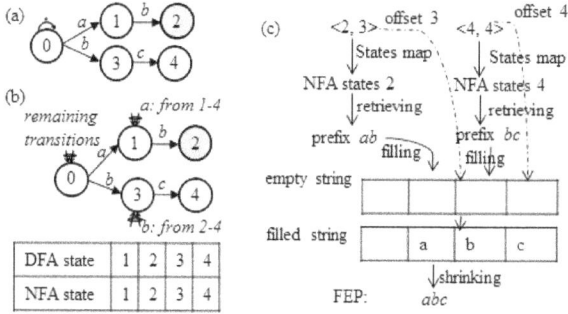

Figure 7. (a) NFA format and (b) equivalent pDFA format with states map built upon prefix set {.*ab.*, .*a, .*bc, .*b}. (c) Construction of functionally equivalent packet to packet P$_2$=eabc.

ments are *abc* and *b*, and the two corresponding concatenated current packets *abcefgh* and *befgh* should be processed serially. This solution can be highly inefficient. However, concurrently concatenating all retrieved segments to the current packet is not straightforward, since many segments may have overlaps. Our proposed solution is the *Functionally Equivalent Packet* (FEP). The main idea is to construct an alternate packet based on all retrieved segments and then deal with the alternate packet instead of the segments. Such an alternate packet contains all effective information (i.e., all detected segments) of the original packet and thus is functionally equivalent to the original one.

Consider the example RegEx *ab.*bcd*; the prefix set is {.*ab.*, .*a, .*bc, .*b}. Figure 7 (a) and (b) are the NFA format and pDFA with a states map for this prefix set. Supposing the input packets are P$_1$=*afab*, P$_2$=*eabc* and P$_3$=*defg*, there is obviously only one matching of *ab.*bcd* across all three packets. Two pDFA states 2 and 4 are recorded after packet P$_2$ is processed, representing two detected segments that match prefixes .*ab.* and .*bc. The retrieved alternate segments are *ab* and *bc*. Directly concatenating both segments to P$_3$ as *abbcdefg* can cause a false-positive matching. Our FEP design needs only one change that recording <*state, offset*> pairs instead of only matched states; the *offset* is the offset of matched segment's last character in the packet. When retrieving segments, all retrieved alternate segments will be filled into an empty string, filling positions accord to their offsets; then, the filled string will be shrunken to get FEP. Figure 7(c) shows the construction of FEP to P$_2$. <2,3> and <4,4> are two recorded <*state, offset*> pairs. The alternate FEP of P$_2$ is *abc*; substituting P$_2$ by FEP in the data stream as *afababcdefg* will not affect the matching results.

5. O³FA-BASED SYSTEM

In this section, we describe the design of a regular expression-matching engine based on our proposed O³FA.

5.1 O³FA Engine Architecture

Our O³FA engine consists of four components: (i) a Regular Expression (RegEx) Parser, (ii) a Finite Automata (FA) Kernel, (iii) a State Buffer, and (iii) a Functionally Equivalent Packet (FEP) Constructor.

The **RegEx Parser** operates offline. It first breaks the regular expressions as described in Section 3 and generates the corresponding prefix and anchored/unanchored suffix sets. It then generates the required regular DFAs (rDFA) and supporting-FAs:

compressed suffix-NFA (csNFA), prefix-DFA (pDFA) and suffix-DFA (sDFA).

The **FA Kernel** is the operational core of the O³FA engine and performs online packet processing. Specifically, it processes every input packet (possibly extended by the FEP Constructor) against regular and supporting-FAs, and stores the matching state information into the State Buffer.

The **State Buffer** is an auxiliary component that assists both the FA Kernel and the FEP Constructor. This component stores the matching state information generated by the FA Kernel, and it provides information required by FEP reconstruction to the FEP Constructor. As discussed in Section 4, the State Buffer stores: final states from the regular DFA traversal, state pairs <*start_state, end_state*> from the csNFA traversal, and <*state, offset*> pairs from the pDFA and sDFA traversal. Specifically, the State Buffer stores an entry for each packet processed. During processing, if neither the predecessor nor the successor of the current packet has been previously processed, the current packet is directly processed by the FA Kernel and the resulting matching information is stored in the State Buffer. Otherwise, the FEP Constructor retrieves the predecessor/successor's entry in the State Buffer, and it constructs the FEP of the arrived predecessor/successor packets based upon that state information. The FEP is then concatenated with the current packet, and the modified packet is processed by the FA Kernel. At the end of FA processing, the matching state information is stored in the current packet's entry of the State Buffer, and the related predecessor/successor entries are deleted from the State Buffer since the corresponding information is part of the current packet's entry. Storing only state information corresponding to previously processed packets (as opposed to the entire packets) and dynamically clearing entries during processing allow limiting the size of this buffer.

FEP Constructor: The FEP constructor uses state information provided by the State Buffer to reconstruct functionally equivalent packets, as described in Section 4.5.

The packet processing flow is summarized in Figure 8.

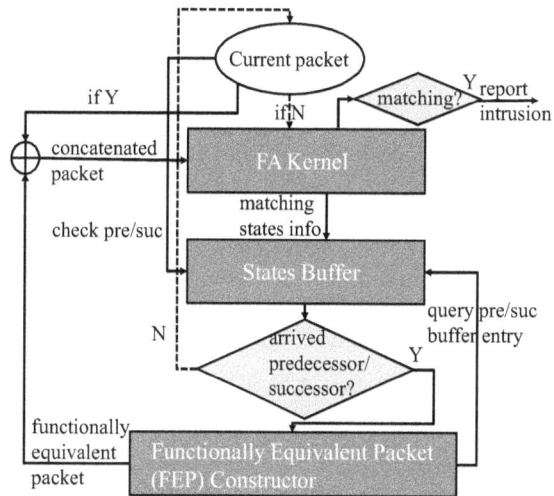

Figure 8. Packet processing flow. Dotted arrows indicate alternative paths if there are no arrived successor/predecessor packets.

6. EXPERIMENTAL EVALUATION

In this section, we provide experimental data to show the feasibility of our O^3FA engine design. Specifically, our experiments are designed to analyze the following aspects: (i) O^3FA memory footprint on reasonably large and complex regular expression sets; (ii) savings in buffer size requirements of O^3FA engine compared to traditional flow reassembly schemes; (iii) memory bandwidth overhead of supporting-FAs; and (iv) O^3FA traversal efficiency.

6.1 Datasets & Streams

In our experiments, we use two real world and six synthetic datasets. The real world datasets contain *backdoor* and *spyware* rules from the widely used Snort NIDS[2] (snapshot from December 2011), and they include 176 and 304 regular expressions, respectively. The synthetic datasets have been generated through the synthetic regular expression generator[3] [29] using tokens extracted from the *backdoor* rules. Each synthetic dataset contains 500 regular expressions. The synthetic *dot-star** datasets contain a varying fraction of dot-star sub-patterns (5%, 10% and 20%); in the synthetic *range** datasets 50% and 100% of the patterns include character sets; finally, the synthetic *exact-match* dataset contains only exact-matching strings.

For each dataset, we generate 16 synthetic traces using the traffic trace generator[3] [29]. This tool allows for generating traces that simulate various amount of malicious activity. This can be realized by tuning parameter p_M, which indicates the probability of malicious traffic. In addition, to allow randomization, a probabilistic seed parameter can be used to configure the trace generation. In our experiments, we use four probabilistic seeds and four p_M values: 0.35, 0.55, 0.75 and 0.95, i.e., 16 traces in total for each dataset. All traces have a 1 MB size. Each of the data points below has been obtained by averaging the results reported on four simulations, each using a different probabilistic seed.

6.2 Packet Reordering

To simulate out-of-order packet arrival, we break each synthetic stream down into multiple packets and reorder these packets. Packet reordering is driven by two parameters: the out-of-order degree k and the stride s. Parameter k indicates the minimum number of arrived packets that are needed for partial stream reconstruction; parameter s indicates the maximum stride between two consecutive packets within each group of k packets.

For example, let us assume a stream consisting of eight packets: P_1 to P_8. If we set $k=2$ and $s=1$, then packets are reordered as $P_2 \to P_1 \to P_4 \to P_3 \to P_6 \to P_5 \to P_8 \to P_7$; if we set $k=4$ and $s=1$, then packets are reordered as $P_4 \to P_3 \to P_2 \to P_1 \to P_8 \to P_7 \to P_6 \to P_5$; if we set $k=4$ and $s=2$, the packets' order will be $P_4 \to P_2 \to P_3 \to P_1 \to P_8 \to P_6 \to P_7 \to P_5$. Obviously, $k=1$ and $s=1$ implies natural ordering, while $k=$(number of packets) and $s=1$ leads to reverse ordering (in the example, from P_8 down to P_1).

This packets' reordering scheme allows us to characterize how the packet order affects the performance of the O^3FA engine, and to compare the O^3FA engine with the traditional input stream reassembly method. In our experiments, we break each 1MB stream into 16 packets, each having the 64KB standard TCP

---
[2] https://www.snort.org/
[3] http://regex.wustl.edu/

Table 1. Memory footprint of FA Kernels (MB)

Dataset	Regular multi-DFAs		Supporting-FAs	
	# of DFA	Memory Footprint	# of FA States	Memory Footprint
Backdoor	8	60	4k	0.62
Spyware	10	56	12k	1.35
Dotstar0.05	15	26	26k	3.58
Dotstar0.1	8	60	25k	3.12
Dotstar0.2	14	100	23k	2.76
Range0.5	1	5.6	24k	2.43
Range1	1	5.8	24k	2.05
Exact-match	1	4.7	17k	1.92

packet size. We reorder packets of each stream using three parameter settings: $k=2/s=1$, $k=4/s=1$ and $k=4/s=2$.

6.3 Experiment Results

6.3.1 O^3FA Memory Footprint

First, we evaluate the memory footprint of the O^3FA supporting each of the considered datasets. The *backdoor*, *spyware* and *dot-star** datasets include sub-patterns (e.g. dot-stars) leading to state explosion. To limit state explosion, for these datasets we break the regular DFA into multiple DFAs [6] (the number of DFA ranges from 8 to 15). Due to their simplicity, the *exact-match* and *range** datasets can be supported by a single regular DFA. The total number of regular DFA states ranges from 9k to 254k across the considered datasets. We recall that the supporting-FAs are of three kinds: compressed suffix-NFA (csNFA), prefix-DFA (pDFA) and suffix-DFA (sDFA). As discussed in Section 4, none of the supporting-FAs suffers from state explosion, leading to relatively small automata. The number of csNFA, sDFA and pDFA states ranges from 2k to 13k, from 1k to 13k and from 1k to 9k, respectively. *Range** datasets have larger supporting-FA sizes. This is because all character sets must be exhaustively enumerated before constructing the supporting-FAs, resulting in large prefix and suffix sets. The number of transitions of the csNFA ranges from 5k to 27k. To achieve memory space efficiency, we apply default-transition compression [22] to DFAs. Table 1 shows the estimated memory footprint of the resulting O^3FA (we assume 32-bit transitions). As can be seen, O^3FA requires about 100MB memory space in the worst case, which does not put pressure to commodity systems. In addition, because supporting-FAs do not suffer from state explosion, their size is in all cases limited, and their memory space overhead is negligible in case of complex datasets including dot-star terms.

6.3.2 Buffer Size Savings

Figure 9 shows the maximum buffer size requirement comparison between the O^3FA engine and a traditional flow reassembly scheme [18]. The O^3FA engine uses the state buffer described in Section 5, while the flow reassembly scheme uses a packet buffer. The optimized flow reassembly scheme reassembles a partial stream once the buffered packets allow it and then processes that partial stream and flushes the corresponding packet buffer entries. For each value of p_M, we average the results reported using four

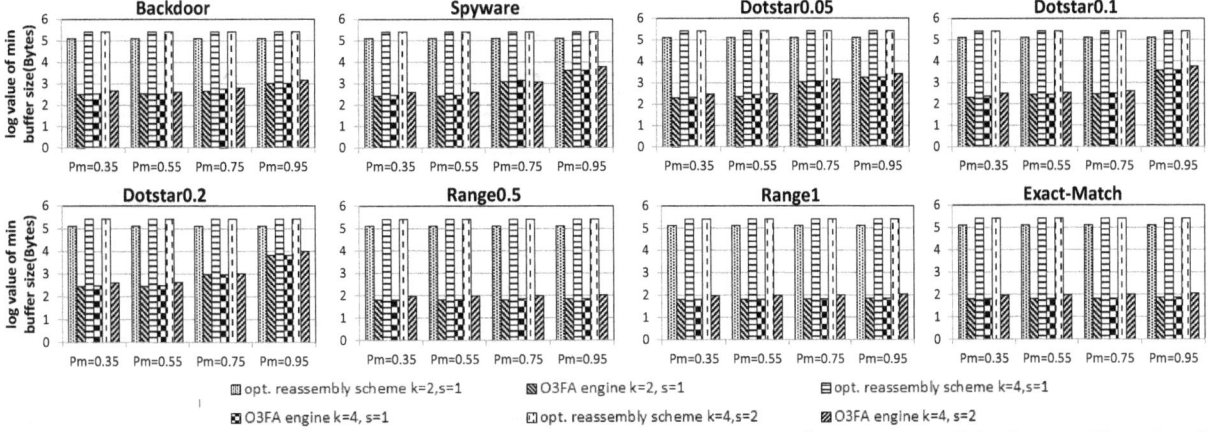

Figure 9. Maximum buffer size requirements for optimized reassembly scheme and O³FA engine on eight datasets. Note that the vertical coordinate is in logarithmic scale.

probabilistic seeds. In the charts, the six bars represent combinations of the two considered packet processing schemes and the three reordered packet sequences ($k=2/s=1$, $k=4/s=1$ and $k=4/s=2$). In all cases, we report the logarithmic value of the buffer size.

Overall, the O³FA engine with state buffer achieves 20x-4000x less buffer size requirement than does the optimized flow reassembly scheme with packet buffer. We can also see how the packet order and malicious traffic probability affect the buffer size: (i) as could be expected, the degree of packet reordering k affects the packet buffer size, while s does not, and the buffer size has a linear relationship with k; (ii) k has a minor effect on the state buffer size, while s has a major effect on it; (iii) p_M has a major effect on the state buffer size: a higher p_M leads to a larger buffer requirement.

These effects can be explained as follow. First, since the considered flow reassembly scheme flushes the packet buffer entries after partial stream reconstruction, the packet buffer size is affected only by the minimum number of packets required for partial reassembly, which is controlled by parameter k; on the other hand, the size of the state buffer is affected by the number and size of non-empty buffer entries, which are related to the detected segments and the arrived predecessors/successors. The former is affected by p_M, while the latter is affected by the stride parameter s. Specifically, $k=2$ and $k=4$ lead to two and four packets being buffered before partial reassembly, while s does not affect this num-

ber; thus, $k=4/s=1$ and $k=4/s=2$ lead to the same packet buffer size, and to twice the packet buffer size than the $k=2/s=1$ case. However, s affects the arrival order of the predecessor/successor of the current packet, thus affecting the size of the state buffer. $s=1$ and $s=2$ lead to two and three entries required (one for previous groups of k packets, the others for packets out of current k packets having neither a predecessor nor a successor), respectively; thus, $k=2/s=1$ and $k=4/s=1$ lead approximately to the same state buffer size requirement, while $k=4/s=2$ leads approximately to a 1.5x larger state buffer. Because a higher probability of malicious traffic leads to the possible detection of more packet segments by supporting-FAs, resulting in more matching state information being stored in buffer entries, a larger p_M can lead to an increased state buffer size requirement.

6.3.3 Memory Bandwidth Overhead

While in traditional solutions the memory bandwidth requirement of the regular expression matching engine is dominated by the processing of the regular DFAs, O³FA engines have a memory bandwidth overhead due to the processing of supporting-FAs. In particular, while DFA components add a single state traversal (or memory access) per input character, NFA components can potentially have a more significant effect on the memory bandwidth requirement. Table 2 shows the ratio between the number of csNFA states traversed and the number of input characters processed. As can be seen, this ratio is generally small (well below 1), leading to limited memory bandwidth overhead. This small

Table 2. Ratio between the number of csNFA states traversed and the number of input characters processed (%)

Dataset	k=2, s=1				k=4, s=1				k=4, s=2			
	$P_M=0.35$	$P_M=0.55$	$P_M=0.75$	$P_M=.95$	$P_M=0.35$	$P_M=0.55$	$P_M=0.75$	$P_M=0.95$	$P_M=0.35$	$P_M=0.55$	$P_M=0.75$	$P_M=0.95$
Backdoor	0.0144	0.0202	0.0278	0.0349	0.0347	0.0337	0.0440	0.1010	0.0144	0.0202	0.0278	0.0349
Spyware	0.0590	0.1002	0.1163	0.1286	0.1158	0.1942	0.2188	0.1853	0.0590	0.1002	0.1163	0.1286
Dotstar0.05	0.0804	0.0838	0.1173	0.2595	0.1733	0.1394	0.1517	0.3927	0.0804	0.0838	0.1173	0.2595
Dotstar0.1	0.0526	0.0715	0.1054	0.2610	0.1129	0.1184	0.1701	0.3974	0.0526	0.0715	0.1054	0.2610
Dotstar0.2	0.0363	0.0611	0.1142	0.2977	0.0531	0.1112	0.1806	0.3622	0.0363	0.0611	0.1142	0.2977
Range0.5	0.0973	0.1015	0.2170	0.2238	0.1839	0.1865	0.3488	0.3831	0.0973	0.1015	0.2170	0.2238
Range1	0.0638	0.1180	0.2181	0.3927	0.1697	0.1910	0.3319	0.6929	0.0638	0.1180	0.2181	0.3927
E-M	0.0391	0.0627	0.1460	0.3140	0.1407	0.1395	0.1959	0.4374	0.0391	0.0627	0.1460	0.3140

Table 3. O³FA traversal overhead compared to conventional stream reassembly methods (%)

Dataset	k=2, s=1				k=4, s=1				k=4, s=2			
	P_M=0.35	P_M=0.55	P_M=0.75	P_M=0.95	P_M=0.35	P_M=0.55	P_M=0.75	P_M=0.95	P_M=0.35	P_M=0.55	P_M=0.75	P_M=0.95
Backdoor	0.0114	0.0102	0.0346	0.3277	0.0211	0.0139	0.0732	0.5140	0.0119	0.0076	0.0288	0.3376
Spyware	0.0059	0.0058	0.1333	2.4362	0.0101	0.0090	0.2635	3.6701	0.0057	0.0049	0.0753	2.4427
Dotstar0.05	0.0103	0.0076	0.2645	1.0132	0.0220	0.0389	0.4492	1.5218	0.0134	0.0221	0.2679	1.0135
Dotstar0.1	0.0041	0.0129	0.0116	2.2671	0.0120	0.0304	0.0183	3.3866	0.0073	0.0136	0.0111	2.2464
Dotstar0.2	0.0083	0.0092	0.0160	3.4655	0.0164	0.0173	0.0225	5.2268	0.0098	0.0101	0.0112	3.4838
Range0.5	0.0007	0.0011	0.0032	0.0137	0.0017	0.0020	0.0054	0.0214	0.0009	0.0012	0.0033	0.0128
Range1	0.0006	0.0011	0.0033	0.0123	0.0014	0.0020	0.0051	0.0153	0.0008	0.0012	0.0033	0.0102
E-M	0.0006	0.0011	0.0033	0.0168	0.0014	0.0022	0.0054	0.0214	0.0008	0.0012	0.0033	0.0159

number of NFA state activations can be explained as follows: since the csNFA is anchored, most state activations will die after processing a small number of input characters.

6.3.4 Traversal Overhead

Because of FEP processing, the O³FA engine may process more characters than inputs. These additional characters processed bring traversal overhead over conventional stream reassembly methods. Table 3 shows the O³FA traversal overhead, expressed as a percentage ratio between the number of extra characters processed and the size of the input stream. As can be seen, the traversal overhead (0.0006%-5%) is small enough to be negligible in practice. In other words, O³FA traversal efficiency is comparable to that of conventional stream reassembly methods.

This traversal overhead is affected by both p_M and the number of packets with a previously processed predecessor/successor. In our experiments, k=4/s=1 packet sequences have longer FEP lengths than do k=2/s=1 and k=4/s=2 sequences. In addition, a larger p_M leads to longer FEPs, since it results in more packet segments being detected by supporting-FAs.

In summary, our experiments have shown that: (i) on datasets consisting of a few hundreds regular expressions with varying complexity, the O³FA memory footprint is typically less than 100MB, and the supporting-FAs size is limited (3.5 MB in the worst case); (ii) O³FA state buffers can be up to 20x-4000x smaller than conventional packet buffers; (iii) the O³FA bandwidth is linear in the number of incoming characters and not significantly affected by the NFA components of O³FA; and (iv) the O³FA traversal efficiency is comparable to that of conventional flow reassembly methods.

7. CONCLUSION AND FUTURE WORK

In this paper we have introduced the O³FA engine, a new regular expression-based DPI architecture that can handle out-of-order packets on the fly without requiring packet buffering and stream reassembly. The O³FA at the core of the proposal consists of regular DFA(s) and supporting-FAs, the latter allowing the detection of matches across packet boundaries. We have proposed several optimizations aimed to improve both the matching accuracy and speed of the O³FA engine. Our experimental evaluation shows the feasibility and efficiency of our proposed O³FA engine.

The main goal of this paper is to demonstrate the O³FA idea and engine design; in the future, we aim to deploy this engine on

real hardware. In particular, because the automata in O³FA can operate concurrently, the O³FA engine can be implemented on parallel architectures such as FPGAs [30] and GPGPUs [31], potentially leading to higher traversal efficiency. Moreover, since the size of the O³FA state buffer is typically at the KB level, better performance can be achieved by storing this buffer in SRAM (rather than in DRAM).

8. ACKNOWLEDGEMENT

This work was supported in part by the Institute for Critical Technology and Applied Science (ICTAS), an institute dedicated to transformative, interdisciplinary research for a sustainable future (http://www.ictas.vt.edu). Becchi has been supported by NSF grant CNS-1319748.

REFERENCES

[1] J. Newsome, B. Karp, and D. Song, "Polygraph: automatically generating signatures for polymorphic worms." pp. 226-241.

[2] R. Sommer, and V. Paxson, "Enhancing byte-level network intrusion detection signatures with context," in Proceedings of the 10th ACM conference on Computer and communications security, Washington D.C., USA, 2003, pp. 262-271.

[3] Y. Xie, F. Yu, K. Achan, R. Panigrahy, G. Hulten, and I. Osipkov, "Spamming botnets: signatures and characteristics," in Proceedings of the ACM SIGCOMM 2008 conference on Data communication, Seattle, WA, USA, 2008, pp. 171-182.

[4] R. M. J. Hopcroft, and J. Ullman, *Introduction to Automata Theory, Languages, and Computation*: Addison Wesley, 1979.

[5] B. C. Brodie, D. E. Taylor, and R. K. Cytron, "A Scalable Architecture For High-Throughput Regular-Expression Pattern Matching," in Proceedings of the 33rd annual international symposium on Computer Architecture, 2006, pp. 191-202.

[6] F. Yu, Z. Chen, Y. Diao, T. V. Lakshman, and R. H. Katz, "Fast and memory-efficient regular expression matching for deep packet inspection," in Proceedings of the 2006 ACM/IEEE symposium on Architecture for networking and communications systems, San Jose, California, USA, 2006, pp. 93-102.

[7] M. Becchi, and P. Crowley, "A hybrid finite automaton for practical deep packet inspection," in Proceedings of the 2007 ACM CoNEXT conference, New York, New York, 2007, pp. 1-12.

[8] S. Kumar, B. Chandrasekaran, J. Turner, and G. Varghese, "Curing regular expressions matching algorithms from insomnia, amnesia, and acalculia," in Proceedings of the 3rd ACM/IEEE Symposium on Architecture for networking and

communications systems, Orlando, Florida, USA, 2007, pp. 155-164.

[9] R. Smith, C. Estan, S. Jha, and S. Kong, "Deflating the big bang: fast and scalable deep packet inspection with extended finite automata," *SIGCOMM Comput. Commun. Rev.,* vol. 38, no. 4, pp. 207-218, 2008.

[10] M. Becchi, and P. Crowley, "Extending finite automata to efficiently match Perl-compatible regular expressions," in Proceedings of the 2008 ACM CoNEXT Conference, Madrid, Spain, 2008, pp. 1-12.

[11] X. Yu, B. Lin, and M. Becchi, "Revisiting State Blow-Up: Automatically Building Augmented-FA While Preserving Functional Equivalence," *Selected Areas in Communications, IEEE Journal on,* vol. 32, no. 10, pp. 1822-1833, 2014.

[12] V. Paxson, "End-to-end Internet packet dynamics," in Proceedings of the ACM SIGCOMM '97 conference on Applications, technologies, architectures, and protocols for computer communication, Cannes, France, 1997, pp. 139-152.

[13] J. Sharad, G. Iannaccone, C. Diot, J. Kurose, and D. Towsley, "Measurement and classification of out-of-sequence packets in a tier-1 IP backbone." pp. 1199-1209 vol.2.

[14] S. Dharmapurikar, and V. Paxson, "Robust TCP stream reassembly in the presence of adversaries," in Proceedings of the 14th conference on USENIX Security Symposium - Volume 14, Baltimore, MD, 2005, pp. 5-5.

[15] T. Ptacek, and T. Newsham, "Insertion, Evasion and Denial of Service: Eluding Network Intrusion Detection," *Secure Networks, Inc. Technical Report*, 1998.

[16] A. E. Saldinger, J. Ding, and S. K. Sathe, "Method and apparatus for ensuring ATM cell order in multiple cell transmission lane switching system," Google Patents, 1999.

[17] A. S. J. Chapman, and H. T. Kung, "Method and apparatus for re-ordering data packets in a network environment," Google Patents, 2001.

[18] A. V. Rana, and C. A. Garrow, "Queue engine for reassembling and reordering data packets in a network," Google Patents, 2004.

[19] M. Zhang, and J.-b. Ju, "Space-Economical Reassembly for Intrusion Detection System," *Information and Communications Security*, Lecture Notes in Computer Science, pp. 393-404: Springer Berlin Heidelberg, 2003.

[20] X. Chen, K. Ge, Z. Chen, and J. Li, "AC-Suffix-Tree: Buffer Free String Matching on Out-of-Sequence Packets," in Proceedings of the 2011 ACM/IEEE Seventh Symposium on Architectures for Networking and Communications Systems, 2011, pp. 36-44.

[21] T. Johnson, S. Muthukrishnan, and I. Rozenbaum, "Monitoring Regular Expressions on Out-of-Order Streams," in Data Engineering, 2007. ICDE 2007. IEEE 23rd International Conference on, Istanbul, Turkey, 2007, pp. 1315-1319.

[22] M. Becchi, and P. Crowley, "An improved algorithm to accelerate regular expression evaluation," in Proceedings of the 3rd ACM/IEEE Symposium on Architecture for networking and communications systems, Orlando, Florida, USA, 2007, pp. 145-154.

[23] S. Kong, R. Smith, and C. Estan, "Efficient signature matching with multiple alphabet compression tables," in Proceedings of the 4th international conference on Security and privacy in communication netowrks, Istanbul, Turkey, 2008, pp. 1-10.

[24] J. Patel, A. X. Liu, and E. Torng, "Bypassing Space Explosion in High-Speed Regular Expression Matching," *Networking, IEEE/ACM Transactions on,* vol. 22, no. 6, pp. 1701-1714, 2014.

[25] S. Kumar, S. Dharmapurikar, F. Yu, P. Crowley, and J. Turner, "Algorithms to accelerate multiple regular expressions matching for deep packet inspection," in Proceedings of the 2006 conference on Applications, technologies, architectures, and protocols for computer communications, Pisa, Italy, 2006, pp. 339-350.

[26] D. Ficara, S. Giordano, G. Procissi, F. Vitucci, G. Antichi, and A. D. Pietro, "An improved DFA for fast regular expression matching," *SIGCOMM Comput. Commun. Rev.,* vol. 38, no. 5, pp. 29-40, 2008.

[27] G. Varghese, J. A. Fingerhut, and F. Bonomi, "Detecting evasion attacks at high speeds without reassembly," in Proceedings of the 2006 conference on Applications, technologies, architectures, and protocols for computer communications, Pisa, Italy, 2006, pp. 327-338.

[28] R. Smith, C. Estan, and S. Jha, "XFA: Faster Signature Matching with Extended Automata." pp. 187-201.

[29] M. Becchi, M. Franklin, and P. Crowley, "A workload for evaluating deep packet inspection architectures." pp. 79-89.

[30] C. R. Clark, and D. E. Schimmel, "Efficient reconfigurable logic circuits for matching complex network intrusion detection patterns," *Field Programmable Logic and Application*, pp. 956-959: Springer, 2003.

[31] X. Yu, and M. Becchi, "GPU acceleration of regular expression matching for large datasets: exploring the implementation space," in Proceedings of the ACM International Conference on Computing Frontiers, Ischia, Italy, 2013, pp. 1-10.

Many-Field Packet Classification for Software-Defined Networking Switches

Cheng-Liang Hsieh
Southern Illinois University
Carbondale, Illinois, USA
hsieh@siu.edu

Ning Weng
Southern Illinois University
Carbondale, Illinois, USA
nweng@siu.edu

ABSTRACT

Packet classification is a core problem for OpenFlow-based software-defined networking switches, which required 38 packet header fields per flow to be examined against thousands of rules in a ruleset. With the trend of continue growing number of fields in a rule and the number of rules in rule set, it will be a great challenge to design a high performance packet classification solution with the capability to easy update new rule and fields. In this paper, we present a scalable many-field packet classification algorithm with varying rulesets and its prototype implementation on a graphics processing unit. The proposed algorithm constructs multiple lookup tables and merges partial lookup results for a small ruleset to accelerate the overall packet classification process by using effective bit positions in a ruleset with three selecting metrics: wildcard ratio, independence index, and diversity index. Those lookup tables made with effective bit positions are flat with a low rule replication ratio. Besides, they are adjustable to meet different implementation environments for a good performance scalability between different ruleset sizes. Our prototype on a single NVIDIA K20C GPU achieves 198 MPPS, 186 MPPS, 163 MPPS throughput for 1K, 32K, and 100K 15-field ruleset.

Keywords

Packet Classification; GPU; SDN

1. INTRODUCTION

Software-defined networking (SDN) abstracts network infrastructures as programmable resources for network applications. OpenFlow-based software-defined networking switches [15] require 38 packet header match fields and 6 pipeline match fields to be examined for a flow. The requirements on latency, throughput, update cost, and storage for a system like OpenFlow Switch become stricter with the increasing complexity of a ruleset. Hence, packet classification remains an open and challenging problem for next generation network device development.

ANCS '16, March 17-18, 2016, Santa Clara, CA, USA
© 2016 ACM. ISBN 978-1-4503-4183-7/16/03...$15.00
DOI: http://dx.doi.org/10.1145/2881025.2881036

Current solutions generate good system performance for traditional 5-tuple packet classification problems [21][9][3][10][1] but they do not scale well to many-field packet classification problems. Longer processing latency and bigger space requirement caused by additional fields in a ruleset are expected. Many-field packet classifications with current 5-tuple TCAM solutions are with high implementation cost due to the bigger size of each rule and arbitrary field types in a many-field ruleset. Many-field implementations with current 5-tuple decision-tree-based solutions will generate a deeper and wider tree due to those additional fields and result in impractical memory usage and inefficient tree traversal to reach leaf nodes. Moreover, many-field implementations with current 5-tuple decomposition-based solutions will increase both process latency and storage requirement due to the merge process for those those additional fields.

Several research groups observed these new challenges in many-field packet classification and tried to come up with different solutions. On the one hand, some solutions avoid the repeated packet classifications on the same packet at different network nodes and free extra processing capacity. For example, tagging approach [2] classifies packets at the edge switch and inserts tags into packets for a fast packet forwarding in a network. Moreover, hashing approach [16] classifies the first packet in a flow and uses hash table lookups for the following packets to improve the performance of packet forwarding. On the other hand, some solutions improve the packet classification performance directly by designing new methods. For example, decomposition-based approach [19] uses bit vector with hash tables, decision-tree-based approach [6] uses 2-d pipeline architecture with tree-to-pipeline mapping scheme, and hybrid-based approach [4] uses effective bits with look-up tables to lower the computation cost and improve the system performance.

In this paper, we propose a scalable many-field packet classification algorithm using multidimensional-cutting via selective bit-concatenation (MC-SBC) for OpenFlow-based SDN switches. MC-SBC uses simple lookup tables to avoid computation divergence problems and leverages the high efficient instructions in a massive computation platform for a higher system throughput. Due to the sparsity and biased rule distribution in a ruleset, MC-SBC is designed to quickly find out few candidate rules using effective bits for the full match as shown in Figure 1. In summary, there are three main contributions of this work:

- MC-SBC demonstrates scalability on both the system performance and rule replication ratio with varying ruleset types and sizes.

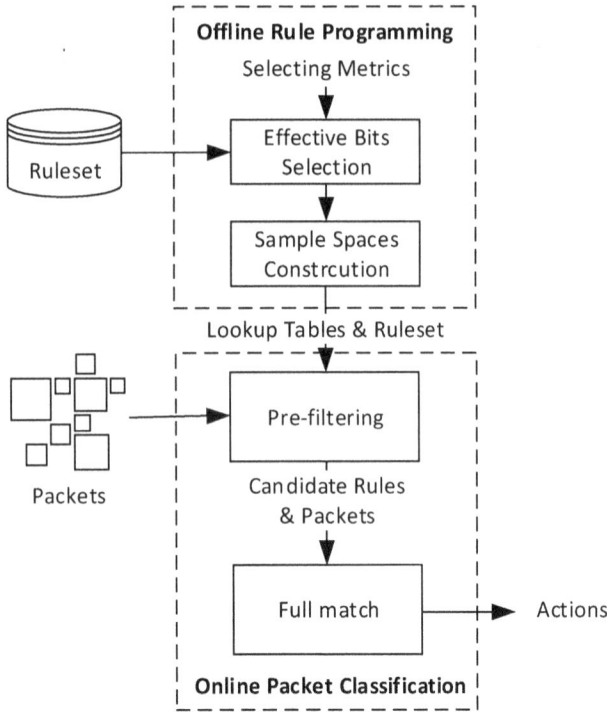

Figure 1: The proposed packet classification architecture. The system consists of off-line rule programming and on-line packet classification. Rule programming is conducted for the first time when a system is initiated or its ruleset is updated.

- MC-SBC designs a two-stage architecture with feasibility and flexibility with easy implementations by leveraging effective bit positions in a ruleset.

- A GPU prototype is implemented with packet classification throughput of 198 MPPS and 163 MPPS for 1K and 100K 15-field rules.

The remainder of this work is organized as follows. Section 2 gives background for related researches on packet classification problems and discusses the motivation of this paper. Section 3 presents the proposed architecture. Section 4 discusses the selecting metrics of effective bits. Section 5 gives an example of algorithm operations. Section 6 discusses the complexity analysis and shows the experiment results. Finally, the paper is concluded in Section 7.

2. BACKGROUND

In this section, we review major types of the packet classification algorithms to show the challenges and the trend of packet classification research area. Then we present the motivations for new many-field packet classification solutions.

2.1 Ternary Content-Addressable Memory Solutions

Ternary content-addressable memory (TCAM) is a specialized memory that can store and query three different types of data: 0, 1, and * (wildcard). TCAM solutions (TCAMs) employ multiple TCAM devices for each rule in a ruleset, and construct a parallel matching architecture for the target packet header fields with those pre-defined rules to fulfill

the line rate requirement. However, for a ruleset with more packet header fields and bigger rule size, TCAMs need more TCAM devices and a complicated hardware implementation. Though TCAMs [9][13] leverage hardware parallel computation power to generate high packet classification throughput, they suffer problems such as high power consumption, high manufacturing cost, and low scalability [21][27].

2.2 Tuple Space Solutions

Besides of the hardware-based implementation like TCAMs, many researchers [16][25] also work on the software-based algorithmic solutions for a better system scalability with a lower implementation cost. Tuple space solutions are software-based and they leverage the fact that the number of distinct tuples is much less than that of rules in a ruleset. A tuple defines the number of significant bits in a prefix match field, the nesting level and range ID of a range field, and the existence of a value for an exact match field in a ruleset. Tuple-space-based solutions efficiently compress a ruleset by storing those valid bits of each field only. Besides, tuple-space-based solutions perform the search of each tuple independently and take advantage of parallelism. With the growth field number in a ruleset, both tuple number and tuple size increase. A longer processing latency could be expected.

2.3 Decomposition-based Solutions

Decomposition-based solutions [7][22][28] work on each field in a ruleset independently and merge the intermediate results from different fields as the final match result. Since each field is processed individually, more intermediate results will be generated with the growth of field number in a ruleset. The increasing merge stages of those additional fields in a ruleset result in a bigger memory requirement and longer processing latency. Recently, many-field decomposition-based solutions [18][17] leverage range-tree and hash functions to process the 15-field packet classification.

2.4 Decision-tree-based Solutions

Decision-tree-based approaches [8][11][24][28] analyze all fields in a ruleset to construct decision trees for efficient packet header lookup. For the matching process, decision-tree-based solutions traverse the tree by using individual field values to make branching decisions at each node until a leaf is reached. Tree depth and rule duplication in a decision tree affect the searching efficiency and memory requirement of one implementation. Both of them increase with the growth of field numbers which results in an exponential increase of memory requirement and increasing processing latency. Recently, many-field decision-tree-based solution [6] divides a ruleset into several subsets which have their own individual optimized decision trees and implement the design as a pipeline architecture on FPGA for good performance on a 12-field ruleset. An improved algorithm [20] leverages similar techniques and designs fine grained processing elements with a 2-dimensional pipelined architecture on FPGA with better performance for a 15-field ruleset.

2.5 Motivation of Many-field Packet Classification Solutions

New applications like OpenFlow Switch examine more than 15 fields in multiple lookup tables to categorize incoming packets into different flows [16]. For the development of

Rules	Field 1	Field 2	Field 3
r_1	0010	1101	1001
r_2	1001	000*	100*
r_3	1010	0110	1110
r_4	1110	1010	10**
r_5	0000	****	0000
r_6	****	110*	101*
r_7	1001	1010	0000
r_8	1111	110*	0000
r_9	0101	1010	101*
r_{10}	****	0110	101*
r_{11}	0001	0110	0000
r_{12}	0010	110*	101*
r_{13}	0100	000*	1110
r_{14}	1100	0010	000
r_{15}	1110	000*	0000
r_{16}	0011	110*	101*

Table 1: An example ruleset of sixteen rules with three fields

advanced network services such as SDN and NFV, the number of packet header fields in a rule are expected to grow in the future. However, the growing field number in a ruleset poses new challenges to packet classification problems in term of system throughput and storage requirement. To address the scalability problem and improve the system performance of many-field packet classification problem, it is necessary to lower the computation complexity with the number of rules and fields in a ruleset. In this paper, MS-SBC leverages the statistical characteristics between different bits in a ruleset to pre-compute lookup tables to lower computation complexity with the growth of field number and ruleset size.

The performance of a network application is affected by not only the implemented algorithm but also by the host platform. Heterogeneous system architecture is proposed to generate high system throughput with low implementation cost and high flexibility. However, it is a challenge to align different computation resources in a heterogeneous system. GPU is a typical commercial off-the-shelf device. Compared to other platforms such as Mulitcore General Processor (GPP) or FPGA, GPU supports fewer instruction but has more computation units to run in parallel. Besides, using GPU to implement an algorithm is a purely software-based solution and the implementation does not change GPU's hardware characteristics. Hence, GPU platforms provide a high flexibility on how to implement an algorithm and a high portability to move the designed algorithm to another GPU with similar architecture. With a proper alignment between the algorithm and GPU, a GPU can generate high throughput. All these benefits make GPU attractive for packet classification problems.

3. MC-SBC ARCHITECTURE

Packet classification multidimensional-cutting via selective bit-concatenation (MC-SBC) is implemented as a two-stage classification system with an off-line rule programming process to construct the lookup tables for the following on-line packet classification process as shown in Figure 1. This two-stage system shifts the computation cost to off-line stage to generate lookup tables to be used later to increase the system performance at on-line stage by doing simple lookups instead of data extracting and composition.

Algorithm 1: The pseudo code of off-line rule programming process.

input : A many-field ruleset, R
output: Effective Bit Sets, EBS

1 **for** *All bits in a ruleset* **do**
      // Get wildcard ratio
2   Get $P_{**}^{R^i, R^j}$;
      // Get diversity index
3   Get Div^{R^i};
      // Get indepedence index
4   Get Ind^{R^i, R^j};
      // Generate selection factor
5   $SF^{R^i, R^j} = \alpha \cdot P_{**}^{R^i, R^j} + \beta \cdot Div^{R^i} + \gamma \cdot Ind^{R^i, R^j}$;
6 **end**
7 Mark all bits as unused;
8 **while** *Unused bits are available* **do**
9   **for** *All unused bits in a ruleset* **do**
10   **if** SF^{R^i, R^j} *is maximum* **then**
11   **if** $P_{**}^{R^i, R^j} > P_{th}$ *and* $Div^{R^i} > Div_{th}$ *and* $Ind^{R^i, R^j} > Ind_{th}$ **then**
12   Append R^i, R^j to current EBS;
13   Mark R^i, R^j as used;
14   **end**
15   **end**
16   **end**
17   Move to next EBS;
18 **end**

3.1 Off-line Rule Programming

Off-line rule programming stage shifts the computation cost of field traversals in many-field packet classification using the pre-computed lookup tables. It stores the partition results of a ruleset into these lookup tables with rules' ID and uses effective bits as indices to access them. These effective bits are selected to provide the best discrimination between rules in a ruleset. Since only few effective bits are used, those bits could be quickly collected from a packet header. A lookup generates preliminary packet classification results without full comparison between rules and packets.

MC-SBC leverages wildcard ratios, independence indices, and diversity indices to identify effective bit positions in a ruleset and uses these bits to generate lookup tables. MC-SBC makes one lookup table by using one set of the effective bit positions of each rule. To save the required memory space and improve the processing latency, MC-SBC constructs multiple lookup tables with high independence to each other. The intermediate lookup results from each table are merged to become a much smaller candidate rule subset for the full match process in on-line packet classification stage.

To update lookup tables with low cost, each lookup table is stored discretely in system memory with two reference tables: the quantity table and the address table. The address table tells the memory address of each location in a lookup table. The quantity table tells the number of rule IDs in that location. Once there is an update in a ruleset, only those affected locations are updated. For example, if we want to add a new rule into a ruleset. By using the pre-defined effective bit position set, we can find the affected locations for

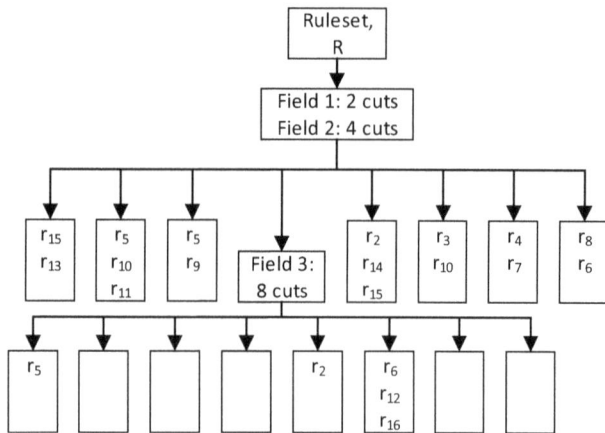

(a) HyperCuts

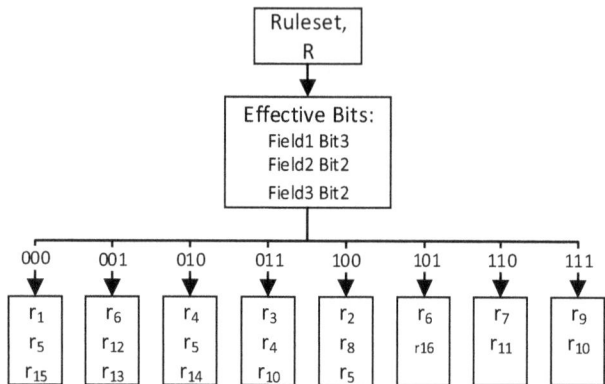

(b) MC-SBC

Figure 2: The examples of (a) HyperCuts and (b) MC-SBC data structures for a ruleset as in Table 1. Both algorithms are set up to have at most 3 rules in a leaf node with minimum rule duplication ratio.

this new rule. The address table tells where to find the data of rule IDs in memory and the quantity table tells how many rule IDs are stored there. MC-SBC modifies rule ID data at this location without interference to others then updates the quantity table.

The pseudo-code of rule programming process is shown in Algorithm 1 where R is the target ruleset, R^i is the bit value of i-th bit, $SF^{i,j}$ is the selection factor for i-th and j-th bits in a ruleset. $P_{**}^{R^i,R^j}$ is the wildcard ratio of i-th and j-th bit in a ruleset and the threshold is P_{th}. Div^{R^i} is the diversity index of i-th bit in a ruleset and the threshold is Div_{th}. Ind^{R^i,R^j} is the independence index of i-th and j-th bits in a ruleset and the threshold is Ind_{th}.

An example of the data structures between HyperCuts [23] and MC-SBC with a ruleset in Table 1 is shown in Figure 2. HyperCuts finds the best way to cut a ruleset heuristically with a bigger processing latency before constructing its data structure. MC-SBC detects those effective bits by using the statistical characteristics in a ruleset deterministically and creates its data structure directly. Besides, more leaf nodes could be found in this example for HyperCuts' data structure resulting in insufficient memory usage. Moreover, when verifying an incoming packet, HyperCuts checks each

header field's value to make branch decisions at each node until a leaf node is reached. MC-SBC saves the time to access each field 's value with the concatenation value of those effective bits to make branch decision. Instead of conducting at most two separate lookups on the data structure used in HyperCuts to reach a leaf node, MC-SBC only needs one lookup on its data structure.

3.2 On-line Packet Classification

The on-line packet classification contains two processes: the pre-filtering process and the full match process. The pseudo code of on-line packet classification is shown in Algorithm 2 where r is the target rule and pkt is an incoming packet. The pre-filtering process is designed to find the related rule IDs for an incoming packet. It takes the values of effective bit position in a packet as lookup table indices and checks with pre-computed lookup tables for preliminary results. To accelerate the merging process, rule IDs in lookup tables are stored in order. Lookup results from different tables are merged to come out candidate rule IDs. All candidate rule IDs are then forwarded to the full match stage.

The full match process is designed to report matches between packets and candidate rules. It checks candidate rule IDs and retrieves both packet data and rule data in full. Then full match process compares them based on each field's characteristics, such as pre-fix match, range match, and exact match. During the matching process, if the match within a field fails, the full match process will move to next candidate rule immediately. Once there is a match with the highest priority rule, it terminates the matching process and reports this match. If there is no match, the full match process conducts the default action.

Algorithm 2: The pseudo code of on-line packet classification process

> **input** : A many-field ruleset, Effective bit position sets, Sample space lookup tables
> **output**: Match results
>
> // Get packet's sample value
> **1 for** *All packet in queue* **do**
> **2**   Get packet sample value;
>   // Find sample space lookups
> **3**   Get the location of each space space based on sample value;
>   // Find common rule ID
> **4**   **for** *All Rule ID in each lookup* **do**
> **5**   Get common rule from different lookups;
> **6**   **end**
>   // Conduct full match
> **7**   Retrive packet data;
> **8**   **for** *All candidate rules* **do**
> **9**   Retrice rule data;
> **10**   **if** $pkt = r^i$ **then**
> **11**   Report match;
> **12**   **end**
> **13**   **end**
> **14 end**

4. SELECTING METRICS FOR EFFECTIVE BIT POSITION

Effective bits are those bits in a ruleset which partition the ruleset evenly at best effort. At the off-line rule programming stage, MC-SBC uses effective bits to cut a ruleset effectively into subsets and generate lookup tables as the cutting results. At the on-line packet classification stage, MC-SBC uses the values of effective bits of a packet to find candidate rules for the full match process. Hence, the aim of MC-SBC is to make the subsets' sizes as small as possible and to distinguish different rules in an efficient way. Therefore, for a set of effective bit positions, any two of them are designed to be with low wildcard ratio ($P_{**}^{(i,j)}$) and high diversity (Div) to lower the total number of duplicated rules. Besides, the independence index (Ind) between any two bits is designed to avoid possible bias of data structure. To find out effective bits, MC-SBC leverages several key statistic characteristics in a many-field ruleset as discussed in the following sections.

4.1 Wildcard Ratio

Wildcard ratio measures how many wildcard symbols (*) appear on two chosen bit positions in a ruleset. A wildcard (*) symbol in a bit position means it could be either 0 or 1. When an effective bit position encounters a wildcard symbol in a specific rule due to the prefix and range fields, this wildcard symbol has to be converted into 0 and 1 to cover all possible matches and causes rule duplication. The duplication of a rule increases sharply when some rules have many wildcard symbols on those effective bits. For example, a rule has its sample value as 01**, and the rule ID of this rule will be duplicated to subsets 0100, 0101, 0110, and 0111 in a sample space. A higher wildcard ratio for a bit position means there are many wildcard symbols on this bit position and more duplications are produced. Therefore, more rules will be duplicated and distributed to different subsets in a lookup table, and it results in a higher replication ratio, bigger averaged number of rules in a subset, and longer processing latency.

MC-SBC chooses those bit positions with a lower wildcard ratio when other parameters are the same, and examines wildcard symbols for any two chosen bit positions in a ruleset to avoid the impacts caused by wildcard ratio. MC-SBC uses Equation 1 to estimate the *combined wildcard ratio* for any two chosen bit positions where N is the number of rules in a ruleset, i and j are for bit positions in a ruleset:

$$P_{**}^{(i,j)} = \frac{N_{**}^{(i,j)}}{N}. \quad (1)$$

4.2 Independence Index

Bit positions with low correlations to each other can draw good distinctions between different rules when checking sample values, and *independence index* ensures that different bit positions are with high independence to each other. MC-SBC chooses a set of effective bit positions to guarantee the high independence among them. MC-SBC determines the independence index by the calculation for any two bit positions by the following Equation 2:

$$Ind^{(i,j)} = \sum_{x=0,1,*} \sum_{y=0,1,*} P_{xy}^{ij} - P_x^i \cdot P_y^j. \quad (2)$$

4.3 Diversity Index

Diversity index ensures the distribution of rule number in the subsets is even for better performance and lower processing latency. The diversity index of a bit position is calculated by calculating the entropy of the distribution on 0 and 1 as Equation 3:

$$Div^i = -\frac{P_0^i}{1-P_*^i} log \frac{P_0^i}{1-P_*^i} - \frac{P_1^i}{1-P_*^i} log \frac{P_1^i}{1-P_*^i}. \quad (3)$$

With a high diversity index, the subset sizes are distributed more evenly, and if the subset sizes are with uniform distribution, the processing latency under the worst case can be greatly reduced for a given duplication.

The above indices can be generalized to the cases of many bit positions (even two sets of bit positions), and the corresponding definition can be derived in a similar way. The proposed algorithm becomes more accurate when more bit positions are evolved. However, more computational cost will arise. Thus, we use these indices of one or two bit positions to reduce the computational complexity and the general cases for them are neglected here. Examples of how to implement MC-SBC are discussed in the next section.

5. EXAMPLES OF MC-SBC IMPLEMENTATION

Examples of MS-SBC algorithm are given in this section to show how MC-SBC works as a two-stage system for many-field packet classification. In the off-line rule programming stage, an example is given to illustrate how MC-SBC detects effective bits from a ruleset, uses those bits to create lookup tables, and updates those tables when a ruleset changes. In the on-line packet classification stage, an example is given to illustrate how the prefiltering process uses a packet header data with those pre-computed lookup tables and extracts candidate rules by merging intermediate results from table lookups.

5.1 Effective Bits Selection

MC-SBC uses only few effective bits in a ruleset to construct lookup tables to accelerate the overall processing speed. Since only those effective bits in the ruleset are used, MC-SBC converts range match fields to prefix match fields with an expanded value to avoid rule explosion problem but still keeps the characteristics of each field for the packet classification. For an effective bit position set, MC-SBC finds any two bit positions where Div is big, Ind is small, and P_{**} is small. Here, $R^{(i,j)}$ is denoted as the bit position j in field i of a ruleset R. For the ruleset as in Table 1, $R^{(1,1)}$, $R^{(1,2)}$, $R^{(1,3)}$, $R^{(1,4)}$, $R^{(2,1)}$, $R^{(2,2)}$, $R^{(2,3)}$, $R^{(3,1)}$, and $R^{(3,3)}$ are with higher Div indices compared to other bits for an effective bit position set. However, if $R^{(1,1)}$, $R^{(1,2)}$, $R^{(1,3)}$, $R^{(1,4)}$ or $R^{(2,1)}$, $R^{(2,2)}$, $R^{(2,3)}$ are in the same set, a higher P_{**} index of that set is found and it results in a higher rule duplication. Hence, there are at most two sets with up to 3 elements in each set: $\{R^{(1,1)} \vee R^{(1,2)} \vee R^{(1,3)} \vee R^{(1,4)}, R^{(2,1)} \vee R^{(2,2)} \vee R^{(2,3)}, R^{(3,3)} \vee R^{(3,4)}\}$ or at most 24 sets with up to 2 elements in each set. To decide the of the elements in a set, Ind indices are used and $\{R^{(2,3)}, R^{(3,3)}\}$, $\{R^{(1,1)}, R^{(2,1)}\}$, and $\{R^{(1,4)}, R^{(3,1)}\}$ are found as effective bit position sets which have smaller Ind values. Thus those effective bit position sets are good to divide a ruleset into smaller groups and construct lookup tables for each group by using other effective bit position sets.

The effective bit position sets decide the size of a lookup table, the number of groups for a ruleset, and how many lookup tables can be generated for a ruleset. We take the same matric as mentioned in Section 4 for differnt types of ClassBench rulesets. Table 2 shows the number of effective bits we can find after the rule programming on 5-tuple ClassBench rulesets. The available number of effective bits varies from one ruleset to another but there are sufficient bits from most fields. With this observation, a many-field synthetic ruleset with sufficient bit position sets is assumed to generate lookup tables with low dependence to each other.

Ruleset	SA	DA	Ptrl	SP	DP
ACL	4.36	6.64	2.93	1.14	8.64
FW	1.64	1.51	2.43	5.14	6.93
IPC	2.05	2.89	2.67	5.01	7.71

Table 2: The experimental average number of effective bits from the traditional 5 tuples for different rulesets

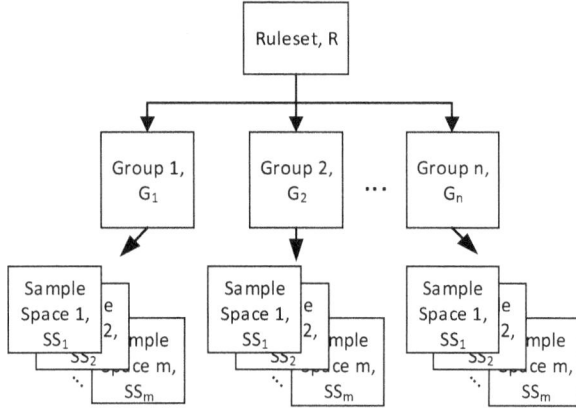

Figure 3: An example of the relationship between ruleset, groups, and sample spaces. A ruleset is divided into several small group. Each subset creates its own sample spaces.

5.2 Lookup tables construction

To improve system scalability and performance, MC-SBC divides a ruleset into smaller groups with minimum overlaps to each other and constructs lookup tables for each group separately. MC-SBC collects the target rules by putting rules with same attributes into a smaller subset and gives each subset a group index. Later, when doing a lookup, MC-SBC can only check those rules with same attributes by using group indices without wasting resources on those unrelated rules. For a big ruleset size, MC-SBC can generate more groups to maintain system scalability and performance. When the groups of a ruleset are ready, MC-SBC creates lookup tables for each group to maintain the system performance and memory requirements. The relationship among a ruleset, groups, and lookup tables is shown in Figure 3.

An example of the lookup table construction process is shown in Figure 5 for a ruleset as in Table 1. From Section 5.1, multiple effective bit position sets could be found from the example ruleset and there are three sets with the

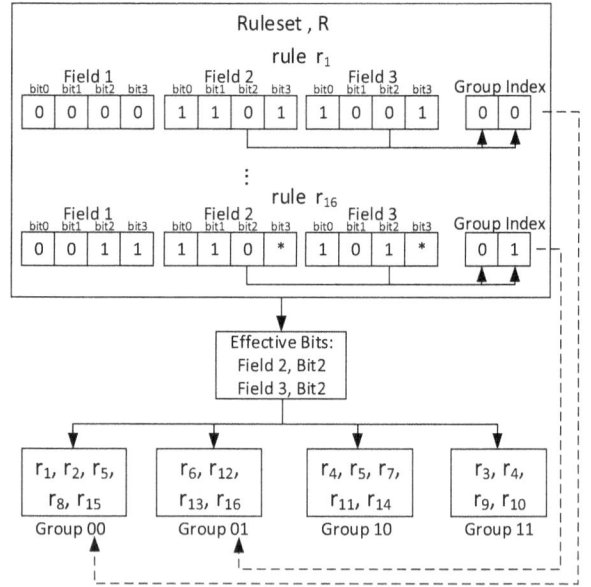

Figure 4: An example of the rule programming process on subset construction. In this example, we use the effective set: $\{R^{(2,3)}, R^{(3,3)}\}$ to generate the group indices. The ruleset is divided into several groups based the group indices.

best ruleset discrimination: $\{R^{(2,3)}, R^{(3,3)}\}$, $\{R^{(1,1)}, R^{(2,1)}\}$, and $\{R^{(1,4)}, R^{(3,1)}\}$. The first set is used to generate the group index and the following two sets are used to construct lookup tables. For example, the concatenation value of $\{R^{(2,3)}$ and $R^{(3,3)}\}$ in rule r_{16} is 01 and it acts as a group index as shown in Figure 4. Set $\{R^{(1,1)}, R^{(2,1)}\}$ and $\{R^{(1,4)}, R^{(3,1)}\}$ are used for lookup tables. In the group 00, there are 5 rules in it: r_1, r_2, r_5, r_8, and r_{15} and the lookup tables are shown in Figure 5.

When a ruleset is updated, only those related groups and lookup tables are updated and the following part remains unchanged. To update these lookup tables, MC-SBC finds which groups the target rule belongs to originally and removes the target rule from all related locations in the sample spaces. For example, to update r_{15}:[1110, 000*, 0000] as r'_{15}:[1110,000*,1111], r_{15} belongs to group 00 but now r'_{15} belongs to group 01. Hence, r_{15} has to be removed from lookup tables of group 00 and r'_{15} has to be inserted into group 01. Instead of checking all group 00 sample spaces, r_{15} is stored in location 10 of the first lookup table and in location 11 of the second table of group 00 by its original sample values. Hence, MC-SBC checks the address table to find where to modify in the memory space, and updates the quantity table with the updated number of rules in both locations. Then MC-SBC inserts r'_{15} into in group 01 lookup tables and updates the associated reference tables accordingly.

5.3 Pre-filtering

The pre-filtering process merges the lookup results from each sample space to extract candidate rules for the full match process. It takes the group index and the sample values of an incoming packet to find out which group's lookup tables should be used to retrieve rule IDs in a target location. The pre-filtering process then extracts candidate rules from the

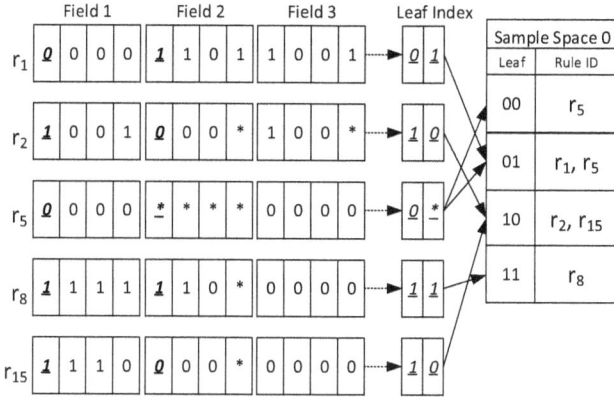

Figure 5: An example of rule programming process on lookup table construction for group 00 with r_1, r_2, r_5, r_8 and r_{15} in it. The concatenation of bit values is used to lookup the different locations in a sample space for the rule IDs. Rule IDs with same sample values are kept in the same location.

lookup results of different sample spaces for the following full match process.

For example, to verify an incoming packet p_y as shown in Figure 6, MC-SBC takes the group index and table indices from p_y, and uses them to check the lookup tables for rule IDs. Hence, p_y has 00 as its group index, 10 and 00 as the table indices for lookup tables. Thus, MC-SBC gets r_2, r_{15} from location 10 of first lookup table and r_5, r_{15} from location 00 of second lookup table in group 00. By merging the lookup results, the pre-filtering process generates r_{15} as the candidate rule ID and passes it to the following full match process.

5.4 Full match

To accelerate the matching process, the pre-filtering process uses only the rule ID to find out the candidate rules for the full match process for each incoming packet. However, a lookup only shows the match result on those effective bit positions between a rule and the incoming packet. To guarantee a match between packets and rules, a full comparison between each header field of a packet and the candidate rules is necessary. The full match process retrieves those candidate rules' data and packet data in full for the matching process and reports the matching results. With only few rules, we are able to implement those efficient match algorithms and derive the match results quickly at the full match stage. Other solutions can be implemented at this stage for a faster matching process without the restrictions caused by the complexity on a ruleset. To demonstrate comparable results with other algorithmic solutions, we only conduct the linear search at the full match process.

6. RESULTS

In this section, the theoretical results of time and space complexity are given to demonstrate how MC-SBC reduces the complexity by using multiple lookup tables. Then the experimental results are given to show the feasibility and effectiveness of the proposed MS-SBC algorithm with the comparison along with other existing many-field packet classification solutions.

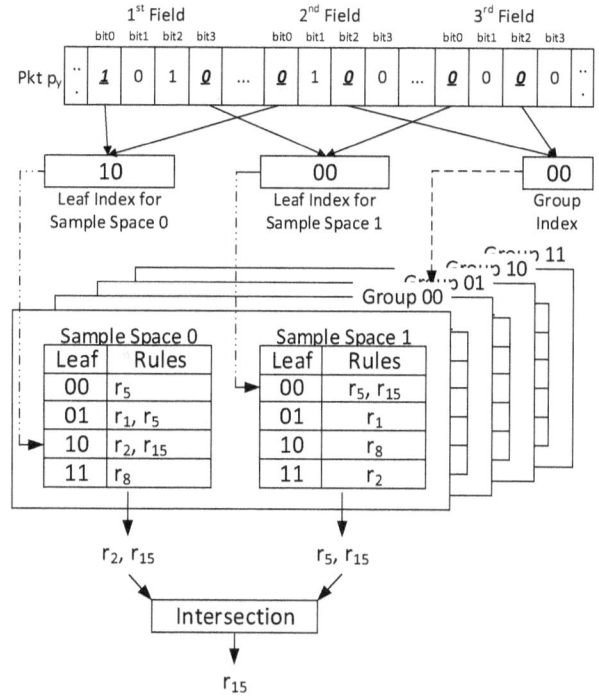

Figure 6: An example of the pre-filtering process for packet p_y. The subset index and sample values of packet p_y are generated with effective bit position sets used for sample space construction. The group index is used to decide which group's sample spaces should be used for the look-ups. The packet's sample values are used for lookups in different sample spaces. The intersection process in pre-filtering derives the candidate rules and pass them to the following full match process.

6.1 Theoretical Results

In this section, the time and space complexity are given for both D^2BS [28] and MC-SBC at first to show how MC-SBC can lower the complexity by using multiple lookup tables. Then a example with practical setting is given to show the performance of MC-SBC.

6.1.1 Time Complexity

Assume there are m rules in a ruleset, R, and each rule has h fields in it. For this ruleset, there are up to q effective bit position sets and each set has up to k bits in it. When using one set of effective bit position to partition R, R could be divided into at most 2^k subset. Due to wildcard symbol in the ruleset, one rule could appear in multiple subsets. Hence, the replication ratio caused by each effective bit is ρ and each subset could have up to $\rho^k \cdot m$ rules. When the partition result is stored as a lookup table and uses the concatenation values of those effective bits as indexes for the table, there are up to q lookup tables for this ruleset and only rule's ID is stored in the lookup table. Based on the selecting metric of effective bits, the rule distribution between different lookup tables is designed to be different. Hence, there are up to α rules will be the same from any subset in two different lookup tables.

D^2BS and MC-SBC use similar effective bit concept to cut a ruleset. By following the definition in D^2BS, the time

Algorithm	Time Complexity	Space Complexity
D^2BS	$O(\rho^k \cdot m \cdot c(h))$	$O((2 \cdot \rho)^k \cdot m)$
MC-SBC	$O(\rho^k \cdot m(q + \alpha^{q-1} \cdot c(h)))$	$O(q \cdot (2 \cdot \rho)^k \cdot m)$

Table 3: Complexity comparison between D^2BS [28] and MC-SBC where ρ is the average replication ratio, m is the number of rules in a ruleset, h is the number of fields in a rule, q is the number of effective bit sets, k is the number of effective bits, and α is the duplicated ratio between subsets in two lookoup tables.

complexity to find a rule ID is $O(\rho^k \cdot m)$. When more effective bits are chosen, less rule IDs are stored in a subset. However, the number of fields in a rule also impacts the time complexity to generate the results of packet classification. Hence, the time complexity of D^2BS with full match process is expanded as $O(\rho^k \cdot m \cdot c(h))$, where $c(h)$ depends on the implemented matching algorithm and the number of field in a rule.

The time complexity of MC-SBC is the sum of the cost to find candidate rules from different tables and the cost to compare candidate rules with a packet. However, MC-SBC allows multiple lookup tables to lower the complexity when doing the full match. Hence, the time complexity of MC-SBC is $O(q \cdot \rho^k \cdot m + \rho^k \cdot m \cdot \alpha^{q-1} \cdot c(h)) = O(\rho^k \cdot m(q + \alpha^{q-1} \cdot c(h)))$ where $q \cdot \rho^k \cdot m$ is the cost to find candidate rules from q different tables with ordered sorting and $q \cdot \rho^k \cdot \alpha^{q-1} \cdot c(h)$ is the cost to match a packet with candidate rules.

6.1.2 Space Complexity

Both D^2BS and MC-SBC store rule IDs in their data structures as pointers to the full rule data. When the classification process is launched, the full rule data will be retrieved and compared with incoming packets. Hence, data structures in D^2BS and MC-SBC are not increasing proportionally with the number of field in a ruleset. By following the definition in D^2BS, the space complexity of D^2BS is $O(2^k \cdot \rho^k \cdot m) = O((2 \cdot \rho)^k \cdot m)$.

MC-SBC provides the flexibility to trade space complexity for time complexity. With the multiple lookup tables, MC-SBC can checks only rule IDs to quickly filter out unrelated rules to lower the number of rules for full match. When there are more lookup tables used in MC-SBC, the space complexity of MS-SBC is increasing proportionally. Hence, the space complexity of MC-SBC is $O(q \cdot (2 \cdot \rho)^k \cdot m)$.

6.1.3 Complexity Comparison

The comparison between D^2BS and MC-SBC is shown as Table 3. MC-SBC provides the level of time and space complexity as D^2BS under the same setting. Moreover, MS-SBC provides the flexibility to lower the time complexity at the cost of the increasing space complexity. The cost to examine each packet for a match result is proportional to the number of fields in a ruleset. For applications like OpenFlow switch that needs more fields in a packet to be examined, MC-SBC is able to support this application development trend.

For example, the probability of 0, 1, and *(wildcard) of for all fields in a random generated ruleset with 100K rules are $(P_0, P_1, P_*) = (0.45, 0.45, 0.1)$. Assume two sets of effective bits are found and each set has 15 effective bits. Hence, there are at most 0.00013 similar rules in average from any subset in two different lookups. Hence, ρ is 0.55

and /alpha is 0.00013 in this case. Assume only linear search is conducted and the cost to match each field is equal for both D^2BS and MC-SBC. With D^2BS, the cost to find a match result is: $0.55^{15} \cdot 100000 \cdot 15 = 191$ unit cost and the storage requirement is: $0.55^{15} \cdot 100000 \cdot 2^{15} = 417725$ unit space. With MC-SBC, the cost to find a match result is: $0.55^{15} \cdot 100000(2 + 0.00013 \cdot 15) = 26$ unit cost and the storage requirement is: $2 \cdot 0.55^{15} \cdot 100000 = 835450$ unit space. By doubling the space requirement, MC-SBC could decrease the time complexity to about one seventh of the original value.

6.2 Experimental Results

In this section, MC-SBC is compared with other solutions in terms of data structure and system performance. The off-line rule programming stage in MC-SBC generates lookup tables for the on-line packet classification stage. The lookup tables are similar concepts with trees in decision-based solutions. The subset of each lookup table is actually the lead node in a decision tree. To show the efficiency of those lookup tables, MC-SBC is compared to those existing decision-based solutions with three key parameters: tree depth (D_t), replication ratio (f), and the maximum number of rules stored on a leaf node $(binth)$. The on-line packet classification stage in MC-SBC affects the overall system performance. To keep the flexibility of implementation with high system throughput, MC-SBC is implemented on a GPU with different optimization strategies. Moreover, MC-SBC is compared with other many-field packet classification solutions on different platforms using the synthetic rulesets with same setting.

6.2.1 Experiment Setup

All experiments are conducted on an Intel Xeon E5410 CPU machine with 4GB DDR2 RAM as the main memory. This machine is equipped a NVIDIA K20C GPU [14] with 13 streaming multiprocessors (SMXs) and 5Gb GDDR5 memory for general computation. Each SMX has 192 single-precision CUDA cores, 64 double-precision units, 32 special function units, and 32 load/store units. Besides, MC-SBC is implemented on the Debian 7.3 64-bit operating system with Cuda 7.0 as the software development environment. All necessary packets and tables are assumed to be ready on GPU before the packet classification process starts. This is a feasible and practical assumption because in the network system there are an abundant number of packets buffered to be processed in a network system [29]. In this paper, the synthetic rulesets are generated by taking ClassBench ruleset for the traditional 5-tuple first [26]. We attach 10 additional fields with wildcard ratio as 0.1 and the unique values setting as in [18] to those ClassBench rulesets to create the synthetic rulesets for the experiments.

6.2.2 Off-line Rule Programming Results

The off-line rule programming stage determines the size of each subset in a lookup table and impacts the overall system performance. The characteristics of a ruleset and the selecting criteria both play key roles at this stage. Both ideal and synthetic rulesets are verified to show the mixed interaction between system setting and varying ruleset characteristics.

6.2.2.1 Results with ideal rulesets.

An ideal ruleset provides more effective bits compared to practical rulesets and the distribution of rule IDs are evenly.

# of Subsets	Wildcard Ratio (%)	Binth Sample Space = 1 Space size (bits)			Candidate Rules Sample Space = 2 Space size (bits)		
		5	10	15	5	10	15
2	0	156K	4K	108	4K	5	11
	0.1	157K	4K	156	5K	6	1
	1	164K	5K	178	6K	11	1
	10	251K	12K	640	23K	280	4
8	0	39K	1K	27	1K	2	1
	0.1	39K	1K	39	1K	2	1
	1	41K	1K	45	1K	3	1
	10	62K	3K	160	5K	70	1
32	0	9K	306	10	306	1	1
	0.1	9K	310	10	315	1	1
	1	10K	355	12	405	1	1
	10	15K	793	40	1K	18	1

Table 4: Binth and candidate rules for a ruleset with 10 M rules by giving different subset and space size settings. All fields in the ruleset varying with the field wildcard ratio for each setting. Binth shows how many rule are stored in a leaf node of a sample space. Candidate rules are the intersection results of any two sample spaces.

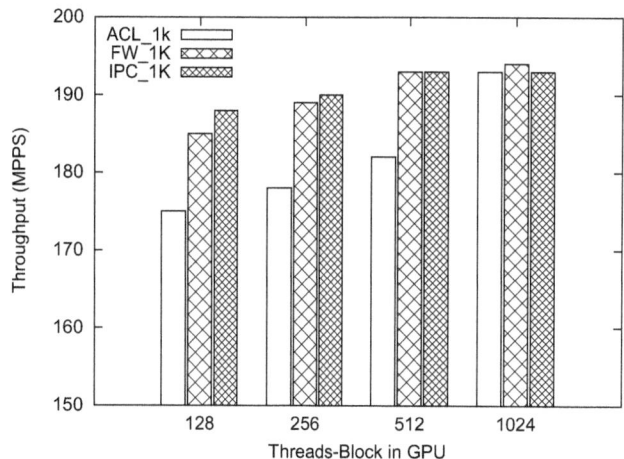

Figure 8: System throughput of GPU prototype implementation with varying GPU thread-block setting.

The analysis of ideal rulesets can show a trend to design a MC-SBC system. The *binth* of a lookup table is affected by bit position wildcard ratio, subset size, sample space size, and the number of lookup tables. We evaluate field wildcard ratio ranging from 0.01 % to 10%. The evaluation of ideal ruleset is summarized as in Table 4. More subsets and bigger sample space will decrease the number of rules stored in each leaf node (binth) for higher system performance. However, the wildcard ratio for each field in a ruleset increases binth and results in longer processing latency and a higher memory requirement. By changing these design factors, an improved system could found with a trade-off between system performance and memory requirement.

6.2.2.2 Results with synthetic rulesets.

The evaluation of MC-SBC with synthetic rulesets is conducted to compare the data structure of MC-SBC with other well-known algorithms like BC, SBC, Hi-Cuts, and Hyper-Cuts to show the effectiveness of the proposed system. MC-SBC is implemented with 3 major types of ClassBench rulesets. The trade-off between *binth* and *f* helps a designer to choose a setting which is suitable for the implementation environment.

Figure 7a shows the maximum number of rules per leaf node and Figure 7b shows the maximum replication ratio in a sampling space with subsets. The number of rules per leaf node (binth) decreases when the number of subsets increases. Binth also increases when the number of rules in a ruleset increases. The replication ratio increases when the number of subsets increases. However, it does not increase when the number of rules in the same ruleset increases. The proposed method controls the replication ratio to achieve better scalability in terms of storage, and provides the flexibility to trade the number of subsets for the number of rules stored in a leaf node, at the cost of memory storage. Besides, the binth of synthetic ruleset is bigger and does not decrease as fast as the ideal ruleset. When more effective bits are chosen,

the dependence between effective bits becomes stronger and it weakens the effectiveness of MC-SBC.

MC-SBC is compared with other decision-tree-based solutions such as BC, SBC, HiCuts, and HyperCuts. Table 5 shows the comparison result with other algorithms. All algorithms are set to have the same number of rules stored in a leaf node (binth) to count accesses of tree traversal (D_t) and the rule replication ratio (f). The proposed method (MC-SBC) is able to maintain the same level of binth and replication ratio with lower and deterministic tree depth and fast searching time.

6.2.3 On-line Packet Classification Results

A GPU prototype is implemented to show the performance of the proposed system with comparisons to the other many-field packet classification solutions on different platforms. Each packet is designed to have 15 fields in it and the size of a packet header is 354 bits as defined in OpenFlow. The system throughput is calculated based on the processing time of GPU kernel by CUDA Visual Profiler. The time duration of the GPU kernel is used as process latency for packet classification process. We make an assumption that packet data could be pre-loaded into GPU memory. This is a feasible and practical assumption because in a network system there are abundant packets in a network device waiting to be processed. Therefore, we can pre-load packet data to hide the transfer latency. However, the up and coming memory architectures may remove this bottleneck and allow for the full performance potential of MC-SBC. To avoid the performance penalty of kernel synchronization, we implement only one kernel to run both pre-filtering and full match with buffers to store packet subset indices, packet sample values, and suspected packets. Once the prefiltering process is done, the same kernel is going to run full match process and report the match results for each thread. Figure 8 shows the impact on system performance with different GPU thread-block setting. MC-SBC is able to mitigate the variance between different types of rulesets and generate consistent performance. Besides, MC-SBC is also able to utilize the massive computation platform by generating a higher system performance with more threads and higher instructions level parallelism.

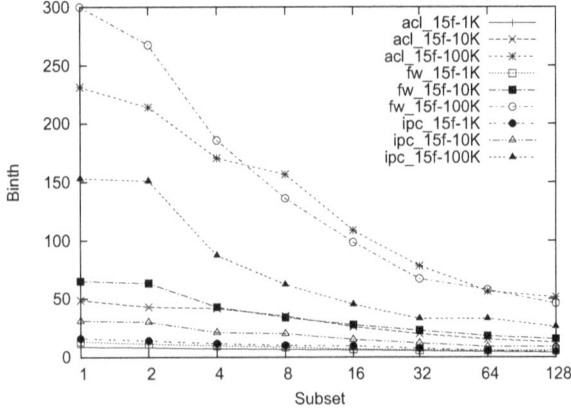

(a) The number of rules in a leaf node (binth)

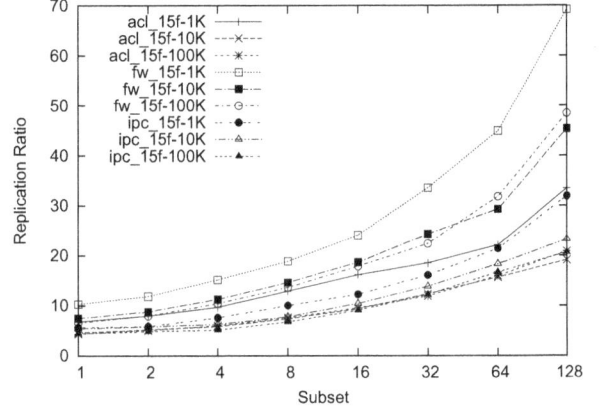

(b) The replication ratio (f)

Figure 7: The experimental maximum number of rules per leaf node (binth) and the replication ratio (f) by dividing a ruleset into 1 to 128 subsets with 15-bit sample space for each subset

Ruleset	binth	BC		SBC		HiCuts		HyperCuts		MC-SBC	
		5-field ruleset								15-field ruleset	
		Dt	f	Dt	f	Dt	f	Dt	f	Dt	f
ACL_1K	6	5	9	5	6	66	20	17	5	2	12
ACL_10K	10	5	41	5	25	63	34	14	3	2	16
ACL_100K	46	5	93	5	56	55	106	14	7	2	28
FW_1K	11	5	42	5	27	64	98	22	3	2	12
FW_10K	17	5	157	5	107	63	454	18	122	2	29
FW_100K	54	6	7683	6	6237	85	151514	18	825	2	48
IPC_1K	5	5	12	4	10	70	11	22	3	2	6
IPC_10K	16	6	66	6	33	78	270	19	279	2	10
IPC_100K	39	6	277	6	101	76	738	18	359	2	16

Table 5: The comparison between different algorithms: Boundary Cutting(BC), Selective Boundary Cutting(SBC), HiCuts, HyperCuts [12], and Multidimensional-Cutting Via Selective Bit-Concatenation(MC-SBC)

Based on the observation of ClassBench rulesets, we can find that a field normally has less than 10% as wildcards for a ruleset. However, the wildcard ratio of a field does impact the effectiveness to sample a ruleset to construct operational lookup tables. Hence, the system performance and memory requirement for varying number of rules with different wildcard setting is shown in Figure 9 to show the feasibility of the proposed system. Normally, only few fields in a ruleset are with high wildcard ratio compared to other fields. MC-SBC can mitigate this problem by finding only effective bits. In Figure 9, all field are set up with a high wildcard ratio as the worst scenario and MC-CBS still maintains a good scalability in term of wildcard ratio.

Figure 10 shows the comparison of system throughput with other many-field packet classification algorithms such as GPP-BV [18] and GPU-BV [19]. The processing latency is about 4 ms in GPP-BV when processing 64 packets with 32 K rules and is about 22 ms in GPU-BV when processing 81920 packets with 32 K rules. However, the processing latency of this work is about 80 ms when processing 26624 packets with 32 K rules. The proposed system is able to maintain scalability with the increasing ruleset size and the growth field number in a ruleset. Although FPGA solutions [5][19] are with a higher throughput (upto 650 MPPS), the FPGA platform is constrained by its limited memory space and

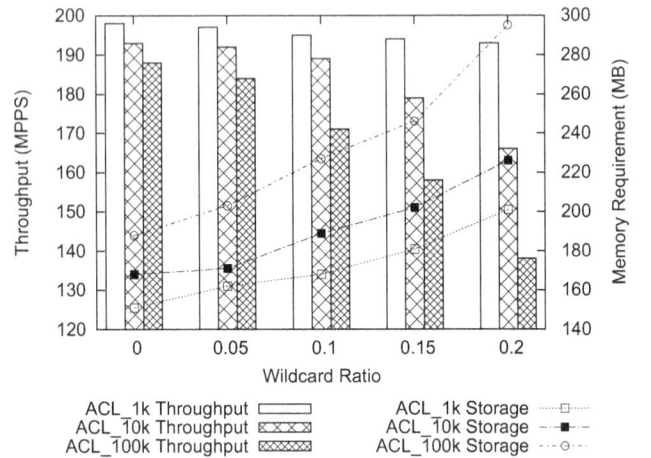

Figure 9: System throughput and memory requirement of GPU prototype implementation for different 15-field rulesets with varying wildcard setting.

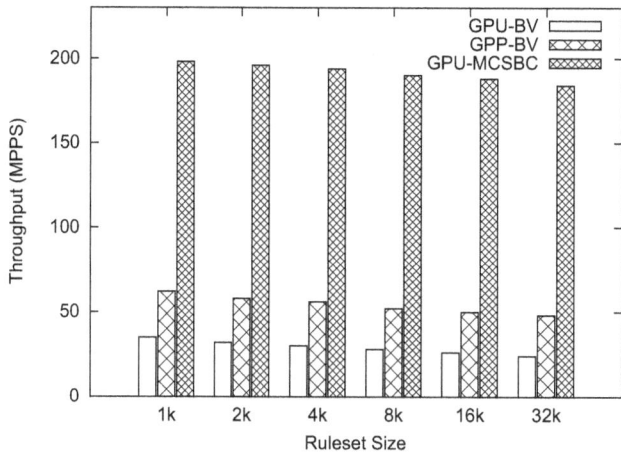

Figure 10: The comparison between GPP-BV [18], GPU-BV [19], and GPU-MCSBC(this paper).

can only support a ruleset with around 1K 15-field rules in it. Hence, the comparison with FPGA platforms is not conducted here.

7. CONCLUSION AND DISCUSSION

In this paper, we present a many-field packet classification algorithm by extracting only few candidate rules for full match process to improve the system performance. The proposed method converts a huge and biased rule space into several small subsets by using key selecting metrics to construct flat data structures for fast processing and easy updating. Both data structures and matching processes in the proposed system are designed for massive computation platforms to hide short latency tasks behind a long access latency task for a better system performance. The proposed method is examined with ideal and synthetic rulesets with all key factors related to system performance. Besides, the cutting results are compared with well known cutting algorithms to show the effectiveness. The throughput of GPU prototype achieves around 198 MPPS for 1K 15-field rules and around 163 MPPS for 100K 15-field ruleset. The prototype result is also compared with other many-field implementations in terms of scalability and throughput. This paper demonstrates the feasibility of Openflow-based SDN switches using software-based packet classification instead of TCAM solutions.

8. ACKNOWLEDGMENTS

We want to thank Dr. Wei Wei from Beihang University for his help on the mathematical problem formulation when he was a visiting professor at Southern Illinois University.

9. REFERENCES

[1] F. Baboescu and G. Varghese. Scalable packet classification. volume 31, pages 199–210, 2001.

[2] H. Farhadi and A. Nakao. Rethinking flow classification in sdn. In *2014 IEEE International Conference on Cloud Engineering (IC2E)*, pages 598–603, 2014.

[3] P. Gupta and N. Mckeown. Classifying packets with hierarchical intelligent cuttings. *IEEE Micro*, 20(1):34–41, 2000.

[4] C. Hsieh and N. Weng. Scalable many-field packet classification using multidimensional-cutting via selective bit-concatenation. In *Proceedings of the Eleventh ACM/IEEE Symposium on Architectures for networking and communications systems*, pages 187–188, 2015.

[5] W. Jiang and V. K. Prasanna. Field-split parallel architecture for high performance multi-match packet classification using fpgas. In *Proceedings of the Twenty-first Annual Symposium on Parallelism in Algorithms and Architectures*, pages 188–196, 2009.

[6] W. Jiang and V. K. Prasanna. Scalable packet classification on fpga. *IEEE Transactions on Very Large Scale Integration (VLSI) Systems*, 20(9):1668–1680, 2012.

[7] W. Jiang, V. K. Prasanna, and T. Ganegedara. A scalable and modular architecture for high-performance packet classification. *IEEE Transactions on Parallel and Distributed Systems*, 25(5):1135–1144, 2014.

[8] A. Kennedy and X. Wang. Ultra-high throughput low-power packet classification. *IEEE Transactions on Very Large Scale Integration (VLSI) Systems*, 22(2):286–299, 2014.

[9] K. Kogan, S. Nikolenko, O. Rottenstreich, W. Culhane, and P. Eugster. Sax-pac (scalable and expressive packet classification). In *Proceedings of the 2014 ACM Conference on SIGCOMM*, pages 15–26, 2014.

[10] T. V. Lakshman and D. Stiliadis. High-speed policy-based packet forwarding using efficient multi-dimensional range matching. In *Proceedings of the ACM SIGCOMM 1998 Conference*, pages 203–214, 1998.

[11] H. Lim, N. Lee, G. Jin, J. Lee, Y. Choi, and C. Yim. Boundary cutting for packet classification. *IEEE/ACM Transactions on Networking*, 22(2):443–456, 2014.

[12] H. Lim, N. Lee, G. Jin, J. Lee, Y. Choi, and C. Yim. Boundary cutting for packet classification. *IEEE/ACM Transactions on Networking*, 22(2):443–456, 2014.

[13] Y. Ma and S. Banerjee. A smart pre-classifier to reduce power consumption of tcams for multi-dimensional packet classification. 42(4):335–346, 2012.

[14] Nvidia Corp. *Nvidia K20 GPU Accelerator*, 2012. http://www.nvidia.com/content/PDF/kepler/Tesla-K20ActiveBD06499001v02.pdf.

[15] Open Networking Foundation. *OpenFlow Switch Specification, Version 1.5.1*, 2015. https://www.opennetworking.org/images/stories /downloads/sdn-resources/onf-specifications /openflow/openflow-switch-v1.5.1.pdf.

[16] B. Pfaff, J. Pettit, T. Koponen, E. Jackson, A. Zhou, J. Rajahalme, J. Gross, A. Wang, J. Stringer, P. Shelar, K. Amidon, and M. Casado. The design and implementation of open vswitch. In *12th USENIX Symposium on Networked Systems Design and Implementation (NSDI 15)*, pages 117–130, 2015.

[17] Y. Qu, S. Zhou, and V. K. Prasanna. Scalable many-field packet classification on multi-core processors. In *2013 25th International Symposium on Computer Architecture and High Performance Computing (SBAC-PAD)*, pages 33–40, 2013.

[18] Y. Qu, S. Zhou, and V. K. Prasanna. A decomposition-based approach for scalable many-field

packet classification on multi-core processors. *International Journal of Parallel Programming*, 438(6):965–987, 2014.

[19] Y. R. Qu, H. H. Zhang, S. Zhou, and V. K. Prasanna. Optimizing many-field packet classification on fpga, multi-core general purpose processor, and gpu. In *Proceedings of the Eleventh ACM/IEEE Symposium on Architectures for Networking and Communications Systems*, pages 87–98, 2015.

[20] Y. R. Qu, S. Zhou, and V. K. Prasanna. High-performance architecture for dynamically updatable packet classification on fpga. In *2013 ACM/IEEE Symposium on Architectures for Networking and Communications Systems (ANCS)*, pages 125–136, 2013.

[21] O. Rottenstreich, I. Keslassy, A. Hassidim, H. Kaplan, and E. Porat. On finding an optimal tcam encoding scheme for packet classification. In *2013 Proceedings IEEE INFOCOM*, pages 2049–2057, 2013.

[22] A. Sanny, T. Ganegedara, and V. K. Prasanna. A comparison of ruleset feature independent packet classification engines on fpga. In *IPDPS Workshops*, pages 124–133, 2013.

[23] S. Singh, F. Baboescu, G. Varghese, and J. Wang. Packet classification using multidimensional cutting. In *Proceedings of the 2003 Conference on Applications, Technologies, Architectures, and Protocols for Computer Communications*, pages 213–224, 2003.

[24] H. Song and J. S. Turner. Abc: Adaptive binary cuttings for multidimensional packet classification. *IEEE/ACM Transactions on Networking*, 21(1):98–109, 2013.

[25] V. Srinivasan, S. Suri, and G. Varghese. Packet classification using tuple space search. *ACM SIGCOMM Computer Communication Review*, 29(4):135–146, 1999.

[26] D. E. Taylor and J. S. Turner. Classbench: A packet classification benchmark. *IEEE/ACM Transactions on Networking*, 15(3).

[27] B. Vamanan and T. N. Vijaykumar. Treecam: Decoupling updates and lookups in packet classification. In *Proceedings of the Seventh COnference on Emerging Networking EXperiments and Technologies*, pages 1–12, 2011.

[28] B. Yang, J. Fong, W. Jiang, Y. Xue, and J. Li. Practical multituple packet classification using dynamic discrete bit selection. *IEEE Transactions on Computers*, 63(2):424–434, 2014.

[29] S. Zhou, S. Singapura, and V. Prasanna. High-performance packet classification on gpu. In *2014 IEEE High Performance Extreme Computing Conference (HPEC)*, pages 1–6, 2014.

HyPaFilter – A Versatile Hybrid FPGA Packet Filter

Andreas Fiessler[†]

Sven Hager[‡]

Björn Scheuermann[‡]

Andrew W. Moore[§]

[†]genua mbH, Germany
andreas_fiessler@genua.de

[‡]Humboldt University of Berlin, Germany
{hagersve,scheuermann}@informatik.hu-berlin.de

[§]University of Cambridge, UK
andrew.moore@cl.cam.ac.uk

ABSTRACT

With network traffic rates continuously growing, security systems like firewalls are facing increasing challenges to process incoming packets at line speed without sacrificing protection. Accordingly, specialized hardware firewalls are increasingly used in high-speed environments. Hardware solutions, though, are inherently limited in terms of the complexity of the policies they can implement, often forcing users to choose between throughput and comprehensive analysis. On the contrary, complex rules typically constitute only a small fraction of the rule set. This motivates the combination of massively parallel, yet complexity-limited specialized circuitry with a slower, but semantically powerful software firewall. The key challenge in such a design arises from the dependencies between classification rules due to their relative priorities within the rule set: complex rules requiring software-based processing may be interleaved at arbitrary positions between those where hardware processing is feasible. We therefore discuss approaches for partitioning and transforming rule sets for hybrid packet processing, and propose HyPaFilter, a hybrid classification system based on tailored circuitry on an FPGA as an accelerator for a Linux netfilter firewall. Our evaluation demonstrates 30-fold performance gains in comparison to software-only processing.

Keywords

Packet classification, FPGA hardware accelerator, Firewall

ANCS '16, March 17 - 18, 2016, Santa Clara, CA, USA

© 2016 Copyright held by the owner/author(s). Publication rights licensed to ACM.
ISBN 978-1-4503-4183-7/16/03... $15.00

DOI: http://dx.doi.org/10.1145/2881025.2881033

1. INTRODUCTION

Software firewalls like `netfilter/iptables` [3], `pf` [4], or `ipfw` [2] are widely used in practice, in both standalone applications and as a basis for professional security appliances [1]. Their main advantages are flexibility and powerful filtering options, as well as their easy setup and handling, since they can be used on top of common operating systems with commercial off-the-shelf (COTS) hardware. These CPU-based architectures, however, hardly meet the line rate packet processing requirements for high link speeds such as 40 Gbps or beyond, which leave only small processing time frames of 8 ns or less for each packet in the worst case [21]. In contrast, packet classification systems based on special purpose hardware, such as network processors (NPUs) [24,26], field-programmable gate arrays (FPGAs) [11, 17, 20, 21], graphics processing units (GPUs) [35], or application-specific circuits (ASICs) [8] provide an abundant amount of parallelism which can be used to process many network packets at once. Furthermore, the matching process for every single packet is often parallelized, which leads to large achievable throughputs of up to 640 Gbit/s [8].

However, dedicated hardware is significantly more constrained with respect to the expressiveness of the supported rule set semantics: while the functionality of software-based classification systems ranges from stateful connection tracking over probabilistic matching to deep packet inspection [2–4], specialized hardware engines are often restricted to simple stateless packet classification with no or only limited connection tracking capabilities [8, 11, 17, 21, 35]. Moreover, while software firewalls can utilize a virtually unlimited amount of memory for storing policies and connection states, hardware firewalls have to operate within fixed boundaries.

In order to combine the advantages of massively parallel matching hardware and powerful inspection capabilities of software-based packet filters, we propose *HyPaFilter*, a hybrid packet classification concept. The HyPaFilter approach aims to reach the packet rate and processing latency of a dedicated hardware firewall for common, easy to classify traffic, while providing the flexibility and functionality of a software firewall for packets which require complex processing. To this end, HyPaFilter partitions a user-defined packet processing policy into a simple part manageable by specialized matching hardware, and a complex part, which is handled in software. We found that a key challenge in such a hybrid design, regardless of its concrete implementation, is the proper handling of dependencies between different rules in the specified policy: if the hardware detects a rule match of an incoming packet in the simple part of the policy, it must ensure that the packet does not match a more highly prioritized rule installed in the software filter *before* the action specified by the hardware-detected rule is applied. However, it is desirable to avoid a full-fledged software packet classification whenever possible in order to achieve the full hardware speedup for a large number of packets. In order to overcome this challenge, the HyPaFilter approach determines the largest rule index in the simple rule set up to which a hardware-only classification is safely possible. Furthermore, even if complex processing for a packet is required, the matching information from the hardware can be reused in order to narrow down the set of rules the software filter has to match against this packet. We also address policy updates, as both the simple and complex part of a policy can change at arbitrary positions after an initial system setup.

As FPGA-based systems are suitable candidates for high performance, low latency network applications [25], we prototyped the HyPaFilter approach using a standard Linux host using `netfilter/iptables` as the software packet filter, combined with the NetFPGA SUME [37] platform. In this setup, the NetFPGA SUME is configured with tailored logic which matches packets against every simple rule in parallel, allowing it to perform basic firewalling tasks without involving the host at all at speeds of up to 40 Gbps for 64 byte frames. Complex rules and policy updates are implemented in `netfilter` in order to allow for comprehensive packet analysis as well as short rule update latencies. Whenever possible, updates that involve simple rules are moved from the software filter to the hardware filter during the next hardware configuration phase.

Of course, the achievable performance of HyPaFilter is dependent on both the structure of the implemented policy as well as on network traffic characteristics. However, previous examination of real-world traffic in [6] showed that the fraction of traffic which can be analyzed by simple packet filter rules is large enough to expect a significant performance gain in practical applications. Our evaluation results indicate that the HyPaFilter system can significantly increase the maximum achievable classification throughput over a software-only approach even for policies with many and widely spread complex rules. In the current state of development, stateful firewalling relies on the software firewall only. Therefore, the intended use case prefers scenarios like bridging firewalls, denial-of-service protection, or demilitarized zone configurations, where many policies can be implemented by stateless firewall rules.

To sum up, the main contributions of this paper are: (1) We present a hybrid packet classification concept which combines the benefits of dedicated matching hardware with powerful matching semantics typically found in software-only approaches. We prototyped this concept on a combination of a NetFPGA SUME and a Linux host system. However, at its core, the HyPaFilter approach does not make any assumptions on the used hardware and can be used with other kinds of hardware, such as GPUs or NPUs. (2) We describe different strategies in order to achieve a good policy separation, which is one of the key challenges in such hybrid designs. (3) We provide a detailed study on how the structure of the implemented policies affects the achievable throughput in our hybrid system.

The remainder of this paper is structured as follows: in Section 2, we discuss related work in this field of research. Next, we briefly introduce the packet classification problem in Section 3. Sections 4 and 5 describe the hybrid matching algorithm as well as the architecture of the HyPaFilter system, respectively. Finally, we present our evaluation results in Section 6 and conclude this paper in Section 7.

2. RELATED WORK

Network packet classification has been of major interest to the research community due to its importance for packet-switched networks [13, 32]. Most of the scientific work in this area focuses on the geometric variant of the packet classification problem, which considers a limited number of packet header fields and does not take other criteria into account, such as packet payloads or connection states. These research efforts can be roughly split into the following categories: *classification algorithms*, *hardware architectures*, and *rule set transformations*.

Classification algorithms traverse an algorithm-specific data structure in order to find the highest prioritized rule that matches on all relevant header fields of an incoming packet. Such approaches exist in many different flavors, such as decision tree algorithms [12, 30, 34], bit vector searches [7, 22], or techniques based on hash maps [31]. In comparison to a straightforward linear search through the rule set, these advanced classification algorithms provide significantly faster classification performances [13]. Despite this fact, many practically used packet classification systems, such as `netfilter` [3] and `pf` [4], implement a linear search in order to discriminate network packets and thus generally suffer from low classification performance [16]. However, these systems also provide powerful rule set semantics which are more expressive than plain stateless header field inspection.

Specialized hardware architectures used for packet classification typically employ large amounts of parallelism in order to achieve high throughput rates. The most common hardware architecture used for packet classification is *Ternary Content Addressable Memory (TCAM)*, which matches the entire rule set in parallel against incoming packet headers [28] and can thus process every incoming packet in a small, fixed number of clock cycles. On the downside, TCAMs are expensive, power-intensive, and cannot natively represent rules with range or negation tests [17]. Other widely used implementation platforms for packet classification are FPGAs [11, 17, 18, 20], NPUs [24, 26], and GPUs [35], which typically also employ a full parallel match [17] or implement a classification algorithm which is amenable for parallelization/pipelining [11, 18, 20, 24, 26, 35]. Although significantly faster than software-based systems, these approaches only support limited stateless matching semantics. In contrast, the HyPaFilter design combines the flexibility of existing software engines with the processing speed of dedicated hardware.

Rule set transformation techniques are orthogonal to the employed classification algorithm/architecture. The goal is to transform an initial rule set $\mathscr{R}$ into an equivalent rule set $\mathscr{R}'$ which can be traversed faster for incoming network packets. Existing approaches for rule set transformation are rule set minimization [23] or the encoding of decision tree data structures into the rule set [16]. HyPaFilter utilizes the latter transformation variant to install complex rules in the software filter which can reuse the hardware classification result in order to accelerate the software matching.

The possibility of hybrid packet filters for FPGA/`netfilter` and NPU/`netfilter` combinations has been previously addressed in [10] and [6], respectively. However, these works do not answer the following key questions: (1) How should a packet processing policy be deployed in a hybrid system in order to reach high classification performance? (2) How does the hybrid system implement rule set updates? In order to provide an answer to these questions, we present three rule set partitioning schemes as well as update mechanisms to handle rule set changes.

3. PROBLEM STATEMENT

In this section, we first introduce the packet classification problem, which serves as the vantage point for the extended packet classification problem, which we define subsequently.

3.1 Packet Classification Problem

The packet classification problem, as it is most often seen in the literature [7, 12, 17, 31], can be formally defined as follows: let

$\mathscr{H} = (H_1 \in D_1, \ldots, H_K \in D_K)$ be a tuple of *header values* and $\mathscr{R} = \langle R_1, \ldots, R_N \rangle$ be an ordered list of *rules* R_i, which is called the *rule set*. Here, D_j is called the *domain* of the jth header field. For the rest of this paper, we assume that each D_j is a range of non-negative integers, in order to cover common header fields like IP addresses, ports, or protocol numbers. Every rule R_i consists of K *checks* $C_i^j : D_j \to \{\text{true}, \text{false}\}$ with

$$R_i = C_i^1 \wedge \ldots \wedge C_i^K.$$

R_i is said to *match* the header tuple $\mathscr{H}$ if $C_i^j(H_j)$ yields true for all $j \in \{1, \ldots, K\}$. The goal of the packet classification problem is to find the smallest index i^* such that rule R_{i^*} matches $\mathscr{H}$. This index can subsequently be used in order to look up and execute an *action* for the corresponding matching rule, such as DROP or ACCEPT. Here, the checks C_i^j are often simple equality, range, or subnet tests. An example for an `iptables` rule which consists of these basic tests is

```
-p tcp --dport 80 --dst 1.2.3.4 -j ACCEPT
```

which accepts incoming TCP packets with destination port 80 addressed to 1.2.3.4.

The most straightforward way to solve the packet classification problem, which is implemented by many practically used classification systems [3, 4], is a linear search through the rule set $\mathscr{R}$. Although a linear search is simple to implement and memory efficient, it does not provide good classification performance. Faster classification algorithms, such as [7, 12, 22], exploit the simplicity of the above mentioned tests in order to translate the rule set $\mathscr{R}$ into search data structures for fast traversal at runtime. However, this is independent of the semantic specification of the rule set, which is typically still done through a linear list of rules, ordered by priority. Any other representation used by the algorithm must not change these rule set semantics, so that HyPaFilter can remain independent of the specific algorithms and data structures used internally in the software classificator.

3.2 Extended Packet Classification Problem

Practical packet filter implementations, such as `netfilter` [3], `pf` [4], and `ipfw` [2], support advanced matching criteria in order to increase the expressiveness of an implemented filtering policy. Examples for such sophisticated checks are connection tracking, rate limiting, unicast reverse path forwarding (URPF) verification, probability-based matching, or deep packet inspection. When used in conjunction with the previously defined basic checks, these tests can greatly foster both the robustness and effectiveness of the used packet filtering policy. In such a system, a rule R_i can be modelled as

$$R_i = C_i^1 \wedge \ldots \wedge C_i^K \wedge A_i,$$

where A_i is a rule-specific combination of advanced matching criteria. An example `iptables` rule which scans the packet payload in addition to basic header checks could look like

```
-p tcp --dport 80 -m string --string "BAD" --algo
                bm -j DROP.
```

Here, the A part of this rule is the test for the string "BAD". In contrast to most other existing hardware-accelerated classification systems, the HyPaFilter approach tackles both the basic and the extended packet classification problems.

4. MATCHING ALGORITHM

In order to support good classification performance, small rule set update latencies and expressive rule set semantics, the HyPaFilter system relies on a hybrid matching algorithm which first processes every incoming packet on the FPGA. After the packet is matched, the FPGA circuitry decides whether the packet requires further, potentially more complex processing in the host-based `netfilter` classification system. For the remainder of this paper, we follow the nomenclature of [36] and denote packets forwarded by the FPGA as *forwarded*, while those diverted to the host are called *shunted*. Although software-based packet processing is significantly more expensive than classification on the FPGA, we will present a strategy how the software rules can be structured in order to keep the number of traversed rules as small as possible in case of a packet shunt. In the remainder of this section, we will explain the architecture of the FPGA-based filter, the dispatch logic which decides whether a processed packet must be shunted to the host, as well as the rule set structure implemented in `netfilter`.

4.1 Hardware Filter

Let $\mathscr{R}_S \subseteq \mathscr{R}$ be the sublist containing the simple rules without advanced matching criteria, and $\mathscr{R}_C \subseteq \mathscr{R}$ be the sublist of complex rules with advanced matching criteria. That is, $\mathscr{R}_S \cup \mathscr{R}_C = \mathscr{R}$ and $\mathscr{R}_S \cap \mathscr{R}_C = \emptyset$. The classification system implemented on the FPGA solves the classic packet classification problem on $\mathscr{R}_S$, as introduced in Section 3.1. It therefore implements every $R_i \in \mathscr{R}_S$. In order to achieve high matching performance on the FPGA with a low deterministic processing latency per packet, we decided to use a rule set specific parallel matching engine, which is generated by translating every rule $R_i \in \mathscr{R}_S$ at setup time into a specialized match unit M_j specified in VHDL, similar to the technique proposed in [17]. Here, j is the index of rule R_i within the sublist $\mathscr{R}_S$. This process is illustrated in Figure 1. Since each rule in $\mathscr{R}_S$ is a conjunction of simple checks, such as subnet tests or port range tests, the match units are composed of a small number of basic comparator circuits. For example, a rule which matches TCP packets if the source IP address is in the subnet 203.0.0.0/8 with destination port 80 is translated into three specific comparator circuits: the first one compares the packet's transport protocol field against the TCP transport protocol number 6, while the second and third comparators compare the first octet of the packet's source IP address against 203 and the packet's destination port against 80, respectively. Finally, the results of these comparators are connected with an AND gate in order to determine whether the rule matches or not. As the match units are arranged in parallel, incoming network packets can be matched against the entire simple rule set $\mathscr{R}_S$ in a single clock cycle, which yields a result bit vector V of size $|\mathscr{R}_S|$. Here, the ith position V_i of the result vector V stores a 1 if rule R_i matches the current packet, otherwise V_i is set to 0. As we are interested in the most highly prioritized matching rule, we employ a priority encoder in order to determine the index of the first enabled bit in

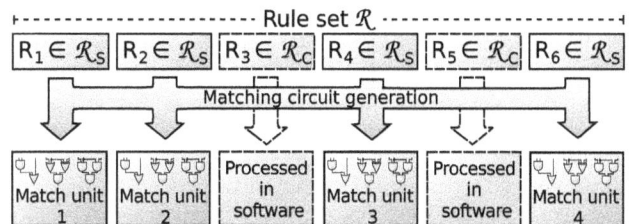

Figure 1: Translating simple rules into matching circuitry.

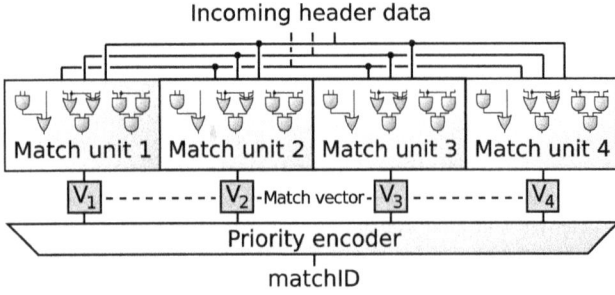

Figure 2: Parallel match of packet header data against $\mathscr{R}_S$.

V, which we will refer to as *matchID* in the following. The entire hardware matching process is sketched in Figure 2.

Up to this point, the packet classification problem is solved for the simple rule set $\mathscr{R}_S$ solely in hardware, as the matchID can be used in order to quickly look up the action $A_{\mathscr{R}_S,P}$ which must be applied for the current packet P. If the installed rule set $\mathscr{R}$ does not specify any rules with complex checks, i.e., if $\mathscr{R}_C = \emptyset$ and thus $\mathscr{R}_S = \mathscr{R}$, then the classification is complete at this point and $A_{\mathscr{R}_S,P}$ is applied to the current packet. However, if $\mathscr{R}_C \neq \emptyset$, then additional processing may be required by the software filter residing on the host system. This is the case when the matchID is greater or equal to the smallest index of a rule in $\mathscr{R}$ that specifies complex checks. In the following, we denote the smallest index of a rule in $\mathscr{R}$ with complex checks by the term *validID*.

For instance, consider the case that the hardware matching circuit for the rule set sketched in Figure 1 computes that matchID is 3 for an incoming packet P (that is, the packet matches the simple rule R_4). In this case, our hardware classification might be incorrect, as rule $R_3 \in \mathscr{R}_C$ is more highly prioritized than rule $R_4 \in \mathscr{R}_S$, and R_3 might also match on the packet P. Thus, whenever matchID $\geq$ validID, we shunt the classified packet to the host for further processing, as described in the next section.

4.2 Software Filter

The task of the software filter running on the host computer (which is `netfilter` in our case) is to classify every shunted packet which cannot be handled solely in hardware. However, simply installing only the complex rule set $\mathscr{R}_C$ in the software filter is not enough, since for every shunted packet P, the hardware classification might have been correct. This is the case when P is not matched by any complex rule with a higher priority than the first matching simple rule. As a consequence, the software filter must be able to reproduce the hardware classification result iff the most highly prioritized matching rule is in $\mathscr{R}_S$ and not in $\mathscr{R}_C$. In the remainder of this section, we present three different strategies how the rule set in the software filter can be organized in order to achieve this goal.

Full set strategy.

The most straightforward way to setup the software filter, which we call the *full set strategy*, is to simply install the entire rule set $\mathscr{R}$. That way, forwarded packets will always traverse rules in the correct order until the first matching rule is found, as sketched in Figure 3a for the example rule set from Figure 1. This approach allows for quick rule updates, since only one rule in the rule set installed in the software filter has to be changed in addition to a possible update of the validID register on the FPGA. This strategy is simple, but comes at the cost of a major disadvantage: the software filter may process a large number of rules for every shunted packet, including simple rules. It thus repeats significant work al-

ready done in hardware. In contrast to the full parallel match in the hardware filter, this can be rather expensive, as the rules are processed linearly in most existing software packet filters.

Cut set strategy.

The amount of redundant work which is done in software for shunted packets can be reduced with a simple modification. We already know that no simple rule with an index less than validID can match a packet which has been forwarded to the software filter—otherwise, the packet would have been processed solely on the FPGA. For example, consider the rule set from Figure 1 and a packet P with matchID 3. As matchID is equal to validID (which is also 3 in the example), P will be forwarded to the software filter, which will superfluously once again test rules R_1 and R_2 against P. In order to avoid this potential extra work on the host system, the *cut set strategy* installs only those rules $R_i \in \mathscr{R}$ in the software filter where $i \geq$ validID, as sketched in Figure 3b.

In comparison to the full set strategy, the cut set strategy has higher rule update costs, as a potentially large number of rules must be inserted or removed from the software filter in case of an update. For instance, if the current validID is 300, and a rule is updated at position 100, then the 200 rules $R_i \in \mathscr{R}$ with $100 \leq i \leq 299$ must be inserted in the software filter. However, our evaluation demonstrates that the update effort can clearly pay off in terms of classification performance, as the software filter will test $|\mathscr{R}| - \text{validID} + 1$ rules at most, in contrast to the worst case of testing $|\mathscr{R}|$ rules in the full set strategy.

Interval strategy.

All strategies described so far implement rule sets in the software filter which are agnostic to the partial classification result tuple <matchID, $A_{\mathscr{R}_S,P}$> previously computed on the FPGA for every shunted packet P. This results in wasted effort on the software side and inflates the software-side rule set—also in case of the cut set strategy. To avoid the recomputation effort, the *interval strategy* relies on metadata handed over from the FPGA to the matching software when a packet is shunted, i.e., the match index and action tuple <matchID, $A_{\mathscr{R}_S,P}$>. Simply put, the goal of the interval strategy is that shunted packets should only be tested against a fraction of the complex rules $\mathscr{R}_C$ and none of the rules in $\mathscr{R}_S$ again in software.

The basic idea behind the interval strategy is that groups of consecutive simple rules $G_k = \{R_i, \ldots, R_{i+\alpha}\}$ in $\mathscr{R}$ can be mapped to intervals $I_k = [M(R_i), M(R_{i+\alpha})]$, where $M(R_i)$ is the index of the generated match unit for R_i. For instance, the simple rules from the example rule set in Figure 4 form three groups $G_1 = \{R_1, R_2\}, G_2 = \{R_4\}$, and $G_3 = \{R_6\}$, with the corresponding intervals $I_1 = [1,2], I_2 = [3,3]$, and $I_3 = [4,4]$, respectively. Each interval represents a range of matchIDs, which may be computed by the FPGA for an incoming packet P. It is important to note that, if P is shunted to the host, then the matchID computed on the FPGA falls into exactly one of these intervals. The interval strategy exploits this fact by precomputing the chain of complex rules C_k for every interval I_k, that could potentially contain a more highly prioritized matching rule for a packet P whose hardware-computed matchID falls into interval I_k (i.e., P matches a simple rule in group G_k). In the example shown in Figure 4, C_1 is empty, since there are no complex rules in $\mathscr{R}$ that are more highly prioritized than the simple rules R_1 and R_2. In contrast, $C_2 = \{R_3\}$, as the complex rule R_3 is more highly prioritized than the simple rule R_4 and thus could match on packets which have been assigned to R_4 by the FPGA. Similarly, C_3 would be set to $\{R_3, R_5\}$, as both complex rules R_3 and R_5 are more highly prioritized than the simple rule R_6.

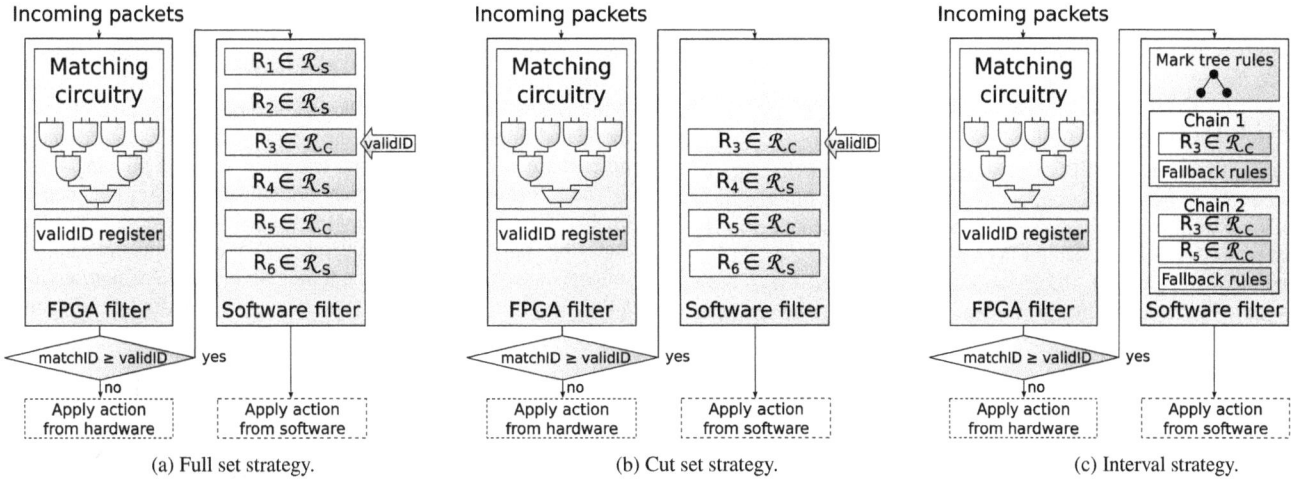

Figure 3: Different strategies to implement the complex rule set $\mathcal{R}_A$ in the software filter.

Now, whenever a packet P is shunted to the host, the FPGA driver fetches the <matchID, $A_{\mathcal{R}_S,P}$> tuple from the hardware, which are 28 and 4 bit values, respectively. Then, the FPGA driver code on the host uses the matchID to perform a binary search over the precomputed intervals in order to find the index k of the interval I_k that contains the matchID. Before the actual `netfilter` packet classification starts, the index k as well as the hardware action code $A_{\mathcal{R}_S,P}$ are written to the most significant 28 and least significant 4 bits of the `netfilter` `mark` field, which is a 32 bit metadata field attached to the packet P.

These efforts are justified by the fact that `netfilter` supports tests on the `mark` field. We exploit this fact in order to achieve two goals: first, we want to limit the set of complex rules which must be tested in `netfilter` to only those which are more highly prioritized than the first matching simple rule. Second, we want to apply the hardware-computed action $A_{\mathcal{R}_S,P}$ in `netfilter` *without* the need to re-traverse any simple rule in software.

To this end, the rules which are installed in `netfilter` for the interval strategy are generated as follows: the `netfilter` rule set starts with a sequence of rules which implement a binary search over the interval index k encoded in the most significant 28 bits of the `mark` field. This is done in order to quickly locate the chain of relevant complex rules C_k during the matching process, as sketched in Figure 3c. The generated rule set also contains each chain C_i as a linear list, which contains the complex rules that are mapped to interval I_i. Finally, the last rule in every chain C_i ends with a jump to a small set of fallback rules (one for each possible action), which use the least significant four bits of the `mark` field in order to apply the action $A_{\mathcal{R}_S,P}$ to the shunted packet P if no complex rule matches.

In comparison to the full set and cut set strategies, the interval strategy requires more complex preprocessing in case of a rule update, as the intervals for the complex rules have to be re-computed and communicated to the hardware driver. Furthermore, the `netfilter` binary search tree encoded in the filter rules must be re-generated. However, this strategy provides the best classification performance in software, as the number of traversed rules for each shunted packet P can be orders of magnitude smaller than in the full set and cut set strategies, as indicated by our evaluation. Furthermore, this approach does not require a change of the `netfilter` source code in order to use the hardware-computed matching information. Instead, we completely rely on existing `netfilter` match functionality in order to accelerate the software match process.

5. SYSTEM ARCHITECTURE

We implemented the hybrid algorithm on our HyPaFilter system, which consists of two functional units. One part is a standard host system, used to run the software firewall and the toolchain for managing the system. This can even be an already existing firewall appliance which should be upgraded in terms of performance. This system is extended by the second part, a general purpose FPGA

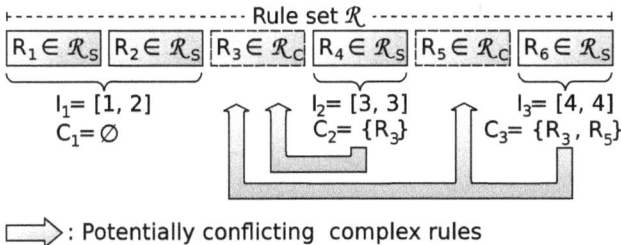

Figure 4: Intervals in the rule set $\mathcal{R}$.

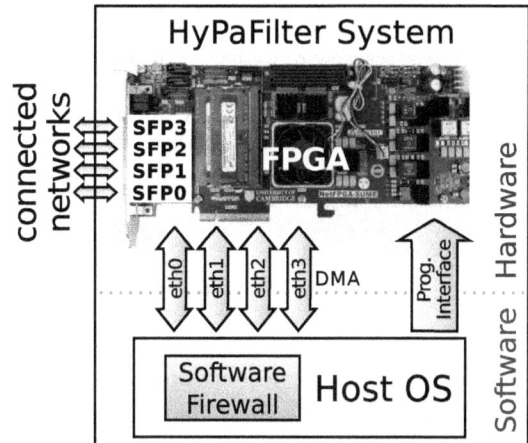

Figure 5: Proposed structure of a HyPaFilter system. The host can be any COTS system capable of carrying the additional FPGA NIC.

addon card, as shown in Figure 5. These units must provide a sufficient communication path for transferring data and settings between them.

FPGA Networking Card

This card is a suitable FPGA platform which can provide the required interfaces to both communicate with external Ethernet networks as well as acting as a regular network interface card in regard to the host system. Both FPGA plug-in cards we used during our evaluation – the VC709 [5] and the NetFPGA SUME – have proven to be suitable. They provide multiple network ports and can be plugged into a COTS system via PCI Express (PCIe). This card acts as the primary network interface connected to both internal (e.g., LAN) and external network (e.g., Internet). The hardware based filtering is handled exclusively on the FPGA on the card.

Host System

The host system carries the FPGA NIC and communicates with it, for example via PCIe. The host runs the operating system where the back-end `netfilter` with `iptables` is installed, supplies the tools to configure the FPGA and provides a user interface for administrating HyPaFilter.

These two units are connected through several communication channels. For quick and simple settings, the host system is able to set and read predefined 32 bit registers on the FPGA. Network traffic between FPGA and host is handled through *direct memory access (DMA)*. On the host side, a driver provides the functionality and interfaces so that the operating system can access the FPGA like a regular NIC. This is important since we do not want to rely on non-standard customizations to `netfilter` or other core components for HyPaFilter to work. By using a programming interface, the configuration of the FPGA can be updated. A software toolchain of the FPGA vendor, in our case Xilinx Vivado, is used to generate the FPGA configuration based on a given rule set. For convenience, it is also installed on the host.

Operation

Packets received from any connected network are first matched against the rules implemented on the FPGA. Based on its decision and the validID, packets are either dropped, forwarded directly (without interaction of the host system), or shunted to the host for further processing. The host can send packets through the supplied driver interface, which applies to both packets shunted through the software firewall and packets generated by the host itself. These packets are directly forwarded by the FPGA to the corresponding network interface. The flow of packets through this structure is visualized in Figure 6.

The two reasons for packets being shunted are a) not synthesizable rules appearing at positions in the rule set that would otherwise be forwarded, or b) an update to the rule set at these positions. For updating, this technique copes with the problem that changes to logic-level optimized rule sets cannot be selectively integrated. While a new filter's source code can be quickly generated, the synthesis and implementation of the new FPGA bitfile requires a significant amount of time – in our test setup about 45 minutes.

The information about which index in the rule set matched on the hardware is not discarded, as it is needed to remove the redundancy by applying the interval strategy. For operation, the administrator uses a central management tool. In our implementation, it is a Python command line interface. The general workflow for using HyPaFilter is shown in Figure 7.

5.1 Rule Set-Specialized Hardware Filter

The dataflow through the FPGA can be shown in two layers. The underlying structure for general networking and communication tasks is based on the NetFPGA SUME pipeline. The actual core which is responsible for filtering is embedded into this pipeline and connected via the AXI4 stream protocol as shown in Figure 8.

Internally, the HyPaFilter core uses a data bus width of 512 bits, with the pipeline running at 180 MHz. The theoretically achievable throughput of 85.83 Gbit/s is therefore enough to fully saturate all four 10 Gbit/s Ethernet ports. The NetFPGA SUME currently uses a bus width of only 256 bits which are converted before and after the hardware core. Packets coming into the hardware core are first distributed (cloned) into a classification path and a data path, with the latter being a simple FIFO queue of 64 kB. In the classification path, the *Header Parser* extracts relevant information from incoming packets. For a versatile operation, the header parser should take care of the data alignment due to VLAN tags or various header lengths. It is therefore implemented as a multi-stage non-blocking pipeline architecture. The preprocessed data is forwarded to the filtering module, which is automatically generated by the management toolchain. After the classification, the decision is forwarded to the *Output Processing*, where the determined action is executed: DROP (read from FIFO and discard), FORWARD, or SHUNT by adapting the output port field in the packet's metadata. The register interface can be accessed from the host directly via PCIe. Figure 9 shows the described parts in the module. The match logic is able to classify packets in constant time. Hence, a reader might note that the separation into data and classification path yields no advantages in terms of maximum throughput. However, as we aim to support more complex decisions in hardware in our future work, this structure allows for more flexible development. Since the hardware filtering logic contains no components that could cause a congestion, it is clear that the HyPaFilter hardware core is never the limiting

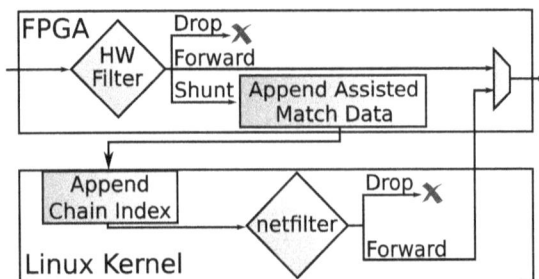

Figure 6: Flow of packets through the HyPaFilter system.

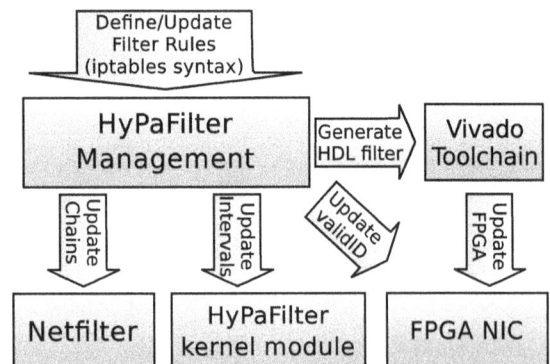

Figure 7: HyPaFilter workflow with the central management tool.

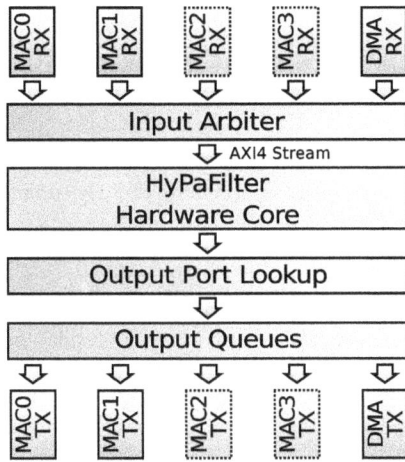

Figure 8: Simplified dataflow structure of the NetFPGA SUME. The dashed elements are available, but not used in our evaluation.

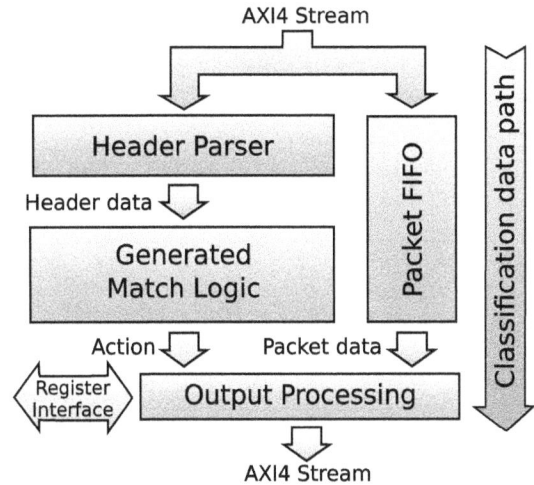

Figure 9: Dataflow inside the HyPaFilter hardware core.

factor for raw data throughput in this setup. The hardware filter core is able to extract and classify incoming packets against a variety of parameters like IPv4 address, IPv6 address, protocol type (UDP, TCP, ICMP, ARP), media access control (MAC) address, TCP/UDP ports, and several flags.

Previous work has shown that the resource utilization of typical rule sets on FPGAs can be significantly reduced by including the actual rule set in the logic optimization process, rather than using a generalized filtering logic [15, 17]. As firewall rule sets in general are not static, an FPGA's reconfigurability allows to exploit this potential in practical applications. Thus, in our HyPaFilter prototype, we combine such a rule set tailored hardware filter with a generic software filter residing on the host. However, the proposed HyPaFilter approach does not strictly rely on this type of specialized hardware filter and could also utilize another hardware matcher (e. g., a TCAM), as long as the driver interface which provides the matching information is maintained.

5.2 Software Filter for Incremental Updates and Complex Rules

Although hardware-based parallel packet filtering, as explained in the previous section, can achieve high throughputs of 40 Gbps or higher, it suffers from two fundamental drawbacks: on the one hand, incremental updates to the rule set are time-consuming. On the other hand, the flexibility of hardware-based filters is much more constrained than that of software-based filters. Most hardware-based approaches are restricted to simple equality, range, or prefix checks on incoming header fields [17, 19, 20]. In contrast, many software-based packet filters, such as netfilter [3] or pf [4], support much more complex matching criteria. Examples are the state of the flow that corresponds to the examined packet, probability-based matches for rate limiting, or even arbitrary Berkeley Packet Filter (BPF) expressions, to name only a few. Furthermore, new filtering functionality like, e. g., support for a new protocol or the addition of further options for an existing one, can be added relatively quickly. However, a full-fledged in-circuit implementation which supports all of these features is notoriously difficult, as dedicated hardware it typically optimized for a very limited functionality.

In order to achieve the advantages of both software- and hardware-based packet processing, i. e., (1) high throughput, (2) fast incremental updates, and (3) powerful rule set semantics, we combine

fast specialized matching circuitry with the flexibility and expressiveness of a CPU-based packet filter, namely netfilter.

6. EVALUATION

In our evaluation, we focus on three of the most important performance metrics for packet classification architectures: packet rate, rule set update latencies and consumption of resources. This stands in contrast to raw data throughput measurements, which are more targeted at the data flow structure. Therefore, we conducted the following experiments:

- determining the maximum number of rules which can be fitted onto the FPGA,

- measuring the maximum packet rate of the NetFPGA SUME architecture,

- measuring the performance of the HyPaFilter system and comparing the impact of rule updates using different strategies,

- measuring the network latency,

- measuring delays of the update process and number of rules and

- comparing against a commercial OpenFlow software-defined networking (SDN) setup.

To generate a high workload on the classification engine, we used small packets at a high rate. Packets carry just five arbitrarily chosen bytes as payload. For our evaluation, we set up a typical bridging firewall scenario as shown in Figure 10.

Traffic is generated and received by two dedicated machines, based on Intel Core i7 960 with a dual-port 10 Gbit/s NIC. The hosts run Ubuntu Linux. We generated rule sets and traffic using the ClassBench suite [33], which is widely used in this context. The system is easily capable of saturating the connected networks with traffic. These sender and receiver hosts are connected to the HyPaFilter system via optical fibre. We counted the number of packets received by the MAC-Core MAC0 on the NetFPGA and those arriving on the network interface of the receiver. Further network connections between the systems to remotely start the test cycles and collect the results are not shown.

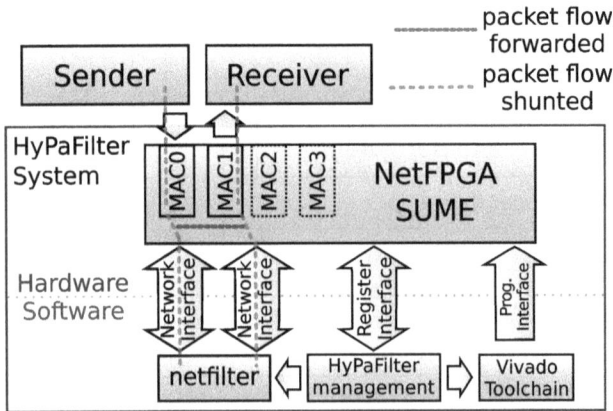

Figure 10: Evaluation setup showing the relevant components. Traffic is generated on the sender and directed through the bridging HyPaFilter firewall.

The HyPaFilter system consists of the following relevant components: Intel Xeon E5-1650 v3 based host, Intel 82599ES dual-port 10 Gbit/s NIC, NetFPGA SUME PCIe card, Ubuntu Linux, `netfilter` framework and `iptables` v1.4.21, Xilinx Vivado 2014.4, as well as the HyPaFilter management tools. The hardware filter core is integrated into a modified data pipeline based on the reference NIC project of the NetFPGA SUME release 1.0.0.

6.1 Test Rule Sets

To evaluate the classification performance under replicable conditions, we generated our test rule sets with ClassBench [33]. The number of rules we could fit onto the FPGA was limited by the timing constraints and resulted in a maximum of 1100 rules. For evaluating our classification algorithm and strategy, we created three different UDP rule sets `acl1k1`, `fw1k1` and `ipc1k1`, with all rules applying the action ACCEPT. This way, the number of dropped packets can be regarded as the packet loss solely due to the architecture.

ClassBench's *trace_generator* was used to generate trace files corresponding to the rule sets. We wrote a C program for generating and transmitting the test packet stream from such a trace file, because no sufficiently fast solution could be found for this task under the given conditions. The rule sets as well as the traces we used are publicly available at [14].

For each test, the rule set was translated by the HyPaFilter management tool, integrated in the NetFPGA SUME pipeline and afterwards synthesized and implemented into an FPGA configuration bitfile. Table 1 shows the resource utilization of the FPGA configuration for a Virtex 7 690T. The relevant parameters are usage of flip-flops (FF), look-up tables (LUT), LUTs used as memory elements (Memory LUT), and block random access memory (BRAM). Differences can be caused by the different rule sets and heuristic algorithms used during the implementation process in Vivado.

To measure the impact of changes or occurrences of complex rules to the rule set we added in each test new rules to certain positions, starting from the end of the rule set. We used string matching rules for this purpose:

```
-m string --algo bm --string BAD -m statistic\
 --mode random --probability 0.99
```

These complex rules are especially interesting as the use of the full capabilities of `netfilter` is one of the core features of HyPaFilter.

Resource	acl1k	fw1k	ipc1k
FF	9.12%/0.86%	9.12%/0.86%	8.26%/0.86%
LUT	15.07%/1.69%	16.22%/2.85%	13.38%/1.83%
Memory LUT	1.07%/0.01%	1.10%/0.01%	1.10%/0.01%
BRAM	16.73%/2.72%	16.73%/2.72%	14.01%/2.72%

Table 1: FPGA resource utilization overall/HyPaFilter core with different rule sets.

6.2 Architecture Packet Rate

Forwarding packets directly in hardware provides the lowest latency and highest packet rate. Therefore, the first experiment was used to measure the maximum packet rate dependent on the percentage of packets bridged to the software. We will later compare the packet rate of the different strategies against these values.

As the generated packets by the sender will match the rule set at certain positions with a predefined distribution, the hardware filter was used in combination with the validID to shunt parts of the traffic to the software. There were no rules loaded into `netfilter`, all incoming packets are forwarded by the Linux bridge.

We compared the number of ingress packets vs. packets received at the receiver, which is the inverse of packets being dropped in the firewall. Each data point shows the average packet rate of ten 20 second test runs, with distribution of the workload being set by the validID as the variable parameter. The average number of ingress packets arriving at the HyPaFilter network interface in each test run before any classification is 2.3 million in 20 s. Figure 11 shows the percentage of packets arriving at the receiver, the standard deviation was too small to be visible in the plot. The architecture of the host system and the NetFPGA SUME used as a simple NIC is only capable of processing on average 6.4% of the packets which arrive at the NetFPGA input interface. Increasing the validID and therefore reducing the fraction of shunted packets increases the overall amount close to 100% when all packets are directly forwarded by the FPGA NIC.

6.3 Strategy Comparison

To evaluate the performance of the different strategies described in Section 4.2, the setup described in Section 6.2 was now adapted to use firewalling. Starting with a hardware only scenario, we measured the impact of rule insertions without updating the hardware filter definition. This subsequently causes an increasing amount of packets to be shunted to the software firewall.

We conducted our experiments by following a certain test cycle for all three strategies and repeated them for each of the three sam-

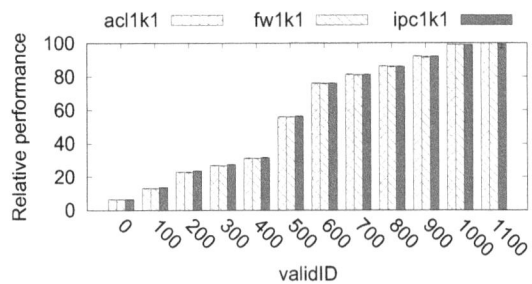

Figure 11: Packet rate of the underlying architecture as a function of the fraction of packets forwarded through hardware. At validID = 0 all packets are shunted to the software, while at validID = 1100 all packets are forwarded.

ple rule sets `acl1k1`, `ipc1k1`, and `fw1k1`. During the test cycle, we measured the average packet throughput rate after iteration n following these steps:

1) implement the sample rule set onto the FPGA and set validID to match everything in hardware

2) for test run $n = 0$ insert a new rule at position $P_0 = 1100$ and set validID $= P_0$

3) for test run $n + 1$ insert a new rule at position $P_{n+1} = 1100 - 100(n+1)$ and set validID $= P_{n+1}$

4) repeat last step until $P_n = 0$.

For the first part of this test, we used the full set strategy and loaded the complete rule set in `netfilter`. As mentioned in Section 4.2, this leads to a high redundancy in the matching. For example, an update at position index $P = 500$ sets validID $= 500$, therefore all packets with matchID ≥ 500 will be shunted. These packets will, however, never match the first 500 rules in `netfilter` (counting from index zero), making them essentially useless.

For large validIDs, the tests confirmed the assumption that significant performance gains can already be achieved by removing the parts of the `netfilter` rule set that correspond to matchID $<$ validID (cut set strategy). The interval strategy proved to be a useful additional measure when the amount of packets shunted to software is large or the hardware and software rule sets intersect at a high priority. Figures 12a, 12b, and 12c show the speedup as a factor of the received packet rate compared to using `netfilter` without any hardware acceleration and string matching rules for insertion. The error bars show the standard deviation.

For the full set strategy, it can be clearly seen that the packet rate behaves non-monotonic and dips near validID $= 800$. This can be explained by the combination of two contrary effects: first, with the validID decreasing, an increasing amount of shunted packets causes the software performance to reach its limit. Second, with the validID increasing, the packets that are shunted will only match a smaller and smaller part at the end of the software rule set. This means that the average number of rules traversed by the packets will also increase, regardless of the constant total number of software rules.

To get a better overview of the performance increase by applying the improved strategies, their packet rate has to be compared against the full set strategy. This relative speedup, again for using complex string matching rules in the insertion process, can be seen in Figures 13a, 13b, and 13c. Large gains of performance of both the cut set and interval strategy can be seen due to the reduction of the long path effect which is causing the equivalent dip for with the full set strategy near validID $= 800$. With an increased amount of complex software rules with high priority (low validID), the advantage of our hardware assisted binary search algorithm used in the interval strategy becomes clear.

6.4 Network Latency

While the packet classification rate is the most interesting parameter to measure for evaluation, the additional latency which is added by security appliances can be a major issue for certain applications, e.g., in data centers. Our network latency measurement splits into two parts: the additional delay of the HyPaFilter hardware core in the NetFPGA SUME pipeline, and the actual delay which can be seen on network packets.

The internal additional delay in the FPGA could be determined in the Vivado Simulator and is fully deterministic at 24 clock cycles. With a clock rate of 180 MHz, the core therefore adds an ad-

ditional delay of 133 ns compared to the NetFPGA SUME in NIC operation.

In order to check for the overall network latency imposed by the HyPaFilter system, the round-trip time (RTT) was measured with `ping`, sending 50 packets per test. While a direct connection between sender and receiver (without the NetFPGA SUME) shows a one way latency of 51 µs ($\sigma = 3.2$ µs), with the HyPaFilter system present and forwarded packets only we saw a tolerable increase to 52 µs ($\sigma = 5.4$ µs). For packets shunted through software without any firewall interaction it further increased to 73 µs ($\sigma = 3.5$ µs), the highest average delay of 96 µs ($\sigma = 7$ µs) occurred with shunted packets and an active software rule set of 1100 rules loaded into `netfilter`.

With the limitation of the uncertainty of the measurement method, the results show that our hardware filtering algorithm is suitable for low latency requirements.

6.5 Rule Set Parameters

The strong influence of the number of rules in a software firewall to its classification performance leads to the question how many rules are loaded into the firewall for the three different strategies after applying the update cycle. These numbers were determined by exporting the rules with `iptables-save` and counting the correspondent lines. As HyPaFilter uses a binary tree searching algorithm, we also evaluated the worst case path length, i.e., the highest number of potentially traversed rules for incoming packets. Figure 14 gives an overview over the actual number of rules which are active in `netfilter` for different strategies, as well as the number of rules which have to be evaluated in the worst case.

The synthesis and implementation process that is used to generate the new bitfile with one of the test rule sets requires about 45 minutes on the described HyPaFilter evaluation host, using Vivado 2014.4. The Xilinx tool `xmd`, which is used to configure the FPGA with this bitfile via the programming interface finishes in 17.38 s. During this time, the network is interrupted. In our test cycles, no hardware update was required to reach the stated results.

6.6 Update Delay

Another interesting parameter is the time required for different types of updates required for different strategies. We therefore measured the time for inserting rules, updating the validID register in the FPGA and uploading a new configuration to the FPGA. According to our test cycle, the delays for the insertion were determined for consecutive insertions of rules at certain positions, i.e., the test at validID = 900 is executed with the assumption of rules preliminary inserted at position 1100 and 1000. The update process involves different operations for each strategy: a) for the full set strategy, inserting a single rule with `iptables` and setting validID b) for the cut set strategy, truncating the rule set, inserting and loading this set with `iptables-restore`, setting validID c) for the interval strategy, calculating intervals, inserting the chained rule set with `iptables-restore`, updating the driver and setting validID. Figure 15 shows the result of this test, as an average of 10 test cycles for each data point. Setting the validID register on the FPGA alone takes 1 µs. The measured time confirms our assumptions about the cost for rule insertions (see Section 4.2). However, even the most demanding updates of the interval strategy could be carried out with a tolerable delay.

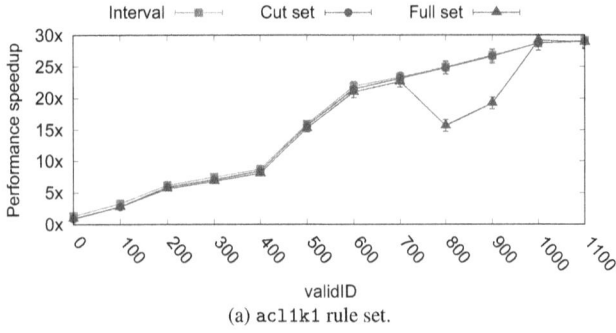

(a) acl1k1 rule set.

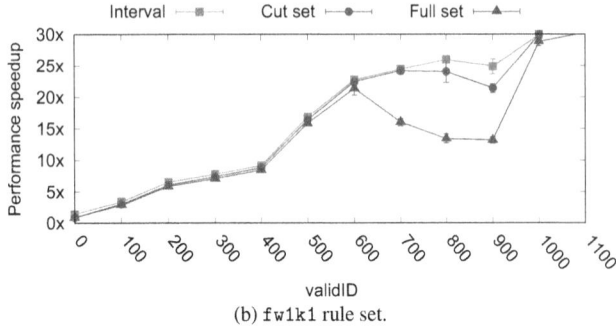

(b) fw1k1 rule set.

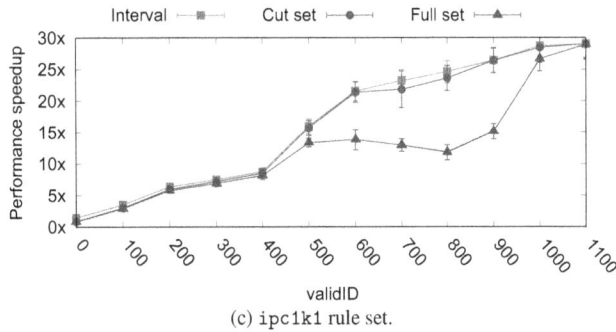

(c) ipc1k1 rule set.

Figure 12: Speedup of HyPaFilter with complex inserted rules and different strategies over a software-only `netfilter` setup.

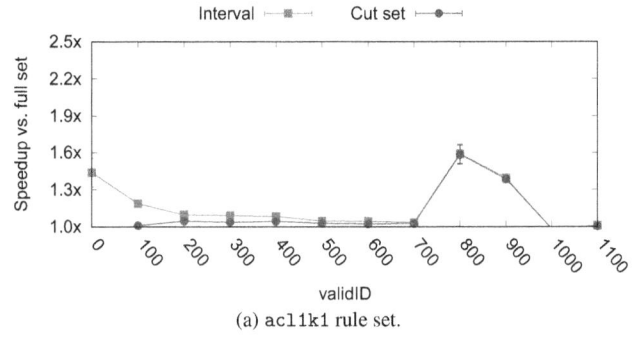

(a) acl1k1 rule set.

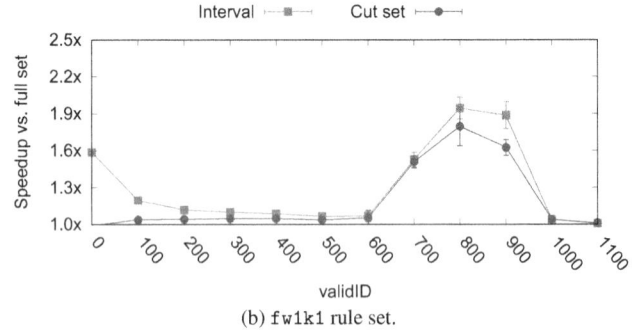

(b) fw1k1 rule set.

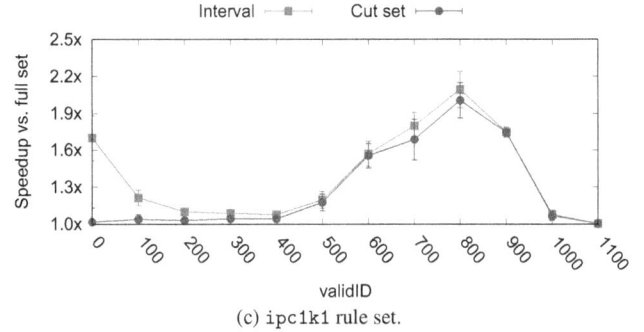

(c) ipc1k1 rule set.

Figure 13: Speedup of the enhanced strategies with complex inserted rules, compared to the full set strategy.

6.7 OpenFlow SDN

The logical division into a hardware filtering unit with a software backend is in several aspects similar to the concept of an SDN. In a typical SDN switch setup, a controller would place *flows* dynamically into the hardware, allowing fast transmission of matching packets. For a firewall application, the requirements are more complicated than for a simple switch. Therefore, a controller with firewalling functionality was required.

We replaced the NetFPGA with a Quanta Computer LB8 48-port SDN [27] switch running PicOS. For a fair comparison, we used a publicly available and stable controller, OpenIRIS v2.2.1 [9], which was installed on the HyPaFilter host system. The OpenFlow 1.3 protocol is used for the communication with the switch. OpenIRIS includes a firewall module which can be controlled via the REST API [29]. The number of incoming packets was determined through the web interface of OpenIRIS.

We noticed several issues of the OpenIRIS firewall module during our evaluation:

- Rules could not be added to certain positions. Although it is possible to define a `ruleid`, the parameter seems to be ignored and replaced by a random value which is not related

to the actual (logical) position of the rule. New rules are always prepended to the current rule set.

- The source and destination port could not be specified as a range.

- The port fields could not be set to values higher than 32767, obviously due to sign conversion problems.

The update process therefore has to be carried out by first deleting all rules and then adding all rules of our rule set in reverse order. Loading 1100 rules into the module with the REST API takes 3.9 s on average. During our evaluation we found out that the firewall only placed flows into the hardware for ICMP ping packets and established TCP sessions. Our test data (UDP packets), as well as generic TCP packets do not trigger this mechanism, therefore forcing each packet into the slow path to the controller. Although not configurable, this behaviour may be a protection against SYN flooding of the flow table, i. e. purposefully trying to fill the flow table with useless entries. We concluded that due to these effects, a fair comparison against our setup was not possible. Further investigation of these issues is out of the scope of this paper.

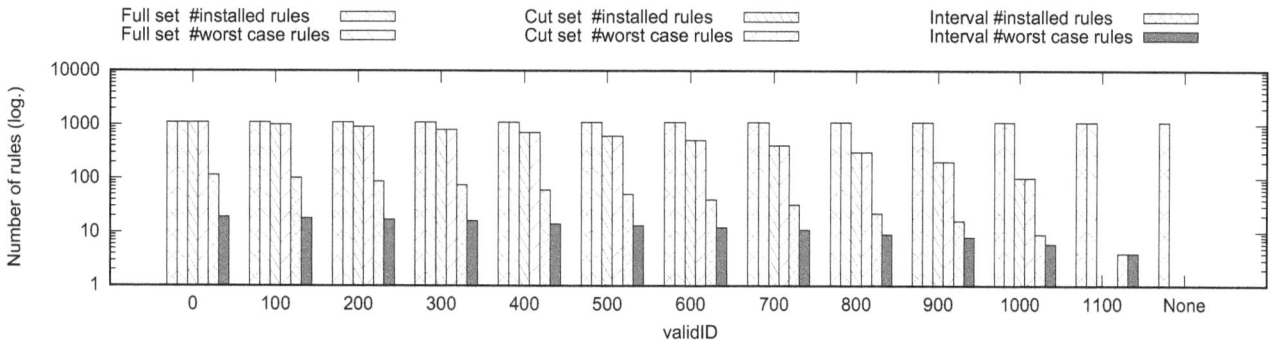

Figure 14: Number of installed/worst case traversed rules for different strategies.

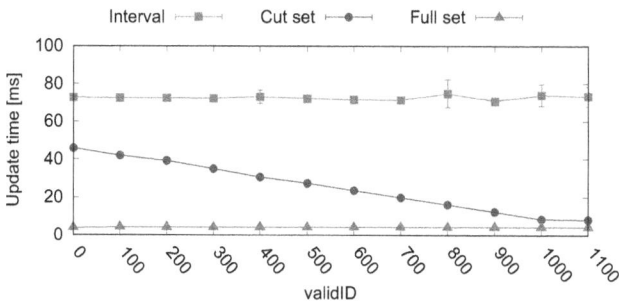

Figure 15: Update latency of different strategies.

7. CONCLUSION

In this work we introduce HyPaFilter, a hybrid packet classification approach which combines the parallel matching capabilities of specialized hardware with the extensive matching semantics of widely used software packet filters. HyPaFilter accomplishes this task by partitioning the implemented packet processing policy into a simple and a complex part, where the simple part can be handled directly in hardware and the complex part is installed in the software filter. Incoming network packets are first processed in hardware and are shunted to the software filter only in the case where complex processing is required. We present a novel strategy how the software-implemented part of the rule set can be organized in order to reuse matching information from the hardware. This strategy can be used on top of `netfilter` and does not require changes of the `netfilter` source code. The actual hardware filter is not limited to our evaluation example, it can be any suitable algorithm which provides the match index. Our evaluation of HyPaFilter based on a combination of a NetFPGA SUME device and a Linux host system demonstrates significant increases in the achievable throughput over a software-only approach, even with rule set constellations where the majority of incoming packets must be processed in software.

Possible future work includes the integration of a fast dynamic state table on the FPGA which can be used to directly handle stateful rules in hardware. This way, stateful rules could be handled entirely in hardware and would not require the bridging of packets. Ideally, this table would still allow access from the host so that the software is able to shunt acknowledged sessions in hardware.

8. ACKNOWLEDGEMENTS

The authors would like to acknowledge the support of the German Federal Ministry for Economic Affairs and Energy, whose grant allowed us to conduct major parts of the fundamental research. Furthermore, we thank the Computer Laboratory of the University of Cambridge for providing the NetFPGA SUME project as a suitable research platform. This work was, in-part, supported by the European Union Horizon 2020 SSICLOPS project (grant agreement 644866).

9. REFERENCES

[1] genugate firewall. www.genua.de/en/solutions/high-resistance-firewall-genugate.html. Last access: Novemver 6, 2015.

[2] IPFW firewall. https://www.freebsd.org/cgi/man.cgi?ipfw. Last access: September 28, 2015.

[3] The netfilter.org project. www.netfilter.org. Last access: September 28, 2015.

[4] OpenBSD packet filter. http://www.openbsd.org/faq/pf/. Last access: September 28, 2015.

[5] VC709 Evaluation Board for the Virtex-7 FPGA. http://www.xilinx.com/support/documentation/boards_and_kits/vc709/ug887-vc709-eval-board-v7-fpga.pdf. Last access: September 29, 2015.

[6] K. Accardi, T. Bock, F. Hady, and J. Krueger. Network processor acceleration for a linux* netfilter firewall. In *ANCS '05: Proceedings of the 2005 Symposium on Architectures for Networking and Communication Systems*, pages 115–123, Oct. 2005.

[7] F. Baboescu and G. Varghese. Scalable packet classification. In *SIGCOMM '01: Proceedings of the 2001 Conference on Applications, Technologies, Architectures, and Protocols for Computer Communications*, pages 199–210, Aug. 2001.

[8] P. Bosshart et al. Forwarding metamorphosis: Fast programmable match-action processing in hardware for SDN. In *SIGCOMM '13: Proceedings of the 2013 Conference on Applications, Technologies, Architectures, and Protocols for Computer Communications*, pages 99–110, Aug. 2013.

[9] L. Byungjoon, J. Shin, and S. H. Park. Openflow Controller by ETRI. https://github.com/openiris/IRIS, 2015. Last access: Oct 25, 2015.

[10] M.-S. Chen, M.-Y. Liao, P.-W. Tsai, M.-Y. Luo, C.-S. Yang, and C. E. Yeh. Using netfpga to offload linux netfilter firewall. In *2nd North American NetFPGA Developers Workshop*, 2010.

[11] J. Fong, X. Wang, Y. Qi, J. Li, and W. Jiang. Parasplit: A scalable architecture on FPGA for terabit packet classification. In *HOTI '12: Proceedings of the 20th*

Symposium on High Performance Interconnects, pages 1–8, Aug. 2012.

[12] P. Gupta and N. McKeown. Packet classification using hierarchical intelligent cuttings. In *HOTI '99: Proceedings of the 7th Symposium on High Performance Interconnects*, pages 34–41, Aug. 1999.

[13] P. Gupta and N. McKeown. Algorithms for packet classification. *IEEE Network: The Magazine of Global Internetworking*, 15(2):24–32, Mar. 2001.

[14] S. Hager. Hypaf rule sets. http://hardfire.de/rule-sets.

[15] S. Hager, D. Bendyk, and B. Scheuermann. Partial reconfiguration and specialized circuitry for flexible FPGA-based packet processing. In *ReConFig '15: 2015 International Conference on ReConFigurable Computing and FPGAs*, Dec. 2015. to appear.

[16] S. Hager, S. Selent, and B. Scheuermann. Trees in the list: Accelerating list-based packet classification through controlled rule set expansion. In *CoNEXT '14: Proceedings of the 10th International Conference on Emerging Networking Experiments and Technologies*, pages 101–107, Dec. 2014.

[17] S. Hager, F. Winkler, B. Scheuermann, and K. Reinhardt. MPFC: Massively parallel firewall circuits. In *LCN '14: Proceedings of the 39th Annual IEEE International Conference on Local Computer Networks*, pages 305–313, Sept. 2014.

[18] W. Jiang and V. Prasanna. Large-scale wire-speed packet classification on FPGAs. In *FPGA '09: Proceedings of the ACM/SIGDA 17th International Symposium on Field Programmable Gate Arrays*, pages 219–228, Feb. 2009.

[19] W. Jiang and V. K. Prasanna. Field-split parallel architecture for high performance multi-match packet classification using FPGAs. In *SPAA '09: Proceedings of the 21st ACM Symposium on Parallelism in Algorithms and Architectures*, pages 188–196, Aug. 2009.

[20] W. Jiang and V. K. Prasanna. A FPGA-based parallel architecture for scalable high-speed packet classification. In *ASAP '09: Proceedings of the 20th IEEE International Conference on Application-specific Systems, Architectures and Processors*, pages 24–31, July 2009.

[21] W. Jiang and V. K. Prasanna. Large-scale wire-speed packet classification on FPGAs. In *FPGA '09: Proceedings of the ACM/SIGDA 17th International Symposium on Field Programmable Gate Arrays*, pages 219–228, Feb. 2009.

[22] T. V. Lakshman and D. Stiliadis. High-speed policy-based packet forwarding using efficient multi-dimensional range matching. In *SIGCOMM '98: Proceedings of the 1998 Conference on Applications, Technologies, Architectures, and Protocols for Computer Communications*, pages 203–214, Aug. 1998.

[23] A. Liu, E. Torng, and C. Meiners. Firewall compressor: An algorithm for minimizing firewall policies. In *INFOCOM '08: Proceedings of the 27th Annual Joint Conference of the IEEE Computer and Communications Societies*, pages 176–180, Apr. 2008.

[24] D. Liu, B. Hua, X. Hu, and X. Tang. High-performance packet classification algorithm for many-core and multithreaded network processor. In *CASES '06: Proceedings of the 2006 International Conference on Compilers, Architecture, and Synthesis for Embedded System*, pages 334–344, Oct. 2006.

[25] A. Putnam, A. Caulfield, E. Chung, D. Chiou, K. Constantinides, J. Demme, H. Esmaeilzadeh, J. Fowers, G. Gopal, J. Gray, et al. A reconfigurable fabric for accelerating large-scale datacenter services. In *ISCA '14: Proceedings of the 41st International Symposium on Computer Architecture*, pages 13–24, June 2014.

[26] Y. Qi, B. Xu, F. He, B. Yang, J. Yu, and J. Li. Towards high-performance flow-level packet processing on multi-core network processors. In *ANCS '07: Proceedings of the 3rd ACM/IEEE Symposium on Architectures for Networking and Communication Systems*, pages 17–26, Dec. 2007.

[27] Quanta Computer Inc. QuantaMesh 5000 Series BMS T5016-LB8D. http://www.qct.io/Product/Networking/Bare-Metal-Switch/QuantaMesh-BMS-T5016-LB8D-p58c77c75c159, 2015. Last access: Oct 25, 2015.

[28] D. Qunfeng, S. Banerjee, J. Wang, and D. Agrawal. Wire speed packet classification without TCAMs: A few more registers (and a bit of logic) are enough. In *SIGMETRICS '07: Proceedings of the 2007 ACM SIGMETRICS International Conference on Measurement and Modeling of Computer Systems*, pages 253–264, June 2007.

[29] J. Shin. REST API List of OFMFirewall. https://github.com/openiris/IRIS/wiki/REST-API-List-of-OFMFirewall, 2014. Last access: Oct 25, 2015.

[30] S. Singh, F. Baboescu, G. Varghese, and J. Wang. Packet classification using multidimensional cutting. In *SIGCOMM '03: Proceedings of the 2003 Conference on Applications, Technologies, Architectures, and Protocols for Computer Communications*, pages 213–224, Aug. 2003.

[31] V. Srinivasan, S. Suri, and G. Varghese. Packet classification using tuple space search. In *SIGCOMM '99: Proceedings of the 1999 Conference on Applications, Technologies, Architectures, and Protocols for Computer Communications*, pages 135–146, Aug. 1999.

[32] D. Taylor. Survey and taxonomy of packet classification techniques. *ACM Comput. Surv.*, 37(3):238–275, Sept. 2005.

[33] D. Taylor and J. Turner. Classbench: a packet classification benchmark. *IEEE/ACM Transactions on Networking*, 15(3):499–511, June 2007.

[34] B. Vamanan, G. Voskuilen, and T. N. Vijaykumar. Efficuts: Optimizing packet classification for memory and throughput. In *SIGCOMM '10: Proceedings of the 2010 Conference on Applications, Technologies, Architectures, and Protocols for Computer Communications*, pages 207–218, Aug. 2010.

[35] M. Varvello, R. Laufer, F. Zhang, and T. Lakshman. Multi-layer packet classification with graphics processing units. In *CoNEXT '14: Proceedings of the 10th International Conference on Emerging Networking Experiments and Technologies*, pages 109–120, Dec. 2014.

[36] N. Weaver, V. Paxson, and J. Gonzalez. The shunt: an FPGA-based accelerator for network intrusion prevention. In *FPGA '07: Proceedings of the ACM/SIGDA 15th International Symposium on Field Programmable Gate Arrays*, pages 199–206, Feb. 2007.

[37] N. Zilberman, Y. Audzevich, G. Covington, and A. Moore. NetFPGA SUME: Toward 100 Gbps as Research Commodity. *Micro, IEEE*, 34(5):32–41, Sept 2014.

Memory-Efficient String Matching
for Intrusion Detection Systems
using a High-Precision Pattern Grouping Algorithm

Shervin Vakili[†], J.M. Pierre Langlois[†], Bochra Boughzala[‡], Yvon Savaria[†]

[†]Polytechnique Montréal, Montréal, Canada
{shervin.vakili, pierre.langlois, yvon.savaria}@polymtl.ca
[‡]Ericsson Canada, Montréal, Canada
bochra.boughzala@ericsson.com

ABSTRACT

The increasing complexity of cyber-attacks necessitates the design of more efficient hardware architectures for real-time Intrusion Detection Systems (IDSs). String matching is the main performance-demanding component of an IDS. An effective technique to design high-performance string matching engines is to partition the target set of strings into multiple subgroups and to use a parallel string matching hardware unit for each subgroup. This paper introduces a novel pattern grouping algorithm for heterogeneous bit-split string matching architectures. The proposed algorithm presents a reliable method to estimate the correlation between strings. The correlation factors are then used to find a preferred group for each string in a seed growing approach. Experimental results demonstrate that the proposed algorithm achieves an average of 41% reduction in memory consumption compared to the best existing approach found in the literature, while offering orders of magnitude faster execution time compared to an exhaustive search.

Keywords

Computer network security; Deep packet inspection; Intrusion detection systems; String matching

1. INTRODUCTION

The utilization of high performance hardware engines is becoming an inevitable choice for real-time Intrusion Detection Systems (IDS), due to their increasing complexity and the ever-growing performance demands of network applications. Deep Packet Inspection (DPI), the most complex part of an IDS, performs the detection of malicious patterns of data in packet payloads. String matching is a key function in the DPI process. A list of suspicious patterns is extracted and regularly updated from known attacks as a library of hazardous rule-sets by network security companies. As the size of these patterns increases, the complexity of real-time string matching grows rapidly.

ANCS '16, March 17-18, 2016, Santa Clara, CA, USA
© 2016 ACM. ISBN 978-1-4503-4183-7/16/03...$15.00
DOI: http://dx.doi.org/10.1145/2881025.2881031

Using hardware string matching engines is necessary to enable real-time DPI in modern high-speed networks. Finite-state machine (FSM)-based algorithms such as Aho-Corasick [1] (AC) are broadly used for string matching hardware design. The memory-based realization of these algorithms can achieve linear time complexity ($O(n)$) for the matching function. However, memory requirements, which are proportional to the number of states and the number of bits in each state, can be a significant limiting factors [2]. Khan et al. [2] and Jony [3] presented comparative analysis and experimental results on various string matching algorithms.

Several algorithms and architectural techniques have been introduced in the literature aiming to improve the efficiency of the AC algorithm. For such realizations, memory consumption and memory accesses are the most limiting factors. Hence, they are the main criteria in evaluating different realization approaches [4-6]. Some previous works proposed new representations for finite state machines aiming at reducing the total number of states or transitions. Such reductions can lead to proportional savings in both the memory consumption and the number of memory accesses.

Kumar et al. introduced a new representation for Deterministic Finite Automata (DFA) that is called Delayed Input DFA (D^2FA) [7]. D^2FA can significantly save memory space by reducing the number of distinct transitions between states. Becchi et al. proposed a compression technique that can achieve comparable memory savings with lower provable bounds on memory bandwidth compared to the D^2FA approach [8].

Crochemore et al. [9] introduced a new algorithm that combines the ideas of the AC algorithm and the directed acyclic word graphs. The time complexity of that algorithm is linear in the worst case. In the average-case, the time complexity is considerably better, assuming the shortest pattern is sufficiently long. Dimopoulos et al. [4] presented the Split-AC algorithm, which is a reconfigurable variation of the AC algorithm. The algorithm employs domain-specific characteristics of intrusion detection to reduce the FSM memory requirements. Arudchutha et al. [10] employed multicore processors to implement the AC algorithm. The objective of that work is to improve the performance of AC algorithm through parallelization. Zha et al. [11] utilized a graphics processing unit (GPU) to accelerate the AC algorithm. Kouzinopoulos et al. [12] evaluated the speedup of the basic parallel strategy and the different optimization strategies for parallelization of five well-known string matching algorithms, including Aho-Corasick, on a GPU.

Bit-splitting is a well-proven technique that can effectively improve efficiency of hardware realizations for FSM-based string matching. Tan *et al.* [13] demonstrated that the bit-splitting technique can reduce memory requirements by a 10-fold factor. Bit-split architectures were used as target architecture design and evaluation of the related works in literature [5, 13-15].

Another effective approach to improve the efficiency of FSM-based string matching is to partition the target strings into multiple subgroups. This leads to the replacement of a large String Matching Unit (SMU) with multiple smaller SMUs that work in parallel. Each subgroup of strings is mapped onto one SMU. The assignment of strings to subgroups significantly impacts the efficiency of the design in terms of performance and overall memory consumption. Finding the optimal grouping scheme requires the exploration of a search space that grows exponentially with the number of strings. Since searching the whole space can be impractical for large designs, heuristic search algorithms are widely preferred to solve this problem [5, 13, 14].

Pattern grouping based on Gray code [5] and Lexicographical [13] sorting aims to reduce the overall number of states required in FSMs by maximizing the shared common prefixes among the strings of each group. For this purpose, these approaches sort the strings based on their prefixes and then assign the strings to the groups in order. Kim *et al.* [14] introduced a pattern grouping algorithm that uses the average length of the strings as a determinant factor in group mapping decision. The goal of Kim's algorithm is to balance the number of target strings mapped onto each SMU. For this purpose, it keeps the average length of each subgroup's strings as close as possible to the overall average length of the strings.

This paper proposes a new heuristic algorithm for string grouping that targets heterogeneous bit-split string matching architectures. The proposed algorithm estimates the correlation between the strings using specific measurements. The correlation values play a key role in deciding how to map the strings onto the groups. This algorithm uses precise string correlation information to make decisions, and it achieves more efficient grouping solutions compared to recent approaches [5, 13, 14].

Existing works on pattern grouping algorithms targeted homogenous architectures which are composed of identical SMUs. In this paper, we introduce and target a heterogeneous architecture in which each SMU can have a different amount of memory resources and configuration. This enables more efficient resource allocation that leads to significant reduction in overall memory usage.

2. TARGET ARCHITECTURE

Figure 1 represents the results of applying three AC-based string matching approaches on a simple set of target strings: {me, he, him, his}. Figure 1(a) shows the basic memory-based AC realization. In Figure 1(b), the target set of strings has been divided into two groups {me} and {he, him, his} using the pattern grouping technique. Then, the AC algorithm has been used to create a state machine for each group. In Figure 1(c) bit-splitting has been added to further parallelize the state machines. Since a single-bit granularity has been adopted for bit-splitting, in this example, 8 bit-level state machines are required for each group of strings.

In this work, we focus on implementing the bit-split AC algorithm as shown in Figure 1(c). To accomplish this, we introduce a hardware architecture made up of heterogeneous memory-based units to process bit-level FSMs.

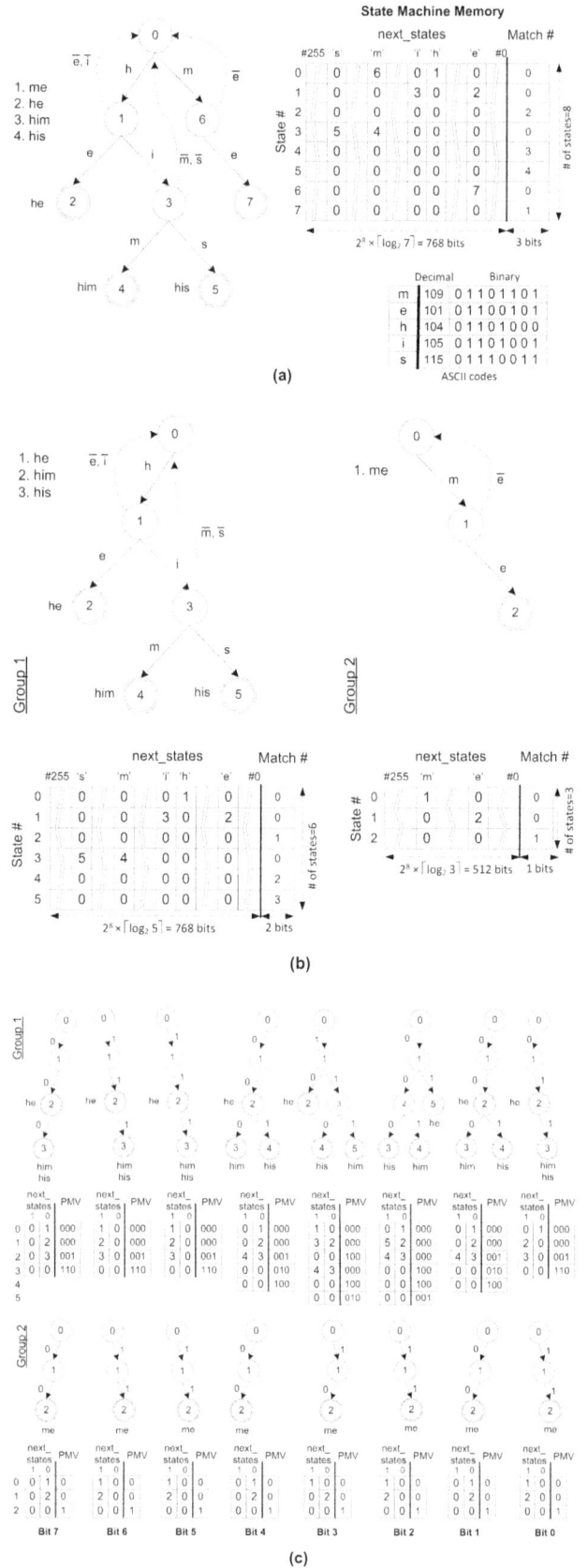

Figure 1. Memory-based string matching for a simple set of target strings using (a) direct realization of AC; (b) pattern grouping and AC; (c) pattern grouping and bit-split AC.

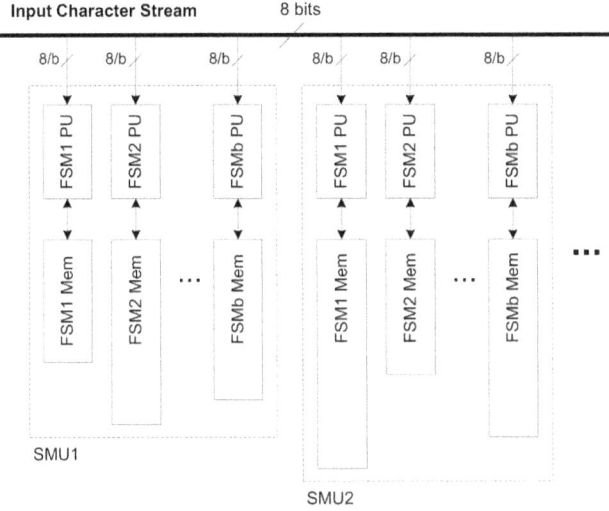

Figure 2. The target string matching architecture with heterogeneous memory-based SMUs.

Figure 2 illustrates the target architecture with arbitrary memory sizes. Each SMU is a bit-split Aho-Corasick machine that performs string matching for one group. Mem units store the FSMs in a specific data structure and Processing Units (PUs) perform the state machine traversal based on the input data. This means that each SMU can have a different memory size. The sizes of memories allocated to the FSMs are determined based on design requirements.

The bit-splitting technique is used in SMU architectures to improve their efficiency. This technique suggests splitting the characters into multiple b-bit chunks, where $b=1,2,4$ or 8, and to use one FSM to process each chunk. When $b=1$, one FSM is utilized to process each single bit of input characters, while $b=8$ gives the original character-level AC algorithm.

Using this technique, each SMU will be composed of $8/b$ FSMs. For each state of an FSM, a Partial Matching Vector (PMV) is stored in memory. In each SMU, the bit-width of the PMVs of all FSMs is equal to the number of strings mapped onto that SMU. In a PMV, the ith bit indicates whether the ith string is matched. A matched string is detected by the logical AND operation of all PMVs in a SMU. The data structure used to represent FSM nodes in memory is similar to Piyachon *et al.*'s work [6].

PUs are relatively small circuits in the memory-based realization of the AC algorithm. Each PU contains a state register which keeps track of the current state for FSM traversal. In each cycle, the memory line at the address indicated by the state register is read from the corresponding FSM memory. The input value is used as an index to extract the next state from the memory line. Then, the state register is updated by the next state value. Since the required memory resources are far more expensive than the PU circuits, memory consumption is usually one of the main factors in evaluating new algorithms and techniques in memory-based AC realization [4-6]. The PU cost is not generally measured or reported.

Although the existing works [5, 13, 14] have similar objectives to the present work, they target a homogenous architecture contrary to the heterogeneous architecture targeted in this work. The homogenous architecture allocates a fixed, predefined and equal

amount of memory to all FSMs. Therefore, the total number of FSM states that can fit in each memory is inherently limited. A larger number of target strings will require more SMUs. The main drawback of using homogeneous architecture is that the number of states allocated to each bit-level FSMs may differ. For instance, in example of Figure 1(c), the bit-level FSMs have 4, 5 or 6 states. Consequently, allocating the same memory space to all FSMs will leave some of the memory units partially unused. Experimental evaluations in related works demonstrate that these unused memory spaces, which can be denoted as wasted memories, constitute a significant part of the overall memory consumption [6]. The heterogeneous architecture, which is used in this work, can save the wasted memory spaces by allowing customized allocation of the memory space to each FSM. Both width and depth of the FSM memories are determined through the proposed optimization process at design time. As illustrated in Figure 1, the width of an FSM memory depends on three factors:

1. fan-out or number of maximum next states that is equal to 2^b, where b is the number of bits processed at a time in an FSM;
2. bit-width of *next_state* fields that depend on the total number of states;
3. the bit-width of the PMV that is equal to the number of strings mapped onto that SMU.

The minimum memory requirement, in terms of bits, for the nth FSM of the mth SMU is as follows:

$$MFSM_{mn} = (2^b \times \lceil \log_2 N\_S_n \rceil + W\_PMV_m) \times N\_S_n \quad (1)$$

where N_S_n and W_PMV_m denote total number of states and PMV bit-width, respectively. In the proposed approach, the minimum memory requirement is calculated for each FSM using (1). An equivalent memory block is allocated to that FSM in hardware. The group partitioning scheme can significantly impact the N_S_n and W_PMV_m factors. The proposed optimization algorithm, described in Section 3, explores the search space to find the group partitioning scheme that minimizes total memory consumption. Total memory consumption is:

$$Total\_Mem = \sum_{m=1}^{G} \sum_{n=1}^{8/b} MFSM_{mn} \quad (2)$$

where G is the number of groups. A customized memory allocation may appear to restrict the scalability and future revisions on the rule-set in our architecture. However, the homogenous architecture of previous works also faces comparable limitations. In that architecture, adding new strings to the rule-set may require the introduction of new string matchers to the engine due to the shortage of memory spaces to accommodate all FSMs. On the other hand, adding a new SMU to the engine introduces an extra cost for the processing units and communication signals. Our approach allows the designer to control the number of SMUs. This can help to achieve higher cost efficiency by preventing unnecessary expansion in the number of SMUs.

3. Proposed Algorithm

The proposed pattern grouping algorithm receives two inputs: the target strings and the number of groups. The algorithm is composed of two phases: 1) a seed selection process, which uses a calculation to estimate the correlation between strings and 2) a seed growing process for mapping strings onto subgroups. Figure 3 illustrates the pseudocode of this algorithm. The following subsections describe the two phases of the algorithm in detail.

```
1.   Function STR_GRP(Target Strings S, No. of GRPs G)
2.   N=number of strings in S;

        /* Seed Selection and Correlation Estimation Phase*/
3.   GRP(1,1)=1;                              /*seed₁*/
4.   FOR i=1 to G-1
5.     FOR j=1 to N
6.       Correlation_Vector(i, j)= Correlation_{GRP(i,1),j};
7.     END FOR
8.     Find the string δ that has the minimum
                correlation with all already assigned seeds
                (seed₁ to seedᵢ) using Correlation_Vector;
9.     GRP(i+1,1)= index of δ;                /*seedᵢ₊₁*/
10.  END FOR

        /*Seed Growing Phase*/
11.  FOR l=S+1 to N
12.    Find the string φ that has largest
                difference in correlation between the two
                most highly correlated groups;
13.    Find the group n that has the largest correlation
                with string φ
14.    GRP(n,end+1)= φ;        /*Assign φ to Group n*/
15.    Update correlation values of group n
                (Correlation_Vector(n, j), 1 < j < N)
                using Eq. (4)
16.  END FOR
17. END FUNCTION
```

Figure 3. The proposed string grouping algorithm

3.1 Seed Selection and Correlation Estimation

In the first phase, the algorithm selects the seed pattern of each group using estimates of correlations between patterns. In the original Aho-Corasick algorithm, each FSM processes one character of the input stream at a time.

Common character-level prefixes between two target strings can reduce the overall number of states in the FSM. Mapping strings with the longest common prefixes onto the same groups can reduce memory consumption. In the bit-split approach, the bit-level prefixes are important, since each FSM works on one or a few bits of each character and two different characters may have up to 7 common bits. Hence, the common prefixes should be measured for each parallel FSM, separately. We define a novel metric for correlation estimation, $Correlation_{ij}$, that estimates the benefit of mapping the ith and j^{th} strings onto the same group as follows:

$$Correlation_{ij} = \frac{NS(string(i))+NS(string(j))}{NS(strings(i),string(j))} \quad (3)$$

where NS is a function that calculates the total number of nodes required to represent the given strings inside one FSM. The proposed algorithm uses the estimated $Correlation$ values to anticipate the appropriateness of mapping a string onto each subgroup.

As illustrated in Line 3 of Figure 3, the seed selection process starts by assigning the first string to the first group as the first seed. In Figure 3, GRP is a 2D array where $GRP(i, j)$ indicates the index of the jth string assigned to the ith group. Then the correlation between this first seed string and the rest of the strings is measured using (3). The results are stored in the first row of a 2D vector called $Correlation\_Vector$. Then, if more than two groups are requested, the algorithm considers the string that is the least correlated to those already assigned to the first group. The selected string is then assigned to the second group. In a similar way, the string that has the smallest correlation distance from all previously assigned strings is selected for the subsequent groups. This process continues until the first members of all groups are identified. These first members can be considered as the seed strings.

3.2 Seed Growing Phase

In the second phase, the algorithm maps the remaining strings onto the groups in an iterative manner. We call this process *seed growing*. In each seed growing iteration, one of the ungrouped strings is selected and assigned to a group. The selection order highly impacts the results. The proposed algorithm defines and uses a criterion to identify and select the most appropriate string to be processed first. The criterion is as follows: the highest priority is given to the string that has the largest difference in correlation with the closest group and with the other groups. In other words, if the correlation of string A and string B with their closest related groups are m and m', respectively, and their correlation with their second nearest groups are n and n', respectively, then A is selected first if $m - n > m' - n'$. The selected string is assigned to the most correlated group.

Thereafter, the assigned string is part of the prototype of that group. The elements related to the assigned string are removed from the $Correlation\_Vector$ since that string is not ungrouped anymore. Instead, the correlation values of all remaining elements with the enlarged prototype are updated. This process continues until all strings have been grouped. The following calculation is used for updating the correlation values:

$$GRP\_Correlation_{ij} = \frac{NS(group(i))+NS(string(j))}{NS(group(i),string(j))} \quad (4)$$

where $group(i)$ is the set of all strings already assigned to the ith group and, thus, $NS(group(i))$ represents the total number of states required to represent all strings in $group(i)$.

Seed growing dominates the time complexity of the algorithm. To group n strings, n iterations are required in the seed growing loop. The correlation of all remaining strings with the enlarged seed must be recalculated for each iteration. Hence, the proposed algorithm has a time complexity of $O(n^2)$. This time complexity is quite adequate for intrusion detection systems in which the signature database is updated every few days or weeks.

4. EXPERIMENTAL RESULTS AND DISCUSSIONS

The proposed algorithm was evaluated using a simulator developed in MATLAB. This simulator reads the strings from the rule-set file and gives them to the pattern grouping algorithm. The grouping solution is given back to the simulator. The simulator creates the FSMs from the target strings using the given grouping solution. Then, it measures the total amount of memory required to store FSMs in a hardware realization based on the proposed architecture of Figure 2. The size of *FSMi Mem* in a SMU is determined based on the size of the ith FSM created for the corresponding string group. In all experiments, each FSM took a single-bit input for the bit-split string matching.

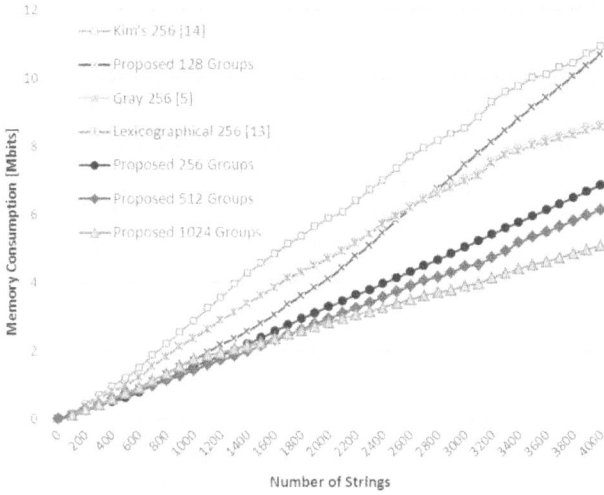

Figure 4. Overall memory consumption with the proposed string grouping algorithm compared to existing approaches.

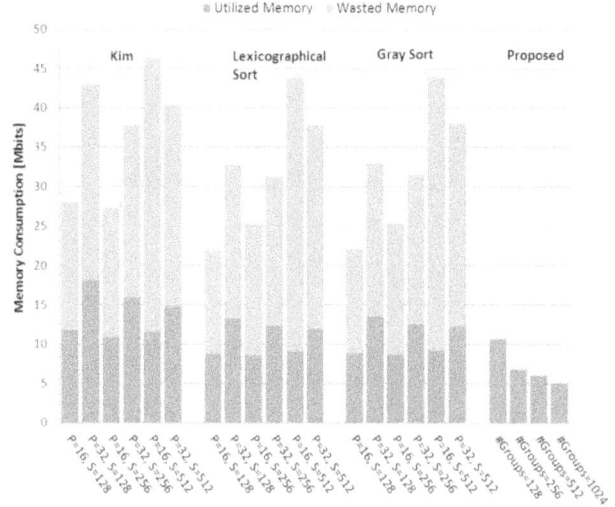

Figure 5. Memory consumption using various parameter values for 4000 strings from the Snort v2.9 rule-set.

Regarding Figure 2, this means that n=8 in the evaluated architectures. The target architecture has a heterogeneous bit-split structure. Snort v2.9 [16] was used as the target rule-set in the experiments.

Figure 4 shows the memory consumption for different sizes of the target set of string using the proposed approach and for Lexicographical sorting [13], Gray code-based sorting [5] and the algorithm proposed by Kim *et al.* [14]. The results show that the proposed algorithm and architecture can save memory consumption by an average of 41% compared the best results obtained by both the Lexicographical sorting and the Gray code sorting. This saving is 53% compared to the Kim's algorithm.

There are two important adjustable parameters in the previous three compared works: p, the bitwidth of a PMV which defines the maximum number of strings that can be mapped onto one group, and s, the number of states in each FSM. We found the best parameter values by examining different values for these parameters in a systematic design space exploration. Figure 4 illustrates the results achieved by the best parameter values for the three existing approaches.

The proposed algorithm was evaluated for 128, 256, 512, and 1024 groups. The results in Figure 4 demonstrate that increasing the number of groups enables more memory saving. The distinction increases in larger sets of strings. The drawback of using a larger number of groups is that more computational circuits are required for extra SMUs and peripheral circuits.

Figure 4 includes only the utilized memory spaces, not the wasted memories. Figure 5 compares the overall memory usage achieved by the four approaches using various parameter values, for the case of 4000 strings from Snort v2.9 [16] rule-set. The pale parts of the bars represent the amount of wasted memory. These results demonstrate that the proposed approach offers 33%, 34% and 48% less memory consumption compared to the utilized memory space in the Lexicographical sorting [13], the Gray code sorting [5] and the Kim's algorithm [14], respectively. These values increase to 69%, 67% and 67% when comparing with the total memory usage, including utilized and wasted memory, in existing works.

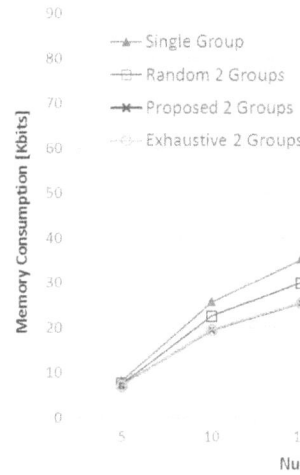

Figure 6. Memory consumption of the proposed algorithm compared with the single grouping, random grouping and exhaustive search approaches.

We have also compared the proposed algorithm with exhaustive search and random grouping methods, and the results are presented in Figure 6. There are G^N/G possible solutions that should be evaluated in an exhaustive search, where G is the number of groups and N is the number of strings. An exhaustive search is thus not feasible for large rule-sets. Therefore, we limited the number of groups to 2 and the number of strings to 30 in the experiments of Figure 6. The proposed algorithm produces a solution that requires at most 2.8% more memory than the optimal solution given by the exhaustive search. However, for the largest experiment with 30 strings, the execution time of the exhaustive search and the proposed algorithm are 230 minutes and 31 seconds, respectively. This means that even for a small set of strings, the proposed algorithm is over 445× faster than an exhaustive search.

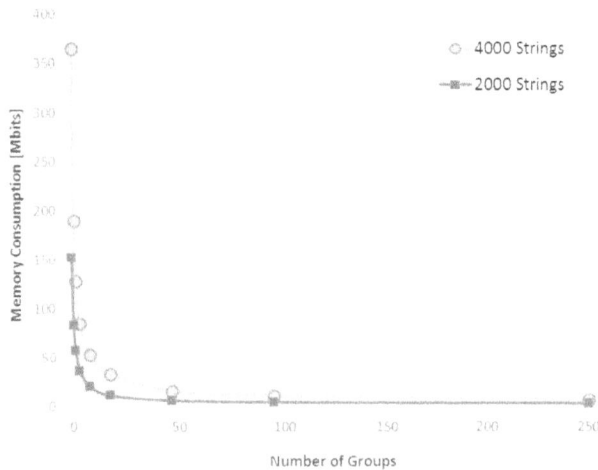

Figure 7. Memory consumption versus number of groups.

Finally, the last experiment studies the impacts of changing the number of groups on the memory requirements. Figure 7 illustrates the total memory consumption versus the number of groups for two sets of 2000 and 4000 target strings. The number of groups varies from a 1 to 256. The proposed algorithm has been used to perform group partitioning. The results show that in small number of groups, a tiny increase in number of groups can cause a significant saving in memory consumption. For instance, for 2000 target strings, moving from a single-group to a double-group solution, which means adding only one group, reduces the memory consumption by up to 1.8 times. However, the memory reduction speed rapidly degrades when the number of groups increases. For example, 50 groups require only 1.8 times less memory resources compared to 20 groups. This means that this time 1.8× memory saving is achieved at the expense of 30 more groups. [8]

5. CONCLUSION

In this paper, we proposed a new string grouping algorithm for designing efficient string matching engines for DPI systems. The algorithm uses a suitable metric proposed to estimate the correlations between strings. The estimated correlations are used to effectively partition the strings onto groups. The target string matching architecture is a memory-based heterogeneous realization of the bit-split Aho-Corasick algorithm. Experimental results demonstrate that the proposed algorithm can offer significantly more efficient solutions in terms of memory consumption compared to existing works. Moreover, the results show that the memory consumption results achieved by the proposed algorithm are very close to the optimal ones offered by an exhaustive search.

6. ACKNOWLEDGMENTS

This work is supported by Canada's Natural Sciences and Engineering Research Council (NSERC) and Ericsson Research.

7. REFERENCES

[1] Aho, A. V. and Corasick, M. J. Efficient string matching: an aid to bibliographic search. *Commun. ACM*, 18, 6 (June 1975), 333-340.

[2] Khan, Z. A. and Pateriya, R. K. Multiple pattern string matching methodologies: a comparative analysis. *International Journal of Scientific and Research Publications*, 2, 7 (July 2012), 1-7.

[3] Jony, A. I. Analysis of multiple string pattern matching algorithms. *International Journal of Advanced Computer Science and Information Technology (IJACSIT)*, 3, 2 (2014), 344-353.

[4] Dimopoulos, V., Papaefstathiou, I. and Pnevmatikatos, D. A memory-efficient reconfigurable Aho-Corasick FSM implementation for intrusion detection systems. In *Proceedings of the Embedded Computer Systems: Architectures, Modeling and Simulation, IC-SAMOS* (Samos, Greece, Jul. 2007), 186-193.

[5] Kim, H., Hong, H., Kim, H.-S. and Kang, S. A memory-efficient parallel string matching for intrusion detection systems. *IEEE Communications Letters*, 13, 12 (Dec. 2009), 1004-1006.

[6] Piyachon, P. and Yan, L. Efficient memory utilization on network processors for deep packet inspection. In *Proceedings of the ACM/IEEE Symposium on Architecture for Networking and Communications systems* (San Jose, USA, December 3-5, 2006), 71-80.

[7] Kumar, S., Dharmapurikar, S., Yu, F., Crowley, P. and Turner, J. Algorithms to accelerate multiple regular expressions matching for deep packet inspection. *SIGCOMM Comput. Commun. Rev.*, 36, 4 (Oct. 2006), 339-350.

[8] Becchi, M. and Crowley, P. An improved algorithm to accelerate regular expression evaluation. In *Proceedings of the Proceedings of the 3rd ACM/IEEE Symposium on Architecture for networking and communications systems* (Orlando, Florida, USA, 2007). ACM, 145-154.

[9] Crochemore, M., Czumaj, A., Gasieniec, L., Lecroq, T., Plandowski, W. and Rytter, W. Fast practical multi-pattern matching. *Information Processing Letters*, 71, 3–4 (1999), 107-113.

[10] Arudchutha, S., Nishanthy, T. and Ragel, R. G. String matching with multicore cpus: performing better with the Aho-Corasick algorithm In *Proceedings of the 8th IEEE International Conference on Industrial and Information Systems (ICIIS)*, (Peradeniya, Sri Lanka, Dec. 2013), 231-236.

[11] Xinyan, Z. and Sahni, S. Multipattern string matching on a GPU. In *Proceedings of the IEEE Symposium on Computers and Communications (ISCC)* (Kerkyra, Greece, June 28 - July 01, 2011), 277-282.

[12] Kouzinopoulos, C. S. and Margaritis, K. G. String matching on a multicore GPU using CUDA. In *Proceedings of the Proceedings of the 13th Panhellenic Conference on Informatics* (Corfu, Greece, 2009). IEEE Computer Society, 14-18.

[13] Tan, L., Brotherton, B. and Sherwood, T. Bit-split string-matching engines for intrusion detection and prevention. *ACM Trans. Archit. Code Optim.*, 3, 1 (March 2006), 3-34.

[14] Kim, H. and Kang, S. A pattern group partitioning for parallel string matching using a pattern grouping metric. *IEEE Communications Letters*, 14, 9 (Sep. 2010), 878-880.

[15] Hyunjin, K., Hong-Sik, K. and Sungho, K. A memory-efficient bit-split parallel string matching using pattern dividing for intrusion detection systems. *IEEE Transactions on Parallel and Distributed Systems*, 22, 11 (March 2011), 1904-1911.

[16] *Snort, Network Intrusion Detection System*, http://www.snort.org.

High Throughput Forwarding for ICN with Descriptors and Locators

Michele Papalini, Koorosh Khazaei, Antonio Carzaniga, Daniele Rogora
Faculty of Informatics
Università della Svizzera italiana (USI)
Lugano, Switzerland

ABSTRACT

Application-defined and location-independent addressing is a founding principle of information centric networking (ICN) that is inherently difficult to realize if one also wants scalable routing and forwarding. We propose an ICN architecture, called TagNet, intended to combine expressive application-defined addressing with scalable routing and forwarding. TagNet features two independent delivery services: one with application-defined and possibly location-independent content descriptors, and one with network-defined host locators. In this paper we develop and evaluate specialized forwarding algorithms for TagNet. We then implement and combine these algorithms in a forwarding engine built on a general-purpose commodity CPU, and show experimentally that, thanks to the dual addressing, by descriptor or by locator, this engine can achieve a throughput of over 20Gbps with large forwarding tables corresponding to hundreds of millions of users.

CCS Concepts

•Networks → **Data path algorithms;** *Naming and addressing; Network layer protocols;*

Keywords

ICN; forwarding; algorithms; locators; content descriptors

1. INTRODUCTION

Addressing by name is a defining feature of information centric networking that poses a crucial trade-off. On the one hand, the network would serve applications better if applications were allowed to choose names to refer directly to information objects or other entities, such as servers or users, without necessarily referring to the network hosts where those entities are located. On the other hand, such application-defined and possibly location-independent addresses may aggregate poorly, which fundamentally limits the scalability of the network.

ANCS '16, March 17-18, 2016, Santa Clara, CA, USA
© 2016 ACM. ISBN 978-1-4503-4183-7/16/03. . . $15.00
DOI: http://dx.doi.org/10.1145/2881025.2881032

One solution could be to restrict applications to use names with globally routable prefixes similar to DNS names. This is the approach taken, for example, by the CCN architecture. The data plane would still be more complex than IP, since it requires longest *name* prefix matching, but fortunately there are good solutions for that [7, 12, 13] and in any case the approach would improve scalability, since names would be forced to aggregate. However, from the application's perspective, this solution amounts to turning names back into network-chosen addresses. And even though the notion of ICN could be beneficial in other ways, those benefits might not be worth a radical redesign of the Internet.

We believe that a radically new network should offer a richer communication service. So our goal is to design an information centric network that allows applications to choose meaningful names, and our challenge is to engineer routing and forwarding systems that can cope with such application-chosen names. In prior work, we developed our design with a network architecture called *TagNet* that, among other things, supports application-defined addressing. In the same prior work we also proposed and evaluated a scalable routing scheme for TagNet [6]. In this paper we develop the TagNet data plane. In particular, we build a software forwarder (matcher) on inexpensive general-purpose CPUs and show that such a forwarder can sustain a throughput of over 20Gbps even with a large forwarding information base.

At the architectural level, our approach is first to disentangle two network functions typically embodied in a single name. Names are supposed to allow applications to refer to content and application-level entities, and at the same time they are the basis for routing and forwarding and therefore they are supposed to allow the network to locate and reach hosts. This double duty is problematic, so we designed a network supporting two types of addresses: one based on application-chosen and typically location independent *content descriptors*, which are intended to be expressive for applications although potentially expensive for routing; and one based on network-chosen *host locators* that are instead very efficient for routing but meaningless to applications.

In particular, we designed TagNet to support content descriptors consisting of sets of tags. For example, a music server might advertise its collection with the descriptor {*concert, classical*} and a music player might request a file for download with the descriptor {*classical, Beethoven, ninth, concert, 360bps*}, and TagNet would forward the request *by descriptor* to the server. We then developed a routing scheme for TagNet that supports descriptors as well as very efficient locators based on a compact routing scheme by Thorup and Zwick [10]. Now we turn to forwarding, by descriptor or locator.

Forwarding a packet using its descriptor D_p (a set of tags) amounts to finding one or more subsets of D_p (possibly the largest subset) in a descriptor FIB containing many tag sets. This is analogous to longest-prefix matching in IP forwarding or to longest name prefix matching in name-based ICN, except that *subset* matching is fundamentally more expressive and therefore also more complex than prefix matching. Our contribution is a descriptor matching algorithm that performs well in practice, especially within a network that supports efficient host locators.

We start by representing the descriptor forwarding table with a trie over which we implement two subset-matching algorithms: *Find All Subsets* and *Find Largest Subset*. We then introduce specific improvements to speed-up both algorithms. We do that by first compressing the trie and then by laying out its structure in memory so as to maximize locality in the memory access patterns of the two algorithms. We then implement and fine-tune the forwarding algorithm for the Thorup and Zwick locators, and finally we integrate descriptor-based and locator-based forwarding algorithms in our TagNet forwarding engine.

We evaluate our TagNet forwarding engine under a variety of workloads. This evaluation shows that the forwarding engine is efficient, and in particular that the descriptor-based matching algorithms perform well under different workloads, and scale well with the size of the FIB as well as with the number of threads. We also show that, thanks to the separation between descriptors and locators, the TagNet forwarding engine can achieve a high throughput, since most of the traffic can be forwarded based on extremely efficient network-defined locators. For example, in the music download flow exemplified above, except for the very first request packet routed by descriptor, all the follow-up data and request packets exchanged between the music server and the music player can be forwarded by their locators. In such mixed flows, the forwarding engine takes advantage of the excellent performance of locator-based matching, exceeding 20Gbps of throughput even with large FIBs.

2. BACKGROUND

We now briefly describe the TagNet architecture, focusing on the formulation of the problems related to forwarding. We then review existing algorithms and systems that solve the same or related problems.

2.1 TagNet: Descriptors and Locators

TagNet is an ICN architecture designed to support push and pull flows with two independent addressing and delivery methods: one with content descriptors, one with host locators (hereafter simply *descriptors* and *locators*). Descriptors are sets of tags and are chosen by applications. Locators are opaque bit strings and are chosen by the network. More specifically, the network allows an application to (1) advertise one or more descriptors $A_1, A_2, \ldots$; (2) obtain the application's own network-assigned locators (one or more); (3) send a packet addressed by descriptor B to up to k applications that advertise a matching descriptor $A_i \subseteq B$; (4) send a packet addressed by locator to the corresponding application. The fan-out limit k, which controls the delivery by descriptor (3), can be used to obtain an anycast ($k = 1$) or multicast ($k = \infty$) delivery semantics.

With these primitive operations, applications can communicate in various ways. For example, this is how a consumer C could "pull" data from a producer P in a pattern typical of ICN architectures such as CCN and NDN: producer P advertises a content object x with a descriptor D_x; consumer C obtains its own locator L_C and then sends an "interest" packet I addressed by descriptor D_I with fan-out limit $k = 1$ (i.e., anycast) and containing C's locator L_C; assuming D_I matches D_x ($D_I \supseteq D_x$), meaning that object x satisfies the interest expressed by consumer C, the network delivers the interest packet I to producer P; producer P obtains its own locator L_P and sends a "data" packet, addressed by locator L_C, containing its locator L_P and the requested object x (or a chunk of x); the network delivers the data packet to consumer C. At this point consumer C knows the locator of the producer, L_P, so C can send follow-up requests (e.g., for other chunks of data) by addressing P directly by locator.

Consumer C could also use a fan-out limit $k > 1$ to try to obtain the data from multiple producers at the same time, or to choose one among many producers. Also, switching roles, producer P could "push" content to C, and similarly a producer could also push data to multiple consumers, either directly pushing the data or by pushing a request to pull.

Descriptors are strictly more expressive than hierarchical names (as in CCN or NDN). In fact, we can emulate the semantics of a hierarchical name with a descriptor by enumerating the components of the name as separate tags. For example, the name */org/gnu/software/* is equivalent to the descriptor {*1:org*, *2:gnu*, *3:software*}. In Section 3.1.3 we describe a specific forwarding algorithm that can also emulate the semantics of longest name prefix matching.

2.2 Forwarding in TagNet

In the TagNet data plane, we need to implement a forwarding engine that supports both locator- and descriptor-based forwarding. We describe the locator-based forwarding implementation later in Section 3.3, where we give an overview of the Thorup and Zwick routing scheme. In this section we focus on descriptors.

Descriptors expressed as sets of string tags may not be ideal for network-level packet forwarding. So, in TagNet we use Bloom filters to compress descriptors into fixed-size bit vectors, which is what we then use for forwarding at the network level. Notice that an individual descriptor is a relatively small set of tags, so the corresponding Bloom filter can also be small. Notice also that the inclusion relation between two Bloom filters (bitwise) corresponds to the subset relation between the tag sets that they represent, except for a controllable small false-positive probability. Concretely, based on a conservative estimate on the typical number of tags in descriptors, we choose to use Bloom filters of 192 bits and 7 hash functions (see Papalini et. al [6] for details).

In summary, a packet addressed by descriptor carries a Bloom filter B and a fan-out limit k, and a router's FIB maps Bloom filters $A_1, A_2, \ldots$ to interfaces. With that, forwarding amounts to finding at most k entries $A_i \subseteq B$ in the FIB. This subset lookup problem is equivalent to and therefore also known as the partial matching problem.

2.3 Forwarding in ICN

The problem of forwarding in ICN has been considered mostly if not exclusively for hierarchical name-based addressing, and more specifically in forwarding interest packets in CCN or NDN. In these cases, forwarding amounts to longest prefix matching (LPM) or more specifically longest name prefix matching (LNPM).

One of the first systems for high-throughput interest forwarding was developed by Wang et al. [12] and exploits the high-parallelism of a GPU. Wang et al. implement LPM on a character trie compressed in a data structure called multi-aligned transition array (MATA). Wang et al. report a throughput of 63.52Mpps with a FIB of 10 million entries (we later refer to this FIB as 10M-CCN). However, this system also incurs high latency [7], which is a common problem for GPU-based systems.

Most ICN forwarding systems implement LNPM with a hash-table: the algorithm stores the FIB in a hash table and, for an input name of ℓ components, proceeds by first looking up the prefix of length ℓ (the whole name), then the prefix of length $\ell - 1$, and so on. On this basis, authors have built a number of variants. For example, Perino et al. use Bloom filters to group multiple prefixes [7], Wang et al. search prefixes in an order based on the distribution of prefix lengths [11], and Yuan and Crowley use a binary search on multiple hash tables organized by prefix lengths [13]. These systems achieve a high throughput in the tens of million packets per second on the 10M-CCN FIB, although notably Yuan and Crowley evaluate their system on a FIB of 1 billion entries, which is the largest FIB used so far to test an interest forwarding algorithm for ICN.

In addition to interest forwarding, CCN and NDN also require a suitable implementation of the pending-interest table (PIT) to forward *data* packets. We know of only two systems that support both forwarding functions. The first, proposed by So et al. [9], is based on hash tables and achieves 8.8Mpps throughput on mixed traffic (interest and data packets) and with FIBs of 64 million entries. Another one is BFAST by Dai et al. [2], and consists of a unified index that supports LNPM in the FIB and exact-match in the PIT and content store, and that can achieve a throughput of up to 81.32Mpps depending on the incoming traffic mix.

The *eXpressive Internet Architecture* (XIA) is a proposed new Internet architecture [3] that supports a notion of flexible addressing that, although not designed specifically for ICN, relates to forwarding in ICN. In essence, flexible addressing in XIA means that each packet may specify multiple addresses of different kinds together with a directed acyclic graph that expresses alternatives or "fallback" relations between those addresses. Based on the partial order defined by the graph, a router then selects the most appropriate address it is capable of using for forwarding.

XIA provides a nice framework within which we could realize the dual addressing of TagNet, by defining descriptors and locators as two types of addresses. However, notice that XIA and its fallback mechanism do not provide specific support for descriptors or locators. Furthermore, the duality of locators and descriptors in TagNet is rather different from, and to some extent *incompatible* with the flexible addressing of XIA. This is because locators are not intended to be fallback addresses for descriptors, or vice-versa, and even though a fallback relation may make sense in some cases, both locators and descriptors are intended to be globally routable in TagNet. Still, XIA is flexible enough to accommodate the dual addressing of TagNet, and possibly to extend it with alternative types of descriptors and locators.

2.4 Subset Matching

The systems discussed so far relate to our work because of the domain (forwarding in ICN) and the nature of the solution (algorithmic, general-purpose multi-core CPU). But notice that they solve a different combinatorial problem, namely prefix matching instead of subset matching. We now review existing results for subset matching.

The theory on subset matching is well established, although unfortunately not very useful in our case. Recall that we are given n sets $A_1, A_2, \ldots, A_n \subseteq \{1, \ldots, m\}$ and a query set $B \subseteq \{1, \ldots, m\}$ (specifically $m = 192$) and we want to find all (or up to k) sets A_i such that $A_i \subseteq B$. There are two trivial solutions: one stores the answers for all possible queries in an index, and requires $O(m)$ time but a prohibitive $O(2^m)$ space; one scans the sets linearly, which requires linear (minimal) space but also linear time $O(nm)$. The first non-trivial improvements are due to Rivest [8], one regarding the index solution that is irrelevant for us, and one based on a trie that is quite similar to the one we develop in this paper. Charikar et al. also propose two improvements over the trivial solutions [1] but their results are not useful in practice, as they either require too much memory or are too slow for a real implementation of a matching engine.

Subset matching has concrete applications in many fields, for example in networking for packet classification, and in information retrieval to search documents containing a given set of words. Most relevant for our purposes are applications in databases, where the base of sets (the FIB in our case) is typically very large. What is traditionally considered the best algorithmic solution in databases and information retrieval is an inverted index that maps each element (tag) to the list of sets the element appears in [4]. However, inverted indexes perform well when the universe of elements is large and the frequencies of individual elements are low, not when the universe is small and therefore each element appears in many sets. But this is precisely the problem we intend to solve, since the Bloom filters already reduce our universe to a small size ($m = 192$).

Perhaps the most relevant work in the database literature is a recent paper by Luo et al. [5] who propose two set-containment algorithms based on tries. The first one, called *PATRICIA trie-based signature join* (PTSJ), encodes each set of tags with a hash-based signature, and then stores the signatures in a trie. This is similar to what we do, but there are also significant differences: in essence, we use a more effective algorithm and layout, and we use more compact Bloom filters. The second algorithm, called PRETTI+, works on the actual elements of the sets (tags) and builds what amounts to an inverted index. Interestingly, Luo et al. evaluate their algorithms with real data sets. The most relevant data set, which is also more similar to our typical workload, is a collection of 3.5 million tagged photos from Flickr with an average of 5.36 tags per photo. Under this workload, PRETTI+ outperforms PTSJ with an average throughput of 17.5K queries per second on a single Intel Xeon 2.27GHz core. These results are interesting for us because we use comparable workloads with which we achieve a throughput of 140K–319K queries (packets) per second, also on a single thread, but on a collection (FIB) that is almost three times larger. Notice however that, even though Luo et al. use a hardware platform almost identical to ours, they implement their algorithms in Java while we use C++.

3. FORWARDING ALGORITHMS

In this section we present the matching algorithms we implement to realize the dual forwarding system of TagNet. We start with the algorithms for descriptor-based forwarding, which we describe in detail, and then at the end of the section we briefly present the algorithm for locator-based forwarding. We do not spend much text to describe this algorithm simply because we implement it directly from a compact-routing scheme by Thorup and Zwick [10].

3.1 Descriptor-Based Matching Algorithms

We develop two algorithms to realize descriptor-based forwarding in TagNet: *Find All Subsets* (FAS) and *Find Largest Subset* (FLS). Both algorithms operate on the same data structure that represents the FIB. We now describe this structure and then detail each algorithm. Recall that we encode descriptors (tag sets) as Bloom filters. Therefore, for the purpose of forwarding and throughout this section, the term *descriptor* refers to the Bloom filter that encodes the descriptor.

3.1.1 FIB Data Structure

We use a prefix trie to store all the descriptors in the FIB. The FIB represents a relation between descriptors and interfaces, therefore we link each full descriptor from the prefix trie to a list of output interfaces. Figure 1 shows an example of this basic data structure. To be more precise, in TagNet we route packets on multiple trees [6], so the FIB represents a relation between filters, interfaces, *and trees*. The FIB is still indexed by descriptor with a prefix trie, but each full descriptor in the trie links to a list of tree–interface pairs. This structure is only relevant for the very last phase of the forwarding algorithm, which has little if any impact on performance. Therefore, for the purpose of this paper and for simplicity, we ignore trees altogether.

Each path in the trie from the root to a leaf represents a descriptor in the FIB. In particular, the trie represents each descriptor as a sequence of positions (from 1 to 10 in the figure, from 1 to 192 in the real implementation) corresponding to the bits set to one in the descriptor (1-bits). Thus each node in the trie represents either the position of a 1-bit in one or more descriptors, or a terminator node, marked with the '$' position in the figure, that represents a full descriptor and that links that descriptor to the output list. For example, the FIB depicted in Figure 1 contains descriptor 0011100010 represented as the sequence $3, 4, 5, 9$ in the trie and associated with interfaces i_6 and i_2.

In each node we also store the maximum and minimum depths reachable through that node. Depth values exclude the terminator nodes, and therefore represent the Hamming weight of a descriptor (the number of 1-bits). In Figure 1 we write the maximum and minimum depths with superscripts and subscripts, respectively. For example, the node marked 1_2^3 is the root of a subtree representing a set of descriptors of Hamming weights between 2 and 3.

Given the descriptor trie, matching an incoming packet with descriptor B amounts to finding one or more descriptors in the trie that are subsets of B. This in essence can be done by performing a walk over the prefix trie guided by the 1-bits in B. This algorithmic structure is the basis for the two algorithms we develop: *Find All Subsets* and *Find Largest Subset*.

3.1.2 Find All Subsets

The forwarder invokes the *Find All Subsets* (FAS) algorithm to forward packets with fan-out limit $k > 1$, and in particular multicast packets with $k = \infty$. FAS takes an input packet p and the fan-out limit k, and in its basic form visits only nodes representing bit positions that correspond to a 1-bit in the packet descriptor ($p.descriptor$). The FAS algorithm is listed as Algorithm 1.

Algorithm 1 *Find All Subsets* (FAS)

Input: packet p, fan-out limit k, FIB trie *root*
Output: set of output interfaces

  $nodes\_to\_visit \leftarrow \{root\}$ *// stack of nodes*
  $out \leftarrow \emptyset$
  while $nodes\_to\_visit \neq \emptyset$ **and** $|out| < k$ **do**
    $n \leftarrow$ pop node from $nodes\_to\_visit$
    if n is a terminator node **then**   *// subset found*
      $out \leftarrow out \cup n.interfaces$ *// up to $|out| = k$*
    else if $p.descriptor[n.pos]$ is a 1-bit **then**
      for all children c of node n **do**
        push c onto $nodes\_to\_visit$
      end for
    end if
  end while
  return out

FAS walks through the trie in depth-first order using an explicit stack of nodes to visit. When the algorithm reaches a terminator node, which means that there is a matching descriptor, the algorithm processes the list of interfaces associated with that descriptor, adding those interfaces to the set of output interfaces for the input packet. The walk terminates immediately if the set of output interfaces reaches a size greater than or equal to the fan-out limit k.

Descriptor		Out ifx
Bit String	**1s Pos**	
1000100000	(1,5)	i_2
1010000100	(1,3,8)	i_4, i_2
0110100000	(2,3,5)	i_3
0011100010	(3,4,5,9)	i_6, i_2
0010101000	(3,5,7)	i_5, i_2
0000100100	(5,8)	i_2

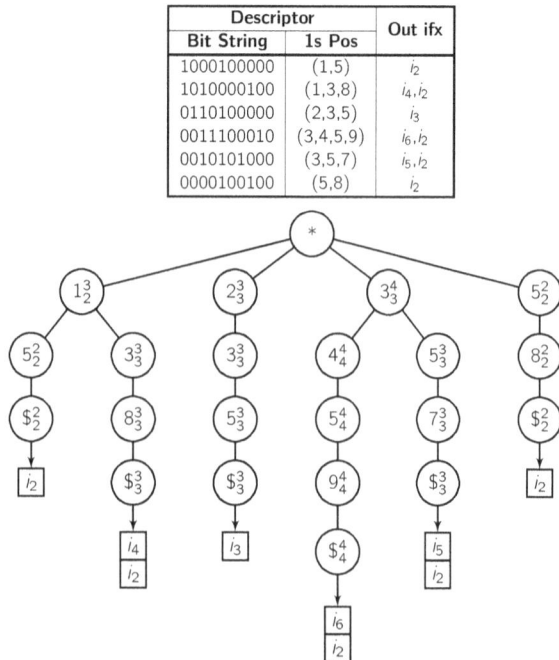

Figure 1: FIB representation using a prefix trie

3.1.3 Find Largest Subset

When the fan-out limit is $k = 1$, which is typically used to send anycast packets such as data or service requests, the forwarder uses *Find Largest Subset* (FLS). This specialized algorithm is intended to select the *most relevant* descriptor among a potentially large number of matching descriptors. FLS is also intended to provide the semantics of longest name prefix matching with TagNet's descriptors. The FLS algorithm is listed as Algorithm 2.

Algorithm 2 *Find Largest Subset* (FLS)

Input: packet p, FIB trie *root*
Output: maximal FIB entry matching *p.descriptor*

$nodes\_to\_visit \leftarrow \{root\}$ // stack of nodes
$best \leftarrow$ null   // leaf node of best match found
while $nodes\_to\_visit \neq \emptyset$ **do**
  $n \leftarrow$ pop node from $nodes\_to\_visit$
  if $best$ is null **or** $n.max\_depth > best.max\_depth$ **then**
    if n is a terminator node **then**   // subset found
      $best \leftarrow n$
    else if $p.descriptor[n.pos]$ is a 1-bit **then**
      for all children c of node n **do**
        push c onto $nodes\_to\_visit$
      end for
    end if
  end if
end while
return $best$

The FLS algorithm is conceptually similar to the FAS algorithm, and therefore FLS also performs a trie walk limited to matching descriptors. The main difference is that FLS keeps track of the matching descriptor with maximal Hamming weight found during the walk (variable *best*). Thus FLS further limits the trie walk to the subtrees that may contain matching descriptors larger than the current best.

3.1.4 Basic Algorithmic Improvements

Having defined the high-level structure of the descriptor matching algorithms, we now introduce three additional pruning strategies to further reduce the complexity of the trie walk. These strategies are based on the Hamming weight of the descriptors.

The first strategy exploits the fact that we search for subsets, so the Hamming weight of the descriptor in the packet must be greater than or equal to the Hamming weight (or depth) of a matching descriptor in the FIB. Therefore, we can check the minimum depth of a node before we push the node onto the stack, and in case the minimum depth exceeds the Hamming weight of the descriptor in the packet, we can safely skip that node.

The second strategy is a refinement of the first one. Before pushing a node c onto the $nodes\_to\_visit$ stack, we compute the number of remaining 1-bits in the input descriptor to the right of the bit position of node c ($c.pos$). We then add this number to the depth of node c in the trie, which represents the number of 1-bits already matched. The result is the maximum potential matching weight. That is, the maximum possible Hamming weight of any matching descriptor under node c. This also means that we can skip c when this maximum weight is less than the minimum depth of c. For example, consider matching input descriptor $(1, 3, 5)$ against

the trie of Figure 1. In this case, the algorithm can skip the descendants of the node labeled 3_3^4 (third child of the root). In fact, the depth of node 3_3^4 is 1, and the number of 1-bits to the right of position 3 in the input descriptor is 1, since there is only one position left unchecked (position 5), which adds up to a maximum potential matching weight of 2, which is less than the minimum depth of 3 under node 3_3^4.

The third strategy is also based on the maximum potential matching weight, and is applicable to the FLS algorithm only. FLS remembers the maximal matching descriptor seen in the walk (*best*). Therefore the algorithm can safely skip subtrees that have a maximum potential matching weight lower than *best*.

3.2 Improvements for Memory Usage

Tries, like other linked data structures, are notoriously inefficient in their use and access of memory. A naïve implementation of the FIB described in Section 3.1.1 requires a lot of memory, and accesses that memory without locality and therefore inefficiently. We now describe how we engineer the FIB to make it efficient in terms of memory usage and access. In summary, we apply four transformations: (1) we permute the bits of the descriptors in the FIB according to their popularity, (2) we factor out node chains (lists of nodes with a single child) from the trie, (3) we implement the trie with a single compact vector, and (4) we lay out the nodes in the vector so as to improve locality in the search algorithms.

3.2.1 Bit Permutation

The first transformation we apply to the trie is global. In essence, we sort the bits in decreasing order of frequency. The effect is that we move the most popular 1-bits to the leftmost positions in the descriptors. This in turn increases the sharing of prefixes in the trie, which means that the trie contains less nodes and also that a trie walk crosses less nodes.

Bit Pos	Bit Freq	New Pos	Original Descriptors	Permuted Descriptors
1	2	3	(1,5)	(1,3)
2	1	5	(1,3,8)	(2,3,4)
3	4	2	(2,3,5)	(1,2,5)
4	1	6	(3,4,5,9)	(1,2,6,8)
5	5	1	(3,5,7)	(1,2,7)
6	0	9	(5,8)	(1,4)
7	1	7		
8	2	4		
9	1	8		
10	0	10		

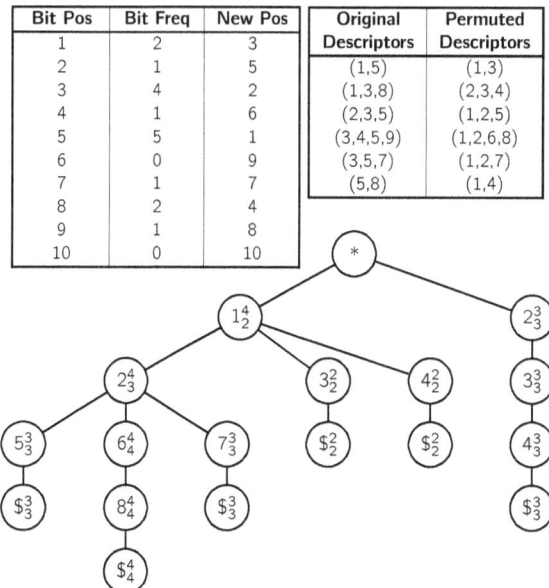

Figure 2: Trie compression with bit popularity (the original trie is the one presented in Figure 1)

Figure 2 shows the application of a bit permutation to the trie of Figure 1. The top-left table in Figure 2 shows the occurrences of each bit in the whole FIB together with the resulting bit permutation. The top-right table then shows the application of that permutation to the FIB. For example, descriptor $(2, 3, 5)$ becomes $(1, 2, 5)$, because the permuted position of 2 is 5, the new position of 3 is 2, and 5 goes to position 1. This technique is very effective and gives us an impressive compression. In order to use this technique we have to permute all the incoming queries accordingly. This overhead is linear in the number of 1-bits in the query and is negligible in practice.

Compare the new trie obtained with the permutation, represented in the lower part of Figure 2, with that of Figure 1. The permutation improves the sharing of prefixes and therefore reduces the size of the trie from 22 to 18 nodes. This improvement might seem small. However, notice that in this example the frequencies of the 1-bits in the FIBs are all small and therefore very similar, necessarily since the trie is itself very small. In large and realistic FIBs, the frequency distribution tends to be much more skewed, as can be deduced from the the popularity distributions for on-line content, which are likely to remain the same in an ICN. And that amplifies the benefits of the permutation transformation.

3.2.2 Chains Removal

To further reduce memory usage for the prefix trie, we remove chains from the data structure. With the term *chain* we indicate a sequence of nodes with a single child that amounts to a linked list of nodes. In our implementation we transform only those chains that lead to a terminator node, namely a node with position '$'. We also experimented with chain removal throughout the trie, but that proved less effective. This is because chains at the top of the trie are shared and there are far more terminal chains than intermediate ones. And crucially, operating on chains in the middle of the trie requires additional checks in the basic trie-walk algorithm that offset the cost savings of chain elimination. Conversely, terminal chains do not require additional processing in the trie walk.

Our intuition is that chains are at the same time costly in terms of memory, and also redundant for the purpose of the search algorithms. In fact, when we reach a chain we can explore only one path, meaning a single descriptor. In other words, a chain exercises the trie-walk algorithm for potentially several iterations, only to produce a simple yes/no answer: either the descriptor matches or it does not. Our approach is therefore to extract each terminal chain from the trie and to store it, together with the corresponding list of output interfaces, in a separate compact data structure that we check in the final stage of matching with a much more efficient comparison operation. Figure 3 shows an example of a terminal chain in the trie (left) and its compact external representation (right).

To remove a chain we simply move the terminator node that closes the chain to the head of the chain, and drop all the other nodes. Notice that the minimum and maximum depths are the same throughout the chain, which means that the shortened trie behaves exactly as the original trie for the purpose of the matching algorithms. We then link the terminator node to a compact vector that represents all the bit positions removed from the trie. See Figure 3 for an explanatory example.

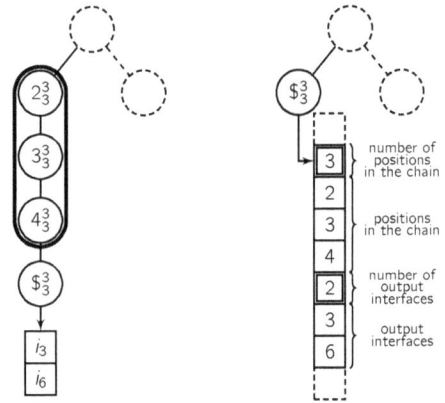

Figure 3: A chain in the trie (left) and its representation (right)

3.2.3 Vector Representation and Memory Layout

One of the main disadvantages in a naïve trie representation is the use of pointers and possibly of tables of pointers. A common way to reduce the use of pointers is first to structure the trie as a binary trie in which each node "points to" the node's first child and the node's next sibling, and then to represent this binary trie within a vector so as to remove one of the two pointers by implicitly linking a node with the following one in the vector.

Figure 4 exemplifies this method by showing the representation of the trie of Figure 2 after chain removal as a binary trie (top), and then the vector representation of the binary trie (bottom). We draw the binary trie with solid arrows to denote first-child links and with dashed arrows to denote next-sibling links.

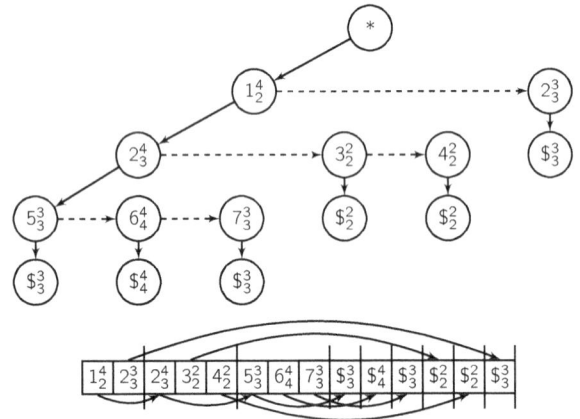

Figure 4: Trie represented as a vector

The binary trie can then be encoded as a vector in which the next-sibling links are implicit in the sequence of nodes, and the first-child links are represented as offsets in the vector. In particular, each node within the vector holds the same data as in the trie (position, minimum and maximum depths) plus an offset to point to the first child, which we depict with a solid arrow in the figure. This, however, is not enough to represent and walk through the trie, since the walk algorithm would know how to start iterating through the children of a given node, but it would not know where to stop. So, to support the trie walk, we add a flag to a node that indicates whether that node is the last child, or in other words the last node in a contiguous sequence of siblings. In Figure 4 we indicate that a node is a last child with a vertical bar.

Having defined the vector representation of the FIB, we also adapt the search algorithms to that representation. Algorithm 3 is the specialization of the *Find All Subset* algorithm that operates on the vector FIB. The structure is the same for the *Find Largest Subset* algorithm.

Algorithm 3 *Find All Subsets* on FIB vector
___
Input: packet p, FIB vector *FIB*
Output: set of output interfaces

$nodes\_to\_visit \leftarrow \{FIB[0]\}$ *// stack of nodes*
$out \leftarrow \emptyset$
while $nodes\_to\_visit \neq \emptyset$ **and** $|out| < k$ **do**
  $n \leftarrow$ pop node from $nodes\_to\_visit$
  while true do   *// iteration through n's children*
    if n is a terminator node **then**   *// subset found*
      $out \leftarrow out \cup n.interfaces$ *// up to $|out| = k$*
    else if $p.descriptor[n.pos]$ is a 1-bit **then**
      push first child of node n onto $nodes\_to\_visit$
    end if
    if n is a last child **then**
      break out of the loop   *// go to next-node loop*
    end if
    $n \leftarrow$ next node in the FIB vector
  end while
end while
return out

The vector representation we just described is generally not unique (for a given tree). In fact, there are different ways to lay out the nodes in the vector that, in combination with the search algorithm, would induce different memory access patterns. In the following we study two node layouts and we compare them through a simple example.

Figure 5 shows the memory access pattern for the FAS algorithm for two different layouts of the vector. In this example we trace the nodes that the algorithm visits when matching the input descriptor $(1, 2, 4, 7)$. In particular, we depict the pointers of the trie structure (first child) with thin gray arrows below the vector, while we depict the sequence of memory accesses with bold black arrows above vector. Under each vector we also represent the evolution of the stack during the search. The values in the stack are the indexes of the vector cells indicated over each vector.

The first node-layout in Figure 5 is the same layout shown in the example of Figure 4. We obtain this layout by storing the descendants of a list of sibling nodes in the same order of the siblings, which is by increasing bit positions. Therefore we call this the *Sibling Order Layout* (SOL).

More specifically, we always store a list of siblings in increasing order of bit position. For example, we store the two sibling nodes in the first level of the trie of Figure 4, 1_2^4 and 2_3^3, at position 1 and 2, respectively. But then we have to choose how to lay out the children of these two nodes, and their children, etc. In the SOL layout we do it left-to-right and with immediate recursion, so we start by visiting the

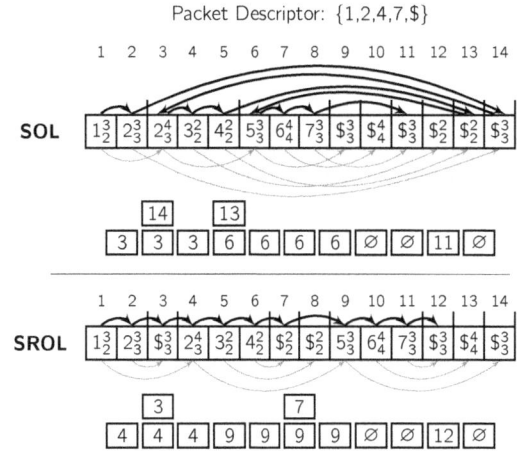

Figure 5: **Different node layouts and related memory access pattern**

children of the first sibling node, and then recursively their children until we lay out the entire subtree rooted at the first sibling, and then we proceed in order of bit position with the subtrees of the second sibling, the third, etc. So, as shown in the top part of Figure 5, we first add the children of node 1_2^4, at positions 3,4,5, then the entire subtree rooted at 1_2^4, and then the child of node 2_3^3 at position 14.

The second layout, shown at the bottom of Figure 5, uses the reverse ordering, and hence we call it *Sibling Reverse Order Layout* (SROL). As usual, we store sibling nodes in consecutive cells sorted by bit position. However, contrary to SOL, with the SROL layout we visit the children of sibling nodes in reverse order, starting from the last sibling node. For example (see the lower part of Figure 5) after nodes 1_2^4 and 2_3^3, we start with the children of 2_3^3, and recursively their children and the entire subtree rooted at 2_3^3, and after that we lay out the children of node 1_2^4 and its entire subtree.

In our implementation we use this latter layout (SROL), because it induces a much more linear and therefore cache-efficient memory access pattern. In fact, as shown in Figure 5, the more natural SOL layout defines an almost random memory access pattern. We first visit nodes 1 and 2, then jump to position 14, then back to position 3, and so on. Instead, the SROL layout produces a nicely sequential memory access pattern that is optimal for caching.

3.3 Locator-Based Matching Algorithm

We now provide an overview of the labeling and forwarding scheme that we use for locators. Labeling is the process by which the network assigns locators and locator FIBs to nodes. In their seminal paper on stretch-3 compact routing schemes for general graphs [10], Thorup and Zwick also propose a lesser-known but still practical compact routing scheme for trees. Since we use trees as a basic routing structure for TagNet, we adopt this Thorup and Zwick scheme for locator-based forwarding, and therefore we refer to the implementation of our locators as TZ-labels. Here we review the scheme only very briefly, without going through the details of the labeling algorithm and its associated forwarding algorithm, and we refer our readers to Section 2 of Thorup and Zwick [10].

49

The most compact scheme for trees by Thorup and Zwick uses both labels and FIBs of $(1 + o(1)) \log_2 n$ bits. We use a simpler and less compact version of that scheme (described in Section 2.1 of their paper) that uses $3.4 \log_2 n$ bits. Along with the labeling algorithm for that scheme, Thorup and Zwick provide a very efficient forwarding algorithm, which is what we use in TagNet and that we reproduce in Figure 6.

To forward a message toward a destination node (on a tree) each intermediate node needs only the TZ-label of the destination node (on that tree) plus its own TZ-label, which also serves as the node's FIB.

```
1  struct TZ_label {
2      uint16_t node_id;
3      uint16_t ifx_list;
4      uint16_t mask;
5  };
6  struct TZ_label my_label;
7  uint8_t k = leftmost_bit(my_label.mask);
8  uint16_t P[2] = {parent_interface, heavy_child_interface};
9  uint16_t f = largest_descendent_id;
10 uint16_t h = heavy_child_id;

12 int forward(struct TZ_label & dest) {
13     v = dest.node_id;
14     L = dest.ifx_list;
15     M = dest.mask;
16     return ((v >= my_label.node_id && v < h)
17            ? (L >> k) & ((M >> k) ^ ((M >> k) −1))
18            : P[v >=h && v <=f]);
19 }
```

Figure 6: Locator-based forwarding algorithm

Figure 6 indicates the local variables that we need to store at each node. A node stores its own label (my_label), which in turn contains the node identifier ($node\_id$), a list of interfaces encoded in a bit string (ifx_list), and a mask used to extract them ($mask$). Each node also stores a constant k that indicates the size of the local mask in bits, the identifier f of the largest descendant, and the identifier h of the node's heavy child, which is the child through which it is possible to reach the majority of the descendants. In addition, a node stores a vector P that contains the interfaces where to forward packets for the parent node and the heavy child.

The forward function extracts all the information needed from the incoming TZ-label, and returns the output interface. Notice that this forwarding decision is taken in a single line of code that amounts to a handful of machine instructions. Using this scheme, TZ-labels computed for the AS-level network topology[1] of 42113 nodes and 118040 edges, are at most 46-bits long and can be represented by the TZ_label struct defined in the code of Figure 6.

4. EVALUATION

The algorithmic complexity of our subset matching algorithms conforms to an analysis of general partial-matching algorithms on search tries developed by Rivest [8]. In our

---

[1]Internet AS-level topology archive (http://irl.cs.ucla.edu/topology/), data retrieved 29/06/2012.

setting, assuming a random FIB, the expected running time is $O(n^{h/m})$, where n is the size of the FIB, h is the Hamming weight of the input set, and $m = 192$ is the size of the Bloom filters we use.[2] For example, with an input set of four tags, a basic subset search would run in time $O(n^{0.15})$. In essence, our subset matching algorithms are efficient with reasonably small input sets, but their complexity grows with the size of the input set.

This analysis is indicative at a high level but does not consider algorithmic improvements, memory-usage, the specific distribution of tag sets in a realistic FIB, and many other issues that are important in practice. We therefore turn to an experimental evaluation. In particular, we evaluate the forwarding engine we developed for TagNet in order to examine the following research questions: (1) How effective are the memory compression techniques that we propose? (2) What are the differences in performance between the SOL and SORL memory layouts? (3) How scalable is our implementation in terms of number of CPU cores and FIB size? (4) What is the effective throughput of our matcher under different traffic workloads?

Our subject is a matcher written in C++ that implements the three algorithms described in Section 3, namely the FAS, which we run with fan-out limit $k = \infty$, and the FLS algorithm, both operating on a vector FIB, plus the locator-based forwarding algorithm of Thorup and Zwick. We run all our experiments on a general-purpose machine equipped with two Intel Xeon E5-2670 v3 processors, each with 12 cores and a clock frequency of 2.30GHz. The machine has 64GB of RAM.

With this subject and test-bed, we measure memory and throughput of the forwarding engine. The throughput corresponds to the total processing time of the forwarding engine, which includes the parsing of the packet header to figure out the type of address (descriptor or locator) and the fan-out limit (for descriptors), the dispatching of the packet to the appropriate algorithm (FAS, FLS, or TZ forwarding), and the execution of that algorithm. In all our experiments, we measure matching times and throughput as an aggregate measure (average) over all the packets in a workload, which is typically over one million packets. These average measurements are extremely consistent over repeated trials, therefore we never report any variance in the charts and in the tables. In fact, time measurements (averages over all packets) are so consistent that the full variability range for repeated trials (maximum minus minimum) is never more than 3% of the mean.

We begin our analysis by characterizing the data sets and the workloads we use for the evaluation, and then we continue with a series of experiments to answer our research questions.

4.1 FIB and Traffic Workloads

We test descriptor-based forwarding under three different FIBs. The first FIB workload, labeled 63M, contains more than 63 million unique descriptors. We generated this set of descriptors for a previous analysis of the scalability of the

---

[2]See Section 4.3 of Rivest [8]. The general complexity is $O(n^{\log_2 (2-s/k)})$, where s/k is the ratio of fixed bits over the total number of bits in the partial-matching query. Since $s/k < 1$, $\log_2 (2 - s/k)$ is approximately $1 - s/k$, which is the ratio of "don't care" bits, which in our case is h/m, since 1-bits in the input Bloom filter play the role of "don't care."

routing protocol we proposed for TagNet [6]. In particular, we derived the 63M FIB from the routing state generated by 500 million users for a variety of classes of applications. The second workload we use, labeled 10M, is a sample of 10 million descriptors taken from the 63M workload. The third workload, labeled 10M-CCN, is composed of almost 10 million descriptors. This workload corresponds to the FIBs used by Wang et al. to test their GPU-based matcher for CCN hierarchical names [12], and was also used to test other implementations [7, 11]. Notice that the workload by Wang et al. consists of hierarchical names, not tag-set descriptors. We therefore compile 10M-CCN by transforming hierarchical names into descriptors as shown in Section 2.1. We use this workload to show that our algorithms perform well also when they emulate the semantics of hierarchical names.

In addition to the FIB, the workload must provide a way to feed traffic into the forwarder, specifically we need to define a way to create the descriptors in the packets. So, in order to obtain valid results, we first analyze various options for the traffic mix. The analysis shows that the matching rate has a fundamentally negative impact on performance. Figure 7 shows the matching time of the two descriptor matching algorithms as a function of the matching rate, for the 10M FIB and for a single thread.

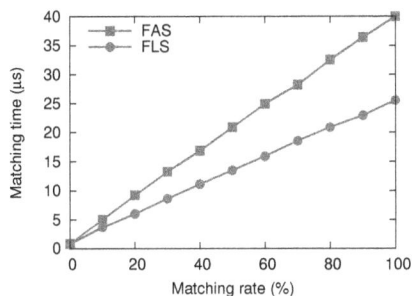

Figure 7: Effect of the matching rate on performance; matching rate is the percentage of messages that match at least one descriptor in the FIB

Notice that even a single thread can handle on average 1.2Mpps (million packets per second) with the FAS algorithm, and 1.3Mpps with FLS, when none of the packets matches a single descriptor (0% matching rate). In fact, non-matching packets can be discarded very quickly after a few checks. However, the matching time grows quickly with the matching rate, especially for the FAS algorithm. Based on these results, to be conservative, in the rest of the evaluation we use workloads with 100% of matching packets. To guarantee the high rate of matching, we generate packet descriptors by drawing descriptors from the FIB itself and then by adding extra tags to those descriptors.

The number of additional tags that we put in the packet descriptors also plays a fundamental role in the performance of our matcher, since it further increases the matching rate. And even without more matches, having more tags and therefore descriptors with higher Hamming weights means more paths to visit in the trie. Figure 8 shows the impact of the additional tags on the average matching time (in microseconds) for the FAS and FLS algorithms. In this experiment we use again the 10M FIB and we run again the

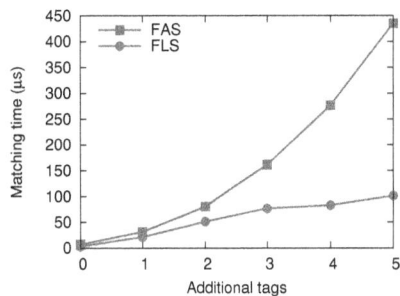

Figure 8: Effect of the descriptor size on the performance of the matcher

matcher with a single thread. It is clear from the figure that the number of tags in the packet descriptors has a very significant impact on the FAS algorithm, with the matching time growing almost exponentially with the number of additional tags, which is also consistent with the complexity analysis discussed earlier. This effect, however, is much less visible for the FLS algorithm. This is because increasing the matching rate also increases the chance of finding a good match at the beginning, which in turn allows the algorithm to skip entire sub-trees. In the remainder of our evaluation we use a workload where we introduce up to two additional tags to the packet descriptors drawn from the FIB.

4.2 Trie Compression

We now present the results of a number of experiments intended to test the effectiveness of our trie compression techniques, namely bit permutation (Section 3.2.1) and chain removal (Section 3.2.2), both in terms of memory usage and in terms of the performance of the matching algorithms.

We start by analyzing the memory usage. We always use the vector representation for the trie, but we apply different combinations of compression. Figure 9a shows the results for all the FIB workloads. The histogram shows the memory used by the trie with no compression ("no compression"), when we apply the bit permutation ("bit perm"), and when we also remove chains ("bit perm+chain"). The bit permutation is quite effective on all the workloads, with a 48% reduction in the FIB size for the 10M FIB, 42% for 10M-CCN, and 46% for 63M. Chain removal is also effective in all cases. In the end, the size of the FIB for 10M and 10M-CCN is 171MB, while it is 1.06GB for 63M.

We then look at the effect of trie compression on matching time. Figure 9b shows the matching time required by the FAS and FLS algorithms using the different trie compression techniques. We run our experiments using a single thread using the 10M workload. The results are in microseconds. We label the different compression techniques as in Figure 9a.

The results show that trie compression is not only useful to reduce the memory footprint of the FIB, but it also reduces the matching times for both FAS and FLS. The bit permutation is the most effective optimization in terms of matching time. This is due to the fact that it reduces the number of prefixes to check, which reduces the search space. Bit permutation alone yields a 29.2% performance improvement for the FAS algorithm, and 16.8% for FLS. In addition to that, chain removal also gives a good improvement, with an additional 8% for FAS and 6.2% for FLS.

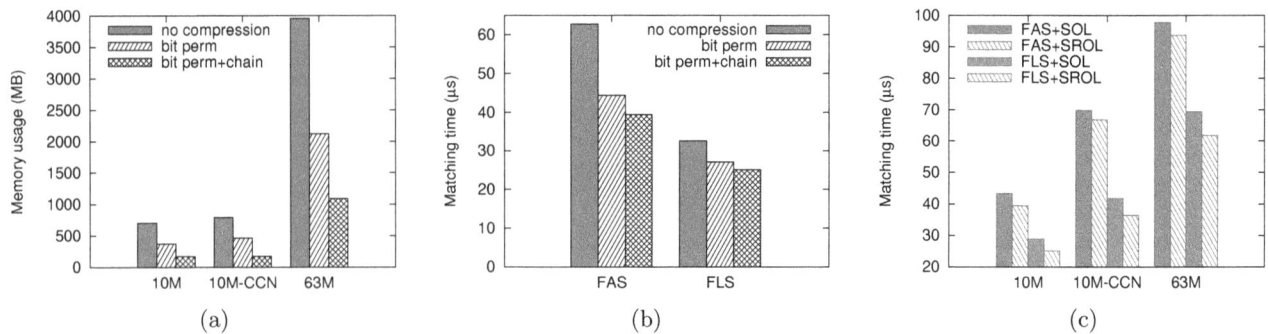

Figure 9: Memory usage for different FIBs with different types of trie compression (a); matching times with the 10M workload with different types of trie compression (b), and with different node layouts (c)

4.3 Memory Layout

We now examine the performance of the matcher in terms of average matching time using the two memory layouts discussed in Section 3.2.3. In Figure 9c we report the average matching time for the SOL and SROL memory layouts. The histogram shows the matching time required by both the FAS and FLS algorithms for all the FIB workloads. The results are for a single thread.

What is immediately clear is that the SROL layout improves performance in all cases. The relative improvements vary. In the worst case, when we use the FAS algorithm with the 10M-CCN and 63M FIBs, we gain 4.1%. However, with the FLS algorithm we always gain more than 10%, with a peak of 13.1% in the case of 10M.

These results are also particularly important to measure the latency of our matcher, since the values reported in Figure 9c represent the average latency introduced by the matcher. In particular, the latency of our implementation is the one of the SROL layout, shown in the histogram with the diagonal pattern. According to Wang et al. the latency should be lower than $100\mu s$ [12], and our implementation satisfies this requirement with all the workloads we tested.

4.4 Implementation Scalability

We now test the scalability of our implementation with respect to the number of threads and with respect to the size of the FIB.

4.4.1 Number of Threads

With modern hardware architectures, it is particularly important that algorithms be capable of exploiting parallelism. In the following experiments we test the scalability of our implementation with respect to the number of CPU threads used within the matcher. In Figure 10a we show the throughput in thousands of packets per second (Kpps) of the FAS algorithm when we vary the number of threads. The plot shows that the implementation scales almost perfectly with higher numbers of threads for all three FIB workloads. Every time we double the number of threads, we gain on average 80.8% in throughput, with a peak of 98.3%, which is very close to linear scaling. However, when we go from 16 to 32 threads, using the 63M FIB, we only obtain a 57.1% improvement. We believe this is due to the fact that our test machine has only 24 real cores, so the 32 threads run using Intel's Hyper-Threading technology. Using the FAS

algorithm, our router can forward on average 499Kpps with 10M, 307Kpps with 10M-CCN, and 183Kpps with 63M.

In Figure 10b we show the multi-threading scalability of the FLS algorithm. Also in this case the implementation scales well, since on average we obtain an incremental (doubling) gain of 83.1%, with a peak of 98.4%. And again the least incremental gain (59.3%) is when we use 32 threads with the 63M FIB. The throughput in the case of FLS is almost twice the throughput of the FAS algorithm. Our matcher processes 914Kpps with 10M, 602Kpps in case of 10M-CCN and 272Kpps using 63M. The gain in the throughput is due to the fact that using this algorithm we can skip more checks and so we need less memory accesses.

Another interesting result visible both in Figure 10a and Figure 10b is that, although the 10M and 10M-CCN workloads require the same amount of memory (see Figure 9a), their performance differs significantly under the two workloads. This is due to the fact that 10M-CCN has more paths in the top part of the trie as compared to 10M. For this reason, the algorithm needs to explore more nodes, which in turn requires more memory accesses.

4.4.2 FIB Size

A crucial measure of scalability for our matcher is the ability to sustain a good throughput with large FIBs. We already have some evidence of good scalability from the results of figures 10a and 10b, since the throughput achieved with the 63M FIB is only 2.59 times lower (on average) than the throughput with the 10M FIB, even though the 63M FIB is more than 6 times larger than the 10M FIB.

To further test the scalability in the size of the FIB, we conduct an experiment in which we vary the size of the FIB, starting with 10 million entries and increasing the size up to 60 million entries in steps of 10 millions. We report the results of this experiment in Figure 10c, where we show the throughput of the matcher with the FAS and FLS algorithms. The chart clearly shows that the throughput decreases, but does so with a flattening slope, which confirms that our implementation scales well with the size of the FIB.

4.5 Performance with Mixed Traffic

So far we tested only the performance of the content-based matcher. However our matcher can also forward packets by locator and therefore benefit from their efficiency. To highlight these benefits, but also to test the performance of the matcher under more realistic workloads than the ones used

52

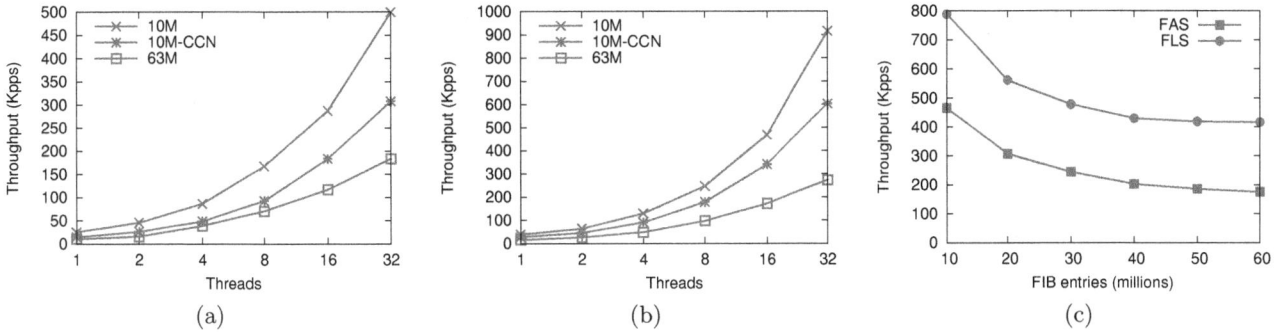

Figure 10: Throughput of FAS (a) and FLS (b) with multiple threads, and with different FIB sizes (c)

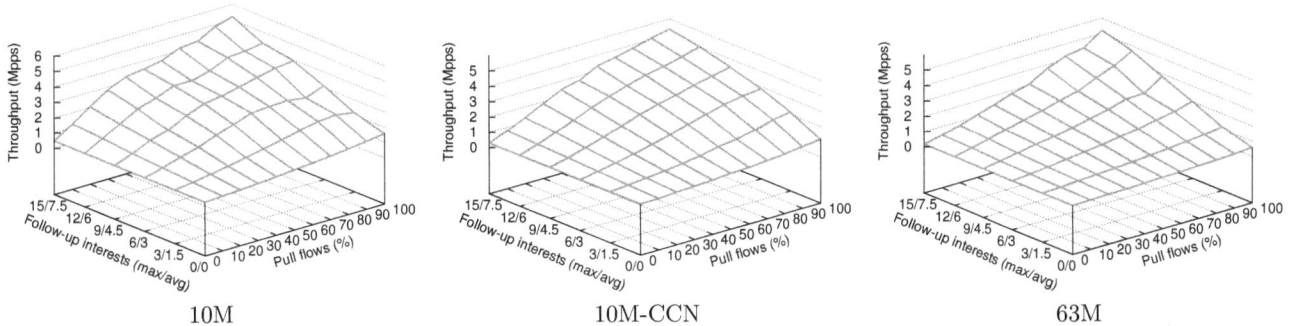

Figure 11: Throughput with different traffic mixes

so far, we create different traffic mixes. In particular, we generate a traffic mix where we vary the percentage of push and pull flows as described in Section 2.1. A push flow always consists of a single packet that we forward using the FAS algorithm ($k = \infty$). A pull flow starts with an anycast "interest" packet addressed by descriptor, and therefore forwarded with the FLS algorithm, and continues with a sequence of follow-up interest packets addressed directly to the producer by locator, and for each interest there is also a data packet forwarded by locator in the opposite direction. In each in pull flow, we choose the number of follow-up interests uniformly at random in a range between 0 and a maximum value that we set as the independent variable of our experiments.

In these experiments we measure the throughput in Mpps for the three different FIBs, varying the percentage of pull traffic and the number of follow-up interests. We display the results in Figure 11. In the charts we indicate the number of follow-up interests on the x-axis, the percentage of pull flows on the y-axis, and the measured throughput on z-axis. Notice that on the x-axis we indicate both the maximum and the average number of follow-up interests that we can have in each pull flow. The results demonstrate that we can easily forward millions of packets per second, even using short pull flows averaging only 7.5 follow-up requests. The throughput also depends on the push traffic, which is quite costly for forwarding. For example, if we consider a traffic mix where we have 80% of pull flows and 20% of push flows, we can forward 2.89Mpps with 63M, 4.27Mpps with 10M, and 3.79Mpps with 10M-CCN.

In this experiment we also estimate the throughput in bits per second. To do that we compute the average packet

Table 1: Throughput (Mpps/Gbps) for different traffic mixes using different FIBs

pull (%)	pkt (B)	Throughput (Mpps/Gbps)		
		10M	10M-CCN	63M
0	1280	0.47/4.8	0.31/3.1	0.17/1.8
20	835	2.04/13.6	1.30/8.7	0.74/5.0
40	775	3.30/20.5	2.44/15.2	1.39/8.7
60	751	3.70/22.2	3.29/19.8	2.08/12.5
80	739	4.27/25.3	3.79/22.4	2.89/17.1
100	731	5.20/30.5	4.33/25.3	4.2/24.6

size for each traffic mix. We hypothesize that push packets and data packets are quite large, since they would typically carry data. In particular, for those packets we consider 1280 bytes, which is the minimum link MTU in IPv6.[3] For the first interest we consider the average size of an HTTP GET header, which is around 800 bytes according to the Google SPDY report.[4] Finally we consider follow-up interests to be small packets of 100 bytes. With these parameters, Table 1 reports the average packet size (in bytes, in the second column) for different percentages of pull traffic. In this table we consider only the case where we have a maximum number of follow-up requests equal to 15. The table reports the throughput in Mpps and in Gbps. Considering again the case where we have 80% of pull flows and 20% of push flows, our forwarder can achieve a throughput of 17.1Gbps using 63M, 22.4Gbps using 10M-CCN and 25.3Gbps with 10M.

[3]RFC2469: Internet Protocol, Version 6 (IPv6) Specification. https://tools.ietf.org/html/rfc2460
[4]SPDY: An experimental protocol for a faster web. https://www.chromium.org/spdy/spdy-whitepaper

5. CONCLUSION

We presented and evaluated a data plane for TagNet, an ICN architecture that features a dual addressing scheme and two corresponding delivery services, one based on expressive, application-defined descriptors, and one based on extremely efficient, network-defined locators. We see this dual addressing, and the algorithms we developed to support it, as an effective way or perhaps simply a first but essential step in designing a true *information centric* network.

In prior work we proposed and evaluated a routing scheme for TagNet. Here we developed the essential algorithms to realize the TagNet data plane. In particular, we developed a forwarding engine that implements specialized subset matching algorithms for descriptor forwarding and an extremely fast locator forwarding algorithm based on a compact routing scheme for trees. The forwarding engine runs on general purpose CPU, and yet it is capable of forwarding over 20Gbps of mixed traffic flows with large forwarding tables corresponding to hundreds of millions of users.

One of our most immediate plans for future research includes the development of a forwarding engine built on massively parallel hardware to increase the throughput of even the descriptor-based forwarding alone. Indeed we have a GPU-based prototype that in a preliminary evaluation can process almost one million descriptors per second with the 63M FIB and the same traffic workload we used in the evaluation presented in this paper.

6. ACKNOWLEDGMENTS

We thank Alessandro Margara and Gianpaolo Cugola for their comments an insights in many useful discussions on the subset matching problem. This work was supported in part by the Swiss National Science Foundation under grant number 200021-132565 and under grant number 200021-157164.

7. REFERENCES

[1] M. Charikar, P. Indyk, and R. Panigrahy. New algorithms for subset query, partial match, orthogonal range searching, and related problems. In *Proceedings of the 29th International Colloquium on Automata, Languages, and Programming (ICALP 2002)*, pages 451–462, July 2002.

[2] H. Dai, J. Lu, Y. Wang, and B. Liu. BFAST: Unified and scalable index for NDN forwarding architecture. In *2015 IEEE Conference on Computer Communications (INFOCOM)*, pages 2290–2298, Apr.–May 2015.

[3] D. Han, A. Anand, F. Dogar, B. Li, H. Lim, M. Machado, A. Mukundan, W. Wu, A. Akella, D. G. Andersen, J. W. Byers, S. Seshan, and P. Steenkiste. Xia: Efficient support for evolvable internetworking. In *Proceedings of the 9th USENIX Conference on Networked Systems Design and Implementation (NSDI'12)*, pages 309–322, Apr. 2012.

[4] S. Helmer and G. Moerkotte. Evaluation of main memory join algorithms for joins with set comparison predicates. In *Proceedings of 23rd International Conference on Very Large Data Bases (VLDB'97)*, pages 386–395, Aug. 1997.

[5] Y. Luo, G. H. L. Fletcher, J. Hidders, and P. De Bra. Efficient and scalable trie-based algorithms for computing set containment relations. In *31st IEEE International Conference on Data Engineering (ICDE'15)*, pages 303–314, Apr. 2015.

[6] M. Papalini, A. Carzaniga, K. Khazaei, and A. L. Wolf. Scalable routing for tag-based information-centric networking. In *Proceedings of the 1st International Conference on Information-centric Networking (ICN'14)*, pages 17–26, Sept. 2014.

[7] D. Perino, M. Varvello, L. Linguaglossa, R. Laufer, and R. Boislaigue. Caesar: A content router for high-speed forwarding on content names. In *Proceedings of the Tenth ACM/IEEE Symposium on Architectures for Networking and Communications Systems (ANCS'14)*, pages 137–148, Oct. 2014.

[8] R. L. Rivest. Partial-match retrieval algorithms. *SIAM Journal on Computing*, 5(1):19–50, Mar. 1976.

[9] W. So, A. Narayanan, and D. Oran. Named data networking on a router: Fast and dos-resistant forwarding with hash tables. In *Proceedings of the Ninth ACM/IEEE Symposium on Architectures for Networking and Communications Systems (ANCS'13)*, pages 215–226, Oct. 2013.

[10] M. Thorup and U. Zwick. Compact routing schemes. In *Proceedings of the thirteenth annual ACM symposium on Parallel algorithms and architectures (SPAA'01)*, pages 1–10, July 2001.

[11] Y. Wang, B. Xu, D. Tai, J. Lu, T. Zhang, H. Dai, B. Zhang, and B. Liu. Fast name lookup for named data networking. In *2014 IEEE 22nd International Symposium of Quality of Service (IWQoS)*, pages 198–207, May 2014.

[12] Y. Wang, Y. Zu, T. Zhang, K. Peng, Q. Dong, B. Liu, W. Meng, H. Dai, X. Tian, Z. Xu, H. Wu, and D. Yang. Wire speed name lookup: A gpu-based approach. In *Proceedings of the 10th USENIX Symposium on Networked Systems Design and Implementation (NSDI'13)*, pages 199–212, Apr. 2013.

[13] H. Yuan and P. Crowley. Reliably scalable name prefix lookup. In *Proceedings of the Eleventh ACM/IEEE Symposium on Architectures for Networking and Communications Systems (ANCS'15)*, pages 111–121, May 2015.

PFPSim: A Programmable Forwarding Plane Simulator

Samar Abdi*, Umair Aftab*, Gordon Bailey*, Bochra Boughzala[†],
Faras Dewal*, Shafigh Parsazad*, Eric Tremblay*

*Concordia University, Canada   [†]Ericsson Research, Canada
Email: samar@ece.concordia.ca
samar@ece.concordia.ca

ABSTRACT

In this paper, we introduce PFPSim, a host-compiled simulator for early validation and analysis of packet processing applications on programmable forwarding plane architectures. The simulation model is automatically generated from a high-level description of the hardware/software architecture of the forwarding device and the behavioral description of the various modules in the architecture. Our high-level architectural description language is capable of defining many-core network processors as well as reconfigurable pipelines. The behavior of the fixed-function processing elements in the architecture is defined in C++. The code targeted for the processor cores, or reconfigurable pipeline stages, is compiled from P4, an emerging programming language for packet processing applications. Application developers can use PFPSim as a virtual prototype to simulate and debug their applications before hardware availability. Moreover, forwarding device architects can use PFPSim to evaluate the trade-offs between different hardware/software design decisions.

Keywords

Forwarding plane, System-level design, P4, Network Processors.

1. INTRODUCTION

Software defined networking (SDN) has seen rapid adoption in recent years, with several switch chip vendors offering support for the Openflow protocol [1]. However, Openflow is restricted to known packet header types, which makes it difficult to implement new headers and protocols. Therefore, researchers have proposed new protocol-independent programming abstractions, such as P4, for the forwarding plane in order to enable programming the forwarding chip to support new protocols [2]. The idea behind these efforts to provide complete flexibility to the application developer in defining *how* packets are processed regardless of the underlying hardware [3]. The forwarding plane hardware providers, on the other hand, may distinguish their devices on cost, performance and power metrics, while providing support for standard programming abstractions.

The concept of a programmable forwarding plane is not new. Network processors (NPUs) and even general purpose CPUs have long been used in forwarding plane hardware [4-7]. Recently, we

ANCS '16, March 17-18, 2016, Santa Clara, CA, USA
© 2016 ACM. ISBN 978-1-4503-4183-7/16/03...$15.00
DOI: http://dx.doi.org/10.1145/2881025.2881029

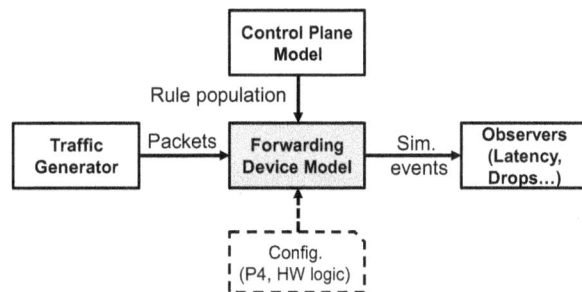

Figure 1. PFPSim simulation environment

have seen emergence of new devices, such as *r*econfigurable *m*atch *t*able (RMT) [8] and FlexPipe [9] that utilize reconfigurable pipelined hardware for fast and programmable packet processing. Based on these trends, we foresee an ecosystem where application developers can simulate, debug and analyze their packet processing programs on top of a simulation model of the programmable forwarding device, much before hardware availability. The hardware vendors, in turn, can use the simulation model and the applications to validate and optimize their designs.

In order to support such an ecosystem, we have developed a *Programmable Forwarding Plane Simulator* (*PFPSim*). Figure 1 illustrates the PFPSim environment. PFPSim uses SystemC [10, 11] to build a host-compiled model of the hardware, and the low-level software services, of the forwarding device. The logic for the modules in the forwarding device is written in C++ by the user. The packet processing program, to be executed by the programmable cores in the forwarding device, is compiled from a P4 description, and linked with the SystemC model of the forwarding device. The control plane model populates the memories in the forwarding device model with match-table rule entries. The final executable SystemC model is stimulated by a traffic generator that feeds the model with a simulated stream of incoming packets. At run time, the model generates simulation events that are processed by user defined observers to derive metrics such as packet latency, drops, and energy consumption.

The paper makes the following contributions: (i) a framework for early validation of programmable forwarding devices, (ii) a high-level language to specify the forwarding element's architecture, and (iii) the integration of the simulation model with P4.

There has been relatively little work on modeling of programmable forwarding plane, given that the majority of switches in the market are fixed function. NePSim, a cycle-level network processor simulator, models the Intel IXP1200 architecture but has not been shown to scale to modern many-core NPUs [12]. Current SDN simulators and emulators, such as

Mininet [13] and fs-SDN [14] do not model the forwarding plane architecture and are therefore unsuitable for making architectural design decisions. Many core simulators, such as MCSimA+ [15], perform full system simulation of complex x86 cores. While these are useful to model performance of soft-switch implementations, they cannot model NPUs and pipelines. To the best of our knowledge, there is currently no published simulator that enables system-level modeling and simulation of programmable forwarding devices.

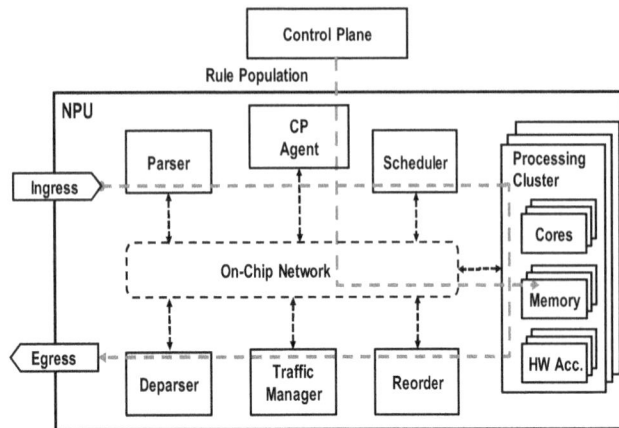

Figure 2. Typical network processor architecture

2. FORWARDING ARCHITECTURES

Packet processing applications exhibit a high degree of data parallelism. In theory, stateless processing can be parallelized indefinitely, given enough processing and memory resources, since each processing thread works independently on a given packet. Moreover, most of the processing actions are fairly simple, often a sequence of arithmetic operations. The complexity, typically, lies in *matching* an incoming packet header against a set of header patterns stored in a table. The match type can be exact, longest-prefix, range or wildcard.

Forwarding device architects exploit the data parallelism in packet processing applications in one of two ways: either by using a large number of multi-threaded RISC cores or a deep pipeline. The former template is used in NPUs, while the latter is used in reconfigurable hardware pipelines. In order to mitigate the complexity of header field matching, architects use efficient search-and lookup data structures such as tries, or hardware accelerators such as *t*ernary *c*ontent-*a*ddressable *m*emories (TCAMs) that perform single cycle match.

2.1 Network Processor

NPUs are widely used in edge routers for performing high-touch functions like encryption and compression. They are also good for CRC and checksum calculation, metering, accounting and keeping statistics: operations that are best done in software. Therefore, NPU architects use a large number of multi-threaded RISC cores to exploit data parallelism, while providing the flexibility of software programming. Figure 2 illustrates the high-level architecture of a simplified NPU, inspired by the SNP 4000 architecture [16]. The NPU consists of configurable hardware units for parsing, scheduling, reordering, traffic management and deparsing of packets. It consists of multiple identical processing clusters, each consisting of a set of RISC cores, memories and hardware accelerators.

The control plane populates the match table entries in the NPU's memory via an agent. Packets arriving at the *ingress* are sent to the *parser* for classification and generation of a packet descriptor. The *scheduler* then assigns the packet to one of the *processing clusters*. The packet processing application runs as concurrent identical threads on the CPU *cores* in the clusters, in a run-to-complete fashion. The application thread transforms the packet header, inspects the associated payload if needed, and then waits for the scheduler to send the next packet. Since any two packets may be processed on different cores, they may encounter different delays and may leave the processing clusters in a different order than the one they arrived. Therefore, a *reorder* module is used to restore the ordering of packets. The packet then goes to a *traffic manager* that sends the packets out according to their priority. The *deparser* generates the deparsed header, and recombines the header with its payload before sending the packet out on *egress*. The on-chip communication architecture of an NPU may vary, but the large number of processing cores and the requirement to access the same set of modules from several cores, naturally lends itself to a network-on-chip architecture.

The bulk of the packet processing on an NPU takes place in the processing cluster, and the majority of the packet latency results from the search-and-lookup operations in memory. Therefore, NPU designers can benefit from executable models that enable them to evaluate the trade-off between the number of cores and the budgeting of on-chip memory in their design. Such an executable model can also help with fast and early functional validation of the NPU architecture before hardware availability.

2.2 Reconfigurable Match Table Pipeline

The RMT architecture consists of a parser and deparser, as in the NPU, but the packet processing is performed in a pipelined fashion. The packet header travels through the pipeline in order, with each stage executing a match action table. The match part of the stage uses TCAM or hash tables for selecting the appropriate action in single cycle. The possible actions for a match-action table are preprogrammed as very wide instructions and stored in an SRAM section, dedicated to the relevant pipeline stage. A VLIW action processor executes the selected instructions, and passes the packet header to the next stage. In RMT, the packet latency is constant and depends on the number of stages. As such, the value addition of using PFPSim is in the functional validation of the RMT design.

3. MODELING METHODOLOGY

The PFPSim modeling methodology is shown in Figure 3. We provide an abstract *f*orwarding *a*rchitecture *d*escription (FAD) language for the designer to create the hierarchical structural model of the forwarding device. FAD provides a few simple declarative constructs to succinctly specify the hardware-software platform. The platform generator utility automatically generates the equivalent SystemC code from the FAD specification.

Logic for the different modules in the platform is input in C++ by the user. The application code to be executed on the NPU cores or RMT match-action processors can be written in C by the user. Alternately, the user may use our P4 compiler to generate code, targeted for the platform model, from a P4 description. The P4 compiler also generates the logic for the parsing module in the platform. If the application code is targeted for the NPU cores, we provide a timing annotation utility that automatically inserts basic-block level timing in the application source. The timed application is compiled along with the SystemC model of the platform and the module logic to generate the final simulation binary.

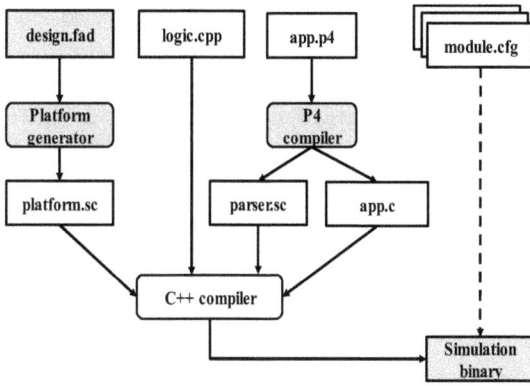

Figure 3. PFPSim modeling methodology

The module instances defined in the FAD specification may be configured by configuration files (*module.cfg*) defined as a separate input to PFPSim. The configuration files contain simply a set of key-value pairs and are loaded into the simulation model, as a map, at run-time. Using the configuration files, the designer may execute batch simulations of multiple design options without having to regenerate the simulation binary.

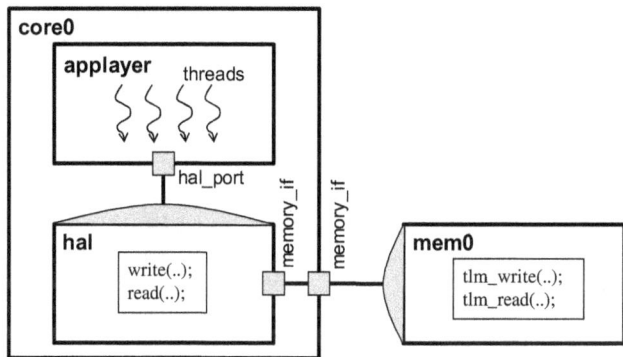

3.1 Transaction-level Modeling in SystemC

Figure 4. SW layers in a core with TLM memory interface

SystemC is a widely used language for System-on-Chip design and validation. It is essentially a discrete event simulation library in C++ that provides modeling abstractions for system-level design. The *transaction-level modeling* (TLM) abstraction in SystemC enables creation of abstract hardware models, particularly of memories, for high speed co-simulation of hardware and embedded software. TLMs abstract away cycle-accuracy and bit-level accuracy using abstract function calls to access memories or hardware services.

Figure 4 illustrates the SystemC TLM representation of a simple design with a single processor core (*core0*) connected to memory (*mem0*). The application layer (*applayer*) and hardware abstraction layer (*hal*) are instantiated as sub-modules inside *core0*. Threads inside the application layer use a port (*hal_port*) to access the memory read and write services provided by the *hal* module. The *hal*, in turn, implements these services via the memory interface ports (*memory_if*) that connect it to the TLM memory module (mem0) that implements the hardware memory services and maintains the memory state. The threads in the *applayer* execute natively on the host, resulting in much faster

simulation than an interpretive instruction-set simulator. Although SystemC provides all the constructs needed to create an executable model of the forwarding device, it is still too detailed as a specification language for forwarding architectures.

Listing 1: FAD example

1:	**interface** MEMI;
2:	**CE** MEMORY **implements** MEMI;
3:	**service** HALS;
4:	**PE** HAL **implements** HALS{
5:	MEMI memory_if; }; // end HAL
6:	**PE** APPLAYER {
7:	HALS hal_port; }; // end APPLAYER
8:	**PE** CORE {
9:	MEMI memory_if;
10:	HAL hal;
11:	APPLAYER applayer;
12:	**bind** applayer.hal_port, hal;
13:	**bind** hal.memory_if, memory_if; }; // end CORE
14:	**PE** *TOP* {
15:	CORE core0;
16:	MEMORY mem0;
17:	**bind** core0.memory_if, memory_if; }; // end TOP

3.2 Forwarding Architecture Description

The FAD language has a few simple constructs to specify the platform's hardware-software structure without having to create a detailed model in SystemC. Listing 1 illustrates the FAD for the design example in Figure 4. We use this example to explain the constructs in FAD.

The *Interface* keyword is used to define a hardware port type for facilitating transactions to memory hardware models (line 1). The behavioral description of an interface is a set of pure virtual functions in C++. Interface functions are defined in communication *elements* (*CEs*) that implement the interface (line 2). *Service,* similar to an interface, is also a port type and its behavioral description is also a set of pure virtual functions. However, service functions are defined in *processing elements* (*PEs*) that implement the service (lines 3-4). We use the distinction between service and interface to distinguish between hardware communication services and software services.

Interfaces and services are instantiated within a PE (lines 5, 7, 9). A service port of a PE instance may be bound to an instance of a PE, which implements the interface, using the *bind* keyword (line 12). An interface port of a PE instance may also be bound to an instance of a CE, which implements the interface, using *bind* (lines 13, 17).

PE defines a processing element type. It can represent either a hardware module, such as parser or CPU core, or a software module, such as application or drivers. PEs may be instantiated within another PE to express structural hierarchy (lines 10, 11, 15). *CE* defines communication element types, such as passive memories or links between modules. A CE instance is the *target* of transactions initiated by PEs (line 16).

The platform generator in PFPSim is a compiler that automatically generates SystemC code for the hardware-software platform defined in the FAD specification using a simple templating engine written in Python. PEs are translated into a hierarchy of SC_MODULES for HW structure. The SC_MODULES contain SC_THREADs to model logic on the PE. Memory CEs are translated into passive transaction-level SC_MODULEs that provides communication services through the implemented interface. Services and interfaces in FAD are translated into SC_INTERFACEs, and their instances are translated in SC_PORTs. The bindings are translated into equivalent port mappings.

3.3 NPU Model Semantics

The C/C++ code targeted for the NPU cores is either provided by the user or generated from P4, as shown in Figure 3. The code is wrapped inside a SystemC thread (SC_THREAD), and instantiated inside the SC_MODULE corresponding to the core. The timing model for this code may also be provided by the user by adding SystemC wait statements at the source level. This is both cumbersome and impractical. Moreover, it hides the memory transactions from the core. If a variable is defined inside a thread, it is mapped to the host's memory because SC_THREADs execute as native threads on the host operating system. Any variables are therefore allocated in the context of the host OS. Such abstraction is acceptable for thread local variables that are used for relatively inexpensive *action* processing. However, the abstraction is insufficient for trie accesses during search and lookup operations for implementing the *match* operations and are major contributors to overall packet latency.

We use a modeling technique to generate trie access transactions during simulation, without requiring the application developer to know about the underlying hardware architecture. We achieve this by defining clear semantics for the memory hardware model, the hardware abstraction layer model instantiated in the CPU cores, and a variable base class, with overloaded operations that use the hardware transaction layer to initiate memory transactions.

Listing 2: HAL write implementation

```
1:    HAL::write (long vaddr, void*VAL, long size) {
2:        mem_id = lookup_mem(vaddr);
3:        mem_addr = lookup_addr(vaddr);
4:        p = lookup_port(mem_id);
5:        p.tlm_write(mem_addr, VAL, size);
6:    } // end hal write
```

The HAL PE implements the virtual memory read/write services for the application threads running on the CPU core. Listing 2 shows the HAL code for the write method that takes the virtual address of the object being written, a pointer to the value and the size as inputs. It translates the virtual address to the memory instance and the physical address within that instance. It then looks up the port bound to that memory and initiates a TLM write to the memory.

The HAL Write and Read functions may be called directly from the application code. However, to facilitate application development and hide the HAL details, we define a base class, named *TLMVAR*, whose allocation, reference and assignment operations are overloaded to call corresponding HAL functions. All objects in the application that need to be explicitly modeled as

residing in the hardware memory models are instantiated from types that derive from TLMVAR.

Listing 3 shows the *write* function of TLMVAR. A TLMVAR object, upon construction, is assigned a virtual address (*vaddr*). To write to the object, we first obtain a pointer to the application layer module it is being accessed from. This is made possible by obtaining the parent module of the current SystemC process handle (line 2). The HAL port of the application layer module is then looked up, followed by calling the write method of the HAL (lines 3-4). Therefore, any read or write operation on a TLMVAR-derived object results in calls to HAL functions, which in turn result in memory transactions in the hardware model.

Listing 3: TLMVAR write implementation

```
1:    TLMVAR::write (void *VAL, long size) {
2:        a = get_applayer(sc_get_current_process());
3:        hal_port = get_hal_port(a);
4:        hal_port.write(vaddr, VAL, size);
5:    } // end write
```

In order to further insulate the application developer from the hardware model details, we have developed a trie library on top of TLMVAR. The search and lookup in the application code use this trie library without having to explicitly create TLMVAR objects. Thus, with clear modeling semantics, we enable the efficient development of applications on the NPU simulation model.

3.4 RMT Model Semantics

The RMT model is composed of three top level submodules: the ingress and egress pipelines, and the queues in between them. The ingress and egress pipelines are both instances of the same module, which contains several submodules: a Parser, a Deparser, and a series of logical Match-Action stages. The parser and deparser modules use the C code generated by the P4 compiler, adding a delay based on the number of states traversed in parsing of each packet. This should result in similar timing to the TCAM-based state machine proposed in the description of the RMT architecture.

The parser generates a *packet header vector* (PHV) which is operated upon in the pipeline. The Match-Action stages are each composed of 3 submodules, mimicking the structure of the logical stages in the RMT architecture. The first submodule is the Selector, which extracts the relevant fields from the PHV, and creates a key for matching. The next submodule is the Match stage, which uses the key to look up a result, which is a pointer to an action specification. The final submodule is the action stage, which takes the action specification and executes it, modifying the PHV accordingly. Each of these stages is given a constant delay, since the RMT architecture executes a match-action stage in a fixed number of cycles.

To implement the table-flow graph specified in the P4 program, we add a *next_table* field to the PHV. When a match-action stage receives a PHV, it checks if its index matches the *next_table* index of the PHV. If there is no match, the stage simply passes the PHV to the next stage in the pipeline without modifying it.

3.5 P4 Compilation for Target Model

We build upon the publicly available P4 compiler to target P4 application to our forwarding device models. The original P4 compiler is targeted for a soft-switch and written entirely in

Python. The compiler front end is a Python module which is included by the back end. The high-level intermediate representation is a collection of data structures in memory. The back end code generation is done using a templating library.

The C code generated by the P4 soft-switch compiler is further compiled into a set of static libraries and headers that are imported into the SystemC model of the forwarding device. Additional templates have been added to the P4 compiler back end to expose an API suitable for use in the SystemC model. These APIs, specifically, implement initialization, parsing, table application and deparsing. The API methods are called directly from the user logic defined in the respective SC_THREADs in the SystemC model. Furthermore, we re-implemented the search and look-up data structures on top of TLMVAR in order to accurately capture the memory transactions during run-time.

4. EXPERIMENTAL RESULTS

We evaluated PFPSim using a sample P4 application and a sample test traffic. We created host-compiled models for various NPU architectures based on Figure 2, where we varied the number of clusters and on-chip memory per cluster to reflect design tradeoff between number of cores and memory. A high-level model of the RMT with 32 stages was also created in PFPSim. Finally, we also developed a soft-switch implementation in SystemC, based on the generated code from the P4 compiler. We used a 2.7 GHz Intel dual-core with 8GB RAM as our simulation host.

We evaluate the quality of PFPSim using the simulation speed metric. In particular, we demonstrate that even complex NPU architectures with a large number of cores can be simulated with realistic applications and traffic in seconds. We also demonstrate the usability of PFPSim by exploring the average packet latency offered by different architectures for the same application.

4.1 Use Cases

The sample P4 program is based off of the *simple_router* application provided with the P4 soft-switch compiler [17]. The program has five match-action tables and three header types (Ethernet, IPv4, and TCP). The program first performs a longest-prefix match on the destination IPv4 addresses and uses this to set egress port and next-hop address metadata fields, additionally decrementing the Ipv4 TTL field. Next an exact match is performed on the next-hop address, and the result is used to rewrite the Ethernet destination address. An exact match is next performed on the TCP source port and the result is used to rewrite the TCP source port. If the TCP source port is not matched, then an exact match is performed on the TCP destination port and the result is used to rewrite the TCP destination port. Finally an exact match is performed on the egress port metadata, and the result is used to rewrite the Ethernet source address. Additionally, the IP and TCP checksums are validated during parsing and updated during deparsing. The match table sizes were set to 2048.

We stimulated the models with 5000 pseudo-randomly generated packets of size 1KB each. The packet trace included all unique IP addresses in the match tables at least once in order to force the search algorithm to access every node in the tries in memory. The packet generator generated packets at a 1 Gpps rate at the ingress.

The soft-switch was modeled as host-compiled C code inside a SystemC wrapper, so that it can be simulated with our traffic pattern. The soft-switch does not have any timing and no underlying platform model. As such, it is only useful for functional validation of the P4 program. The RMT model uses the pipeline stage models written in SystemC. Based on the

architecture shown in Figure 2, we created six NPU models with 1, 2, 4, 8, 12 and 16 clusters. Each cluster consisted of four 4-way hardware multi-threaded RISC cores. Each cluster had 1 eDRAM block with single cycle access. There was only one 256 MB off-chip DRAM with access latency of 10 cycles. The scheduling policy is round-robin over the clusters.

Table 1. PFPSim simulation results

Design	Processing	On-chip mem. model	Sim. time (s)	Latency
soft-switch	dual-core host	host mem.	0.456	N/A
RMT	32 stages	TCAM+hash	0.339	102 ns
NPU-1	4 cores	64K eDRAM	8.438	23.8 µs
NPU-2	8 cores	32K eDRAM	8.639	11.3 µs
NPU-4	16 cores	16K eDRAM	8.947	5.1 µs
NPU-8	32 cores	8K eDRAM	10.41	1.9 µs
NPU-12	48 cores	6K eDRAM	13.501	**0.9** µs
NPU-16	64 cores	4K eDRAM	18.967	24.0 µs

Table 1 presents our experimental results. The NPU design space exploration consisted of increasing the number of cores, while reducing the on-chip eDRAM capacity to fit within the chip area budget. The total eDRAM capacity (in Table 1, Column 3) is distributed equally across the clusters. For instance, in NPU-8, each of the 8 clusters have 1Kb eDRAM for a total eDRAM capacity of 8Kb. The tries corresponding to the match-tables were copied into each of the identical eDRAMs in the clusters by the control plane agent. The structures were spilled over into the singleton off-chip DRAM if needed. Therefore, all application threads running on a core, in a given cluster, could access only the cluster's eDRAM or the off-chip DRAM.

The SystemC model generation from the FAD took only a few seconds and had little correlation to the complexity of the design. However, the reported packet latency and simulation speed showed interesting trends as discussed below.

4.2 Simulation Speed

The soft-switch implementation derived from the P4 example processed all the packets under a second on the host. The RMT model simulation was faster than the soft-switch simulation because of the underlying parallelism of the pipeline stage models and the mapping of SystemC threads to the dual-core CPU. The simulation speed for the NPU models decreases with the increasing number of cores. This is to be expected since the processing of the same 5000 packets in different models is being executed on more threads on the host. As such there are more context switches between the simulation threads leading to slower simulation. However, compared to the untimed soft-switch execution, simulating a 64 core NPU with cycle-level timing results in a slowdown of only 40X. While this may seem like a huge factor, the absolute simulation times are still in the order of few seconds, which is acceptable considering the architectural details captured in the NPU model. The simulation speed can be increased by using a more powerful host or utilizing a parallelized or a GPU-accelerated SystemC simulation kernel.

4.3 Average Packet Latency Estimation

The packet latency for the RMT was constant because parsing and deparsing took 3 cycles each, while each of the 32 stages took 3 cycles, leading to an overall latency of 102. Indeed, if the P4 headers are more complex, and if there are hash conflicts during match stages, the delays would be much larger.

For the NPUs, the average packet latency decreases as we increase the number of clusters from 1 to 12. Although we decrease the total eDRAM size, the corresponding tries still fit in the on-chip memory, given the modest table size of 2048 entries in our synthetic examples. However, when we increase the number of clusters to 16 and reduce the per-cluster eDRAM size to only 256B, the tries spill over into the DRAM. Hence, there are a significant number of slow DRAM accesses in the NPU-16 design. As a result, we notice a marked increase in average packet latency in NPU-16, undoing all the benefits of higher parallelism.

A somewhat unexpected trend is the factor of improvement in average packet latency when we increase the number of clusters. A naïve assumption would be that doubling the number of cores would result in at most 2X average latency reduction. However, recall that the scheduler at the NPU level assigns the packets to clusters in a round robin fashion. Given the constant packet arrival rate at the ingress, the packet inter-arrival delay at a cluster increases with the increase in the number of clusters. As a result, the cores inside the clusters have fewer conflicts on the shared eDRAM, leading to faster packet processing within the cluster. Therefore, we observe a super linear improvement in packet processing latency with respect to the number of clusters, until the tables can no longer fit in the on-chip memory.

4.4 Accuracy

Accuracy of the underlying model is an important metric for any simulator. In the case of PFPSim, we rely on the designer to supply timing annotations as part of the module logic (see Figure 3). In our experiments, we have used timing data from component datasheets. As part of our ongoing work, we are looking into implementing methods for timing back-annotation from cycle-accurate models in order to support fast and accurate simulation.

5. CONCLUSION

In this paper, we presented PFPSim, a simulation environment for programmable packet processors such as NPUs and reconfigurable match-table pipelines. We demonstrated the value of PFPSim as an early modeling, validation and performance analysis tool for programmable forwarding devices. In the future, we plan to improve the PFPSim simulation speed, create more complex NPU models with hardware accelerators and perform accuracy comparisons versus cycle accurate simulations.

6. ACKNOWLEDGMENTS

This work was supported by the National Science and Engineering Research Council of Canada, and Ericsson, Canada under the Collaborative Research and Development program, award number CRDPJ 462474-13.

7. REFERENCES

[1] Nick McKeown, Tom Anderson, Hari Balakrishnan, Guru Parulkar, Larry Peterson, Jennifer Rexford, Scott Shenker, and Jonathan Turner. 2008. OpenFlow: enabling innovation in campus networks. *SIGCOMM Comput. Commun. Rev.* 38, 2 (March 2008), 69-74.

[2] Pat Bosshart, Dan Daly, Glen Gibb, Martin Izzard, Nick McKeown, Jennifer Rexford, Cole Schlesinger, Dan Talayco, Amin Vahdat, George Varghese, and David Walker. 2014. P4: programming protocol-independent packet processors. SIGCOMM Comput. Commun. Rev. 44, 3, pp. 87-95.

[3] Haoyu Song. 2013. Protocol-oblivious forwarding: unleash the power of SDN through a future-proof forwarding plane. In *Proceedings of the second ACM SIGCOMM workshop on Hot topics in software defined networking* (HotSDN '13). ACM, New York, NY, USA, 127-132.

[4] H. Jonathan Chao, Bin Liu, "High Performance Switches and Routers," Wiley-IEEE Press, 2007, ISBN: 978-0-470-05367-6.

[5] Panos C. Lekkas, "Network Processors: Architectures, Protocols and Platforms," McGraw-Hill, 2003, ISBN: 0-07-140986-6.

[6] Ran Giladi, "Network Processors: Architecture, Programming, and Implementation," Morgan Kaufman, 2008, ISBN: 978-0-12-370891-5

[7] P. Crowley, M. Franklin, H. Hadimioglu, "Network Processor Design: Issues and Practices," Morgan Kaufman, 2003, ISBN: 978-0121981570

[8] Pat Bosshart, Glen Gibb, Hun-Seok Kim, George Varghese, Nick McKeown, Martin Izzard, Fernando Mujica, and Mark Horowitz. 2013. Forwarding metamorphosis: fast programmable match-action processing in hardware for SDN. SIGCOMM Comput. Commun. Rev. 43, 4 pp. 99-110

[9] Intel Ethernet Switch Silicon FM6000." http://www.intel.com/content/dam/www/public/us/en/docum ents/white-papers/ethernet-switch-fm6000-sdn-paper.pdf

[10] T. Grötker, S. Liao, G. Martin, and S. Swan, "System Design with SystemC," Kluwer, 2002.

[11] Open SystemC Initiative (OSCI), "Transaction Level Modeling 2.0," available www.systemc.org

[12] Yan Luo, Jun Yang, Laxmi N. Bhuyan, and Li Zhao. 2004. NePSim: A Network Processor Simulator with a Power Evaluation Framework. *IEEE Micro* 24, 5, pp. 34-44.

[13] Nikhil Handigol, Brandon Heller, Vimalkumar Jeyakumar, Bob Lantz, and Nick McKeown. 2012. Reproducible network experiments using container-based emulation. In *Proceedings of the 8th international conference on Emerging networking experiments and technologies* (CoNEXT '12). ACM, New York, NY, USA, 253-264.

[14] Mukta Gupta, Joel Sommers, and Paul Barford. 2013. Fast, accurate simulation for SDN prototyping. In *Proceedings of the second ACM SIGCOMM workshop on Hot topics in software defined networking* (HotSDN '13). ACM, New York, NY, USA, 31-36.

[15] Jung Ho Ahn; Sheng Li; Seongil, O.; Jouppi, N.P., "McSimA+: A manycore simulator with application-level+ simulation and detailed microarchitecture modeling," in *Performance Analysis of Systems and Software (ISPASS), 2013 IEEE International Symposium on* , vol., no., pp.74-85, 21-23 April 2013

[16] Ericsson SNP 4000 Smart Network Processor, http://www.ericsson.com/ourportfolio/products/ssr-8000-family

[17] P4.org. http://p4.org/

A Study of Speed Mismatches Between Communicating Virtual Machines

Luigi Rizzo, Stefano Garzarella, Giuseppe Lettieri, Vincenzo Maffione
Dipartimento di Ingegneria dell'Informazione
Università di Pisa

ABSTRACT

This work addresses an apparently simple but elusive problem that arises when doing high speed networking on Virtual Machines. When a VM and its peer (usually the hypervisor) process packets at different rates, the work required for synchronization (interrupts and "kicks") may reduce throughput well below the slowest of the two parties.

The problem is not peculiar to VMs: I/O on magnetic tapes and rotating disks has similar issues. What is challenging with VM networking is the timescale at which interactions may occur: down to tens or hundreds of nanoseconds, versus the 1..100 milliseconds in mechanical I/O devices.

In this paper we study the impact of producer/consumer synchronization on throughput and overall efficiency of the system; identify different operating regimes depending on the operating parameters; and validate the accuracy of our model on an actual prototype that resembles the operation of a VM and its hypervisor.

Our goal, to be expanded in future work, is to use these findings to derive strategies that can provide good or optimal throughput while being cost effective, robust and practical, i.e., without unnecessarily keeping cores active all the time, or depending on precise timing measurements or unreasonable assumptions on the system's behaviour.

1. INTRODUCTION

Computer systems have many components that need to exchange data and synchronize with each other (i.e. determine when new data can be sent or received). The timescales of these interactions span from the nanosecond range for on-chip hardware (CPU, memory), to hundreds of nanosecond or microseconds for processes or Virtual Machines and their hypervisors, up to milliseconds or more for peripherals with moving parts (such as disks or tapes), or long distance communication.

Synchronization can be implicit, e.g. when a piece of hardware has a guaranteed response time, or explicit, requiring asynchronous *notifications* (e.g. interrupts) and/or *polling*,

i.e. repeatedly reading memory or I/O registers to figure out when to proceed.

The cost of synchronization can be highly variable, and sometimes even much larger than the data processing costs. This used to be a well known problem with when accessing magnetic tapes, which must be kept streaming to avoid abysmal performance (and mechanical wear) due to frequent start/stops. Large buffers in that case came to help in achieving decent throughput; the inherently unidirectional (and sequential) nature of tape I/O does not call for more sophisticated solutions.

We are interested in a similar problem in the communication between user processes (or virtual machines) and physical or virtual network devices. In these cases, we aim at throughputs of tens of Gigabits per second, millions of packets per second, and reasonably low delays (microseconds or less) in the delivery of data. The latency aspect, tightly related with the bidirectional nature of network communication, is what makes the problem a hard one.

Synchronization here typically requires interrupts, context switches and thread scheduling for incoming traffic, system calls and I/O register access (which translates in expensive "VM exits" on virtual machines) for outgoing traffic. The high cost of these operations (often in the microsecond range) means we cannot afford a synchronization on each packet without killing throughput.

Amortizing the synchronization cost on batches of packets [3, 10, 11] greatly improves throughput, but has an impact on latency, which is why several network I/O frameworks [2, 4, 6, 14] rely on polling (or busy wait) to remove the cost of asynchronous notifications and keep latency under control.

Pure polling however has a significant drawback related to resource usage: it consumes a full CPU core, may keep busy the datapath to the device or memory being monitored, and the power dissipated in the polling loop may prevent the use of higher clock speeds on other cores on the same chip.

A middle ground between asynchronous notifications and pure polling is implemented by modern "paravirtualized" VM devices [12] and interrupt handling [1] strategies. In these solutions, the system uses polling under high load conditions, but reverts to asynchronous notifications after some unsuccessful poll cycles.

The key problem in these solutions is that strategies to switch from one to another mechanism are normally not adaptive, and very susceptible to fall into pathological situations where small variations in the speed of one party cause significant throughput changes. In our tests, we have fre-

ANCS '16 March 17-18, 2016, Santa Clara, CA, USA

© 2016 Copyright held by the owner/author(s).

ACM ISBN 978-1-4503-4183-7/16/03.

DOI: http://dx.doi.org/10.1145/2881025.2881037

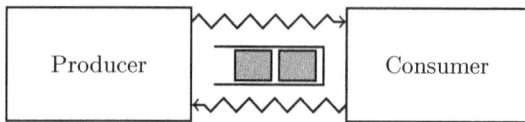

Figure 1: System model. Producer and consumer exchange messages through a queue, blocking when full/empty, and exchanging notifications to wake up the blocked peer.

quently seen system moving from 100-200 Kpps to 1 Mpps with minuscule changes in operating conditions [11]. Even when the throughput shows less dramatic variations, the system's resource usage may be heavily affected, which is why we need to understand and address this instability.

To this purpose, in Section 2, we provide a model of the system explaining how different operating regimes may arise and what kind of impact on performance comes by speed differences, delays and queues. We use this model to derive criteria to select reasonable operating regimes basing on operating parameters, and also understand the impact of erroneous decisions due to incorrect estimates of the parameters.

2. SYSTEM MODEL

To gain a better understanding of the problem of our interest, in this Section we will study the behaviour of a system made of two communicating *parties*, as in Figure 1: a *Producer* P and a *Consumer* C, where P sends one or more messages at a time to C, either continuously or periodically, through a shared queue with L slots.

When P (or C) cannot proceed because the queue is full (or empty), they either **poll** the queue's status for opportunities to do more work, or go to sleep and wait for a **notification** from the other party to restart. Polling can waste large amounts CPU cycles when there is no communication. Notifications on the other hand involve extra work to be sent and received, and may be delivered with some delay.

As defined above, our model is very general and covers a large number of actual situations. P and C are typically processes running on one of the CPUs of a system, with the queue implemented in memory. However the model also applies to cases where P and/or C are implemented as part of a peripheral device, such as a network or disk controller, and the queue may be supported by I/O registers.

Ideally, we would like our system to process messages at a rate set by the slowest of the two parties, and with the minimum possible latency and energy per message. As we will see, actual performance may be very far from our expectations and from optimal values.

Before starting our analysis, we define below the parameters used to model the system.

Name Description

L	the length of the queue
W_P	cost for P to process one message and enqueue it
W_C	cost for C to dequeue one message and process it
k_P	threshold used by P to notify C. When C is blocked and P queues a message, a notification is sent when the queue reaches k_P messages (**typically** $k_P = 1$)
k_C	threshold used by C to notify P (notifications are sent when k_C slots are available)
N_P	the cost for P to notify C about the state change
N_C	the cost for C to notify P about the state change
S_P	the cost for P to start after a notification from C
S_C	the cost for C to start after a notification from P

We measure the cost (i.e. the amount of work) of the various operations in **clock cycles** rather than time. This will ease reasoning about efficiency when our system has the option to use different clock speeds to achieve a given throughput.

We assume that P always sends a message as soon as it can. Moreover, we assume that all the time spent in S_C and S_P is actual work that the CPU must perform to complete the notification and schedule the notified task.

2.1 Operating regimes

The combinations of parameters can give rise to a large number of operating regimes, which we describe next. As we will see, some regimes are more favourable than others, so we will try to determine the conditions that cause the system operate in a given regime x, and for each of them we will determine the **average time between messages,** T_x (the inverse of the throughput), and the **total cost per message** E_x (which includes the work of both P and C).

In the following we consider greedy regimes, where P sends messages as fast as it can, constrained only by the processing times of the P and C.

2.1.1 GP (polling)

When the system uses polling, P and C are always active, and the slowest of the two spins for the other to be ready. On each message, this requires on average a number of cycles $P_{GP} = |W_P - W_C|$ equal to the difference in processing work between the two parties. Hence we have

$$T_{GP} = \max\{W_P, W_C\}$$
$$E_{GP} = 2T_{GP} = W_P + W_C + |W_P - W_C| \quad (1)$$

2.2 Notification based regimes

When the system uses notifications instead of polling, we can identify five different regimes depending on whether the producer is faster or slower than the consumer, and also depending on whether the the queue between P and C is sufficiently long to absorb the startup times S_P and S_C.

With a sufficiently long queue, the slowest party will determine the overall throughput, but the need to periodically stop and restart using notifications will add an overhead (which can be significantly large) to the message processing time.

When the queue becomes too short to absorb the notification latency, one party may block despite being slower than the other one, significantly reducing throughput.

Two non intuitive results of our analysis are that i) the system's performance can be improved by slightly slowing down the fastest party, in order to reduce the overhead of notifications, and ii) the threshold for notifications has opposite effects depending on whether we are in a long or short queue regime.

As a consequence, correctly identifying the operating regime is fundamental for properly tuning (either manually, or automatically) the system's parameters.

In our model the system may be in one of five operating regimes, depending on the relative size of the system parameters. The conditions to check can be grouped in three inequalities, whose possible states are summarized in Table 1 together with the corresponding regime. Each regime

	$\lfloor (L-k_P)W_P - W_C \rfloor$	$\lfloor (L-k_C)W_C - W_P \rfloor$	
$W_C < W_P$	$> S_C$	—	FC
	$< S_C$	$> S_P$	SCS
$W_C > W_P$	$> S_C$	$< S_P$	SPS
	—	$> S_P$	FP
—	$< S_C$	$< S_P$	SS

Table 1: Conditions for the notification based regimes ('—' means 'don't care'). Detailed explanations are in Sections 2.2.1 to 2.2.5.

is identified by an acronym (FC, FP, SCS, SPS and SS) which is explained below.

2.2.1 FC (fast consumer)

When C is faster than P (i.e., $W_C < W_P$), C will start after the notification from P and eventually drain the queue and block. If C starts fast enough (i.e., $S_C < (L-k_P)W_P - W_C$), the queue will never become full and therefore P will never block. The (periodic) evolution of the system over time is shown below. Grey blocks represent message processing, whereas the triangles indicate notifications and wake-ups.

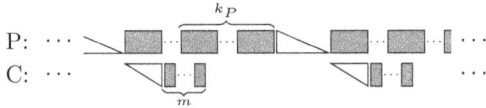

In this regime P is always active, and periodically generates notifications when C is blocked and the queue contains k_P messages. The number of messages processed by C (and P) in each round is $m = \left\lfloor \frac{S_C + (k_P - 1)W_C}{W_P - W_C} \right\rfloor + k_P$. The number m is derived noting that C starts processing with an initial delay S_C, and then catches up draining the queue a little bit at a time. Knowing m, it is easy to determine T_{FC} and E_{FC}, considering that the notifications and startup costs are amortized over batches of m messages:

$$T_{FC} = W_P + \frac{N_P}{m}$$
$$E_{FC} = W_P + W_C + \frac{N_P + S_C}{m} \qquad (2)$$

A large m improves the performance of the system, and since $m \geq k_P$ we would like k_P to be large. However, systems normally use $k_P = 1$ for two reasons: a larger k_P often increases the latency of the system (latency is not one of our metrics, but it is an important one for some systems), and more importantly, P often cannot tell whether there will be more messages to send after the current one.

2.2.2 FP (fast producer)

When $W_C > W_P$ we can identify a different regime, which we call FP (fast producer) regime, which behaves like FC but with the roles of P and C reversed. P is faster than C, so the queue eventually fills up and P blocks. The notification from C to restart P is sent when there are k_C empty slots in the queue. If P starts fast enough (i.e., $S_P < (L-k_C)W_C - W_P$) it refills the queue before it becomes empty and therefore C never blocks.

We omit the formulas for brevity, but the graphs and experiments in the rest of the paper also cover this regime.

Note that as W_P approaches W_C, the burst m grows to

infinity in both FC and FP, and P and C proceed in lockstep at the ideal rate of one message every $W_P = W_C$ cycles.

2.2.3 SCS (slow consumer startup)

SCS differs from regime FP in that C is fast but has a long startup delay, so P can fill the queue before C has a chance to remove the first message. This forces P to block until k_C messages are drained and C generates a notification. The situation then repeats periodically once C has drained the queue, as shown by the following diagram:

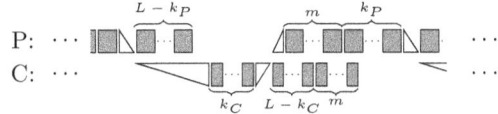

The cycle contains $L + m$ messages, where

$$m = \left\lfloor \frac{(L-k_C)W_C - (S_P + W_P)}{W_P - W_C} \right\rfloor + 1. \qquad (3)$$

We omit the formulas for T_{SCS} and E_{SCS} as they are long and not particularly useful. However, important insights on the performance in this regime come from the analysis of the above diagram and Equation (3). The slow party (P) has to wait because of a large S_C, and **increasing k_C harms in two ways**: it extends the idle time for P, and reduces m, thus increasing the amortized cost of notifications and startups.

Note that k_C has opposite effects on performance in the two regimes SCS and FP, due to the slow startup time: in FP, a large k_C improves performance, whereas in SCS we should use a small k_C.

2.2.4 SPS (slow producer startup)

This regime is symmetric to SPS, and it appears when the producer is faster than the consumer, but slow to respond to a notification. For brevity we omit the formulas, which be obtained from the SCS case by swapping every P with C. The long startup time leads to different choices for the parameter k_P: in regime FC we aim for a large k_P, whereas in regime SPS we should use a small value for that parameter.

2.2.5 SS (slow producer and consumer startup)

This regime combines the previous two, and alternates operation of the producer and consumer due to the large startup delays. Individual speeds only matter in relation to the startup times, and operation in the system alternates between P and C as shown in the following diagram.

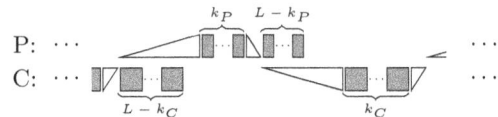

Each round in this case comprises exactly L messages, and T_{SS} and E_{SS} have a relatively simple form:

$$T_{SS} = \frac{k_P W_P + k_C W_C + N_P + S_P + N_C + S_C}{L}$$
$$E_{SS} = W_P + W_C + \frac{N_P + S_P + N_C + S_C}{L} \qquad (4)$$

Just looking at the equation, it might seem that there is a good amortization of the notifications and wakeup costs (once per L messages). However the timing diagram shows

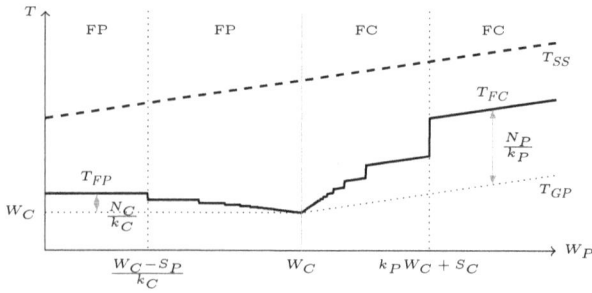

Figure 2: The time for each message as a function of W_P, in the greedy regimes. Note that the message rate decreases as we move away from $W_P = W_C$. The curve for T_{SS} represent the best case for regime SS, actual values may be much larger.

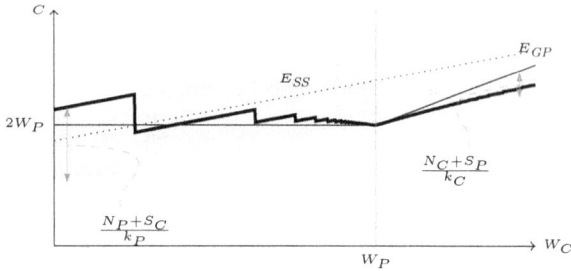

Figure 3: The total cost for each message as a function of W_C. There may be regions where polling (thin line) is more energy efficient than notifications (thick and dotted lines).

clearly that P and C alternate their operation, making the throughput less than half of that of the fastest party.

In general, the regimes with short queues are unfavourable and we should avoid operating the system in them.

3. THROUGHPUT AND COST ANALYSIS

In the rest of this Section we explore how throughput and efficiency change depending on the parameters, using the equations for T_x and E_x derived in Section 2. These equations use an idealized model where the various times are constant. We then validate the model using both a simulator and an actual prototype with variable costs, whose values and distributions are derived from actual measurements.

3.1 Throughput

We start our analysis looking at the time between messages, T_x. In Figure 2 we plot T_x in the greedy regimes for a given W_C (processing time on the consumer) and variable W_P (processing time on the producer). The region to the left of $W_P = W_C$ corresponds to a fast producer.

There are three curves of interest here. The dotted line at the bottom represents the minimum distance between messages, which is $T_{GP} = \max\{W_P, W_C\}$. This corresponds to the best throughput we can achieve if efficiency is not an issue, and **can be obtained with pure polling**, i.e. keeping the fastest party continuously spinning for new opportunities to work.

The next curve (solid line) represents T_{FC} and T_{FP}, corresponding to the first two non-polling regimes. Here the

distance between messages is higher than in the ideal case due to the effect of notifications and startup times. These are amortized on the number m of messages per notification; m changes in a discrete way with the ratio W_P/W_C, hence the curve the staircase shape.

It should be noted that depending on the queue size L and the values of the operating parameters, we cannot guarantee that the system operates in regimes FC or FP. Sections 2.2.3, 2.2.4 and 2.2.5 indicate the conditions for which we may enter one of the three regimes SCS, SPS or SS, all of which have a larger inter message time than FC and FP.

Hence our third curve of interest is labeled T_{SS}, which corresponds to $W_P + W_C + N_P/L + N_C/L$ and marks the best possible performance in regime SS. Operating curves for SCS and SPS lay between T_G and T_{SS}.

IMPORTANT: performance can jump between T_{FC}, T_{FP} and T_{SS} even for small variations of the operating parameters. Hence it is imperative to either make the region between the two curves small, or set parameters to minimize the change of regime changes.

Going back to the analysis of operating regimes, we note that both FC and FP have two different regions, separated by the vertical dotted lines in the figure. These boundaries occur when the batch of messages processed on each notification reaches the minimum value, respectively k_P and k_C. The fact that k_P is usually 1 makes the jump much higher in regime FC than in regime FP.

Since the equations governing the system are completely symmetric, the curves for a fixed W_P and variable W_C have a shape similar to those in Figure 2. This shows that there are regions of operation where **increasing the processing costs (W_P in FP, W_C in FC) increases throughput**.

While the graphs focus on variations of W_P and W_C, they also show the sensitivity of the curves to other parameters. As an example, the distance between T_{FC}, T_{FP} and the optimal value T_{GP} is bounded by N_C/k_C and N_P/k_P, so we have knobs to reduce the gaps. Also, the position of the last big jump in throughput in regime FC can be controlled by increasing S_C. This means that, all the rest being the same, a slower wakeup time improves performance.

3.2 Efficiency

While regime GP is always the one with the highest throughput, its performance may come at a high cost in terms of CPU usage. In regime GP, the fast party must burn cycles proportionally to the difference of processing times, $|W_C - W_P|$. This can possibly double the total overall cost in terms of time/cycles, and can have even worse impact on performance if the fast party has higher cost per cycle. As an example, the fast party could be an expensive, dedicated CPU/NIC/controller.

As a consequence, another metric of interest is one that takes into account the *total cost per message*. In our model, assuming for simplicity that both P and C have the same cost per cycle, this number is represented by the values E_x determined in Section 2.1. We see that the E_x values have the form $W_P + W_C + X$ where the additional term X depends on the operating regime.

Similarly to the previous analysis for throughput, in Figure 3 we show the cost per message in different regimes. For simplicity, here we use only one graph with variable W_C, having already established that the system is symmetric and we can repeat the same reasonings for variable W_P. Even in this case we have three curves of interest, but they are not as nicely ordered as in Figure 2.

3.2.1 Greedy regimes

Figure 3 show that the curve for the polling regime GP (solid thin line) is no more the absolute best in terms of efficiency. This is because the additional term X in E_{GP} is $|W_C - W_P|$, whereas in other cases the term X is upper bounded by some constant independent of the difference $W_C - W_P$. As a consequence, the slope of E_{GP} is twice that of the other curves, and when W_C becomes too large (or more precisely, when $|W_C - W_P|$ becomes large) polling is the worst option in terms of cycles (or energy) per message.

The energy curve (solid thick in Figure 3) for regimes FC and FP has the same stepwise behaviour as the ones for inter-message time. The slope is however unitary (it grows as $\max\{W_P, W_C\}$), and lies within the grey region in the figure depending on the actual parameters. As the graph shows, the curves for polling (solid thin) and non polling (solid thick) regimes may intersect in several points, whose values and position depend heavily on the actual parameters.

The shape of the curves and their discontinuities make it difficult to identify intervals in which one regime is preferable to another. We can compute them using the equations in Section 2.1, but these rely on perfect knowledge of the operating parameters, hence the information is of little practical use.

Comparing the total cost per message in regime GP with the other regimes however can give some useful practical insight. Polling consumes an extra $|W_P - W_C|$ cycles per message, so it is convenient when the cost is lower than the extra notification and startup cost, which is $\frac{N_P + S_C}{m}$ in FC, $\frac{N_C + S_P}{m}$ in FP. Since in FP we have $m \geq k_C$ and k_C is typically large, it very unlikely that polling can be cost effective.

3.2.2 Short queue

The energy efficiency when the queue fills up is heavily dependent on the values of the parameters. Equation 4 for E_{SS} shows that the extra term includes all the four startup and notification times instead of only two of them for E_{FC} and E_{FP}. Given that we expect one of S_C, S_P to be large, this might be a significant cost.

On the other hand, the energy efficiency of these regimes is not too bad, because producer and consumer tend to have significant idle times, and the overheads are amortized over relatively large batches (e.g. the entire queue size in regime SS). This phenomenon is evidenced by the curve E_{SS} (dotted) in Figure 3, which also intercepts the others.

3.3 Model validation

The model of Section 2, and the subsequent analysis, assume constant processing times. To validate how the results hold with variable times and/or in a real system, we have developed a simulator and a synthetic system.

The simulator is a classical event-based simulator. It is written in go to keep the producer and consumer inside their own (go)routine, instead of scattering them into several event handlers. This gives full control on the model parameters, but of course does not provide any insight on value and distribution of the parameters in a real system.

To address this limitation, we have developed a synthetic system using OS processes that exchange messages through

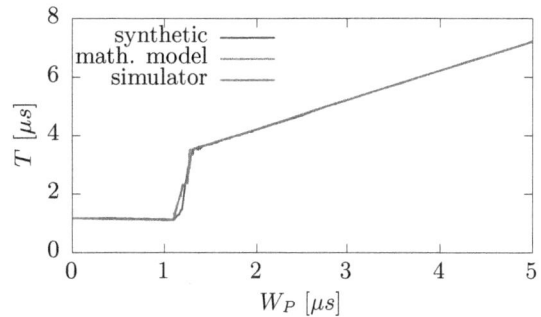

Figure 4: Average per-packet time as a function of W_P with a fixed $W_C = 1.1\,\mu s$. The throughput observed on the synthetic system agrees with the value predicted by the mathematical model and the simulator.

shared memory, and use OS and hypervisor primitives for scheduling and notifications.

The per-packet work is replaced by a configurable amount of spinning, so we can run the experiments with different values of W_P and W_C. The purpose of such synthetic system is to observe the behaviour of real world notifications and startup times, distilled from the unrelated complexity of real application workloads.

Specifically, the producer runs in a thread inside a QEMU/KVM [5] virtual machine (guest), while the consumer runs in a kernel thread in the host. Notifications involve interrupts, VM exits and thread wakeups in the OS, mimicking mechanisms commonly used in modern hypervisors.

By our measurements on an Intel Core i7-3770K with clock fixed at 3.5 GHz and C-states disabled, we have found $N_P = 2.4\,\mu s$, $S_P = 3.9\,\mu s$, $N_C = .2\,\mu s$ and $S_C = .2\,\mu s$. The Producer parameters are much larger than the ones for the Consumer, but this is expected due to the asymmetric nature of our prototype: the Consumer is a kernel thread in the host, ready to react to events, whereas the Producer runs within a guest VM hence requiring more expensive operations such as VM exits and multiple thread handoffs to be notified.

We have then used the measured parameters into the equations from Section 2, as well as in the simulator. Figure 4 shows that in all three cases the curves may be made to agree with great accuracy, suggesting that we have actually captured the most relevant features of the system.

4. CONTROLLING THE SYSTEM

Since our goal is not only to observe the behaviour of the system but modify it to our advantage, we try to identify which regimes are more interesting, and how we can modify operating parameters (either statically or dynamically) to achieve the desired results. Our ability to change operating parameters is limited to queue size (L) and wakeup thresholds (k_C, k_P), but these already help moving between regimes and operating points. We can also make a judicious use of a mixture of polling and sleeping to reduce the cost of notifications. Somewhat surprisingly, slowing down the fast party in the communication can also lead to improved performance.

Maximising throughput

The first (and obvious) indication that the graphs give us is that for maximum throughput, using pure polling is always a winning strategy. This however is conditioned to the fact that we have enough CPU resources to keep both producer and consumer active at all times, even when there are no messages to send.

Maximising efficiency

From an efficiency standpoint, things are not as clear. We can only tell that polling becomes the worst option as $|W_P - W_C|$ becomes large. Intuitively, with pure polling we never know when it is time to stop spinning, and we end up with both parties using 100% of their capacity even with little or no messages to deliver.

For all other cases, the regions where one regime is more or less convenient depends on the actual values of the parameters. Outside of polling, we see that the size of the queue between producer and consumer may significantly impact the performance of the system. Depending on the operating conditions, small changes in one or more parameters may cause the queue to fill up and introduce sudden changes of throughput (between the curves T_{SS} and T_{FC} in Figure 2).

While the regimes where queues saturate are not horrible in terms of energy efficiency, their impact on throughput suggests that we should avoid ending up in one of them. Depending on the operating environment, it is possible that the notification and/or startup costs (N_P, N_C, S_P, S_C) are 1-2 orders of magnitude larger than the work times W_P and W_C, and throughput variations of 5-10 times are not unheard of.

4.1 Towards a practical control scheme

Throughput depends on sometimes non intuitive ways on the parameters:

- exiting from the "short queue" regimes requires reducing the thresholds k_P and k_C. Conversely, in regimes FC and FP we would like to keep these thresholds larger in order to improve the throughput;

- in regimes FC and FP, a higher wakeup time (S_P, S_C) helps improving the throughput (much like an increased notification threshold);

- still in regimes FC and FP, when the producer and consumer's speeds are different, slowing down the fast party improves performance. This is shown by the negative slope of the curves T_{FP} in Figure 2.

We have tried to use these dependencies to steer the system towards more favourable operating regimes.

Our preliminary (but not conclusive) experiments on adapting thresholds k_C and k_P have not given good results, probably because they do not prevent the fast peer from blocking or entering a short queue regime.

Instead, a more promising avenue seems to be the use of schemes where the fast peer reacts to an upcoming blocking situation by increasing its processing time. This can be done in multiple ways, e.g. by doing I/O in smaller batches, or executing short busy wait loops, or opportunistically running short, low priority housekeeping tasks or short sleeps.

The judicious use of spinning and sleeping instead of blocking, based on the state of the peer and some practical running estimate of the system parameters, can prevent

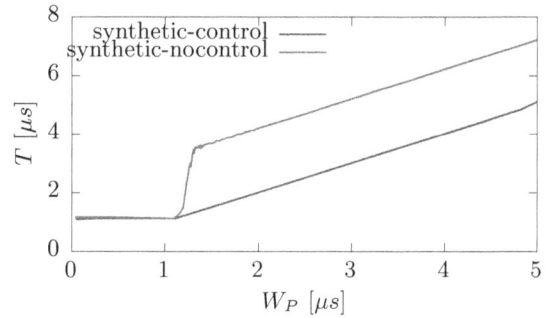

(a) Average per-packet time as a function of W_P.

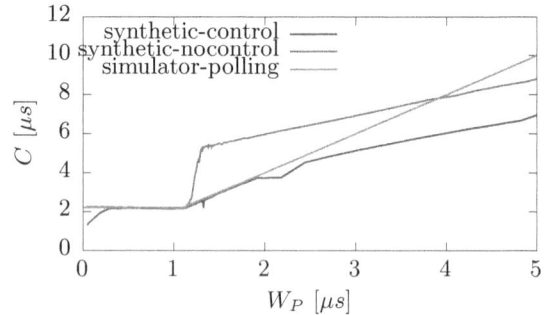

(b) Average per-packet cost as a function of W_P.

Figure 5: Experimental control for the same setup as Fig. 4. For all values of W_P, the control is able to reduce per-packet time at a reduced cost with respect to polling.

peers from using expensive synchronisation primitives, thus retaining both high throughput, and reasonable efficiency.

Fig. 5 shows some preliminary results where the previous strategy is applied to the simple scenario of Fig. 4, where we can see that this control scheme is able to achieve optimum throughput at a reduced cost with respect to pure polling.

5. RELATED WORK

Pure polling (also known as "busy wait" or "spinning") is probably the oldest form of synchronization, and the most expensive in terms of system resource usage. Its use is mostly justified by its simplicity and not reliance on any hardware support. Pure polling is used by a number of high speed networking applications such as the Click Modular Router [6], Intel's DPDK [4], and Luca Deri's PFRING/DNA [2].

Aside from high energy consumption, polling may also abuse of shared resources, such memory or I/O buses. This changes the problem from a simple annoyance (high energy consumption) to a threat to other parts of the system, and requires some form of mitigation.

In the FreeBSD polling architecture [9], polling occurs periodically on timer interrupts and opportunistically on other events. An adaptive limit on the maximum amount of work to be performed in each iteration is used to schedule the CPU between user processes and kernel activities. Adaptive polling schemes are also widely used in radio protocols, sensor networks, multicast protocols.

A seminal work on interrupt moderation [7] points out how mixed strategies (notifications to start processing, followed by polling to process data as long as possible) can reduce system's overhead. The linux NAPI architecture [1,13] is based on the above ideas. When an interrupt comes, NAPI activates a kernel thread to process packets using polling, and disables further interrupts until done with pending packets. A bound on the maximum amount of work to be performed by the polling thread in each round helps reducing latency and fairness on systems with multiple interfaces. NAPI does not use any special strategy to adapt the speed of producer and consumer, and as such it is subject to the performance instabilities discussed in this paper.

The Virtio framework [8,12] is used to provide high performance network support to QEMU guests, and uses a notification system similar to the one presented in Section 2. The notification thresholds in this model are typically chosen as $k_P = 1$, $k_C = 2/3$ of queue occupation at start. This form of adaptivity is not particularly useful, and it is only effective with high load and slow consumers. In particular, it often degenerates to use a threshold $k_C = 1$ even for the consumer side, making the system unnecessarily inefficient.

6. CONCLUSIONS AND FUTURE WORK

We have presented a model of the operation of a packet producer and consumer in a typical Virtual Machine environment; described how throughput and efficiency are affected by operating parameters; and validated the model against a simplified prototype running on a hypervisor. We have discussed some options to implement a control mechanism that can steer the operating regime of the system towards a more favourable region, and presented preliminary results on its behavuiour.

We plan to further explore the ideas discussed in Section 4.1, and integrate them in the network path of common hypervisors.

7. ACKNOWLEDGEMENTS

This paper has received funding from the European Union's Horizon 2020 research and innovation programme 2014-2018 under grant agreement No. 644866. This paper reflects only the authors' views and the European Commission is not responsible for any use that may be made of the information it contains.

8. REFERENCES

[1] Linux Net:NAPI ("New API"). http://www.linuxfoundation.org/en/Net:NAPI.

[2] L. Deri. PFRING DNA page. http://www.ntop.org/products/pf_ring/dna/.

[3] S. Garzarella, G. Lettieri, and L. Rizzo. Virtual device passthrough for high speed vm networking. In *Proceedings of ACM/IEEE ANCS 2015*, pages 99–110, 2015.

[4] Intel. Intel data plane development kit. *http://edc.intel.com/Link.aspx?id=5378*, 2012.

[5] A. Kivity, Y. Kamay, D. Laor, U. Lublin, and A. Liguori. kvm: the linux virtual machine monitor. In *2007 Linux Symposium, Ottawa*, volume 1, pages 225–230, 2007.

[6] E. Kohler, R. Morris, B. Chen, J. Jannotti, and M. Kaashoek. The click modular router. *ACM Transactions on Computer Systems (TOCS)*, 18(3):263–297, 2000.

[7] J. C. Mogul and K. Ramakrishnan. Eliminating receive livelock in an interrupt-driven kernel. *ACM Transactions on Computer Systems*, 15(3):217–252, 1997.

[8] G. Motika and S. Weiss. Virtio network paravirtualization driver: Implementation and performance of a de-facto standard. *Computer Standards & Interfaces*, 34(1):36–47, 2012.

[9] L. Rizzo. Polling versus interrupts in network device drivers. *BSDConEurope 2001*, 2001.

[10] L. Rizzo. netmap: A Novel Framework for Fast Packet I/O. In *USENIX ATC'12*, Boston, MA. USENIX Association, 2012.

[11] L. Rizzo, G. Lettieri, and V. Maffione. Speeding up packet I/O in virtual machines. In *Proceedings of the Ninth ACM/IEEE Symposium on Architectures for Networking and Communications Systems*, ANCS '13, pages 47–58, Piscataway, NJ, USA, 2013. IEEE Press.

[12] R. Russell. virtio: towards a de-facto standard for virtual I/O devices. *ACM SIGOPS Operating Systems Review*, 42(5):95–103, 2008.

[13] J. H. Salim, R. Olsson, and A. Kuznetsov. Beyond softnet. In *Proceedings of the 5th annual Linux Showcase & Conference*, volume 5, pages 18–18, 2001.

[14] D. Zhou, B. Fan, H. Lim, M. Kaminsky, and D. G. Andersen. Scalable, high performance ethernet forwarding with cuckooswitch. In *Proceedings of the ninth ACM conference on Emerging networking experiments and technologies*, pages 97–108. ACM, 2013.

BASEL (Buffer mAnagement SpEcification Language)

Kirill Kogan
IMDEA Networks Institute
kirill.kogan@imdea.org

Danushka Menikkumbura
Purdue University
dmenikku@purdue.edu

Gustavo Petri
Université Paris Diderot - Paris 7
gpetri@liafa.univ-paris-diderot.fr

Youngtae Noh
Inha University
ytnoh@inha.ac.kr

Sergey Nikolenko
Steklov Math. Institute at St. Petersburg
National Research University Higher School of Economics
sergey@logic.pdmi.ras.ru

Patrick Eugster
Purdue University
TU Darmstadt
p@cs.purdue.edu

Abstract

Buffering architectures and policies for their efficient management constitute one of the core ingredients of a network architecture. In this work we introduce a new specification language, BASEL, that allows to express virtual buffering architectures and management policies representing a variety of economic models. BASEL does not require the user to implement policies in a high-level language; rather, the entire buffering architecture and its policy are reduced to several comparators and simple functions. We show examples of buffer management policies in BASEL and demonstrate empirically the impact of various settings on performance.

1. INTRODUCTION

Buffering architectures define how input and output ports of a network element are connected [17, 36]. Their design and management must thus be done with care, as it directly impacts performance and cost of each network element.

Traditional network management only allows to deploy a predefined set of buffer management policies whose parameters can be adapted to specific network conditions. The incorporation of *new* management policies requires complex control/data plane code changes and sometimes respin of implementing hardware. Objectives beyond *fairness* and the consideration of additional traffic properties lead to new challenges in the implementation and performance for traditional switching architectures [16, 18, 20]. Unfortunately, current developments in software-defined networking mostly sidestep these challenges by concentrating on flexible and efficient representations of *packet classifiers* (e.g., OpenFlow [32]) which do not really capture buffer management aspects. This calls for novel abstractions that enable the definition of buffer management policies that can be deployed on real network elements at runtime (without respin of implementing hardware and complex code changes). Designing such abstractions however is non-trivial, as they must satisfy a number of possibly conflicting requirements: (1) EXPRESSIVITY: expressible policies should cover various buffering architectures representing a large majority of existing and future deployment scenarios; (2) SIMPLICITY: policies for different

objectives should be expressible concisely with a limited set of basic primitives and should not impose specific hardware choices; (3) PERFORMANCE: the implementations of policies should be efficient on "virtual switches", that is with various resolutions ranging from a single network element to the whole network (e.g., an interconnect for geographically distributed data centers [18, 20]).

We address these challenges with BASEL (*Buffer mAnagement SpEcification Language*), a flexible way to define buffer management policies.

2. BASEL SPECIFICATION LANGUAGE

2.1 Language Overview

BASEL's design follows existing buffering architectures by considering only two types of objects: *ports*, and *queues* assigned to ports; in the buffered crossbar architecture [22, 23], cross-points can also be represented as ports. An *admission control policy* for a queue determines which packets are admitted or dropped [12, 14, 35]. A *scheduling policy* for a port selects a queue whose *head-of-line* (HOL) packet will be processed next [9, 31]; in each queue, the HOL packet is defined by a *processing policy*. Shared memory switches with several queues sharing the same *buffer space* [4, 10, 11] and architectures with synchronous management policies [24, 26] are out of scope of this paper.

In summary, to define a buffering architecture and its management policy one needs to create instances of ports, queues, and buffers, and specify relations among them; admission control, processing, and scheduling policies attached to the corresponding instances. These constructs suffice to achieve EXPRESSIVITY (cf. Section 1).

Fortunately, buffer management policies are generally concerned with boundary conditions (e.g., for admission a packet with *smallest* value can be dropped; to implement FIFO processing order, a packet with *smallest* arrival time is chosen next). Hence, *priority queues* arise as a natural choice for implementing actions related to the user-defined priorities. The priority criteria does not change at runtime (e.g., a queue's order can not be changed from FIFO to LIFO). We believe that this is a reasonable compromise to achieve conciseness for the policies without compromising expressiveness and performance. Each admission, processing, and scheduling policy in BASEL thus maintains its priority queue whose behavior is defined by a *comparator* – a Boolean function comparing two objects of same type via arithmetic/Boolean operators and accessing packet and object attributes.

2.2 BASEL API

In the following we present how BASEL's abstractions achieve SIMPLICITY (cf. Sec. 1) by means of simple declarations of data

ANCS '16, March 17-18, 2016, Santa Clara, CA, USA
© 2016 ACM. ISBN 978-1-4503-4183-7/16/03. . . $15.00
DOI: http://dx.doi.org/10.1145/2881025.2881027

```
Queue {
// user-specified at declaration
size          // size in bytes        [r, cons]

 // primitive properties
currSize      // current size         [r, dyn]
getHOL()      // head-of-line pkt     [packet fun]

// admission - user-specified at declaration
congestion()  // congestion predicate [bool fun]
admPrio(p1,p2) // pushOut prio comp.   [bool fun]
postAdmAct()  // {MARK,NOTIFY,..}      [action fun]
weightAdm     // priority for adm.     [rw, dyn]

// processing - user-specified at declaration
procPrio(p1,p2)// process. prio comp.  [bool fun]

// scheduling - user-specified at declaration
weightSched    // prio. for scheduling [rw, dyn]
}
```

Listing 1: BASEL's queue primitive.

```
Port {
// primitive properties
getBestQueue() // on weightSched      [queue fun]
getCurrQueue() // scheduled one       [queue fun]

// scheduling user-specified at declaration
schedPrio(q1,q2)// compare q-s         [bool fun]
postSchedAct() //{MARK,NOTIFY,..}      [action fun]
}
```

Listing 2: BASEL's port primitive.

```
Packet {
size        // size in bytes     [r, cons]
value       // virtual value     [r, cons]
processing  // # of cycles       [r, dyn]
arrival     // arrival time      [r, cons]
slack       // offset in time    [r, cons]
queue       // target queue id   [r, cons]
}
```

Listing 3: BASEL's packet primitive.

structures. For each entity, we define its properties, some of which are primitives of the domain (e.g., packet size), and others which have to be set by the programmer[1]. For functions we provide the return type (e.g., **bool fun**).

2.2.1 Queues

List. 1 summarizes the API to declare queues. The standard property `size` is defined by the user at declaration time. The `currSize` property changes dynamically as the queue changes its size. Abstractly, a queue contains packets ordered according to user-defined priorities for admission control and processing. In BASEL, we consider two user-defined priorities at the queue level:

(a) `procPrio(p1,p2)` is a packet comparator defined as a function taking two abstract packets and returning *true* if p1 has a higher processing priority than p2. We are only concerned with the highest processing priority packet at any point, so the only way to access a queue ordered by `procPrio` is through the `getHOL()` primitive which returns the HOL (i.e., highest processing priority as defined by `procPrio`) packet in the queue. E.g., the user can set

        procPrio(p1,p2) = p1.arrival < p2.arrival

to encode FIFO processing. Hence, each call to `getHOL()` returns the packet with the oldest arrival time.

(b) `admPrio(p1,p2)` is also a packet comparator used in case of congestion to choose the packets that should be dropped from the queue. We could have simply chosen to use the least valuable packets according to `procPrio` for drops, but we will see in Sec. 3 that separate priorities for admission and processing gives more flexibility and improves performance.

The user-defined predicate `congestion()` indicates when a queue is virtually *congested*. Usually, `congestion()` is a set of different buffer occupancies and drop probabilities [14]. A capability to *push out* already admitted packets is supported in BASEL. To avoid different implementations for the push-out and non-push-out cases, an admission control policy always virtually admits an incoming packet. In the event of a virtual congestion, admission control drops the least valuable packets until congestion is lifted.

The optional function `postAdmAct()` returns an action applied after admission and can update `weightAdm` (if necessary). Function `postAdmAct()` can also be used to implement *explicit congestion notifications* [6] or *backpressure*; `postAdmAct()` can return actions such as **MARK** or **NOTIFY**. For cases when bandwidth is allocated not only with respect to packet attributes, queues maintain a `weightSched` variable that can be updated dynamically after each scheduling operation. With `weightSched` one can for example define static bandwidth allocation among queues of the same port during scheduling decisions; `weightSched` can be updated in the `postSchedAct()` function defined at the port level.

2.2.2 Ports

The interface provided for ports is presented in List. 2. A port manages a set of queues assigned at its declaration.[2] A user-defined scheduling property `schedPrio(q1,q2)` (queue comparator) defines which HOL packet is scheduled next (this packet is accessed through function `getBestQueue()`). For example, a priority based on packet values which implements several levels of strict priorities is declared simply as follows:

```
schedPrio(q1,q2) =
        q1.getHOL().value > q2.getHOL().value
```

Finally, `postSchedAct()` is similar to the `postAdmAct()` function of queues which can be used to define new services.

2.2.3 Packets

The notion of a packet is *primitive*, meaning that the user cannot modify or extend packets; packet fields can be used to implement policies. Every incoming packet is prepended with three mandatory parameters — an *arrival* time, a packet *size* in bytes, and a destination *queue* — and three optional parameters — an intrinsic *value* (whose meaning is application-specific), the *processing* requirement in virtual cycles, and *slack* (maximal offset in time from *arrival* to transmission). We assume that these properties are set by an external *classification unit* (e.g., OpenFlow [32], if a virtual switch is defined with the finest possible resolution), except for *arrival* (set by BASEL when a packet is received) and *size*.

---

[1]For each property we indicate in comments whether it is **r** read-only or **rw** writable, and **cons** if it's value is fix at runtime, or **dyn** if it's value can change.

[2]We leave the `new` operator used to create network objects in BASEL implicit; its usage will be clear from the examples in Sec. 3.

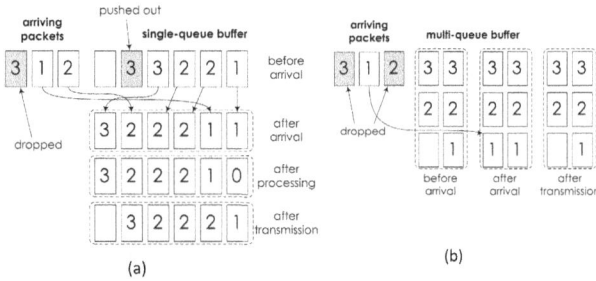

Figure 1: Left: single priority queue with buffer $B = 6$; right: multi-queued switch with three queues ($k = 3$) and buffer $B = 2$ each. Dashed lines enclose queues.

List. 3 depicts the `Packet` data structure. Intrinsic *value* and *processing* requirements can be useful to define prioritization levels [8, 23]. *Slack* is a time bound which used in management decisions of latency-sensitive applications; e.g., if buffer occupancy already exceeds the *slack* value of an incoming packet, the packet can be dropped during admission even if there is available buffer space [25]. Sec. 3 shows specific examples exploiting some of these characteristics.

We postulate that all decisions of buffer management policies (during admission, processing, or scheduling) are based only on the specified packet parameters and internal state variables of a buffering architecture (e.g., buffer occupancy).

3. BASEL AT WORK (EXAMPLES)

3.1 Performance Impact of Admission Control

Consider throughput maximization in a single queue buffering architecture (buffer of size B), where each unit-sized and unit-valued packet is assigned the number of required processing cycles ranging from 1 to k (see Fig. 1(a)). Defining a new admission control policy in BASEL requires only one comparator (admission order upon congestion) and one congestion condition (when an event of congestion occurs). The processing policy is defined by one additional comparator (defining in which order packets are processed). Note that admission and processing comparators actually can be different. List. 4 shows the comparators and congestion conditions used in the following examples.

```
// priorities for admission and processing
fifo(p1,p2)  = (p1.arrival < p2.arrival)
srpt(p1,p2)  = (p1.processing < p2.processing)
rsrpt(p1,p2) = (p1.processing > p2.processing)

// congestion condition for all policies considered
// satisfied when occupancy exceeds queue size.
defCongestion() = lambda q, (q.currSize >= q.size)
```

Listing 4: Example priorities and congestion conditions

List. 5 shows the full specification of a single queue buffering architecture and its optimal throughput policy.

Table 1 lists implementations for `admPrio` and `procPrio` in this architecture and analytic competitiveness results for various online policies versus the optimal offline OPT algorithm [21, 27, 29, 30]. Each row represents a buffer management policy for a single queue; e.g., the first row shows a simple greedy algorithm that admits every incoming packet if possible (see `congestion()`), and

```
// Specification of the buffering architecture
q1=Queue(B); out=Port(q1);
// Admission control
q1.admPrio(p1,p2)=rsrpt(p1,p2);
q1.congestion=defCongestion(q1);
// Processing policy
q1.admPrio(p1,p2)=srpt(p1,p2);
```

Listing 5: Single queue: optimal buffer managment policy for throughtput optimization.

admPrio	procPrio	OPT/ALG
fifo()	fifo()	$O(k)$
rsrpt()	fifo()	$O(\log k)$
rsrpt()	srpt()	1 (optimal)

Table 1: Sample BASEL policies for single queue architecture; k is the maximal processing requirement, OPT/ALG is the competitive ratio between the throughput of optimal offline OPT and online algorithm ALG.

processes them in `fifo()` order; it is $O(k)$-competitive for maximum processing requirement k. In BASEL, this algorithm looks as follows:

```
q1.admPrio=fifo; q1.procPrio=fifo;
```

Changing `fifo()` admission order to `rsrpt()` significantly improves performance and this version of the greedy policy is already $O(\log(k))$-competitive. With the third greedy algorithm processing packets in `srpt()` order and admitting them in `rsrpt()` order, we get an optimal algorithm for throughput maximization regardless of traffic distribution [21]. Since here a port manages only one queue, a *scheduling policy* is just an implicit call to `getHOL()`.

3.2 Performance Impact of Scheduling

One alternative architecture for packets with heterogeneous processing requirements is to allocate queues for packets with the same processing requirements (see Figure 1(b)). The following code creates this buffering architecture in BASEL, where `k` queues share an equal portion of memory `B`.

```
q1=Queue(B);...qk=Queue(B);
out=Port(q1,..,qk);
```

In this architecture, there is no need for advanced processing and admission orders since only packets with the same processing requirement are admitted in the same queue. The following BASEL code instantiates `admPrio`, `procPrio`, and `congestion` in the k created queues.

```
q1.admPrio=fifo; ...; qk.admPrio=fifo;
q1.procPrio=fifo; ...; qk.procPrio=fifo;
q1.congestion=defCongestion(q1); ...;
qk.congestion=defCongestion(qk);
```

This change of buffering architecture is not for free since the buffer of these queues is not shareable. But even here, the decision of which packet to process in order to maximize throughput is non-trivial since it is unclear which characteristic is most relevant for throughput optimization: buffer occupancy, required processing, or a combination. BASEL code in List. 6 presents six different scheduling priorities and `postSchedAct` actions in the cases when this action is used.

Table 2 summarizes various online scheduling policies as shown in [28]. Observe that buffer occupancy is not a good characteristic for throughput maximization: `lqf()` and `sqf()` have bad

71

```
// LQF: HOL packet from Longest-Queue-First
lqf(q1,q2)  = (q1.currSize > q2.currSize);
// SQF: HOL packet from Shortest-Queue-First
sqf(q1,q2)  = (q1.currSize < q2.currSize);
// MAXQF: HOL packet from queue that
// admits max processing
maxqf(q1,q2)= (q1.weightSched > q2.weightSched);
// MINQF: HOL packet from queue that admits
// min processing
minqf(q1,q2)= (q1.weightSched < q2.weightSched);
// CRR: Round-Robin with per cycle resolution
crr(q1,q2)  = (q1.weightSched < q2.weightSched);
crrPostSchedAct() = lambda port,
         (port.getCurrQueue().weightSched += k);
// PRR: Round-Robin with per packet resolution
prr(q1,q2)  = (q1.weightSched < q2.weightSched);
prrPostSchedAct() = lambda port,
   (let q = port.getCurrQueue() in
     if (q.getHOL().processing == 0)
       q.weightSched += k*k));
```

Listing 6: BASEL example of scheduling priorities and postSchedAct actions for multiple separated queues.

init. weightSched	postSchedAct	schedPrio	OPT/ALG
unused	unused	lqf()	$\Omega(\frac{B}{2})$
unused	unused	sqf()	$\Omega(k)$
unused	unused	maxqf()	$\Omega(k)$
qi.weightSched=i	unused	minqf()	upper bound 2
qi.weightSched=i	crrPostSchedAct()	crr()	$\Omega(\frac{k}{\ln k})$
qi.weightSched=i	prrPostSchedAct()	prr()	$\Omega(\frac{3k(k+2)}{4k+16})$

Table 2: Examples of policies in BASEL for multiple queues architecture. k is the maximal processing requirements, B is a buffer size of a single queue. OPT/ALG is the throughput of an optimal offline OPT algorithm vs. online algorithm ALG.

competitive ratios, while a simple greedy scheduling policy Min-Queue-First (MQF) that processes the HOL packet from the non-empty queue with minimal required processing (minqf()) is 2-competitive. This means that MQF will have optimal throughput with a moderate speedup of 2 [28]. The other two policies that implement fairness with per-cycle or per-packet resolution (CRR and PRR respectively) have relatively weak performance; this demonstrates the fundamental tradeoff between fairness and throughput. The following code snippet in BASEL, for instance, corresponds to the CRR policy:

```
// initializing schedWeight for CRR
q1.weightSched=1; ... qk.weightSched=k;
// initial. postSchedAct to update schedWeight
out.postSchedAct = crrPostSchedAct(out);
```

Currently, the best tools available to evaluate performance of buffering architectures are discrete simulators such as NS-2 [3] or OMNet++ [1] that can use traffic traces and/or various traffic distributions to analyze performance of buffer management policies in a high level language. Due to its simplicity, BASEL can be used as a discrete simulator whose configuration is limited to several user-defined expressions. For instance, Fig.s 2 and 3 show the impact of admission, processing, and scheduling policies on throughput optimization for a single queue and multiple queues buffering architectures with packets of heterogeneous processing requirements; in these examples, traffic was generated with an ON-OFF Markov modulated Poisson process (MMPP) with Poisson arrival processes with intensity λ, and required processing chosen uniformly at ran-

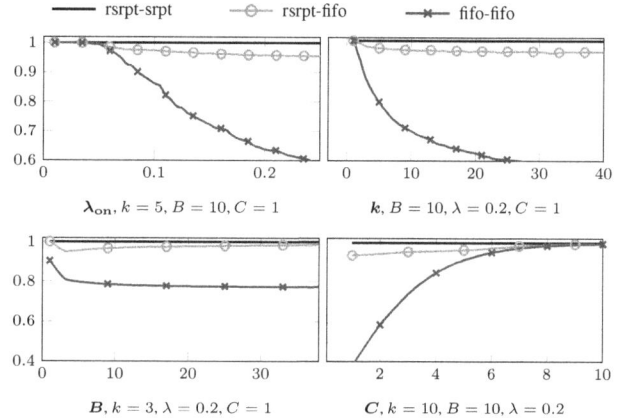

Figure 2: Optimal vs three online algorithms for a single queue architecture with heterogeneous processing; y-axis, competitive ratio; x-axis, top to bottom, left to right: λ; max required processing k; buffer size B; speedup C.

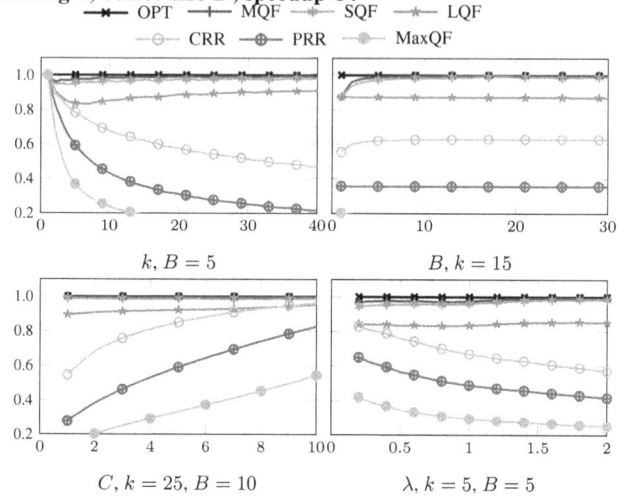

Figure 3: Online vs optimal algorithms for multiple queues with heterogeneous processing; y-axis, competitive ratios; x-axis, top to bottom, left to right: max required processing k, buffer size B, speedup C, intensity λ.

dom from $1..k$. But even if we know how to represent arrivals and analyze them, the applicability of these results will be limited to specific settings. Hence, BASEL is being developed for deployment on real systems.

4. FEASIBILITY OF BASEL

A fundamental building block in BASEL is the *priority queue* data structure where the order of elements is based on user-defined priority. The implementation keeps a single copy of each packet and uses pointers to encode priorities (see Fig. 4). So BASEL implementation is reduced to efficient implementation of priority queues [19, 34] (cf. PERFORMANCE, Sec. 1), making BASEL attractive for hardware implementation.

4.1 BASEL Implementation in Open vSwitch

Open vSwitch (OVS) implements the control plane in user space and the data plane in the kernel [2, 37]. Since OVS exploits Linux TC (Traffic Control) kernel modules via the netdev-linux library to manipulate queuing and scheduling disciplines (qdisc),

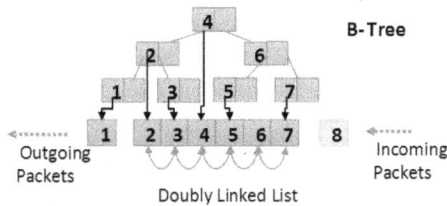

Figure 4: Priority queue implementation.

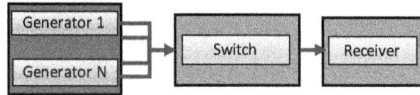

Figure 5: Testbed: 3-node topology

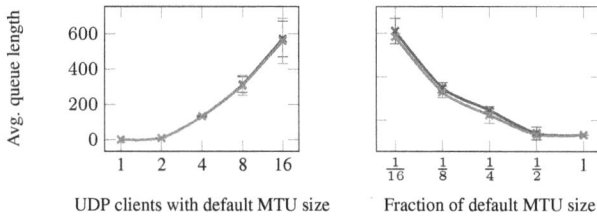

Figure 6: *Left:* **average queue length as a function of number of clients generating UDP traffic with default MTU size.** *Right:* **fraction of default MTU size; blue: FIFO with prioritization; red: regular FIFO.**

we have added configuration options to TC to express BASEL's admission, processing, and scheduling policies. Similar extensions are being added on the data plane via Linux kernel TC loadable kernel modules.

4.2 Performance Impact of Priority Queue

We have extended Linux's default qdisc[3] (i.e., pfifo_fast) to support packet prioritization based on arrival time. Instead of modifying the underlying default packet queue (a doubly linked list), we use an existing B-Tree implementation on top of a default FIFO queue to manage packet prioritization while preserving backward compatibility to existing qdisc solutions. As shown on Fig. 4, we add a reference to the enqueuing packets to the B-Tree and the highest priority packet (i.e., the earliest arrival time) is dequeued first. We remark that FIFO does not need to utilize a B-Tree in general; we use it as a baseline to explore the performance overhead of a generic implementation of prioritization.

In our testbed we set a 3-node line topology to measure the performance overhead of our packet prioritization logic. Fig. 5 shows that the middle node runs OVS with modified data plane (Linux kernel) and acts as a pass-through switch. We vary the number of parallel traffic generators on the first node and measure average queue length (i.e., number of packets in the default queue) in a receiver node on the third for two qdiscs: default FIFO and extended FIFO with prioritization, reporting the average value of 50 runs with 95% confidence interval. Fig. 6(left) shows the average queue lengths for the two qdiscs; in both cases, average queue length increases with the number of UDP clients. In FIFO with 16 clients, the most congested case, regular FIFO has average queue length 559.333 vs. 571 for FIFO with prioritization, only a 2% degradation. We also varied MTU sizes in the same 3-node line topology testbed with 4 parallel UDP generators, which is a good enough case to observe queue build-ups but not dropping packets in the pass-though switch.

---

[3] Queuing Discipline (qdisc) is a part of Linux Traffic Control (TC) used to shape traffic of an interface; qdisc uses dequeue to handle outgoing packets and an enqueue to fetch incoming ones.

We measured average queue lengths of the two qdiscs by varying MTU sizes from $\frac{1}{16}$ of the default MTU size to its default size (1500 bytes). Fig. 6(right) shows that for both qdiscs the average queue length decreases as MTU size increases; FIFO with prioritization incurs only 4% overhead: for MTU size of $\frac{1500}{16}$ bytes the result is 584.3 vs. 610.7. Hence, we conclude that packet prioritization on top of FIFO incurs negligible performance overhead.

5. RELATED WORK

The active networks [42] approach to programmable networks is to execute code contained within packets on the switches. However, we argue that running arbitrary code can hamper switch performance. Frenetic [15], Pyretic [33], among others, have proposed abstractions to express management policies in packet networks. These approaches focus on service abstractions based on flexible *classifiers*, and do not try to manage buffering architectures. Other systems [13, 41] allow for setting a *predefined set* of parameters for buffer management, which intrinsically limits expressivity. Another line of research abstracts the representation of the southbound API (e.g., OpenFlow) in the data plane [7, 40], while languages such as P4 [7] are very successful in representing packet classifiers, they are less suitable to express buffer management policies. The closest work to BASEL is [39] which introduces a set of primitives to specify only admission control policies for a single queue buffering architecture. On the other hand BASEL considers a composition of admission control, processing, and scheduling policies to optimize desired objectives on user-defined buffering architectures. Various frameworks have proposed mechanisms for specifying desired policies in packet networks such as bandwidth allocations [5, 38].

6. CONCLUSION

We propose a concise yet expressive language to define buffer management policies at runtime. The proposed language can define buffering architectures and their management policies with any resolution from a single network element to a virtual switch that can represent a part of the network. We believe that BASEL can enable and accelerate innovation in the domain of buffering architectures and management, similar to programming abstractions that exploit OpenFlow for services with sophisticated classification modules. The conciseness of BASEL and ability to implement priority queue data structures at line-rate, make BASEL attractive for hardware implementations.

Acknowledgments

The work of S. Nikolenko was supported by by the Government of the Russian Federation grant 14.Z50.31.0030 and by the President Grant for Young Ph.D. Researchers MK-7287.2016.1. P. Eugster was partly funded by ERC grant "Lightweight Verification of Distributed Software" and German Research Foundation grant "Multi-Mechanism Adaptation for Future Internet".

7. REFERENCES

[1] OMNeT++. http://www.omnetpp.org/.
[2] Open vSwitch. http://www.openvswitch.org.
[3] This is the ns-2 wiki. http://nsnam.isi.edu/nsnam/index.php/Main_Page.
[4] W. Aiello, A. Kesselman, and Y. Mansour. Competitive buffer management for shared-memory switches. *ACM Trans. on Algorithms*, 5(1), 2008.

[5] H. Ballani, P. Costa, T. Karagiannis, and A. I. T. Rowstron. Towards predictable datacenter networks. In *SIGCOMM*, pages 242–253, 2011.

[6] S. Bauer, R. Beverly, and A. Berger. Measuring the state of ECN readiness in servers, clients, and routers. In *IMC*, pages 171–180, 2011.

[7] P. Bosshart, D. Daly, G. Gibb, M. Izzard, N. McKeown, J. Rexford, C. Schlesinger, D. Talayco, A. Vahdat, G. Varghese, and D. Walker. P4: programming protocol-independent packet processors. *CCR*, 44(3):87–95, 2014.

[8] P. Chuprikov, S. Nikolenko, and K. Kogan. Priority queueing with multiple packet characteristics. In *INFOCOM*, pages 1418–1426, 2015.

[9] A. Demers, S. Keshav, and S. Shenker. Analysis and simulation of a fair queueing algorithm. In *SIGCOMM*, pages 1–12, 1989.

[10] P. Eugster, A. Kesselman, K. Kogan, S. Nikolenko, and A. Sirotkin. Essential traffic parameters for shared memory switch performance. In *SIROCCO*, pages 61–75, 2015.

[11] P. Eugster, K. Kogan, S. Nikolenko, and A. Sirotkin. Shared memory buffer management for heterogeneous packet processing. In *ICDCS*, pages 471–480, 2014.

[12] W. Feng, K. G. Shin, D. D. Kandlur, and D. Saha. The BLUE active queue management algorithms. *IEEE/ACM Trans. Netw.*, 10(4):513–528, 2002.

[13] A. D. Ferguson, A. Guha, C. Liang, R. Fonseca, and S. Krishnamurthi. Participatory networking: an API for application control of sdns. In *SIGCOMM*, pages 327–338, 2013.

[14] S. Floyd and V. Jacobson. Random early detection gateways for congestion avoidance. *IEEE/ACM Trans. Netw.*, 1(4):397–413, 1993.

[15] N. Foster, R. Harrison, M. J. Freedman, C. Monsanto, J. Rexford, A. Story, and D. Walker. Frenetic: a network programming language. In *ICFP*, pages 279–291, 2011.

[16] J. Gettys. Low latency requires smart queuing:traditional AQM is not enough!, 2013. http://www.internetsociety.org/sites/default/files/pdf/accepted/29_bis_ISOC_Workshop_2.pdf.

[17] M. Goldwasser. A survey of buffer management policies for packet switches. *SIGACT News*, 41(1):100–128, 2010.

[18] C. Hong, S. Kandula, R. Mahajan, M. Zhang, V. Gill, M. Nanduri, and R. Wattenhofer. Achieving high utilization with software-driven WAN. In *SIGCOMM*, pages 15–26, 2013.

[19] A. Ioannou and M. Katevenis. Pipelined heap (priority queue) management for advanced scheduling in high-speed networks. *IEEE/ACM Trans. Netw.*, 15(2):450–461, 2007.

[20] S. Jain, A. Kumar, S. Mandal, J. Ong, L. Poutievski, A. Singh, S. Venkata, J. Wanderer, J. Zhou, M. Zhu, J. Zolla, U. Hölzle, S. Stuart, and A. Vahdat. B4: experience with a globally-deployed software defined wan. In *SIGCOMM*, pages 3–14, 2013.

[21] I. Keslassy, K. Kogan, G. Scalosub, and M. Segal. Providing performance guarantees in multipass network processors. *IEEE/ACM Trans. Netw.*, 20(6):1895–1909, 2012.

[22] A. Kesselman, K. Kogan, and M. Segal. Packet mode and QoS algorithms for buffered crossbar switches with FIFO queuing. *Distributed Computing*, 23(3):163–175, 2010.

[23] A. Kesselman, K. Kogan, and M. Segal. Best effort and priority queuing policies for buffered crossbar switches. *Chicago J. Theor. Comput. Sci.*, 2012, 2012.

[24] A. Kesselman, K. Kogan, and M. Segal. Improved competitive performance bounds for cioq switches. *Algorithmica*, 63(1-2):411–424, 2012.

[25] A. Kesselman, Z. Lotker, Y. Mansour, B. Patt-Shamir, B. Schieber, and M. Sviridenko. Buffer overflow management in QoS switches. In *STOC*, pages 520–529, 2001.

[26] A. Kesselman and A. Rosén. Scheduling policies for CIOQ switches. *J. Algorithms*, 60(1):60–83, 2006.

[27] K. Kogan, A. López-Ortiz, S. Nikolenko, G. Scalosub, and M. Segal. Balancing work and size with bounded buffers. In *COMSNETS*, pages 1–8, 2014.

[28] K. Kogan, A. López-Ortiz, S. Nikolenko, and A. Sirotkin. Multi-queued network processors for packets with heterogeneous processing requirements. In *COMSNETS*, pages 1–10, 2013.

[29] K. Kogan, A. López-Ortiz, S. Nikolenko, A. Sirotkin, and D. Tugaryov. FIFO queueing policies for packets with heterogeneous processing. In *MedAlg*, pages 248–260, 2012.

[30] K. Kogan, A. López-Ortiz, S. I. Nikolenko, and A. Sirotkin. A taxonomy of semi-fifo policies. In *IPCCC*, pages 295–304, 2012.

[31] P. McKenney. Stochastic fairness queueing. In *INFOCOM*, pages 733–740, 1990.

[32] N. McKeown, G. Parulkar, S. Shenker, T. Anderson, L. Peterson, J. Turner, H. Balakrishnan, and J. Rexford. OpenFlow switch specification, 2011. http://www.openflow.org/documents/openflow-spec-v1.1.0.pdf.

[33] C. Monsanto, J. Reich, N. Foster, J. Rexford, and D. Walker. Composing software defined networks. In *NSDI*, pages 1–13, 2013.

[34] A. Morton, J. Liu, and I. Song. Efficient priority-queue data structure for hardware implementation. In *FPL*, pages 476–479, 2007.

[35] K. M. Nichols and V. Jacobson. Controlling queue delay. *Commun. ACM*, 55(7):42–50, 2012.

[36] S. I. Nikolenko and K. Kogan. Single and multiple buffer processing. In *Encyclopedia of Algorithms*. Springer, 2015.

[37] B. Pfaff, J. Pettit, T. Koponen, E. J. Jackson, A. Zhou, J. Rajahalme, J. Gross, A. Wang, J. Stringer, P. Shelar, K. Amidon, and M. Casado. The design and implementation of open vswitch. In *USENIX NSDI*, pages 117–130, 2015.

[38] L. Popa, G. Kumar, M. Chowdhury, A. Krishnamurthy, S. Ratnasamy, and I. Stoica. Faircloud: sharing the network in cloud computing. In *SIGCOMM*, pages 187–198, 2012.

[39] A. Sivaraman, K. Winstein, S. Subramanian, and H. Balakrishnan. No silver bullet: extending SDN to the data plane. In *HotNets*, pages 19:1–19:7, 2013.

[40] H. Song. Protocol-oblivious forwarding: unleash the power of SDN through a future-proof forwarding plane. In *HotSDN*, pages 127–132, 2013.

[41] R. Soulé, S. Basu, P. J. Marandi, F. Pedone, R. D. Kleinberg, E. G. Sirer, and N. Foster. Merlin: A language for provisioning network resources. In *CoNEXT*, pages 213–226, 2014.

[42] D. L. Tennenhouse and D. Wetherall. Towards an active network architecture. *Computer Communication Review*, 26(2):5–17, 1996.

Is Memory Disaggregation Feasible?
A Case Study with Spark SQL

Pramod Subba Rao and George Porter
UC San Diego

Abstract

This paper explores the feasibility of entirely disaggregated memory from compute and storage for a particular, widely deployed workload, Spark SQL [9] analytics queries. We measure the empirical rate at which records are processed and calculate the effective memory bandwidth utilized based on the sizes of the columns accessed in the query. Our findings contradict conventional wisdom: not only is memory disaggregation possible under this workload, but achievable with already available, commercial network technology. Beyond this finding, we also recommend changes that can be made to Spark SQL to improve its ability to support memory disaggregation.

1. INTRODUCTION

Achieving efficiency in data processing requires balanced computing, meaning that a system has the right mix of CPU, memory, storage IO, and network IO so that one part of the computation is not bottlenecked waiting for results from another part of the computation. Getting this balance just right is a moving target, since the input data, number and type of queries, presence of failures, and network conditions are in a constant state of flux. Correctly provisioning bare-metal servers is a challenge since one must determine their specific configuration at entirely the wrong timescales, well before they are put into production. While virtual machines play an important role in providing more flexibility in balancing resources, they are not enough. Even with VMs, you are limited to configurations implementable in a single server, you are subject to "fragmentation" of resources, and you are not able to upgrade individual components like CPU and memory independently of each other.

These challenges have led to disaggregated server designs, where individual components such as CPU, memory, and storage are interconnected over a network, rather than over a bus within a single chassis [12]. The advantages of disaggregation include more efficient utilization of resources, and the ability to independently upgrade different system components. The challenge for disaggregation is the "memory wall" [21]. Today storage is commonly disaggregated via SANs and other network-based file storage protocols, and Facebook has introduced a disaggregated system-on-chip (SoC) platform called Yosemite [5], which relies on networked storage. Yet there is a growing gap in the rate at which CPUs can execute instructions and the rate at which data can be fetched into the CPU from main memory. For this reason in Yosemite (as well as other designs), memory and CPU are still tightly integrated in the same chassis.

This paper puts aside the issue of disaggregating memory in general, and instead examines disaggregating memory for a common and increasingly deployed type of application: analytics queries. Using Spark SQL [9] as a motivating platform, we measure the actual rate at which threads of execution access memory and process records, and using these measurements, determine the feasibility of disaggregating memory. Spark is an example of a growing set of data-parallel frameworks which exhibit minimal data-dependent branches, and as such, can take advantage of significant amounts of pipelining. For this reason, they are largely latency insensitive, further enabling the use of disaggregated memory.

Our initial results show that even after significant optimization, Spark SQL analytics queries access memory an order of magnitude slower than the underlying components permit, opening up the possibility of disaggregating memory from compute. In fact, the requirements on the underlying network are modest, and can be met with existing commercial products such as 40- and 100-Gb/s NICs (e.g., the Mellanox ConnectX-4 NIC [17]). We conclude by recommending further changes that improve Spark SQL's ability to support memory disaggregation.

2. MOTIVATION

Two major reasons that server disaggregation attempts have avoided memory is that, at a component level, (1) the bandwidth required between memory and the CPU is too large to be supported by commercial network equipment, and (2) network latency is too high. In the first case, we demonstrate experimentally using microbenchmarks that memory bandwidth indeed exceeds network capabilities (in Section 2.1). Yet users do not run microbenchmarks, they run applications, which might not have such stringent requirements, including for memory latency. We explore one such application in Section 2.2, chosen because of its highly efficient use of memory, serving as a compelling motivating application.

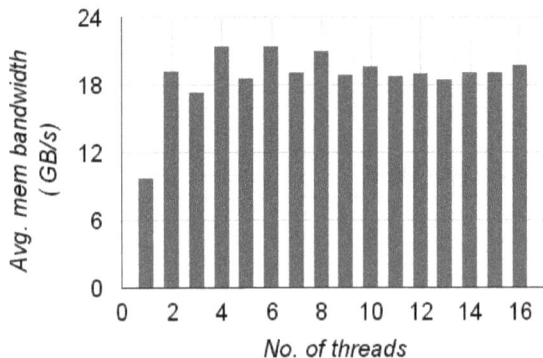

Figure 1: Aggregate memory bandwidth of STREAM benchmark

2.1 The memory wall: barrier or paper tiger?

We start by examining an upper-bound on the bandwidth requirements of a memory disaggregated system through the STREAM benchmark [16], which is a synthetic benchmark that measures sustainable memory bandwidth and the corresponding computation rate for simple vector kernels. A wrapper tool called stream-scaling [7] automates the process of executing STREAM over the various core counts is used in this study. We have deployed STREAM onto an 8-core Intel Xeon 2.27 GHz E5520 processor-based HP ProLiant DL380 G6 server. This machine has 24GB of DDR3 Synchronous RAM (1333 MHz), configured as 12x2GB banks in the Advanced Error Correction Code mode.

Figure 1 shows the results of the STREAM Copy benchmark on the experiment hardware, which copies data from one array of doubles to another. The total memory bandwidth of the system with all cores active is approximately 21 GB/sec (or 168 Gb/s), a result that matches the HP ProLiant datasheet [2]. Not only does 168 Gb/s exceed any commercially available network interface card (NIC), it exceeds the PCIe 3.0 bandwidth capacity (a x16 device is limited to 15.75 GB/s, of which approximately 14.2 GB/s are usable), meaning that modern servers are simply unable to keep up with such demand. Thus, absent additional constraints, memory disaggregation is not feasible. Lim et al. [14, 15] explore partial memory disaggregation, where memory is partitioned into local and remote blades. In this paper, we examine entirely remote disaggregated memory constrained to a specific, though popular and widely deployed, application.

2.2 Analytic queries with Spark SQL

Spark SQL [9] is a relational data processing system implemented in Scala and built on top of the functional programming API of Apache Spark [22]. It bridges the gap between traditional analytics queries and machine learning algorithms by offering both an SQL interface and a procedural programmatic interface.

Analytics queries are used to generate summary reports from large amounts of raw data in order to glean insights. They are characterized by: (1) accessing the source data in a read-only manner, (2) accessing a large number of rows from a table (frequently the entire table), but only for a small subset of all the available columns in the table, (3) performing aggregation operations (count, sum, average, group by) on one or more columns or tables, and (4) consisting of CPU-intensive operations for advanced analytics and machine learning algorithms. To this last point, Ousterhout et al. [18] have shown that for a large set of realistic workloads, Spark is CPU-bound, not memory, network, or storage bound. Due to the nature of aggregation-based queries, the size of the working set can decrease, in some cases significantly, after every stage of aggregation.

In this paper, we chose Spark SQL due to its highly-efficient use of memory, due in part to three major factors: (1) it stores data in a column oriented format, making it efficient to access all the rows of a column, (2) it generates Java bytecode directly for commonly used aggregation operations like *count*, *min*, and *max*, thus avoiding the overhead of multiple, and possibly virtual, function calls, and (3) it applies operators to entire data sets (called RDDs) in parallel, without data-dependent branching. This lack of branching reduces the impact of higher memory latency on overall application throughput. We deploy a series of analytic queries taken from the literature and published benchmarks, and for each thread of execution, we measure the rate at which records are processed and calculate the effective memory bandwidth based on the sizes of the columns accessed in the query multiplied by the number of threads. This results in the overall aggregate memory bandwidth.

Specifically, if there are *threadcount* threads accessing *size* bytes from each record, during a time interval of $AvgTime_{100000}$ between every 100,000 records (averaged across all the threads), the aggregate memory access rate is:

$$Mem\_access\_rate = \frac{(size \times 100000)}{AvgTime_{100000}} \times threadCount \quad (1)$$

We use this formula to calculate the actual memory access rate, rather than potential access rate, for sets of queries.

2.3 High-speed networking

Today 10- and 40-Gb/s Ethernet is commercially available and widely deployed within production data centers [11]. Commercial 100 Gb/s NICs and switches are now available from vendors such as Mellanox [17], and 400 Gb/s Ethernet is in the standardization process [10]. A key aspect of these new standards is that their high overall speeds are obtained by joining multiple, parallel, underlying links together. For example, 100 Gb/s Ethernet is largely 4 25 Gb/s lanes, and 400 Gb/s is currently 16 25 Gb/s lanes (eventually to be replaced with 4 100 Gb/s lanes when those become available). Simply put, the ability to increase a single lane of Ethernet cannot keep pace with overall bandwidth demands, and so parallelism is used in new standards.

3. EXPERIMENTAL SETUP

3.1 Hardware and software

The hardware used for the following experiments is a cluster of five nodes, consisting of a single master node and four workers. Each server is the same configuration as described above in Section 2.1, and they are interconnected with a 10 Gb/s network. We rely on the cluster to distribute jobs to servers, however our measurements are limited to a single server, and thus the network is not a bottleneck for profiling the bandwidth requirements of the memory system.

We use Apache Spark 1.3.0 [1], deployed in standalone mode on Ubuntu Linux 14.04.2. One executor process is run on each worker node and is allotted 18GB of RAM out of the 24GB. To read CSV files, we use the spark-csv library [6]. The Java Virtual Machine used is Java HotSpot 1.6.0_45-b06. No other software is running on this cluster apart from the default system processes.

3.2 Spark SQL

Apart from allocating ample memory (18 GB) to each node, we have set up Spark in a way that increases the demand on the memory subsystem compared to more general configurations, in an effort to provide a conservative upper-bound on the memory bandwidth requirements. Unless mentioned as follows, we maintain the default Spark configuration. We have modified the following settings:

1. We ensure all memory accesses are to local memory. In production workloads, off-node memory might be accessed as well.

2. *spark.storage.memoryFraction* is increased to 0.8 (default: 0.6). This is the fraction of Java heap to use for Spark's memory cache; increasing this value ensures that resilient distributed datasets (RDDs) are cached entirely in memory.

3. We set *spark.shuffle.spill* to false. This ensures that data does not spill over to disk during the reduce phase.

4. Memory compression is turned off (*spark.sql.inMemory-ColumnarStorage.compressed*) to reduce extra overhead on the CPU during query processing.

5. Our instrumentation measures access times after every 100,000 records, and so we set *spark.sql.inMemory-ColumnarStorage.batchSize* to 100001 (from its default of 1000) to ensure we have a sufficient number of records in each batch.

6. We turn on dynamic code generation (*spark.sql.code-gen*). This optimization within Spark SQL generates Scala code at runtime which is specialized for the types and the number of expressions used in the query. It also avoids autoboxing overhead where primitive types are being used. In the absence of code generation, simple operations like extracting a column from a row, or adding two literals, can result in branching and virtual function calls. The code generation feature generates inline Scala code for the same and compiles them to JVM bytecode before execution.

7. To prevent Spark from writing data to disk during the shuffle phase, we ensure intermediate data is written to memory by setting the partition to a *tmpfs* filesystem.

8. We disable the OS swap partition (via *swapoff -a*).

9. Whenever measurements are needed for a specific number of threads, we achieve that by splitting up the data into an equivalent number of RDD partitions.

3.3 Workloads

We evaluate the feasibility of memory disaggregation using three workloads. The first is the STREAM benchmark, described previously, which measures the raw capacity of the memory subsystem, setting the upper bound on what application could obtain. The second is a microbenchmark of Spark SQL's memory access performance, achieved by measured a simple *COUNT(1)* query, which simply scans a synthetic RDD with rows and columns of different lengths, using a varying number of threads, all while incrementing a counter. This sets an upper-bound on the performance of Spark SQL, as it forms one of the simplest queries possible to express. Third, we evaluate a series of more complex queries drawn from the UC Berkeley AMPLab "Big Data" benchmark [3].

3.4 Measurement technique

We measure memory bandwidth at the application level by instrumenting Spark SQL, and validate these measurements by comparing to CPU-level performance counters.

Spark SQL instrumentation: Spark SQL loads data into an in-memory table accessed via the *InMemoryColumnarTableScan* class. Data for all rows of a column is stored in a Java byte array. The first 4 bytes of the array are used to specify the data type, and the rest contain the actual data. We request that the data for the query be cached in memory through Spark's *rdd.persist()* mechanism. When the query is executed for the first time, a CSV file is read to populate the in-memory table; subsequent executions of the query access only the in-memory representation. We log timing information within *InMemoryColumnarTableScan* during iterations over the table, at intervals of 100,000 records in each of the threads. Equation 1 is used to calculate the access rate to memory. All measurements are taken at one of the worker nodes in the cluster.

CPU performance counters: Intel processors provide a set of counters and associated monitoring software [4] to measure CPU utilization and bytes read/written from memory. We use these during query processing to validate the application-level measurements, and our findings (not shown) match those reported by the Spark-level instrumentation.

4. EXPERIMENTAL RESULTS

We examine the memory demands of analytical queries first by examining a trivial query that provides an upper-bound on the bandwidth that can be achieved by Spark SQL, and then by considering two more complex queries drawn from the AMPLab's Big Data Benchmark [8].

4.1 Microbenchmark queries

```
———————— Query 1 ————————
SELECT COUNT(1) from SingleColumnTable;
```

Spark SQL implements Query 1 by fetching the data from the smallest column in the row and then incrementing a counter. If the row contains only one column, this is equivalent to fetching the entire row. We chose Query 1 as an example of a query with minimum CPU usage in order to measure baseline performance of the system. Based on the time taken to count every 100,000 records, the memory access rate is calculated according to Equation 1.

Columns of data, of various lengths, were generated and mapped to different numbers of partitions in order to create

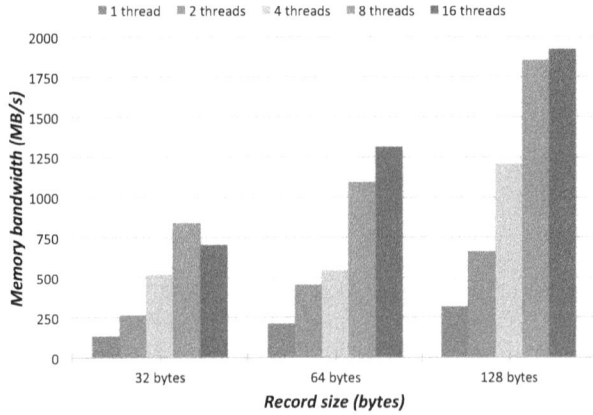

Figure 2: *Select count(1)* query

the appropriate number of threads. Figure 2 shows that a maximum average throughput of 1.9 GB/sec is seen when running with 16 threads on 128 bytes of data, all from the in-memory cache. While the throughput increases with the number of threads, it tapers off as it reaches 16 threads. Since the hardware has only 16-cores, running more than 16 threads is not representative of the CPU intensive nature of analytics queries.

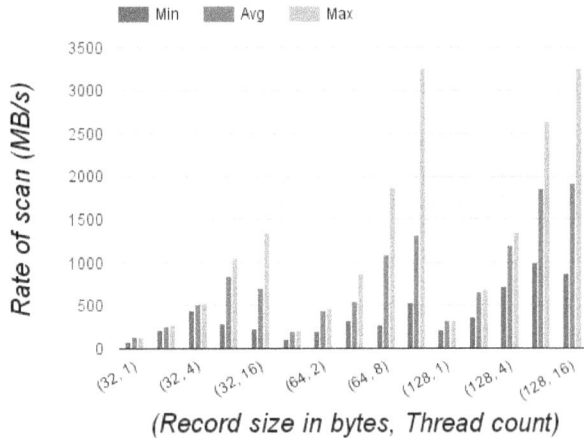

Figure 3: Summary statistics for Query 1

Figure 3 shows the average, max and minimum rates of memory access for Query 1. It can be seen that a maximum throughput of 3.3 GB/sec is observed while scanning records of size 128 bytes in 16 threads. A distribution of this data is shown in Figure 4. The key takeaway from this result is that while under optimal conditions, Spark SQL is capable of driving, in aggregate, an impressive 26.4 Gb/s of network bandwidth on our hardware, it requires 16 independent threads to do so.

4.2 AMPLab Benchmark queries

The previous section has looked at microbenchmark queries, which are significantly memory-intensive, and found that they are satisfiable with 40 or 100 Gb/s Ethernet devices currently available from vendors such as Mellanox [17]. We now turn our attention to more realistic queries, provided

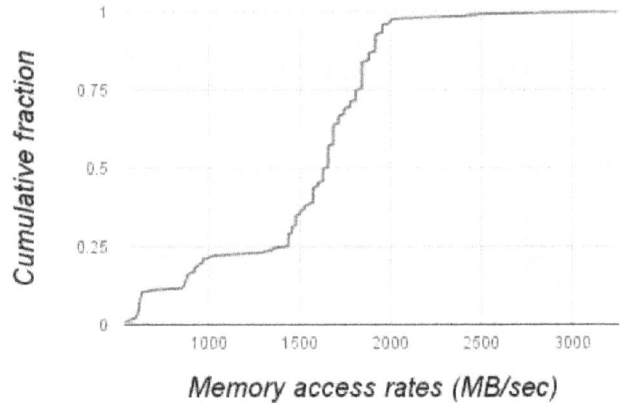

Figure 4: CDF of memory access rates for Query 1 (60M records, 64 bytes, 16 threads)

Column name	Column size	Comments
sourceIp	19 bytes	4 byte length; 15 byte IP
adRevenue	4 bytes	sizeof(FLOAT)
Total	23 bytes	

Table 1: Data accessed per row for Query 2

by the AMPLab "Big Data" benchmark suite [8].

4.2.1 "Group by" query

```
———————————— Query 2 ————————————
SELECT sourceIp, SUM(adRevenue) FROM
 uservisits GROUP BY sourceIp
```

We next look at an Aggregation Query from the Big Data Benchmark [3], shown as Query 2. It shows the advertisement revenue obtained from each end user IP address based on all the sites visited by that IP address and grouping the total revenue obtained from each of those addresses. The *uservisits* table has 10 million entries. For each row, the following columns are accessed: sourceIp and adRevenue. Table 1 shows that the data accessed per row of this query is 23 bytes.

Spark SQL creates 8 threads to process this data on each node. The data accessed per row is 23 bytes, and the average time interval between every 100,000 records is 63.7 ms, and the minimum is 51.0 ms. Based on Equation 1, this translates to an access rate of 289 MB/s (2.3 Gb/s), and a maximum rate of 361 MB/s (2.9 Gb/s). Per thread, however, the demands are a relatively paltry 289 Mb/s on average, 361 Mb/s max.

Effect of code generation: Since Query 2 is more resource intensive (in terms of both CPU and memory) than Query 1, it is instructive to look at the performance of the query without bytecode generation. Figure 5 shows the time spent in various phases of Query 2 in the absence of code generation. Due to the creation of a large number of temporary helper objects for aggregation, and the accompanying garbage collections, the time spent for iterating over data is larger than needed, showing that to get high memory utilization, it is essential to run with code generation enabled. Even with this optimization, it is still practical to support this result with existing network technology.

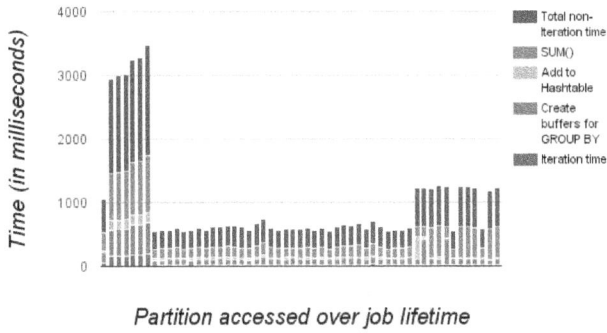

Figure 5: Code generation optimizes memory access rates for Query 2

Column name	Column size	Comments
url	59 bytes	4 byte length; 55 bytes data
pageRank	4 bytes	sizeof(FLOAT)
Total	63 bytes	

Table 2: Data accessed per row for Query 3 (Rankings table)

4.2.2 "Join" query

```
─────────────────── Query 3 ───────────────────
SELECT sourceIp, AVG(pageRank) as avgPageRank,
  SUM(adRevenue) as totalRevenue
        FROM
            Rankings AS R, Uservisits AS UV
        WHERE
            R.pageUrl = UV.destinationUrl AND
            UV.visitDate > '1980-01-01' AND
            UV.visitDate < '2015-05-20'
        GROUP BY
            UV.sourceIp
        ORDER BY totalRevenue DESC LIMIT 1
```

We next examine a *join* query taken from the Big Data Benchmark [3], shown here as Query 3. Along with the advertisement revenue obtained from each end user IP address, it also displays the average rank of the pages visited by that IP address, by joining with a Rankings table. The Uservisits table has 10 million rows as earlier, and the Rankings query also has 10 million rows. To analyze this query it is necessary to inspect the in memory representation more closely (shown in Tables 2 and 3). Since the data for Rankings is split into 2 partitions on the given node and the data for Uservisits is split into 7 partitions, the number of threads operating upon the two tables are also respectively 2 and 7.

For the *Rankings* table, the data accessed per row is 63 bytes, and the time interval between every 100,000 records was an average of 131.6 ms, and a minimum of 67 ms. Based

Column name	Column size	Comments
adRevenue	4 bytes	sizeof(FLOAT)
destinationUrl	59 bytes	4 byte length; 55 bytes data
visitDate	4 bytes	sizeof(FLOAT)
sourceIp	19 bytes	4 byte length; 15 byte IP
Total	86 bytes	

Table 3: Data accessed per row for Query 3 (Uservisits table)

on Equation 1, this translates to an average access rate of 45.1 MB/s (0.4 Gb/s) and a maximum access rate of 94.0 MB/s (0.8 Gb/s). For the *Uservisits* table, the data accessed per row is 86 bytes, and the time interval between every 100,000 records was an average of 504.2 ms, with a minimum of 285.0 ms, translating into an average access rate of 17.1 MB/s (0.1 Gb/s), and a maximum average rate of 30.2 MB/s (0.2 Gb/s).

The relatively lower speed of access on the *Uservisits* table can be explained by the need to filter each row based on the range condition given in the query. Since the above two operations happen in parallel, the total average memory throughput during this phase is $45.1 + 17.1 = 62.2$ MB/sec (0.5 Gb/s). Maximum throughput, assuming both tables are scanned together in an optimal way, is $94.0 + 30.2 = 124.2$ MB/s (1.0 Gb/s). With 7 threads, that's approximately a total memory throughput of 7 Gb/s.

5. FEASIBILITY

We now discuss the potential feasibility of disaggregating memory for analytical queries.

5.1 Reasons to be optimistic

We have purposefully chosen settings and workloads to increase the overall memory access rates of Spark SQL to the extent possible with our hardware. For this reason we are optimistic in the above results, since in real-world deployments, these results are likely to be an upper bound on Spark SQL's potential performance. Additional reasons for this are:

1. Since Spark SQL runs on the Java Virtual Machine, garbage collection pauses - major collections in particular - can interfere with system throughput. We mitigate this by allocating a large amount of heap memory relative to the size of the data set and avoiding major collections entirely, though in a deployed system GC events would reduce memory demand.

2. Concurrency is achieved by partitioning the data and processing different subsets of the data in parallel. Concurrency does not exist within the context of a partition. If a series of operations have to be performed on a row (e.g,. filter, compute an expression on the value, then aggregate), they are performed in sequence and only then is the next row in the partition accessed.

3. It is a new framework, and possibly lacks advanced query optimization features. Since the queries run during this experiment do not benefit from such optimization, their absence should not affect the results.

5.2 Reasons to be pessimistic

Our study is still preliminary, and faces a number of limitations. We focus only on one kind of query (analytical) and restricts its measurement to the rate of consumption of input data. Of course other workloads may result in different bottlenecks and need a different model for analysis, and even within this approach, we have limited our analysis to a subset of published benchmark queries. Considering the limitations of Spark SQL listed in above, the viability of this approach needs to be tested using other frameworks like Impala [13], Redshift [19], and Tez [20].

Finally, we are limited in our hardware in terms of the number of CPU cores that are available. To this last point, a major research question addressing the feasibility of memory disaggregation is to understand the scaling behaviors of the hardware, as well as the query engine. In particular, if the bandwidth available at the NIC grows at a rate comparable to the number of threads available to Spark SQL, then our results will hold up in the future. However if the growth of CPU threads dedicated to query processing grows faster than the aggregate bandwidth of the NIC, then disaggregation will not be feasible without affecting query performance. Such a limitation might not rule out disaggregated designs, however, since it provides a number of other benefits (such as easier management, and incremental upgrades of individual components).

5.3 Suggested improvements

Based on the above experiments and a study of the Spark SQL source code, some improvements to the software architecture present themselves in the context of disaggregated memory. First, the data storage system should provide the ability to address and serve specific data items such as columns, partitions of rows, etc. This will keep aggregate bandwidth requirement to a minimum. Second, prefetching of rows should be implemented for queries which are known to scan all or most of the data set. Pipelining of different phases of a row (as explained above) can help towards this.

For the queries we analyzed, the per-thread memory access rates were all below 25 Gb/s (in some cases much lower). As new Ethernet standards make their way into the market, based on aggregating multiple, parallel, underlying lanes, it would be advantageous to match up these per-thread bandwidth demands with the lanes. For example, 4 Spark SQL threads would match well to a four-lane 100 Gb/s NIC.

6. CONCLUSION

This paper has described a preliminary approach to evaluating the feasibility of disaggregated memory. The approach consists of measuring memory access rates of analytics queries based on the amount of input data accessed per row of the query. A few sample queries drawn from the Big Data Benchmark [3] were used to benchmark this metric for Spark SQL. The results show that it is possible to disaggregate the memory for such workloads using currently available network hardware. Improvements in software architecture can help in performing better in a disaggregated memory environment. While care has been taken to set up Spark SQL so as to get a conservative set of results, more extensive testing needs to be done using different queries and configurations.

Acknowledgements

This work was sponsored in part by the National Science Foundation (CNS-1314921).

7. REFERENCES

[1] Apache Spark version 1.3.0. https://github.com/apache/spark/tree/branch-1.3.
[2] Best Practice Guidelines for ProLiant Servers with the Intel Xeon 5500 processor series Engineering Whitepaper, 1st Edition, Figure 6. ftp://ftp.hp.com/pub/c-products/servers/options/Memory-Config\--Recommendations\--for-Intel-Xeon\--5500-Series-Servers-Rev1.pdf.
[3] Big Data Benchmark. https://amplab.cs.berkeley.edu/benchmark/.
[4] Intel Performance Counter Monitor - A better way to measure CPU utilization. https://software.intel.com/en-us/articles/intel-performance-counter-monitor/.
[5] Introducing Yosemite: the first open source modular chassis for high-powered microservers. https://code.facebook.com/posts/1616052405274961/introducing-yosemite-\-the-first-open-source\--modular-chassis-for\--high-powered-microservers-/.
[6] Spark CSV. https://github.com/databricks/spark-csv.
[7] stream-scaling. https://github.com/gregs1104/stream-scaling.
[8] Amplab big data benchmark. https://amplab.cs.berkeley.edu/benchmark/.
[9] M. Armbrust, R. S. Xin, C. Lian, Y. Huai, D. Liu, J. K. Bradley, X. Meng, T. Kaftan, M. J. Franklin, A. Ghodsi, and M. Zaharia. Spark sql: Relational data processing in spark. In *Proceedings of the 2015 ACM SIGMOD International Conference on Management of Data*, SIGMOD '15, pages 1383–1394, New York, NY, USA, 2015. ACM.
[10] IEEE P802.3bs 400 Gb/s Ethernet Task Force. http://www.ieee802.org/3/bs/index.html.
[11] Introducing data center fabric, the next-generation facebook data center network. https://code.facebook.com/posts/360346274145943/introducing-data-center\--fabric-the-next-generation-\-facebook-data-center-network/.
[12] S. Han, N. Egi, A. Panda, S. Ratnasamy, G. Shi, and S. Shenker. Network support for resource disaggregation in next-generation datacenters. In *Proceedings of the Twelfth ACM Workshop on Hot Topics in Networks*, HotNets-XII, pages 10:1–10:7, New York, NY, USA, 2013. ACM.
[13] Impala. http://impala.io/.
[14] K. Lim, J. Chang, T. Mudge, P. Ranganathan, S. K. Reinhardt, and T. F. Wenisch. Disaggregated memory for expansion and sharing in blade servers. In *Proceedings of the 36th Annual International Symposium on Computer Architecture*, ISCA '09, pages 267–278, New York, NY, USA, 2009. ACM.
[15] K. Lim, Y. Turner, J. R. Santos, A. AuYoung, J. Chang, P. Ranganathan, and T. F. Wenisch. System-level implications of disaggregated memory. In *Proceedings of the 2012 IEEE 18th International Symposium on High-Performance Computer Architecture*, HPCA '12, pages 1–12, Washington, DC, USA, 2012. IEEE Computer Society.
[16] J. D. McCalpin. Stream: Sustainable memory bandwidth in high performance computers. https://www.cs.virginia.edu/stream/, 1995.
[17] ConnectX-4 single/dual-port adapter supporting 100 Gb/s with VPI. http://www.mellanox.com/page/products_dyn?product_family=201&mtag=connectx_4_vpi_card.
[18] K. Ousterhout, R. Rasti, S. Ratnasamy, S. Shenker, and B.-G. Chun. Making sense of performance in data analytics frameworks. In *Proceedings of the 12th USENIX Conference on Networked Systems Design and Implementation*, NSDI'15, pages 293–307, Berkeley, CA, USA, 2015. USENIX Association.
[19] Amazon AWS RedShift. http://aws.amazon.com/redshift/.
[20] Apache Tez. https://tez.apache.org/.
[21] W. A. Wulf and S. A. McKee. Hitting the memory wall: Implications of the obvious. *SIGARCH Comput. Archit. News*, 23(1):20–24, Mar. 1995.
[22] M. Zaharia, M. Chowdhury, M. J. Franklin, S. Shenker, and I. Stoica. Spark: Cluster computing with working sets. In *Proceedings of the 2Nd USENIX Conference on Hot Topics in Cloud Computing*, HotCloud'10, pages 10–10, Berkeley, CA, USA, 2010. USENIX Association.

Stick to the Script: Monitoring The Policy Compliance of SDN Data Plane

Peng Zhang[†‡], Hao Li[†], Chengchen Hu[†], Liujia Hu[†], and Lei Xiong[†]
[†]Department of Computer Science and Technology, Xi'an Jiaotong University
[‡]Science and Technology on Information Transmission and Dissemination in Communication Networks Laboratory

ABSTRACT

Software defined networks provide new opportunities for automating the process of network debugging. Many tools have been developed to verify the correctness of network configurations on the control plane. However, due to software bugs and hardware faults of switches, the correctness of control plane may not readily translate into that of data plane. To bridge this gap, we present VeriDP, which can monitor "whether actual forwarding behaviors are complying with network configurations". Given that policies are well-configured, operators can leverage VeriDP to monitor the correctness of the network data plane. In a nutshell, VeriDP lets switches tag packets that they forward, and report tags together with headers to the verification server before the packets leave the network. The verification server pre-computes all header-to-tag mappings based on the configuration, and checks whether the reported tags agree with the mappings. We prototype VeriDP with both software and hardware OpenFlow switches, and use emulation to show that VeriDP can detect common data plane fault including black holes and access violations, with a minimal impact on the data plane.

1. INTRODUCTION

In traditional networks, when a fault (*e.g.*, routing black hole) occurs in the network, it will be firstly noticed by some end hosts that may become unreachable. Then, customers complain and issue tickets to the network operators, who use simple tools like ping and traceroute to localize the fault and resolve it. The above process lacks automation, and inevitably incurs a long service downtime.

Since networks know every single detail of a packet's lifetime, why not let themselves raise alters to operators, instead of end hosts or customers? There are many potential benefits by letting networks take an active role in network monitoring and debugging. First, by automatically raising alters, operators can resolve the faults more efficiently, thereby reducing the network downtime. Second, some faults (*e.g.*, access violation) that may not be explicitly noticed by any end hosts can be captured by networks. Finally, networks can provide more useful information for the operators to pinpoint the fault location.

One reason that networks keep passive in monitoring and debugging may be the distributed nature of networks: no single switch can reason about the global policies in traditional networks. For example, consider a packet is dropped, the switch does not know whether it is due to faults or access control policies. As another example, if a packet is received twice by a switch, it is a fault of loop in most cases, while it also can happen with a normal policy in flexible middle-box traversal scenarios [8].

We observe that networks have the potential to take a more active role in the monitoring in the context of SDN. First, the SDN controller knows the global network policy, *i.e.*, how the data plane should behave, and there are many tools to guarantee the correctness of the network policy, either off-line [19, 15, 26] or on-the-fly [16, 14, 24]. Secondly, switches can record and report packet forwarding behaviors to the controller, through standard south bound interfaces (*e.g.*, OpenFlow [20]). By comparing the packet forwarding behaviors to the global network policy, the controller is in a good position to detect faults of the data plane.

Previous efforts on automatic network debugging are mostly focused on checking correctness of network configurations [19, 15, 16, 14, 24, 26]. However, even the controller and configurations are correct, the data plane may still experience faults due to switch software bugs [17], hardware failures [25], or malicious attacks [22]. Existing data plane verification tools either solely check reachability and thus miss path information [25], use probe packets that can be poor indicators of real traffic [25, 6], require a large number of flow rules [27, 21], depend on specific data center topology [23], or incur too much data plane traffic [9, 10].

Noted of the above limitations, we propose VeriDP, a new tool that can monitor the policy compliance of SDN data plane. In contrast to path tracers that solely rely on switches to imprint packet paths, VeriDP combines it with the network policies/configurations on the control plane. This combination delivers the following benefits. (1) With the network policy at hand, VeriDP can distinguish packet drops due to access violation from black holes, and strategic multi-traversals [8] from infinite loops. (2) It is not necessary to optimize the path encoding method so as to fit the path info into the limited header space as in [27, 21, 23], since the controller already knows the correct path, and the only task is to judge whether the path taken by packet is the same with it.

The basic idea of VeriDP is quite simple. The controller pre-compute a *path table* which records all mappings from packet headers to forwarding paths. When a packet enters the network, the entry switch decides whether to mark it according to some sampling strategies. If a packet is marked, each switch *en route* tags it with the forwarding information. Before a marked packet leaves the network, the exit switch reports its header and tag to the controller. The controller verifies whether the information encoded in the tag

ANCS'16, March 17–18, 2016, Santa Clara, California, USA.
© 2016 ACM. ISBN 978-1-4503-4183-7/16/03. . . $15.00
DOI: http://dx.doi.org/10.1145/2881025.2881038

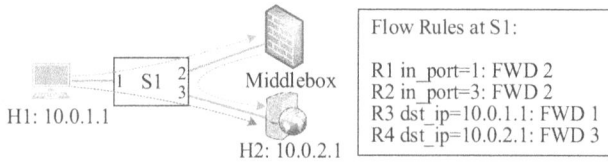

Figure 1: Middlebox traversal example. The security policy of $H1 \rightarrow Middlebox \rightarrow H2$ is violated.

is the same with the path that the packet should take according to the path table.

Indeed, packet tagging is not a new idea for tracing packet trajectories [27, 21, 23]. VeriDP differs from them in that it is not trying to encode path information into packet headers for the receivers to decode it. Rather, VeriDP uses control-plane policies to "infer" paths, and use packet tags to "test" the correctness of real paths. The advantage is that VeriDP does not need complicated encoding methods or a large number of flow entries, in order to compress path info into limited header space.

Our contribution is two-fold:

- We propose VeriDP, a new tool to monitor the policy compliance of SDN data plane, i.e., "whether packet forwarding behaviors agree with the policy configured by the controller".
- We implement VeriDP on software- and hardware-based data plane, and demonstrate that it can detect common faults like black holes, access violation, loops, while incurring minimal overhead on the data plane.

In the rest of this paper, we will first give our notion of policy compliance (§2), and then present the design of VeriDP (§3). We continue to test the function of VeriDP, and evaluate its performance (§4). After discussing some related work (§5), we conclude the paper (§6).

2. INTRODUCING POLICY COMPLIANCE

2.1 Observations

Before introducing our notion of policy compliance, we first elaborate the fact that verifying the policy compliance of data plane necessitates checking packet paths with real traffic.

Path Check Is Important. Pairwise reachability is a key invariant for a network. However, only checking reachability is not enough to reveal data plane faults. Consider an example of middlebox traversal. As shown in Figure 1, rules at switch $S1$ indicate that traffic from the client $H1$ to the server $H2$ must go through the middlebox. To test all these rules based on reachability, we can send two probe packets $H1 \rightarrow H2$ and $H2 \rightarrow H1$. They will follow the path of $H1(H2) \rightarrow S1 \rightarrow M \rightarrow S1 \rightarrow H2(H1)$, respectively, and thus trigger all rules in this network. Now, consider that the high-priority rules $R1$ and/or $R2$ fail, then the probe packets will take the path of $H1(H2) \rightarrow S1 \rightarrow H2(H1)$ instead. However, probe packets will still be received as normal, thus missing the faults. This example shows that to monitor the policy compliance of data plane, we need to check the paths of packets, instead of only checking pairwise reachability.

Real Packets Are Necessary. Verification using probe packets can only verify that the forwarding paths of probe packets agree with the rule. It does not necessarily mean the forwarding paths of real traffic do. For example, consider an ACL rule that only permits HTTP traffic from IP address 10.0.0.1:

match: $src\_ip = 10.0.0.1, dst\_port = 80$, action="ALLOW"

A probe packet with source address 10.0.0.1 and destination port 80 can trigger this rule. However, even the packet is successfully received, it may not mean the rule is correctly configured at the switch. For example, consider the above rule is prioritized by a ill-inserted rule:

match: $src\_ip = 10.0.0.1, dst\_port = *$, action="ALLOW"

The probe packet can still be received. However, Non-HTTP traffic, e.g., SSH, from 10.0.0.1 will also be allowed, violating the controller's policy. This is because the probe packets cannot exhaust all possibilities in the header space in order to detect such ill-inserted rules. Thus, to monitor the policy compliance of data plane, we still need to inspect the real packets.

2.2 Policy Compliance Model

Notations. A port p is defined as a pair $\langle SwitchID, PortID \rangle$, where $PortID \in \{1, 2, 3, \ldots, n, \bot\}$ is the local port ID, and $\bot$ represents the dropping port. A header h is defined as a point in the $\mathcal{H} = \{0, 1\}^L$ space. A header set H is defined as a subset $h \subset \mathcal{H}$. A flow f is defined as a pair $\langle h, p \rangle$, where h is the header of the flow, and p is the port where the flow enters the network. A rule r is defined as a tuple $\langle p_1, H, p_2 \rangle$, meaning that packets received from port p_1 with header $h \in H$ should be forwarded to port p_2. For a dropping rule, $p_2 = \langle SwitchID, \bot \rangle$. A link can be seen as a special kind of rule $\langle p_1, \mathcal{H}, p_2 \rangle$, meaning that packets forwarded to port p_1 of one switch will be received at port p_2 of another switch.

Packet Path. When a packet pkt of flow f is received at port p_1^{in} of S_1, S_1 looks up in its flow table. When the first rule $r = \langle p_1^{in}, H, p_1^{out} \rangle$ satisfying $h \in H$ is found, S_1 forwards pkt to port p_1^{out}, and applies the link rules so that pkt is received at port p_2^{in} of another switch S_2. This process continues until pkt reaches an output port p_n^{out} of switch S_n, such that either p_n^{out} is connected to an end host, or it is a dropping port. The path of flow f is defined as the sequence of traversed ports, i.e., $Path(\mathcal{R}, f) = \langle p_1^{in}, p_1^{out}, p_2^{in}, \ldots, p_n^{out} \rangle$.

Let $\mathcal{R}$ be the set of all rules in the network (including the link rules), and $\mathcal{R}'$ be the counterpart that is actually enforced by switches. The policy compliance of data plane is defined as follows.

DEFINITION 1. *The data plane is said to be policy compliant iff $Path(\mathcal{R}', f) = Path(\mathcal{R}, f)$ for every flow f in the network, where $\mathcal{R}$ and $\mathcal{R}'$ are the set of rules configured by the controller and enforced by switches, respectively.*

VeriDP is aimed to verify the policy compliance of the SDN data plane according to the above definition. Note that there are cases that $\mathcal{R}' \neq \mathcal{R}$ but $Path(\mathcal{R}', f) = Path(\mathcal{R}, f)$ for all f. We do not consider it as a fault since the forwarding behaviors remain the same. Specifically, Definition 1 allows us to detect common faults on the data plane, including black holes, access violation, and loops:

Black Holes. In this case, there exists a flow f, such that $Path(\mathcal{R}', f) = \langle p_1^{in}, p_1^{out}, p_2^{in}, \ldots, p_m^{in}, \bot \rangle$, meaning that the flow is dropped by a switch that receives f from port p_m^{in}. Suppose f is destined to an host connected to port p_n^{out}, then we should have $Path(\mathcal{R}, f) = \langle p_1^{in}, p_1^{out}, p_2^{in}, \ldots, p_n^{in}, p_n^{out} \rangle \neq Path(\mathcal{R}, f)$.

Access Violation. In this case, there exists a flow f, such that $Path(\mathcal{R}', f) = \langle p_1^{in}, p_1^{out}, p_2^{in}, \ldots, p_m^{in}, p_m^{out} \rangle$, where p_m^{out} is connected to an end host that f is forbidden to reach. Then, we should have $Path(\mathcal{R}, f) = \langle p_1^{in}, p_1^{out}, p_2^{in}, \ldots, p_n^{in}, \bot \rangle$, where the switch with p_n^{in} should drop f. Obviously, $Path(\mathcal{R}', f) \neq Path(\mathcal{R}, f)$.

Loops. In this case, there exists a flow f, such that the length of $Path(\mathcal{R}', f)$ exceeds the maximum TTL, say $MaxTTL$. On

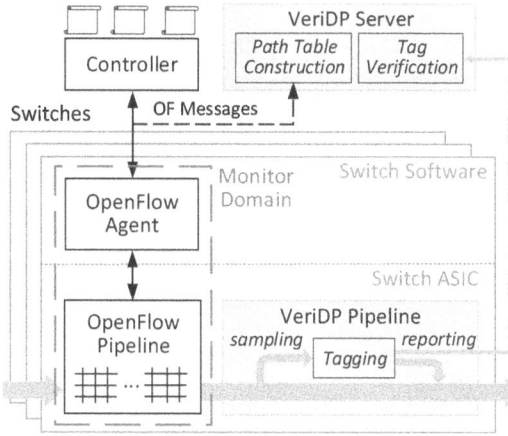

Figure 2: System architecture. The shaded components belong to VeriDP; those within the dashed rectangle are the components that VeriDP monitors.

the other hands, the length of $Path(\mathcal{R}, f)$ should be less than $MaxTTL$, and thus $Path(\mathcal{R}', f) \neq Path(\mathcal{R}, f)$.

3. DESIGN

As shown in Figure 2, VeriDP consists of two major components: the *VeriDP pipeline* on the data path, the *VeriDP server* on the control plane. The pipeline is responsible for sampling, tagging, reporting packets to the VeriDP server. The server intercepts the bidirectional OpenFlow messages exchanged between the controller and switches, in order to construct the *path table*, which records all header-to-tag mappings. With the path table, the server verifies reported packets sent from switches. The dashed rectangle represents the domain that VeriDP monitors, *i.e.*, VeriDP is expected to detect the faults caused by the components inside the domain. The monitor domain includes: (1) the OpenFlow agent that terminates the OpenFlow channel, and (2) the OpenFlow pipeline that manages the hardware flow table and forwards packets through table lookups.

3.1 VeriDP Pipeline

The VeriDP pipeline is responsible for generating tags for packets at entry switches, updating tags for packets at core switches, and reporting packet headers and tags to the controller at exit switches. The VeriDP pipeline is implemented in a switch's fast path, separated from the OpenFlow pipeline. The reason is avoid faults caused by OF flow tables to propagate into the tagging module. Since a typical switch can contain a cascade of flow tables, each of which may hold thousands flow entries, flow entries used for tagging may be override by other rules, replaced when flow table is full, and even incorrectly modified/deleted by applications.

The VeriDP pipeline processing is shown in Algorithm 1. The entry switch initializes the packet tag to zero, and the ttl to the maximum path length (Line 1-3). Each switch updates the tag as:

$$tag = tag \oplus \mathtt{hash}(inport \| switchID \| output) \quad (1)$$

, and decrements the ttl value by one (Line 4-5). When the packet is output to an edge port connected with an end host, output to the dropping port $\perp$, or its ttl hits zero, the switch sends a *tag report* to the server (Line 6-7). Here, a tag report is a 4-tuple $\langle inport, outport, header, tag \rangle$, where *inport/outport* are the entry/exit port of the packet; *header* is a portion of packet header

---

Algorithm 1: $\mathtt{Tag}(S, x, y, p)$

Input: S: the switch ID; x/y: the local input/output port ID of packet p, which is received from the OpenFlow pipeline.

1 **if** $\langle S, x \rangle$ *is an edge port* **then**
2    $p.tag \leftarrow 0$; // initialize the tag
3    $p.ttl \leftarrow \mathtt{MAX\_PATH\_LENGTH}$; // initialize the ttl
4 $p.tag \leftarrow p.tag \oplus \mathtt{hash}(x\|S\|y)$; // update the tag
5 $p.ttl \leftarrow p.ttl - 1$; // decrement the ttl
6 **if** $\langle S, y \rangle$ *is an edge port or* $y = \perp$ *or* $p.ttl = 0$ **then**
7    $\mathtt{Report}(inport, \langle S, y \rangle, p.header, p.tag)$; // send report

---

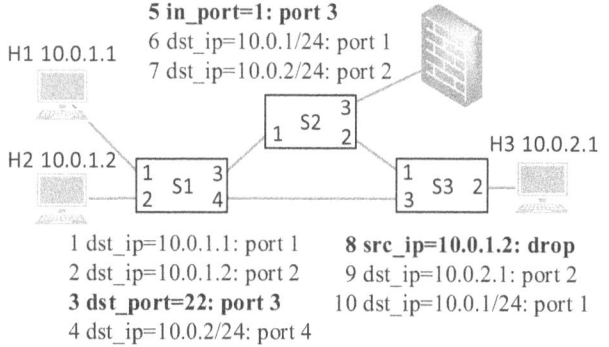

Figure 3: A simple example for path table construction. The network consists of three switches and a total of 10 rules.

(*e.g.*, TCP 5-tuple); *tag* is the tag of the packet. One thing to note is that switches should send tag reports for dropped and looped packets. This is necessary to ensure the visibility of verification server into black holes and loops.

3.2 VeriDP Server

The VeriDP server is responsible for parsing and verifying tag reports sent by switches. Central to the VeriDP server is the *path table*, which maps a pair of $\langle inport, outport \rangle$ a list of paths that enter the network at *inport* and exit at *outport*. Each path is again a pair of $\langle headers, tag \rangle$, where *headers* is a set of headers allowed for the path, and *tag* is the tag represents the path.

For a concrete example, consider the toy network in Figure 3. Rule 3 redirects all SSH traffic to $S2$, and Rule 4 forwards all other packets towards $10.0.2/24$ to $S3$. Rule 5 directs all traffic from port 1 to the middlebox. Rule 8 at switch $S3$ drops all traffic from $H2$. Other rules are plain forwarding rules ensuring connectivity. Table 1 is a part of the path table for this topology.

3.2.1 Representing the Header Set

A problem for constructing path table is how to represent header sets. A straightforward way is to use wildcard expressions, just as in Header Space Analysis [15] and ATPG [25]. However, wildcard expressions are suitable for representing suffix, while very inefficient for representing arbitrary header set. For example, the header set for $dst\_port \neq 22$ in the second row of Table 1 is a union of 16 wildcard expressions. In addition, wildcard expressions have a poor support of set operation like union, conjunction, and complement. For a typical network of tens of switches, each of which has thousands of flow rules, a huge number of wildcard expressions are needed to represent all the possible packet sets. According to [13], characterizing the Stanford backbone network (16 switches) needs 652 million wildcard expressions.

Inspired by the previous work [24], we decide to use the Binary Decision Diagrams (BDDs) [7] to represent header sets. BDD is an efficient data structure for Boolean expressions, and has a better

Table 1: Part of the path table for Figure 3. $[\cdot]$ represents the hash function.

inport	outport	headers	tag
$\langle S_1, 1\rangle$	$\langle S_3, 2\rangle$	$src\_ip = 10.0.1.1, dst\_ip = 10.0.2.1, dst\_port = 22$	$[1\|\|S_1\|\|3] \oplus [1\|\|S_2\|\|3] \oplus [3\|\|S_2\|\|2] \oplus [1\|\|S_3\|\|2]$
		$src\_ip = 10.0.1.1, dst\_ip = 10.0.2.1, dst\_port \neq 22$	$[1\|\|S_1\|\|4] \oplus [3\|\|S_3\|\|2]$
$\langle S_1, 2\rangle$	$\langle S_3, \bot\rangle$	$src\_ip = 10.0.1.2, dst\_ip = 10.0.2.1, dst\_port = 22$	$[2\|\|S_1\|\|3] \oplus [1\|\|S_2\|\|3] \oplus [2\|\|S_2\|\|2] \oplus [1\|\|S_3\|\|\bot]$
		$src\_ip = 10.0.1.2, dst\_ip = 10.0.2.1, dst\_port \neq 22$	$[2\|\|S_1\|\|4] \oplus [3\|\|S_3\|\|\bot]$

Algorithm 2: $\texttt{Traverse}(inport, \langle S, x\rangle, H, t)$

Input: $inport$: the input port of the header; $\langle S, x\rangle$: the currently visited port; H: the header set; t: the tag

1   $\bar{H} \leftarrow H$; // headers of dropped packets
2   $H \leftarrow H \wedge P_x^A$; // ACL predicate of port x
3   **foreach** *port y of switch S* **do**
4      $\hat{H} = H \wedge P_y^F$ // FWD predicate of port y
5   **if** $\hat{H} \neq \emptyset$ **then**
6         $H \leftarrow H - \hat{H}$;
7         $\hat{H} = \hat{H} \wedge P_y^A$ // ACL predicate of port y
8   **if** $\hat{H} \neq \emptyset$ **then**
9            $\bar{H} \leftarrow \bar{H} - \hat{H}$;
10           $t \leftarrow t \oplus \texttt{hash}(x\|\|S\|\|y)$ // update the tag
11   **if** $\langle S, y\rangle$ *is an edge port* **then**
12              $\texttt{Insert}(inport, \langle S, y\rangle, \hat{H}, t)$;
13   **else**
14              $\texttt{Traverse}(inport, \texttt{Link}(\langle S, y\rangle), \hat{H}, t)$;

15   $t \leftarrow t \oplus \texttt{hash}(x\|\|S\|\|\bot)$;
16   $\texttt{Insert}(inport, \langle S, \bot\rangle, \bar{H}, t)$;

Algorithm 3: $\texttt{Verify}(inport, outport, header, tag)$

Input: $inport/outport$: the input/output port of the packet; $header$: the header of the packet; tag: the tag of the packet.
Output: True (pass), or False (fail).

1   **foreach** $p \in \texttt{PathTable}(inport, outport)$ **do**
2   **if** $header \prec p.headers$ **then**
3   **if** $tag = p.tag$ **then**
4   **return** True; // the path is correct
5   **else**
6   **return** False; // the path is wrong

7   **return** False; // the packet should not reach here

---

support of set operations. With BDDs, we can expect to significantly reduce the size of path table.

3.2.2 Constructing the Path Table

We show how to construct the path table from a configuration similar to the Stanford backbone network configuration [3]. For simplicity, we assume the configuration files have already been transformed into a set of predicates using the method in [24]. For each input port x, there is an ACL predicate P_x^A, meaning that packets that satisfy P_x^A are allowed to input from port x. Similarly, for each output port y, there is an ACL predicate P_y^A, meaning that packets that satisfy P_y^A are allowed to output to port y. Finally, each outport y also has a FWD (forwarding) predicate P_y^F which guard which packets will be forwarded to port y.

Algorithm 2 summarizes the process of constructing path table from the above predicates. For each edge port connected with end hosts, we inject a header set H initialized to all-headers (*i.e.*, a BDD of True), and a tag t initialized to zero. When the header H is received at a port $\langle S, x\rangle$, the algorithm intersect H with the ACL predict of port x (Line 2), and then iteratively intersect the resultant header set $\hat{H}$ with the forwarding rules of all output ports (Line 3-4). For each port y that intersection is non-empty, the header set $\hat{H}$ is intersected further with the ACL rules of y (Line 5-7). If $\hat{H}$ is still non-empty, the algorithm updates the tag t, and either inserts an path entry if y is an edge port, or recursively calls the algorithm with the new header and tag (Line 8-14). If there are still headers that are not forwarded to any ports (recorded by $\bar{H}$), they would be dropped, and the algorithm updates the tag and inserts an entry (Line 15-16).

3.2.3 Verifying the Tags

Algorithm 3 specifies the simple process of tag verification. On receiving a tag report $\langle inport, outport, header, tag\rangle$, the server looks up in the path table with index $\langle inport, outport\rangle$, and for each path p, it tries to match $header$ with the header set of path p (Line 1-2). If matched, tag is compared with the tag of path p. The verification succeeds if these tags are equal (meaning that the packet followed the right path), or fails otherwise (Line 3-6). If no matched path is found (meaning that the packet should not have reached here), then the verification also fails (Line 7).

Let us turn back to Figure 3, and assume H_1 sends a packet to port 22 of H_3. The packet should take the path of $S_1 \rightarrow S_2 \rightarrow S_2 \rightarrow S_3$, and the tag should be $[1\|\|S_1\|\|3] \oplus [1\|\|S_2\|\|3] \oplus [3\|\|S_2\|\|2] \oplus [1\|\|S_3\|\|2]$. With $(\langle S_1, 1\rangle, \langle S_3, 2\rangle)$ as the index, the server would find two paths: one for $dst\_port = 22$ and the other for $dst\_port \neq 22$. The header of the packet would match the packet set of the first path. If the tag of the packet is the same with that of that path, the verification succeeds. Now consider that rule $R3$ fails. Then, the packet will take the path of $S_1 \rightarrow S_3$, and the tag would be $[1\|\|S_1\|\|4] \oplus [3\|\|S_3\|\|2]$, disagreeing with that of the path.

3.3 Sampling

Tagging and verifying every packet in the network can incur a large overhead. This overhead can be made significantly smaller since packets of the same flow will very likely experience the same forwarding behaviors. In this paper, we use a simple method which samples packets based on flows at entry switches. Each flow f is associated with a parameter $T_s^f > 0$, termed the *sampling interval*. The entry switch S of f maintains the last sampling instant t^f. For each packet received by S at time t, if $t - t^f > T_s^f$, S marks the packet and updates $t^f \leftarrow t$.

4. IMPLEMENTATION AND EVALUATION

4.1 Implementation

Packet Format. VeriDP needs each data packet to carry three additional elements: marker, tag, and inport. Here, marker is just 1 bit indicating whether the packet is sampled for verification or not; tag is the XORs of the lower 16 bits of hash output (currently we use CRC32); inport is the input port of the packet: 10 bits for switch ID, and 6 bits for local port ID. Thus, VeriDP currently can support 1024 switches, each of which can have up to 63 ports (one reserved for drop port). We put the 1-bit marker into the IP TOS field, and use two VLAN tags[1] to carry `tag` and `inport`. Finally, tag reports are sent to the verification server using UDP packets, each carrying four fields, *i.e.*, `inport`, `outport`, `header`, `tag`.

VeriDP Server. The server is responsible for constructing the path table based on network configuration, and searching the path table for tag verification. The path table construction is based on codes from [24], which iterates over all possible paths in the network to detect bugs (*e.g.*, black holes, loops) in the configuration files. We modify the codes by computing the tag for each path using Eq(1) to construct the path table. In addition, we add a virtual dropping port to each switch, and compute paths that end at this dropping port (*i.e.*, the header sets corresponding to headers that should be dropped by this switch). Before looking up in the path table, we first construct a BDD predicate from the *header* field in the tag report. To determine whether *header* $\prec$ *p.headers* (Line 2 in Algorithm 3), we check whether the intersection of their BDD representation is not `False`.

VeriDP Pipeline. The VeriDP pipeline is responsible for sampling and marking packets, updating tags for marked packets, and sending tag reports to the VeriDP server. We implement the VeriDP pipeline with both the CPqD OpenFlow-1.3 software switch [2] and ONetSwitch [12], a hardware SDN switch we previously built. For the software switch, the VeriDP pipeline functions after all actions have been executed on a packet, and before the packet is sent out. For the hardware switch, the VeriDP and OpenFlow pipeline are both implemented using the FPGA resource. Since it requires switches to maintain the sampling instance for each physical flow, we have not yet implemented the sampling components on the hardware switch due to limit of time.

4.2 Correctness

We use Mininet [4] to emulate a $k = 4$ fat tree topology, and use `pingall` to establish routes between each pair of end hosts. Both the verification server and the Mininet run on the same PC, with Intel i3 3.4GHz CPU and 8GB Memory.

Black Holes. We initiate a UDP flow from one host $H1$ to another host $H2$, at a rate of 100 packets/sec. We set up the verification server and set the sampling interval to 0.1 second. At 15.8 seconds, we manually remove the forwarding rule for $H2$ from the flow table of a switch on the path, in order to simulate a black hole. The effect is shown in Figure 4(a).

Access Violations. Suppose S is the access switch of a host $H2$. We manually add an ACL rule to let S block all packets from another host $H1$. Then, we set up the verification server and initiate a UDP flow from $H1$ towards $H2$. The sampling interval and packet rate is still set to 0.1 second and 100 packets/sec, respectively. At 17.2 seconds, we manually remove the ACL rule from the flow table of S to simulate an access violation. The effect is shown in Figure 4(b).

4.3 Performance

Verification Throughput. We saturate the verification server with tag reports, and measure how many can the server process per second. For the $k = 4$ fat tress, we observe the throughput is around 4×10^6 verifications/sec. We also use the topology of the Stanford backbone network, which consists of 16 routers and 10 switches. We observe a lower throughput of 0.7×10^6 verifications/sec. S-

Table 2: Processing delay of the VeriDP pipeline and native Open-Flow pipeline on the hardware switch.

	Packet Size (bytes)				
	128	256	512	1024	1500
VeriDP (μs)	0.19	0.20	0.20	0.20	0.19
Native (μs)	5.62	8.63	14.65	26.69	37.88
Overhead	3.41%	2.31%	1.32%	0.73%	0.50%

ince the verification is still single-threaded without optimization, we expect a higher throughput with multi-threading in the future.

For the above verification, we generate the configuration with simple `pingall`. Therefore, only shortest paths are computed for each pair of hosts, *i.e.*, there is only one entry for each inport-outport pair in the path table, and Algorithm 3 only needs to check one entry. In real networks, there may be multiple paths between each pair of hosts, and packets with different headers can traverse via different paths. Thus, we continue to measure how many linear searches will Algorithm 3 perform in real networks.

Real Network Policies. We construct the path table with the configuration files of the Stanford backbone network [3] and Internet2 [5]. The Stanford network consists of 757,170 forwarding rules, and 1584 ACL rules; Internet2 has 126,017 forwarding rules without ACL rules. The time to construct the path table is 3830 ms for Stanford network, and 1327 ms for Internet2. We count the number of paths per inport-outport pair. The distribution is reported in Figure 5. We can see that the number of paths for each entry is relatively small, meaning that Algorithm 3 only needs a few time of searches to match the header (if the header can be matched).

4.4 Overhead

Our implementation of VeriDP on the hardware switch can process packets at line speed (1Gbps). We use simulation to find that it takes 24 clock cycles to tag a packet. As the FPGA has a frequency of 125MHz, the additional delay is $24 \times \frac{1}{125 \times 10^6} = 0.192 \mu s$ per hop. Then, we send packets to one port of the switch, receive them from another one, and record the elapsed times. Let $T1$ be the elapsed time for native switch with OpenFlow pipeline only, and $T2$ be that with the modified switch with OpenFlow+VeriDP pipeline. Then, the processing delay of VeriDP pipeline is $\Delta T = T2 - T1$. Table 2 reports the value of ΔT, $T1$, and the overhead $\Delta T/T2$, for packet sizes from 64 bytes to 1500 bytes. Table 2 reports the delay of VeriDP pipeline, native OpenFlow pipeline, and the relative overhead. We can see that the delay of VeriDP pipeline is around $0.20 \mu s$, agreeing with the simulation results. Besides, the overhead drops when packet size increases, and is strictly less than 5%.

5. RELATED WORK

Recently there are many verification tools proposed for SDN [11]. We broadly classify them into two groups: *control plane verification* and *data plane verification*.

Control Plane Verification. Some tools are aimed to check the correctness of network configuration files. **Anteater** [19] models key network invariants (reachability, loop-freedom, black-hole-freedom, etc.) as SAT problems, and uses general solvers to check them. **Header Space Analysis** [15, 14] represents packet headers as points in n-bit space, and switches as transform functions that operate on the space. By analyzing the composite transform functions of switches, Header Space Analysis can check whether the key invariants are satisfied. **VeriFlow** [16] can incrementally check whether a new rule will violate the network invariants in real time. **NoD** [18] allows operators to check the correctness of net-

---

[1] Double VLAN tags are supported by 802.1ad [1]; each tag consists of 12 bits VLAN ID, which can be used to carry our data.

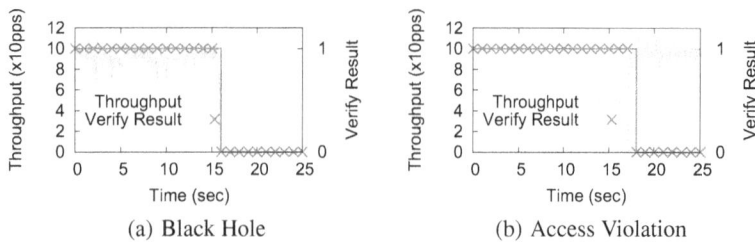

(a) Black Hole (b) Access Violation

Figure 4: Example detection of black hole and access violation with VeriDP.

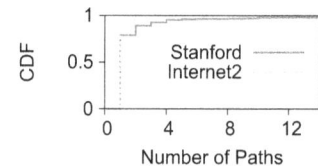

Figure 5: CDF of number of paths per inport-outport pair in the Stanford backbone network and Internet2.

work configuration at a higher abstraction (termed beliefs). The above tools are orthogonal to VeriDP which checks the compliance of data plane to network policies. They complement VeriDP by ensuring the network polices are correct, a premise for VeriDP to detect bugs.

Data Plane Verification. ATPG [25] generates a minimum number of probe packets to trigger all rules in the network. However, it only checks the reception of probe packets, without verifying their trajectories which are vital to configuration correctness. **SDN Traceroute** [6] enables the SDN controller to trace the trajectory of a flow, also based on probe packets. A limitation of them is that real packets may experience different forwarding behaviors with probe packets, making the verification results less convincing. Packet trajectory tracers like **PathletTracer** [27], **PathQuery** [21], and **CherryPick** [23] let each switch to imprint path information into packet headers, so that packet trajectories can be decoded by the receivers. However, packet trajectories by themselves are not very useful unless we know whether they are correct. In contrast, VeriDP not only traces packet trajectories, but also enables the controller to reason about whether the trajectories are compliant with high-level policies.

6. CONCLUSION AND FUTURE WORK

This paper presented VeriDP, a new tool to monitor the policy compliance of SDN data plane. VeriDP checks whether packet forwarding behaviors are agreeing with the network configuration files, based on packet tagging. We implemented VeriDP on both software and hardware switches to demonstrate its feasibility, and used emulation to show it can detect common data plane faults like black holes and access violation. Our future work includes designing a fault localization method to pinpoint root causes when policy incompliance is detected.

Acknowledgement. The authors would like to thank all the anonymous reviewers for their comments. This work is supported by NSFC (No. 61402357), the China Postdoctoral Science Foundation (2015M570835), the Fundamental Research Funds for the Central Universities, and the open project of Science and Technology on Information Transmission and Dissemination in Communication Networks Laboratory (ITD-U14001/KX142600008).

7. REFERENCES

[1] 802.1ad - Provider Bridges. http://www.ieee802.org/1/pages/802.1ad.html.

[2] CPqD: The OpenFlow 1.3 compatible user-space software switch. http://cpqd.github.io/ofsoftswitch13/.

[3] Hassel, the header space library. https://bitbucket.org/peymank/hassel-public.

[4] Mininet. http://mininet.org/.

[5] The Internet2 Observatory. http://www.internet2.edu/research-solutions/research-support/observatory/.

[6] K. Agarwal, E. Rozner, C. Dixon, and J. Carter. SDN traceroute: Tracing SDN forwarding without changing network behavior. In *HotSDN*, 2014.

[7] R. E. Bryant. Graph-based algorithms for boolean function manipulation. *IEEE Transactions on Computers*, 100(8):677–691, 1986.

[8] S. K. Fayazbakhsh, L. Chiang, V. Sekar, M. Yu, and J. C. Mogul. Enforcing network-wide policies in the presence of dynamic middlebox actions using flowtags. In *USENIX NSDI*, 2014.

[9] N. Handigol, B. Heller, V. Jeyakumar, D. Maziéres, and N. McKeown. Where is the debugger for my software-defined network? In *HotSDN*, 2012.

[10] N. Handigol, B. Heller, V. Jeyakumar, D. Mazieres, and N. McKeown. I know what your packet did last hop: Using packet histories to troubleshoot networks. In *USENIX NSDI*, 2014.

[11] B. Heller, C. Scott, N. McKeown, S. Shenker, A. Wundsam, H. Zeng, S. Whitlock, V. Jeyakumar, N. Handigol, J. McCauley, et al. Leveraging SDN layering to systematically troubleshoot networks. In *HotSDN*, 2013.

[12] C. Hu, J. Yang, H. Zhao, and J. Lu. Design of all programmable innovation platform for software defined networking. In *Open Networking Summit*, 2014.

[13] T. Inoue, T. Mano, K. Mizutani, S.-i. Minato, and O. Akashi. Rethinking packet classification for global network view of software-defined networking. In *IEEE ICNP*, 2014.

[14] P. Kazemian, M. Chan, H. Zeng, G. Varghese, N. McKeown, and S. Whyte. Real time network policy checking using header space analysis. In *USENIX NSDI*, 2013.

[15] P. Kazemian, G. Varghese, and N. McKeown. Header space analysis: Static checking for networks. In *USENIX NSDI*, 2012.

[16] A. Khurshid, W. Zhou, M. Caesar, and P. Godfrey. Veriflow: Verifying network-wide invariants in real time. In *USENIX NSDI*, 2013.

[17] M. Kuzniar, P. Peresini, M. Canini, D. Venzano, and D. Kostic. A SOFT way for openflow switch interoperability testing. In *ACM CoNEXT*, 2012.

[18] N. P. Lopes, N. Bjørner, P. Godefroid, K. Jayaraman, and G. Varghese. Checking beliefs in dynamic networks. In *USENIX NSDI*, 2015.

[19] H. Mai, A. Khurshid, R. Agarwal, M. Caesar, P. Godfrey, and S. T. King. Debugging the data plane with Anteater. In *ACM SIGCOMM*, 2011.

[20] N. McKeown, T. Anderson, H. Balakrishnan, G. Parulkar, L. Peterson, J. Rexford, S. Shenker, and J. Turner. OpenFlow: enabling innovation in campus networks. *ACM SIGCOMM Computer Communication Review*, 38(2):69–74, 2008.

[21] S. Narayana, J. Rexford, and D. Walker. Compiling path queries in software-defined networks. In *HotSDN*, 2014.

[22] G. Pickett. Staying persistent in software defined networks. In *Black Hat Briefings*, 2015.

[23] P. Tammana, R. Agarwal, and M. Lee. CherryPick: Tracing packet trajectory in software-defined datacenter networks. In *SOSR*, 2015.

[24] H. Yang and S. S. Lam. Real-time verification of network properties using atomic predicates. In *IEEE ICNP*, 2013.

[25] H. Zeng, P. Kazemian, G. Varghese, and N. McKeown. Automatic test packet generation. In *ACM CoNEXT*, 2012.

[26] H. Zeng, S. Zhang, F. Ye, V. Jeyakumar, M. Ju, J. Liu, N. McKeown, and A. Vahdat. Libra: Divide and conquer to verify forwarding tables in huge networks. In *USENIX NSDI*, 2014.

[27] H. Zhang, C. Lumezanu, J. Rhee, N. Arora, Q. Xu, and G. Jiang. Enabling layer 2 pathlet tracing through context encoding in software-defined networking. In *HotSDN*, 2014.

Links as a Service (LaaS):
Guaranteed Tenant Isolation in the Shared Cloud

Eitan Zahavi
Mellanox Technologies
eitan@mellanox.com

Alexander Shpiner
Mellanox Technologies
alexshp@mellanox.com

Ori Rottenstreich
Princeton University
orir@cs.princeton.edu

Avinoam Kolodny
Technion
kolodny@ee.technion.ac.il

Isaac Keslassy
VMWare & Technion
isaac@ee.technion.ac.il

ABSTRACT

The most demanding tenants of shared clouds require complete isolation from their neighbors, in order to guarantee that their application performance is not affected by other tenants. Unfortunately, while shared clouds can offer an option whereby tenants obtain dedicated servers, they do not offer any network provisioning service, which would shield these tenants from network interference.

In this paper, we introduce *Links as a Service (LaaS)*, a new abstraction for cloud service that provides isolation of network links. Each tenant gets an exclusive set of links forming a virtual fat-tree, and is guaranteed to receive the exact same bandwidth and delay as if it were alone in the shared cloud. Consequently, each tenant can use the forwarding method that best fits its application. Under simple assumptions, we derive theoretical conditions for enabling LaaS without capacity over-provisioning in fat-trees. New tenants are only admitted in the network when they can be allocated hosts and links that maintain these conditions. LaaS is implementable with common network gear, tested to scale to large networks and provides full tenant isolation at the worst cost of a 10% reduction in the cloud utilization.

Keywords

Data centers; High performance computing; Tenant isolation

1. INTRODUCTION

Many owners of private data centers would like to move to a shared multi-tenant cloud, which can offer a reduced cost of ownership and better fault-tolerance. For some of these tenants it is vital that their applications will not be affected by other tenants, and will keep exhibiting the same performance[1] [11,36,37]. For example, a banking application may need to roll-up all accounts data overnight,

---

[1]By *performance*, we refer to the inverse of either the total application run-time, including both the computation and

ANCS '16, March 17-18, 2016, Santa Clara, CA, USA

© 2016 ACM. ISBN 978-1-4503-4183-7/16/03...$15.00

DOI: http://dx.doi.org/10.1145/2881025.2881028

and a weather prediction software should similarly complete within a highly predictable time. For such tenants, run-time predictability is a key requirement.

Unfortunately, distributed applications often suffer from unpredictable performance when run on a shared cloud [12, 27]. This unpredictable performance is mainly caused by two factors: *server sharing* and *network sharing* [7,14,17, 20,24,26,32,34,35,38,41,47,49,52–54,56]. The first factor, *server sharing*, is easily addressed by using bare-metal provisioning of servers, such that each server is allocated to a single tenant [3]. However, the second factor, *network sharing*, is much more difficult to address. When network links are shared by several tenants, network contention can significantly worsen the application performance if other tenant applications consume more network resources, e.g. if they simply want to benchmark their network or run a heavy backup [31]. This can of course prove even worse when other tenants purposely generate adversarial traffic for DoS or side-channel attacks [48].

As detailed in Section 2, current solutions either (a) require tenants to provide and adhere to a specific traffic matrix declared in advance, which often proves impractical [14, 56]; (b) follow the hose model by providing enough throughput for any set of admissible traffic matrices [12, 21, 54], but also significantly reduce the link bandwidth and burst size that can be allocated to each VM; or (c) attempt to track the current traffic matrix, but cannot guarantee constant performance [24,35,47,49,53]. In addition, while it is known that tailoring the packet forwarding method to the specific tenant application can increase its performance, none of the current cloud solutions allow multiple forwarding algorithms to co-exist on the same network without impacting performance.

In this paper, we introduce a simple and effective approach that eliminates any interference in the cloud network. This approach allows each tenant to use a network forwarding algorithm that is optimized for its own application. Keeping with the notion that good fences make good neighbors, we argue that the most demanding tenants should be provided with exclusive access to a subset of the data center links, such that each tenant receives its own dedicated fat-tree network. We refer to this cloud architecture model as *Links as a Service (LaaS)*. The LaaS model guarantees that these tenants can obtain the exact same bandwidth and delay as

---

communication times, or of the response time of online services.

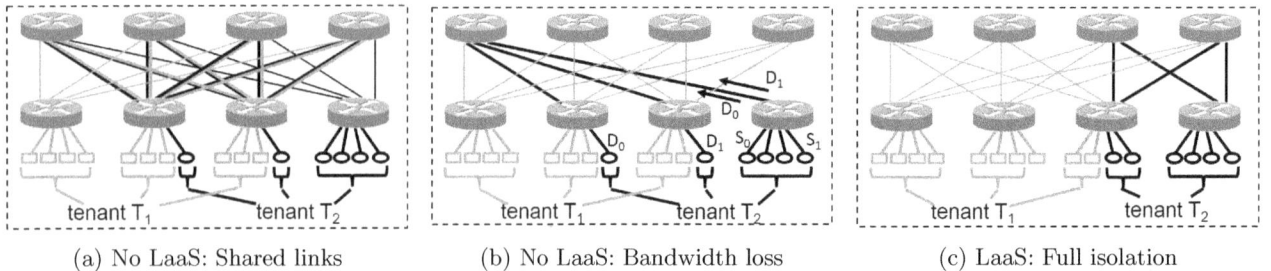

| (a) No LaaS: Shared links | (b) No LaaS: Bandwidth loss | (c) LaaS: Full isolation |

Figure 1: Two tenants hosted on a cloud. (a) Their traffic interferes on many shared links. (b) There are no shared links, but the second tenant cannot service an admissible traffic from S_0 and S_1 to D_0 and D_1. (c) Under LaaS conditions of tenant placement and link allocation, the network can service any admissible tenant traffic demands.

if they were alone in the shared cloud, independently of the number of additional tenants. We show that allocation of links to tenants is cost-effective and implementable by using common hardware. Note that LaaS can similarly support a relaxed model that splits physical links into time-domain-multiplexed channels. This relaxed model allows multiple tenants per server, but requires accurate packet pacing [29] not provided by common hardware today.

While the LaaS abstraction is attractive, Figure 1 illustrates why it can be a challenge to provide it given any arbitrary set of tenants. First, Fig. 1(a) illustrates a bare-metal allocation of distinct hosts (servers) to two tenants that does not satisfy the LaaS abstraction, since the tenants share common links. Likewise, the allocation of hosts and links in Fig. 1(b) also does not satisfy LaaS, even though no links are shared between tenants. This is because, regardless of the packet forwarding algorithm, internal traffic of the second tenant from the two hosts S_0 and S_1 in the right leaf switch to hosts D_0 and D_1 would need to share a common link, and so some admissible traffic patterns would not be able to obtain full bandwidth. Interestingly, for this host placement, we find that there is in fact no link allocation that can provide full bandwidth to all the admissible traffic patterns of both tenants. Finally, Fig. 1(c) fully satisfies the LaaS conditions. All tenants obtain dedicated hosts and links, and can service any admissible traffic demands between their nodes, independently of the traffic of other tenants. To generalize the above examples, we further analyze the fundamental requirements for providing LaaS guarantees to tenants in 2- and 3-level homogeneous fat-trees. Under minor assumptions, our analysis provides the necessary and sufficient conditions to guarantee the same bandwidth and delay performance over the shared fat-tree networks as when being alone in the shared cloud. These conditions are novel and greatly reduce the complexity for the online allocation algorithm presented in Section 3.

We implement a standalone LaaS scheduler that automates tenant placement on top of OpenStack, as well as configures an InfiniBand SDN controller to provide forwarding without interference. Our open-source code is made available online [1]. We show that using this code, our LaaS algorithm responds to tenant requests within a few milliseconds, even on a cloud of 11K nodes, i.e. several orders of magnitude faster than the time it takes to provisioning a new virtual machine. In addition, when the average tenant size is smaller than a quarter of the cloud size, we find that our LaaS algorithm achieves a cloud utilization of about 90%,

for various tenant-size distributions. For larger tenant sizes, our LaaS allocation converges to the maximal utilization obtained by a bare-metal scheduler that packs tenants without constraints. Finally, to demonstrate LaaS strength, we show performance improvements of 50%-200% for highly-correlated tenant traffic generated by a Bulk Synchronous Parallel (BSP) application relying on data exchanges along a virtual three-dimensional axis system. Thus, the performance improvement exceeds the utilization cost for such applications, uncovering an economic potential (Section 4).

While we focus, for brevity, on full-bisectional-bandwidth fat-trees, we show how LaaS can be extended to support over-provisioned (slimmed) fat-trees. We also describe how LaaS can fit more general cloud cases, e.g. when mixing highly-demanding tenants with regular tenants (Section 5).

Our evaluations show that LaaS is practical and efficient, and completely avoids inter-tenant performance dependence.

2. RELATED WORK

Application variability. Several studies about the variability of cloud services and HPC application performance were presented by [12, 13, 27, 31, 40, 51]. They show significant variability for such applications, which strengthens the motivation for using LaaS.

Network isolation. Specific high-dimensional tori supercomputers like IBM BlueGene, Cray XE6, and the Fujitsu K-computer provide scheduling techniques to isolate tenants [5, 13, 42]. However, they all rely on forming an isolated cube on 3 out of the 5- or 6-dimensional torus space, and thus cannot be used in clouds with fat-tree topologies. They also exhibit a significantly lower cluster utilization, measured as the amount of servers used over time, than the 90% utilization obtained by LaaS on fat-trees. Another approach, reduces the interference between jobs running on same fat-tree by applying hard placement constraints [33]. This work reduces but does not guarantee jobs isolation from each other.

Packet forwarding. Many architectures rely on Equal Cost Multiple Path (ECMP) [25] to spread the allocated tenant traffic and avoid the need to allocate exact bandwidth on each of the used physical links [12,30,46]. However, while ECMP load-balancing is able to balance the average bandwidth of many small bandwidth flows, it suffers from a heavy tail of the load distribution. When traffic contains a relatively small number of large flows, ECMP is known to provide poor load-balancing. Thus, other tenants will affect the application performance.

Silo [29] aims to provide guaranteed latency, bandwidth and burst size to multiple tenants for a worst-case traffic pattern, assuming that tenants do not optimize their forwarding scheme. Silo achieves its guarantees by applying accurate rate- and burst-size moderation to enforce centrally-calculated values obtained from network calculus. Unfortunately, Silo does not take forwarding into account. For instance, consider a tenant of 200 VMs placed across more than one 2-level sub-tree (which normally can contain thousands of VMs). If 100 VMs need to send traffic to the other VMs through the same uplink because of the forwarding rules, then each would be restricted to use at most 1/100th of the link bandwidth and 1/100th of the switch buffer size, which is unacceptable for current large tenants. LaaS allows the tenants to adapt their forwarding to the traffic pattern without introducing inter-tenant interference, thus allowing them to fully consume the full network bandwidth.

Time separation. Some systems like Cicade [34] accept the need for handling the varying nature of tenant traffic instead of relying only on the average demand. They assume that traffic demands change at a pace that is slow enough to enable them to react. Alternatively, scheduling the MapReduce shuffle stages was proposed by Orchestra [16]. A generalization of this approach that allows a tenant to describe its changing communication needs is suggested by Coflow [15]. On the same line of thought, scheduling at a finer grain was proposed by Hedera [7]. However, since these schemes propose a fair-share network bandwidth to the current set of applications, they actually change the performance of a tenant when new tenants are introduced. Even though fairness does improve, the tenant performance variability grows.

Tenant resource allocation. Cloud network performance has received significant attention over the last few years. An overview of the different proposals to allocate tenant network resources is provided by [38].

Virtual Network Embedding maps tenants' requested topologies and traffic matrix over arbitrary clusters [14,56]. However, tenants must know and declare their exact traffic demands which is mostly impractical. Moreover, valid embedding is calculated by variants of linear programming, which are known not to scale as the size of the data centers and number of tenants grow. In addition, as most of these solutions rely on the tenant traffic matrix, they consider only the average demands, falling short of representing the dynamic nature of the application traffic. For example, they prove problematic when an application alternates between several traffic permutations, each utilizing the full link bandwidth.

Other proposals, such as Topology Switching and Oktopus [12,54], propose an abstraction for the topology and traffic demands to be allocated to the tenants. They are similar to the hose model proposed for Virtual Private Networks in the context of WAN [8]. In addition, [10] attempts to provide a feedback-based fair-share bandwidth using edge-based rate-limiting. However, to guarantee tenant latency predictability and isolation, such solutions would need strict time-pacing of packets, small limits on allowed VM bandwidth and burst-size allocation, as shown in [29]. As mentioned above, these are impractical in current networks.

Another approach for isolation may rely on distributed rate limiting like [47], NetShare [35], ScondNet [24], Sea-wall [53], Gatekeeper [49] and Oktopus [12]. But distributed rate limiting at the network edge requires tenant-wide coordination to avoid bottlenecks due to load-imbalance. This coordination leads to response time in the order of milliseconds [30], while the life time of a traffic pattern for high-demanding applications may be 2 to 3 orders of magnitude shorter.

Fairness. FairCloud provides a generalization of the required fairness properties of the shared cloud network [45]. LaaS tenant isolation satisfies these requirements, and avoids the allocation complexity of the general case.

Application-based routing. The above schemes for network resource allocation ignore the fact that each tenant application may perform best with a different routing scheme. Routing algorithm types span a wide range. Some are completely static and optimized for MPI applications [22, 57]. Others rely on traffic-spreading techniques like ECMP [25], rely on traffic spray as in RPS or DeTail [18,58], use adaptive routing as proposed by DARD [55], or even rely on per-packet synchronized schemes like FastPass [43]. LaaS isolates the sub-topology of each tenant, and therefore allows each tenant to use the routing that maximizes its application performance. Without link isolation the different routing engines must continuously coordinate the actual bandwidth each one of them utilize from each link. It is clear that the involved complexity of such scheme renders it slow and impractical.

3. LAAS ALGORITHM

In this section, we describe online algorithms for *tenant placement* and *link allocation* in the LaaS scheduler. Online placement algorithms require the existing tenant placement to be maintained when a new job is placed, and therefore do not move existing tenants. Similarly we provide online link-allocation algorithms to avoid any traffic interruption when a new tenant is introduced. The algorithm we describe provably guarantees that a tenant will obtain a dedicated set of hosts and links, with the same bandwidth as in its own private data center. The algorithm relies on the required properties of the placement to trim the solution space and achieve fast results.

We first study 2-level fat-trees, and then generalize the results to 3 levels. We first present a *Simple* heuristic algorithm, and then extend it with a *LaaS* algorithm that achieves a better cloud utilization.

3.1 Isolation for 2-level Fat Trees

Consider a 2-level full-bisectional-bandwidth fat-tree topology, i.e. a Full Bipartite Graph between leaf switches and spine switches, as in Fig. 1 above. For brevity we denote Full Bipartite Graphs that make the fat-tree connections between switches at levels lvl_i and lvl_{i+1}: FBG_i. It is composed of r leaf switches, denoted L_i for each $i \in [1, r]$, and m spine switches. Each leaf switch is connected to $n \leq m$ hosts as required to meet the rearrangeably non-blocking condition for fat-trees [28].

Problem definition. Given a pre-allocation of tenants (with pre-assigned links and hosts), when a new tenant arrives with a request for N hosts, we need to find:

(i) Host placement: Find which free hosts to allocate to the new tenant, i.e. allocate N_i free hosts in each leaf i such that $N = \sum_{i=1}^{r} N_i$.

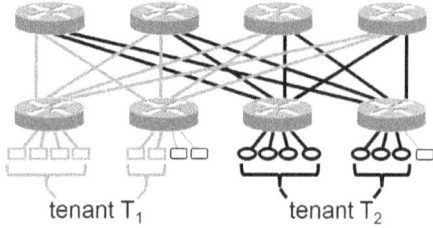

Figure 2: Two tenants of sizes 6 and 7 hosts placed by the *Simple* heuristic, where each tenant fills a number of complete sub-trees.

(ii) Link allocation: Find how to support the tenant traffic, i.e. allocate a set S_i of spines for each leaf i, such that the hosts of the new tenant in leaf i can exclusively use the links to S_i, and the resulting allocation can fully service any admissible traffic matrix.

We want to fit as many arriving tenants as possible into the cloud such that their host placement and link allocation obey the above requirements, and without changing pre-existing tenant allocations.

Simple heuristic algorithm. We first introduce a *Simple* heuristic algorithm, as basis for the discussion of our algorithm. It relies on a property of fat-trees and minimum-hop routing: if a single tenant is placed within a sub-tree, then traffic from other tenants will not be routed through that sub-tree. Note that for 2-level fat-trees a sub-tree is a leaf switch.

Let N denote the number of tenant hosts, and n the number of hosts per leaf. The *Simple* heuristic simply computes the minimal number s of leaf switches required for the tenant: $s = \lceil N/n \rceil$. Then, it finds s empty leaf switches to place the tenant hosts in. Finally, if $s > 1$, it allocates all the up-links leaving the s leaf switches; else, no such links are needed.

Fig. 2 illustrates the *Simple* algorithm, showing how tenant T_1 obtains a placement for $N = 6$ hosts. First, $s = \lceil 6/4 \rceil = 2$. Assuming T_1 arrives first, the two left leaves are available when it arrives, and they are used to host T_1. Also, all the up-links of these 2 leaf switches are allocated to T_1. When it arrives, tenant T_2 is similarly allocated the two right leaves and their up-links.

In the general case, any placement obtained by *Simple* supports any admissible traffic pattern. This is because the dedicated sub-network of the tenant is a single leaf switch if $s = 1$, and a 2-level fat-tree if $s > 1$, which is a folded-Clos network with $m \geq n$. It is well known that such a topology supports any admissible traffic pattern, because it meets the rearrangeable non-blocking criteria and the Birkhoff-von Neumann doubly-stochastic matrix-decomposition theorem [28].

LaaS placement analysis. This section describes a required condition on placement and sufficient condition on link allocation that are key to make the LaaS algorithm correct and efficient. The placement condition requires the allocation of N tenant hosts as Q leaves of D hosts and optionally additional leaf of $R \mid R < D$ hosts such that $N = QD + R$. The sufficient link allocation condition requires that the links of R spines connecting to the Q leaves and the optional single leaf of R hosts. A subset of size $D - R$ of these spines should connect just to the Q leaves.

Consider a single leaf i with N_i tenant hosts. In the analysis below, we make the following simplifying assumption: on every leaf switch, the number of leaf-to-spine links (and the corresponding number of spines) allocated to a tenant equals the number of its allocated hosts:

$$|S_i| = N_i. \tag{1}$$

Our simplifying assumption is based on the following intuition. On the one hand, for tenants occupying several leaves, if $|S_i| < N_i$, we may not be able to service all admissible traffic demands (since we may have up to N_i flows that need to exit leaf i, but only $|S_i|$ links to service them). On the other hand, allocating $|S_i| > N_i$, is wasteful, because the number of remaining spine switches would then be less than the number of available hosts, and therefore future tenants spanning more than one leaf may not be able to obtain enough links to connect their hosts.

Without loss of generality, we also make a notational assumption that the N_i's are sorted such that $0 < N_1 \leq N_2 \leq \cdots \leq N_t$, where t is the number of leaves connected to hosts allocated to the tenant.

We will now see that our assumptions lead (by a sequence of lemmas) to a simple rule that greatly simplifies the possible placements that need to be evaluated by our LaaS scheduling algorithm.

LEMMA 1. *The number of common spines that connect two leaves must at least equal their minimal number of allocated hosts:*

$$\forall i < j \in [1, t] : N_i = \min(N_i, N_j) \leq |S_i \cap S_j| \tag{2}$$

PROOF. Consider a traffic permutation among the tenant hosts. There are up to N_i full-link-capacity host-to-host flows going from L_i to L_j (or back). Since each flow has to use a different link and each link goes to a different spine switch, we will need at least N_i common spine switches in $|S_i \cap S_j|$. □

LEMMA 2. *The number of common spines that connect two leaves to a third must at least equal the minimal number of allocated hosts, either in the union of the first two leaves or in the third, i.e.* $\forall i, j, k \in [1, t] : \min(N_i + N_j, N_k) \leq |S_i \cup S_j|$.

PROOF. Let $c = \min(N_i + N_j, N_k)$. There are at most c flows going from L_k to either L_i or L_j (or back). Since each flow has to use a different link and each link goes to a different spine switch, we will need at least c spines in the union $S_i \cup S_j$ of the spines connected to the two leaves. □

LEMMA 3. *The number of allocated hosts in any leaf cannot exceed the number in the union of any two other leaves, i.e.* $\forall i \neq j \neq k \in [1, t] : N_i, N_j, N_k > 0 \rightarrow N_i + N_j \geq N_k$

PROOF. Assume the contrary: $N_i + N_j < N_k$. There are only two cases: $N_i \leq N_j < N_k$ or $N_j \leq N_i < N_k$. W.l.o.g., we assume the first. If so, $\min(N_i + N_j, N_k) = N_i + N_j$. By Lemma 1, to enable connectivity between N_i and N_j, they must have at least N_i spines in common: $|S_i \cap S_j| \geq N_i$. Substituting the above into Lemma 2 we obtain: $\forall i, j, k \in [1, t] : \min(N_i + N_j, N_k) = N_i + N_j \leq |S_i \cup S_j| = |S_i| + |S_j| - |S_i \cap S_j|$. But since $N_i = |S_i|$ and $N_j = |S_j|$ in LaaS by Equation (1), we get $0 \leq -|S_i \cap S_j|$. But $S_i \cap S_j$ is nonempty because otherwise traffic from hosts in leaf i to hosts in j wouldn't be able to pass. So we get a contradiction, thus $N_i + N_j \geq N_k$. □

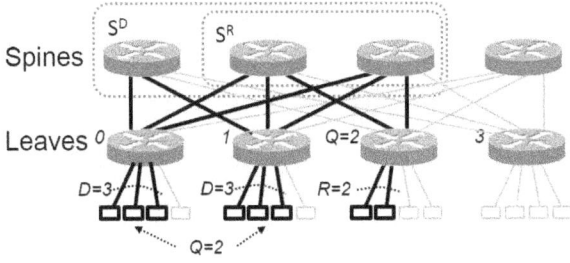

Figure 3: A tenant of $N = 8 = Q \cdot D + R$ hosts. To implement LaaS, there must be Q leaves of D hosts and optionally one leaf of $R < D$ hosts.

Necessary host placement. We will now provide two theorems showing necessary and sufficient conditions to get the LaaS conditions of tenant traffic isolation and support for any admissible traffic matrix. Interestingly, the first theorem requires *necessary conditions on the host placement*, while the second theorem provides *sufficient conditions on the link allocation*. We continue to assume throughout the rest of the paper that $|S_i| = N_i$ for all i, and $N_1 \leq N_2 \leq \cdots \leq N_t$.

THEOREM 1. *A necessary condition for LaaS is*

$$N_1 \leq N_2 = N_3 = \cdots = N_t, \qquad (3)$$

implying that all leaf switches of a tenant should hold the exact same number of hosts except for a potential smaller one.

PROOF. We show that $N_2 = N_t$. By Lemma 1, L_1 and L_2 must have at least $N_1 = |S_1|$ spines in common, i.e. $S_1 \subseteq (S_1 \cap S_2)$. Therefore, S_1 is a subset of S_2, so $|S_1 \cup S_2| = |S_2| = N_2$. By Lemma 3, when $i = 1$, $j = 2$ and $k = t$, $N_1 + N_2 \geq N_t$ thus $\min(N_1 + N_2, N_t) = N_t$. So, when N_t flows are sent from L_t to L_1 and L_2, we must have at least N_t common spines: $|S_1 \cup S_2| = N_2 \geq N_t$. But since $N_2 \leq N_t$, it follows that $N_2 = N_t$. □

Given Theorem 1, the tenant placement should follow the form: $N = Q \cdot D + R$, where Q is the number of repeated leaves with D hosts each, and we optionally add one unique leaf with a smaller number of hosts R. This notation follows the <u>D</u>ivisor, <u>Q</u>uotient and <u>R</u>emainder of N. This result is useful because it greatly simplifies the solution of the host placement problem defined above.

Fig. 3 demonstrates this result. It shows Q leaf switches of D hosts each, and optionally another leaf switch of $R < D$ hosts. We denote by S^D the set of spines connected by allocated links to the Q leaves of D hosts, and by S^R those that connect via allocated links to the optional leaf of R hosts.

Sufficient link allocation. We can now prove sufficient conditions on the link allocation to satisfy LaaS.

THEOREM 2. *A sufficient condition for LaaS is that the link allocation satisfies $\forall i \in [1, Q] : S_i = S^D$ and if $R > 0$: $S^R \subset S^D$, i.e. all the allocated leaf up-links of a given tenant go to the exact same set of spine switches (or a subset of it for the remainder leaf).*

PROOF. For the case $R = 0$, the link allocation above means there is a group of D spine switches that connect to all leaf switches. Thus the tenant sub-topology reduces to

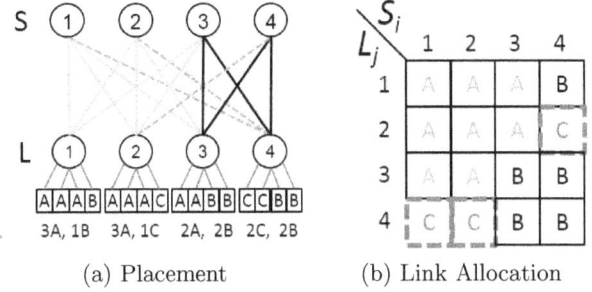

(a) Placement　　　　(b) Link Allocation

Figure 4: Illustration that a simple host placement is not sufficient, and a joint host placement and link allocation is necessary for LaaS. (a) All tenants satisfy the host placement necessary conditions, e.g. the placement of C is $3 = Q \cdot D + R = 2 \cdot 1 + 1$. A and B support any admissible traffic matrix by the sufficient link allocation conditions. (b) However, the link allocation for C is impossible. There is no way to find a common set of spines with free ports.

an *Full Bipartite Graph* (FBG) with $m' = D$ spine switches and $n' = D$ hosts per leaf. Since $m' = n'$ such topology is rearrangeable non-blocking folded-Clos which is known to support any admissible traffic matrix as mentioned above.

For the case of one additional leaf L_{j_R} of R hosts, we provide a constructive method for routing arbitrary permutations. We consider the FBG sub-topology formed by the tenant hosts and links, where L_{j_R} connects to all S^D spines. For this topology $m' = n' = D$ and $r' = Q + 1$. Again, $m' = n'$ so it is guaranteed by the rearrangeable non-blocking theorem that every full permutation of $n' \cdot r'$ flows is route-able. Routing is symmetric with respect to the spine switches. Moreover, to avoid congestion, each spine needs to carry exactly 1 flow from each leaf and 1 flow to each leaf. So any full permutation of our original topology where L_{j_R} has only R flows will be $D - R$ flows short. We extend these flows with $D - R$ flows going from L_{j_R} to L_{j_R}. Since these flows share the same leaf switch they must be routed through $D - R$ different spines. After completing the full permutation routing, and since all spines connect to all leaves, we swap between each spine that carries one of the added $D - R$ flows with a spine that is not included in S^R. As the links allocated to the extra flows are not needed, any permutation is fully routed by the original topology. □

A necessary host allocation is not sufficient. The above theorems provide us with guidelines for implementing LaaS. We now show that due to previous tenant allocations, a host placement as in Theorem 1 is not always sufficient to provide a needed link allocation as in Theorem 2. This is why Theorem 2 proves essential. If the link allocation cannot be found for a specific placement our algorithm will need to search for another host allocation.

LEMMA 4. *A host placement that meets Theorem 1 does not guarantee the existence of a link allocation that meets Theorem 2, and therefore does not guarantee LaaS.*

PROOF. We prove Lemma 4 by the example provided in Fig. 4. Three tenants are shown placed according to the provided heuristic of the previous section: A has $8 = 2 \cdot 3 + 2$ hosts, B has $5 = 2 \cdot 2 + 1$, and C has $3 = 1 \cdot 2 + 1$. We track allocated up-links of the leaf switches in a matrix where rows represent the leaf switches and columns represent the spines each port connects to. As can be observed, there is no possible link allocation for tenant C, since the leaves it is placed on do not have free links connected to any common spine. There is no link allocation possible for C even though it was placed according to the conditions of Theorem 1. The online link allocation algorithm for C (after A and B are placed) cannot allocate the links. In fact, even an offline version of link allocation - reassigning the links of A and B - cannot solve the problem once the placement of A and B does not change. □

According to Lemma 4, some tenant requests may be denied because the scheduler cannot find a proper link allocation. Thus any LaaS algorithm has to validate the feasibility of a link allocation for each legal host placement.

3.2 Isolation for 3-level Fat Trees

So far we have discussed the LaaS allocation for 2-level fat-trees. We now extend the results to 3-level fat-trees, which form the most common cloud topology [6, 9]. We use the notation of Extended Generalized Fat Trees (XGFT) [39], which defines fat-trees of h levels and the number of sub-trees at each level: $m_1, m_2, \ldots, m_h$. and the number of parent switches at each level: $w_1, w_2, \ldots, w_h$.

We consider three approaches to this problem: a *Simple* heuristics, a *Hierarchical* decomposition, and an *Approximated* scheme. We conclude with a description of the final *LaaS* algorithm that we implemented, relying on the *Approximated* scheme.

Simple heuristic for 3-level fat-trees. The *Simple* algorithm described in sub-section 'Simple heuristic algorithm' is easily extended to any fat-tree size. For an arbitrary XGFT, first define the number of hosts R_l under a sub-tree of level l: $R_0 = 0$, and $R_l = \prod_{i=1}^{l} m_i$. Given a tenant request for N hosts, *Simple* first determines the minimum level l_{min} of the tree that can contain all N tenant hosts:

$$l_{min} = \min \{l|\, (R_{l-1} < N) \wedge (R_l \geq N)\} \qquad (4)$$

and the number s of required sub-trees of level l_{min}: $s = \lceil N/R_{l_{min}-1} \rceil$. Then, it places the tenant hosts in s free sub-trees of level l_{min}. It also allocates to the tenant all the links internal to these s sub-trees; and if $s > 1$, it allocates as well all the links connecting the sub-trees to the upper level.

It is clear that the *Simple* heuristic algorithm, by rounding up the number of nodes, trades off cluster utilization for simplicity, non-fragmentation, and greater locality with lower hop distances. As we show in the evaluation section, the utilization obtained by this algorithm is low, making it potentially unacceptable to cloud vendors, so we keep looking for a better one.

Hierarchical decomposition. In this section we describe how LaaS can be provided to a 3-level fat-tree using a hierarchical decomposition approach following the recursive description of fat-trees in [44].

Fig. 5 shows an example of 3-level fat-tree. We denote the switches on the tree by their levels (from bottom up) lvl_1, lvl_2 and lvl_3. We show that for a LaaS link allocation to be feasible, the condition of Theorem 1 needs to hold not only for each 2-level sub-tree but also for each lvl_2 - lvl_3 Full Bipartite Graph (FBG_2) at the top of the tree. One of these FBGs is highlighted in Fig. 5.

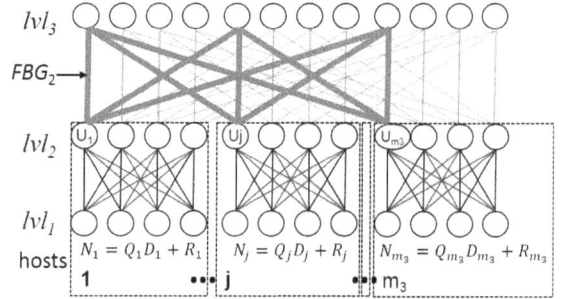

Figure 5: A 3-level fat-tree showing the host allocation on each 2-level sub-tree matching Theorem 1. One of the lvl_2 - lvl_3 Full Bipartite Graphs (FBG_2) is highlighted. We denote as U_j the maximal number of flows injected into this FBG_2 from the jth 2-level sub-tree.

As we showed in the previous sections, since the tenant traffic pattern may be completely contained within each 2-level tree, host allocation in each 2-level tree must adhere to Theorem 1. So the number of tenant hosts within the 2-level sub-tree j must be of the form $N_j = Q_j \cdot D_j + R_j$. Note that an allocation that fits in a single leaf switch also follows this scheme with $Q_j = 1$.

Fig. 5 depicts a Theorem 1-compliant host allocation within each of the 2-level sub-trees. It follows the form: $N_j = Q_j \cdot D_j + R_j | j \in \{1...m_3\}$. Note that the link assignment within the 2-level sub-trees must also adhere to Theorem 2 such that $S_j^R \subset S_j^D$. Consequently, the maximum number U_j of flows leaving the 2-level sub-tree from switch s can be either 0 in case $s \notin S_j^D$, Q_j in case $s \in S_j^D \setminus S_j^R$, or $Q_j + 1$ if $s \in S_j^R$.

When we consider the conditions required for the highlighted FBG_2 to support any admissible traffic pattern, it is strikingly similar to the analysis we provided for the 2-level fat-tree. For the 2-level tree we already proved that in order to support any admissible traffic pattern, the sequence of U_j values must meet the rule $U_1 \leq U_2 = U_3 = \cdots = U_{m_3}$. Applying the same to the 3-level tree we obtain a requirement for the assignments of U_j on each of the FBG_2. However, each one of the FBG_1 (there are m_3 such 2-level sub-trees) could select a different set of S_j^D and S_j^R. This means that a solution could allow each 2-level sub-tree to select a different set of FBG_2 to carry its flows, as long as the above rule is maintained for each FBG_2.

Unfortunately the above rule still allows a vast amount of legal tenant-placement and link-allocation possibilities, which make the full 3-level fat-tree LaaS problem too hard to be solved in practical time even on high-end processors. If we were to provide an optimal allocation we would conclude here that our problem is too hard. But our task is not to find the *optimal* solution, or even *any* solution at a specific iteration. Our target is to show that there is a simple enough algorithm that would be able to handle the online LaaS problem in reasonable time and with reasonable success rate such that the cluster utilization remains high and LaaS is guaranteed. We do that by applying a restriction on the solution space of the hierarchical decomposition.

Approximated algorithm. We provide a simpler algorithm that compromises cluster utilization in favor of reduction of the solution search space. Our approximation

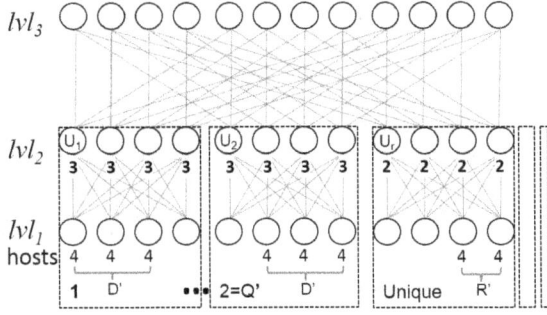

Figure 6: An example of host placement with $N = 32$ hosts on a 3-level fat-tree using the *Approximated* method. Using a notation similar to the 2-level fat-tree, this allocation is of the form: $Q' = 2$, $D' = 3$ and $R' = 2$.

requires the allocation to be symmetrical with respect to all the FBG_2, i.e. that the allocation on all the FBG_2 is identical and thus calculated just once. So the solution must use the same number of flows U_j leaving any one of the lvl_2 switches in the same 2-level sub-tree. Note that any allocation where the number of tenant hosts N_i connected to leaf switch i does not include all the hosts on that leaf switch $N_i < m_1$, will not utilize all the links from that switch to the upper-level switches. So only a subset of the lvl_2 switches in the same FBG_1 is going to pass traffic of that tenant. Thus if we now consider the lvl_2 to lvl_3 traffic, not all FBG_2 will see the same U_j. To avoid this we require that D is either 0 or m_1 for all 2-level sub-trees, except where the tenant fits within the same 2-level fat-tree and thus $U_j = 0$. As a consequence, if a tenant cannot fit within a single sub-tree, we round up its size to a multiple of m_1. The host placement can now be performed in complete leaf switches of m_1 hosts. For instance, if each leaf switch can hold 10 hosts, and a tenant requests $N = 267$ hosts, then we effectively allocate it $N' = m_1 \lceil N/m_1 \rceil = 270$ hosts.

Moreover, since the approximation in 3-level fat-tree allocates complete lvl_1 switches, it is equivalent to the 2-level LaaS problem: lvl_1 switches are equivalent to hosts, lvl_2 switches are like leaf switches and lvl_3 switches are like spines. Thus the approximated 3-level fat-tree LaaS problem has to comply to the same conditions as for the 2-level tree. We denote the allocation of full lvl_1 switches using a similar notation to the 2-level: Q' is the number of allocated 2-level sub-trees, each with $D' = Q$ leaves. Optionally there may be one additional 2-level sub-tree with R' allocated leaves. $N' = \lceil N/m_1 \rceil = Q' \cdot D' + R'$.

An example of such allocation for a tenant of 32 hosts on a 3-level fat-tree, with $m_1 = 4$ hosts per leaf, is provided in Fig. 6. On the left $Q' = 2$ sub-trees, the tenant uses $D' = 3$ leaves and thus $U_1 = U_2 = 3$ for all FBG_2. In addition a single unique sub-tree r with $R' = 2$ leaves is also allocated and thus $U_r = 2$ for all FBG_2. So all the FBG_2 are thus identical. Each one of them has to support Q' lvl_2 switches of $D' = 3$ flows and one lvl_2 switch with $R' = 2$ flows. These requirements meet the condition of Theorem 1 and thus may be feasible.

LaaS algorithm.

We now want to implement our final *LaaS* algorithm for concurrent host placement and link allocation in fat-trees.

Algorithm 1 FLAP($D, Q, R, l, l_e, r, \{ports\}, \{rl\}$)

```
1:  // find next Q size leaf
2:  for i = l to l_e do
3:      if |M[i]| >= Q then
4:          {nPorts} = {ports} ∩ M[i]
5:          if |nPorts| ≥ Q then
6:              {newRL} = {rl} ∪ i
7:              if r = D then
8:                  // found all repeated leaves
9:                  if findUniqueLeaf(R, l_s, l_e; {nPorts} {rl}) then
10:                     {D_PORTS} = {nPorts}
11:                     {D_L} = {newRL}
12:                     return true
13:                 end if
14:             else
15:                 j = i + 1; s = r + 1
16:                 if FLAP(D,Q,R,j,l_e,s,{nPorts},{newRL}) then
17:                     return true
18:                 end if
19:             end if
20:         end if
21:     end if
22: end for
23: return false
```

Algorithm 2 LAAS(N)

```
1:  // Try 1 level allocation
2:  if N ≤ m_1 then
3:      for l = 0 TO m_2 · m_3 − 1 do
4:          if FLAP(N, 1, 0, l, l, 0, {}, {}) then
5:              return true
6:          end if
7:      end for
8:  end if
9:  // Try 2 level allocation
10: if N ≤ m_1 · m_2 then
11:     for D = max(N, m_1) to 1 do
12:         Q = ⌊N/D⌋
13:         R = N − Q · D
14:         for l = 0 TO m_3 − 1 do
15:             if FLAP(D, Q, R, l · m_2, (l + 1) · m_2 − 1, 0, {}, {}) then
16:                 return true
17:             end if
18:         end for
19:     end for
20: end if
21: // Try 3 level allocation
22: U = ⌈N/m_1⌉
23: for D = max(U, m_2) to 1 do
24:     Q = ⌊U/D⌋
25:     R = U − Q · D
26:     if Q ≤ m_3 then
27:         if FLAP2(D, Q, R, 0, m_3 − 1, 0, {}, {}) then
28:             return true
29:         end if
30:     end if
31: end for
32: return false
```

To do so, we rely on our *Approximated* approach, and track the allocated up-links in a matrix similar to Fig. 7(a). The required set of leaves and links is of the form $N = Q \cdot D + R$. As described in the sub-section 'LaaS placement analysis', in a general fat-tree, this translates to R spines that connect to all the $Q+1$ allocated leaves and $D-R$ spines connected just to the Q repeated leaves. These requirements are equivalent to finding a set of Q leaves that have D free up-ports to a common set of spines, and a single leaf that has only R free up-ports that form a subset of the spines used by the previous Q leaves.

The search for Q leaves with enough common spines is performed recursively. In the worst case, it may require examining all $\binom{m_2}{Q}$ combinations. Our *LaaS* algorithm returns

---

93

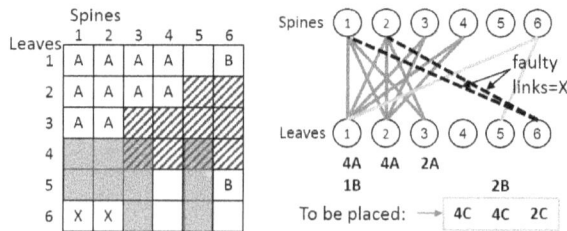

(a) Link Allocation Table   (b) Corresponding Topology

Figure 7: Example of allocation with 2 potential placements. (a) Table of leaf up-links holding the link assignments of tenants A and B, as well as 2 faulty links X. (b) Corresponding topology. The new tenant C of 10 hosts, arranged as $Q \cdot D + R = 2 \cdot 4 + 2$, can be assigned one of two allocations. In (a), the first link allocation is shown in solid, and the second with slanted lines.

the first successful allocation, so trying the most-used leaves first packs the allocations and achieves the best overall utilization results.

Fig. 7 demonstrates the process of evaluating a specific D, Q, R division. Consider a new tenant C of 10 hosts, arranged as 2 leaves of 4 hosts plus 1 leaf of 2 hosts. We show 2 possible placements: The first would use 4 hosts on leaves 4 and 5, and 2 hosts on another leaf 6. The second would use 4 hosts on leaves 3 and 4, and 2 hosts on another leaf 2. We also illustrate how we could take into account two faulty links in our link allocation if needed.

In the following section we describe the algorithm for mapping free leaves. The algorithm to perform the above example is provided in Algorithm 1. The recursive function is assuming the availability of matrix $M[l]$ of free ports on each leaf switch. It is given the following constants: D, R, Q and the start and end leaf switch indexes l_s, l_e. The recursive function provides its current state on the recursion using the following variables: l represents the current leaf index to examine, r the number of Q size leaves that were already found, $\{ports\}$ the set of ports that are possible for this allocation, $\{rl\}$ the collected set of, so far, Q size leaves. Eventually the recursion provides the following results: $\{D_L\}$ set of leaves with Q hosts, $\{D_{PORTS}\}$ the set of ports to be used by the Q size leaves, U_L the unique, sized R, leaf and $\{U_{PORTS}\}$ the ports on that leaf. The higher level algorithm considering the possible valid combinations of Q, D and R, for 2-level and 3-level fat-trees is provided in Algorithm 2.

Extension for over-subscribed fat trees. In order to reduce the network equipment cost, some cloud vendors use over-subscribed fat-trees, also known as *slimmed fat-trees* [50]. In an over-subscribed fat-tree, the number of uplinks is smaller than the number of downlinks in the switches, contrarily to the full bisectional bandwidth fat-tree, where they are equal. (We assume equal-bandwidth links). In such trees, we denote O_i the ratio between the two total number of links: those connecting switches at level i to the previous level $i-1$, and those connecting to the next level $i+1$. By this definition for XGFT:

$$O_i = \frac{m_i}{w_{i+1}} \qquad (5)$$

We describe here how to provide LaaS for over-subscribed fat-trees, without requiring hardware-assisted accurate TDMA link sharing. For simplicity we do not support tenant selection of their requested bandwidth. Since we allow no link-sharing between tenants, and we have no preference between tenants, a tenant placed across a level i of the tree has at least O_i permutation flows shared on each link. So for crossing level i we only require S common switches at level $i+1$:

$$S = \left| S^D \right| = \left\lceil \frac{D}{\lceil O_i \rceil} \right\rceil \qquad (6)$$

Clearly, a selection of D such that it is not divisible by $\lceil O_i \rceil$ reduces the cluster utilization, so the order by which we search for sub-trees should reflect that priority. The changes to Algorithm 1 are a new function argument S which defines the number of spines required, and its usage in line 7: *if $r = S$ then*. The changes to Algorithm 2 involve adding an S of Equation (6) to the calls of $FLAP$ and also adding an external loop around the *for* statements in lines $11 - 19$ and $23 - 31$ to try D values divisible by $\lceil O_i \rceil$ first.

4. EVALUATION

Our evaluation is reported in three sub-sections. The first deals with the resulting *cloud utilization* when applying LaaS conditions. It shows that our *LaaS* algorithm reaches a reasonable cloud utilization, within about 10% of bare-metal allocation. The second part describes the system implementation on top of OpenStack, and the third part shows how the LaaS architecture improves the performance of a tenant in the presence of other tenants by completely isolating the tenants from each other.

4.1 Evaluation of Cloud Utilization

Cloud utilization. We want to study whether our LaaS network isolation constraints significantly reduce the number of hosts that can be allocated to tenants. We define the *cloud utilization* as the average percentage of allocated hosts in steady state. Assuming that tenants pay a fee proportional to the number of used hosts and the time used, the cloud utilization is a direct measure of the revenue of the cloud provider.

Scheduling simulator. To evaluate the different heuristics on large-scale clouds, we developed a scheduling simulator that runs many tenant requests over a user-defined topology. The simulator is configured to run any of the above algorithms for host and link allocation. This algorithm may succeed and place the tenant, or fail. We use a strict FIFO scheduling, i.e. when a tenant fails, it blocks the entire queue of upcoming tenants. Note that this blocking assumption forms an extremely conservative approach in terms of cloud utilization. In practice, clouds would typically not allow a single tenant to block the entire queue and use resource reservation with back-filling techniques to overcome such cases. Since smaller tenants are easier to place, for any tenant size distribution, not letting smaller tenants bypass those waiting means that we fill fewer tenants into the cloud. Thus, the result should be regarded as an intuitive lower-bound for a real-life cloud utilization.

Simulation settings. We simulate the scheduler with LaaS algorithm on the largest full-bisectional-bandwidth 3-level fat-tree network that can be built with 36-port switches, i.e. a cloud of 11,662 hosts. The evaluation uses a randomized

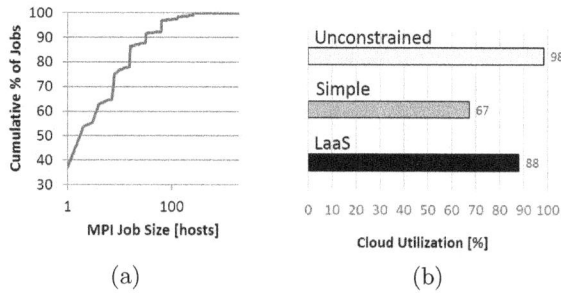

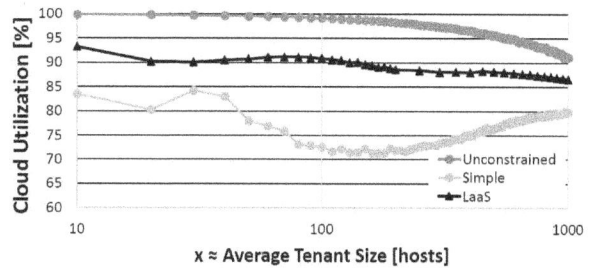

Figure 8: (a) Measured job-size Cumulative Distribution Function (CDF) for the Julich JUROPA scientific-computing cloud. (b) Resulting cloud utilization. *LaaS* achieves 88%.

Figure 9: Cloud utilization for a truncated exponential distribution of tenant host sizes in a cloud of 11,662 hosts.

sequence of 10,000 tenant requests. A random run-time in the range of 20 to 3,000 time units is assigned to each tenant. The variation of run-time makes scheduling harder as it increases fragmentation.

We evaluate 2 distribution types for the number of hosts requested by incoming tenants. First, we randomly generate sizes according to a job size distribution extracted from the Julich JUROPA job scheduler traces. These previously-unpublished traces represent 1.5 years of activity (Jan. 2010 - June 2011) of a large high-performance scientific-computing cloud. Second, we use a truncated exponential distribution of variable average x. It is truncated between 1 and the cluster size.

In order to measure the utilization loss we fill the cluster with tenants by assuming all tenant requests are available at simulation start. Tenants' run-time is randomized with uniform distribution from 10 to 3000 time units.

As a baseline algorithm, we implement an *Unconstrained* placement approach that simply allocates unused hosts to the request, as in bare-metal allocation. Note that some requests may still fail if the tenant requests more hosts than the number of currently-free cloud hosts. We compare this baseline to the *Simple* and *LaaS* algorithms, as described in Section 3.

Simulation results. Fig. 8(a) illustrates the Cumulative Distribution Function (CDF) of the tenant sizes (in number of hosts) collected from the Julich JUROPA cluster. The CDF shows peaks for numbers of hosts that are powers of 2 (1, 2, 4, 8, 16, and 32). We further generated 10,000 tenants with this job-size probability distribution, and the same random run-time distribution as above (instead of the original run-times, since they resulted in a low load, and therefore in an easy allocation). Fig. 8(b) shows the tenant allocation results: again, the cost of our *LaaS* allocation versus the *Unconstrained* bare-metal provisioning is about 10% of cloud utilization (88% vs. 98%).

To further test the sensitivity of our algorithm to the tenant sizes, we use a truncated exponential distribution for tenant host sizes and modify the exponential parameter x. The distribution of the JUROPA tenant sizes is similar to such a truncated exponential distribution. Fig. 9 illustrates the cloud utilization for *Unconstrained*, *Simple*, and *LaaS*, is plotted as a function of the exponential parameter x, which is close to the average tenant host size due to the truncation. The *Unconstrained* line shows how the utilization degrades with the job size, even without any network isola-

tion. This is an expected behavior of bin packing. As the job size grows, so does the probability for more nodes to be left unassigned when the cloud is almost full. The utilization of our *LaaS* algorithm stays steadily at about 10% less than the *Unconstrained* algorithm. Finally, *Simple* has the lowest cloud utilization for the entire tenant size range. Note that it is less steady, since its utilization is more closely tied to the sizes of the leaves and sub-trees. Once the tenant size crosses the leaf size (18 in our case), it is rounded up to a multiple of that number. Likewise, once it crosses the size of a complete sub-tree (324 hosts), it is rounded up to the nearest multiple of that number. These results show that our LaaS algorithm provides an efficient solution for avoiding tenant variability, as its cost is only about 10% for a wide range of tenant sizes. *Simple* suffers from a particularly large fluctuation in utilization. *LaaS* is more stable over the entire range, with about 90% utilization. There are a few points where the *Simple* heuristic provides a better utilization than *LaaS*. But, note that utilization stability is key to cloud vendors, since changing the allocation algorithm dynamically would require predicting the future size distribution, and thus may produce worse results when the distribution does not behave as expected.

4.2 System Implementation

We implemented the LaaS architecture by extending the *OpenStack Nova scheduler* with a new service that first runs the LaaS host and link allocation algorithm, and then translates the resulting allocation to an SDN controller that enforces the link isolation via routing assignments.

Host and link allocation. The integration of the *LaaS* algorithm was done on top of OpenStack (Icecube release), utilizing filter type: *AggregateMultiTenancyIsolation*. This filter allows limiting tenant placement to a group of hosts declared as an "aggregate", which is allocated to the specific tenant-id. Our automation, provided as a standalone service on top of OpenStack's *nova* controller, obtains new tenant requests, and then calls the *LaaS* allocation algorithm. If the allocation succeeds, we invoke the command to create a new aggregate that is further marked by the tenant-id. The allocated hosts are then added to the aggregate. The filter guarantees that a new host request, conducted by a user that belongs to a specific tenant, is mapped to a host that belongs to the tenant aggregate.

Network controller. We further implement a method to provide the link allocation to the InfiniBand SDN controller [2], which allows it to enforce the isolation by chang-

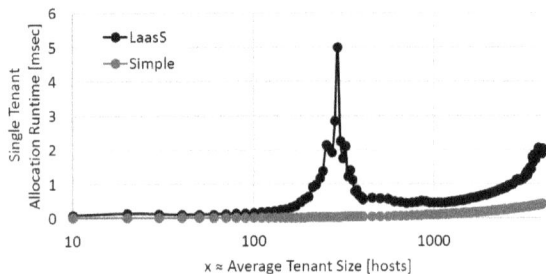

Figure 10: Average run-time of single tenant allocation versus average tenant size.

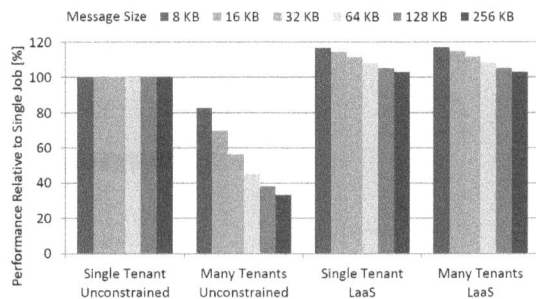

Figure 11: Simulated relative performance for tenants running Stencil scientific-computing applications on a cloud of 1,728 hosts, either alone or as 32 concurrent tenants. While tenant performance degrades when placed unconstrained (without link isolation), the performance of single and multiple tenants with LaaS appears identical, fulfilling the promise of LaaS.

ing routing. The controller supports defining sub-topologies, by providing a file with a list of the switch ports and hosts that form each sub-topology. Then each sub-topology may have its own policy file that determines how it is routed.

Run-time. The LaaS Approximation scans through all possible placements for valid link allocation. This involves evaluating all possible valid combinations of R and Q values. Fig. 10 presents the average run-time per tenant request for placing tenants on 11,664 nodes cluster providing a truncated exponential tenant size distribution. Run time was measured on an Intel® Xeon® CPU X5670 @ 2.93GHz. The peak in run-time of about 5 msec appears just below the average tenant size of 324, which is the exact point where our algorithm first scans all possible placements under a single sub-tree and continues with multiple sub-tree placement.

4.3 Evaluation of Tenant Performance

Since LaaS guarantees tenant isolation, tenant performance should be independent of the number of other tenants that run on the same network. To demonstrate LaaS tenant isolation, we simulate a large cluster using a well known InfiniBand flit level simulator used by [19,23,57].

Fig. 11 presents the relative performance of single and multiple tenants running Stencil scientific-computing applications on a cloud of 1,728 hosts, under either *Unconstrained* or *LaaS*, normalized by the performance of a single tenant placed without constraints. The figure illustrates many effects. First, the performance of a single tenant with *Unconstrained* significantly degrades when other tenants are active, e.g. to 45% with 32-KB message sizes. This is because the bare-metal allocation of *Unconstrained* does not provide link isolation. Second, under our *LaaS* algorithm, *the single-tenant performance is not impacted when the other tenants become active* (the third and fourth sets of columns look identical). This was the key goal of this work. *LaaS* prevents any inter-tenant traffic contention. Finally, we can observe an additional surprising effect (first vs. third sets of columns): the tenant performance is slightly improved for small messages under *LaaS* versus the *Unconstrained* allocation. The reason is that *LaaS* does not accept tenants unless it can place them with no contention, and therefore the resulting placement tends to be tighter, thus improving the run-time performance with small message sizes when the synchronization time of the tasks is not negligible. The lower network diameter of *LaaS* improves the synchronization time, which is latency-dominated.

5. DISCUSSION

Recursive LaaS. When talking to industry vendors, they pointed out simple extensions that would easily generalize the use of LaaS. First, LaaS could be applied recursively, by having each tenant application or each sub-tenant reserve its own chunk of the cloud within the tenant's chunk of the cloud. Second, LaaS could also be applied in private clouds, with cloud chunks being reserved by applications instead of tenants. Third, shared-cloud vendors could easily restrict LaaS to a subset of their cloud, while keeping the remainder of their cloud as it is today. This can be done by reserving large portions of the topology to a *virtual* tenant that is shared between many real tenants. Pre-allocation and modification of that sub-topology is already supported by our code. As a result, LaaS offers a smooth and gradual transition to better service guarantees, enabling cloud vendors to start only with the tenant owners who are most ready to pay for it.

Off-the-shelf LaaS. LaaS is implementable today with no extra hardware cost in existing switches and no host changes. The algorithm requires only a moderate software change in the allocation scheme, which we provide as open source. It also relies on an isolated-routing feature of the SDN controller, which is already available in InfiniBand and could be implemented in Ethernet SDN controllers like OpenDaylight.

Proportional network power. LaaS eases the use of an elastic network link power that would be made proportional to cloud utilization [4]. This is because it explicitly mentions which links and switches are to be used, and therefore can turn off other links and switches. In other approaches the control has to happen as a result of traffic load change and thus is not realistic for common switch hardware for which the turn-ON time is much larger than a microsecond.

Heterogeneous LaaS. Host allocation in heterogeneous clouds involves allowing tenants to express their required host features in terms of CPU, memory, disk and available accelerators. On such systems, the host allocation algorithm should allow the provider to trade off the acceptance of a new tenant versus the cost of the available hosts, which may be higher as their capabilities may exceed the user needs. Our

LaaS algorithm could support these requirements. *Although this requirement complicates the allocation algorithm, it is feasible to support it in LaaS.* First, it should use the host costs to order the search. Second, it should try all the possible divisors and select the one with best accumulated cost. A trade-off between the resulting fragmentation and the cost difference could extend it.

LaaS with VMs. LaaS could easily support multiple tenants running as virtual machines (VMs) on the same host, assuming accurate packet pacing and burst control is provided by hosts and switches. LaaS could then treat each link as a set of isolated links and assign them to different tenants. This includes the links leaving the host.

Non-FIFO tenant scheduling. We conservatively evaluated our *LaaS* allocation algorithm assuming FIFO scheduling of incoming tenants. To improve the cloud utilization, we could equally rely on a non-FIFO policy, e.g. by using back-filling, reservations, or a jointly-optimal allocation of multiple tenants [42].

Fault Tolerance. When a link is down before being allocated it is easy to avoid allocating it to new tenants. However, if a link was already allocated to a tenant, it is not always possible to provide an alternative link without breaking the current operation of the tenant. Similarly to losing a link on the private cloud, the tenant will see some degradation until the link is fixed or the forwarding plane is adapted.

6. CONCLUSIONS

In this paper, we demonstrated that the interference with other tenants causes a performance degradation in cloud applications that may exceed 65%. We introduced LaaS (Links as a Service), a novel cloud allocation and routing technology that provides each tenant with the same bandwidth as in its own private data center. We showed that LaaS completely eliminates the application performance degradation. We further explained how LaaS can be used in clouds today without any change of hardware, and showed how it can rely on open-source software code that we contributed. Finally, we also used previously-unpublished tenant-size statistics of a large scientific-computing cloud, obtained over a long period of time, to construct a random workload that illustrates how isolation is possible at the cost of some 10% cloud utilization loss.

7. ACKNOWLEDGMENTS

We would like to appreciate our gratitude to our colleagues in the Technion and Mellanox Technologies for their support and enthusiasm about our approach.

This work was partly supported by the Technion Funds for Security Research, the Intel ICRI-CI Center, the Hasso Plattner Institute Research School, the Gordon Fund for Systems Engineering, the Israel Ministry of Science and Technology, and the Shillman, Erteschik and Greenberg Research Funds.

8. REFERENCES

[1] LaaS source code, experiments and simulation conditions. https://www.dropbox.com/sh/uzla7rcmdiqrxig/AADpw5ALG-q8VFzMSVcmYvmJa/.

[2] OpenSM - InfiniBand Open SDN Controller.

[3] OpenStack ironic. https://wiki.openstack.org/wiki/Ironic.

[4] D. Abts, M. R. Marty, P. M. Wells, P. Klausler, and H. Liu. Energy proportional datacenter networks. *SIGARCH Comput. Archit. News*, 2010.

[5] Y. Ajima, S. Sumimoto, and T. Shimizu. Tofu: A 6d mesh/torus interconnect for exascale computers. *Computer*, 2009.

[6] M. Al-Fares, A. Loukissas, and A. Vahdat. A scalable, commodity data center network architecture. *SIGCOMM Comput. Commun. Rev.*, 2008.

[7] M. Al-Fares, S. Radhakrishnan, B. Raghavan, N. Huang, and A. Vahdat. Hedera: Dynamic flow scheduling for data center networks. *NSDI*, 2010.

[8] A. Altin, H. Yaman, and M. C. Pinar. The robust network loading problem under hose demand uncertainty. *INFORMS Journal on Computing*, 2010.

[9] A. Andreyev. Introducing data center fabric, the next-generation Facebook the next generation datacenter network, 2014.

[10] S. Angel, H. Ballani, T. Karagiannis, G. O'Shea, and E. Thereska. End-to-end performance isolation through virtual datacenters. *USENIX OSDI*, Berkeley, CA, USA, 2014.

[11] D. Artz. The secret weapons of the AOL optimization team. *Velocity Conference*, 2009.

[12] H. Ballani, P. Costa, T. Karagiannis, and A. Rowstron. Towards predictable datacenter networks. *SIGCOMM*, 2011.

[13] A. Bhatele, K. Mohror, S. H. Langer, and K. E. Isaacs. There goes the neighborhood: Performance degradation due to nearby jobs. *ACM SC*, 2013.

[14] M. Chowdhury, M. R. Rahman, and R. Boutaba. ViNEYard: Virtual network embedding algorithms. *IEEE/ACM ToN*, 2012.

[15] M. Chowdhury and I. Stoica. Coflow: A networking abstraction for cluster applications. *ACM HotNets*, 2012.

[16] M. Chowdhury, M. Zaharia, J. Ma, M. I. Jordan, and I. Stoica. Managing data transfers in computer clusters with orchestra. *ACM SIGCOMM*, 2011.

[17] A. Curtis, W. Kim, and P. Yalagandula. Mahout: Low-overhead datacenter traffic management using end-host-based elephant detection. *IEEE Infocom*, 2011.

[18] A. Dixit, P. Prakash, Y. Hu, and R. Kompella. On the impact of packet spraying in data center networks. *IEEE Infocom*, 2013.

[19] J. Domke, T. Hoefler, and W. E. Nagel. Deadlock-free oblivious routing for arbitrary topologies. *IEEE IPDPS*, 2011.

[20] R. Doriguzzi Corin, M. Gerola, R. Riggio, F. De Pellegrini, and E. Salvadori. VeRTIGO: Network virtualization and beyond. *EWSDN*, 2012.

[21] N. G. Duffield, P. Goyal, A. Greenberg, P. Mishra, K. K. Ramakrishnan, and J. E. van der Merive. A flexible model for resource management in virtual private networks. *ACM SIGCOMM '99*, New York, NY, USA, 1999.

[22] Y. Gong, B. He, and J. Zhong. Network performance aware MPI collective communication operations in the cloud. *IEEE TPDS*, 2013.

[23] E. Gran, S.-A. Reinemo, O. Lysne, T. Skeie,

E. Zahavi, and G. Shainer. Exploring the scope of the InfiniBand congestion control Mechanism. *IEEE IPDPS*, 2012.

[24] C. Guo, G. Lu, H. J. Wang, S. Yang, C. Kong, P. Sun, W. Wu, and Y. Zhang. Secondnet: a data center network virtualization architecture with bandwidth guarantees. *ACM CoNext*, 2010.

[25] C. E. Hopps. Analysis of an equal-cost multi-path algorithm. http://tools.ietf.org/html/rfc2992, 2015.

[26] A. Iosup, S. Ostermann, M. N. Yigitbasi, R. Prodan, T. Fahringer, and D. H. J. Epema. Performance analysis of cloud computing services for many-tasks scientific computing. *IEEE TPDS*, 2011.

[27] A. Iosup, N. Yigitbasi, and D. Epema. On the performance variability of production cloud services. *CCGrid*, 2011.

[28] A. Jajszczyk. Nonblocking, repackable, and rearrangeable clos networks. *IEEE Communications Magazine*, 2003.

[29] K. Jang, J. Sherry, H. Ballani, and T. Moncaster. Silo: predictable message latency in the cloud. *ACM SIGCOMM*, 2015.

[30] V. Jeyakumar, M. Alizadeh, D. MaziÃĺres, B. Prabhakar, C. Kim, and A. Greenberg. EyeQ: practical network performance isolation at the edge. *NSDI USENIX*, 2013.

[31] A. Jokanovic, G. Rodriguez, J. Sancho, and J. Labarta. Impact of inter-application contention in current and future HPC systems. *IEEE HotI*, 2010.

[32] A. Jokanovic, J. Sancho, J. Labarta, G. Rodriguez, and C. Minkenberg. Effective quality-of-service policy for capacity high-performance computing systems. *IEEE HPCC*, 2012.

[33] A. Jokanovic, J. C. Sancho, G. Rodriguez, A. Lucero, C. Minkenberg, and J. Labarta. Quiet neighborhoods: key to protect job performance predictability. *IEEE IPDPS 2015*, Hyderabad, India, 2015.

[34] K. LaCurts, J. C. Mogul, H. Balakrishnan, and Y. Turner. Cicada: Introducing predictive guarantees for cloud networks. *USENIX HotCloud*, 2014.

[35] V. T. Lam, S. Radhakrishnan, R. Pan, A. Vahdat, and G. Varghese. Netshare predictable bandwidth allocation for data centers. *SIGCOMM Comput. Commun. Rev.*, 2012.

[36] G. Linden. Make data useful, 2006.

[37] M. Mayer. In search of a better, faster, stronger web. *Velocity Conference*, 2009.

[38] J. C. Mogul and L. Popa. What we talk about when we talk about cloud network performance. *SIGCOMM Comput. Commun. Rev.*, 2012.

[39] S. Ohring, M. Ibel, S. Das, and M. Kumar. On generalized fat trees. *IPPS*, 1995.

[40] J. Orduna, F. Silla, and J. Duato. A new task mapping technique for communication-aware scheduling strategies. *ICPP Workshops*, 2001.

[41] S. Ostermann, A. Iosup, N. Yigitbasi, R. Prodan, T. Fahringer, and D. Epema. A performance analysis of EC2 cloud computing services for scientific computing. LNICST. Springer, Jan. 2010.

[42] J. A. Pascual, J. Navaridas, and J. Miguel-Alonso. Effects of topology-aware allocation policies on

scheduling performance. *Job Scheduling Strategies for Parallel Processing*. 2009.

[43] J. Perry, A. Ousterhout, H. Balakrishnan, D. Shah, and H. Fugal. Fastpass: A centralized zero-queue datacenter network. *ACM SIGCOMM*, 2014.

[44] F. Petrini and M. Vanneschi. k-ary n-trees: high performance networks for massively parallel architectures. *IPPS*, 1997.

[45] L. Popa, G. Kumar, M. Chowdhury, A. Krishnamurthy, S. Ratnasamy, and I. Stoica. FairCloud: Sharing the network in cloud computing. *ACM SIGCOMM*, 2012.

[46] L. Popa, P. Yalagandula, S. Banerjee, J. C. Mogul, Y. Turner, and J. R. Santos. ElasticSwitch: Practical Work-conserving Bandwidth Guarantees for Cloud Computing. *ACM SIGCOMM*, New York, NY, USA, 2013.

[47] B. Raghavan, K. Vishwanath, S. Ramabhadran, K. Yocum, and A. C. Snoeren. Cloud control with distributed rate limiting. *ACM SIGCOMM*, 2007.

[48] T. Ristenpart, E. Tromer, H. Shacham, and S. Savage. Hey, you, get off of my cloud. *ACM CCS*, 2009.

[49] H. Rodrigues, J. R. Santos, Y. Turner, P. Soares, and D. Guedes. Gatekeeper: Supporting bandwidth guarantees for multi-tenant datacenter networks. In *WIOV*, 2011.

[50] G. Rodriguez, C. Minkenberg, R. Beivide, R. Luijten, J. Labarta, and M. Valero. Oblivious routing schemes in extended generalized Fat Tree networks. *IEEE CLUSTER*, 2009.

[51] J. Schad, J. Dittrich, and J.-A. QuianÃľ-Ruiz. Runtime measurements in the cloud. *VLDB Endowment*, 2010.

[52] R. Sherwood, G. Gibb, K.-K. Yap, G. Appenzeller, M. Casado, N. McKeown, and G. Parulkar. Flowvisor: A network virtualization layer. *OpenFlow Switch Consortium, Tech. Rep*, 2009.

[53] A. Shieh, S. Kandula, A. Greenberg, and C. Kim. Seawall: performance isolation for cloud datacenter networks. *USENIX HotCloud*, 2010.

[54] K. C. Webb, A. C. Snoeren, and K. Yocum. Topology switching for data center networks. *Hot-ICE Workshop*, 2011.

[55] X. Wu and X. Yang. DARD: Distributed adaptive routing for datacenter networks. *IEEE ICDCS*, 2012.

[56] M. Yu, Y. Yi, J. Rexford, and M. Chiang. Rethinking virtual network embedding. *SIGCOMM Comput. Commun. Rev.*, 2008.

[57] E. Zahavi. Fat-tree routing and node ordering providing contention free traffic for MPI global collectives. *JPDC*, 2012.

[58] D. Zats, T. Das, P. Mohan, D. Borthakur, and R. Katz. DeTail: reducing the flow completion time tail in datacenter networks. *SIGCOMM Comput. Commun. Rev.*, 2012.

Optimizing VM Live Migration Strategy Based On Migration Time Cost Modeling

Ziyu Li
School of Software
Shanghai Jiaotong University
No.800 Dongchuan Road, Shanghai, China
+86 15216708853
lzy9059@sjtu.edu.cn

Gang Wu
School of Software
Shanghai Jiaotong University
No.800 Dongchuan Road, Shanghai, China
+86 13636378962
wugang@cs.sjtu.edu.cn

ABSTRACT

The live migration technology of virtual machine is very helpful for dynamic workload balance, server consolidation and fault tolerance in cloud computing environment. It is important to build live migration strategies which lead to low migration time, thus helping reduce migration cost while achieving migration goal. So we look into the topic of building a model to quantitatively predict live migration time. We thoroughly analyze the key parameters that affect the migration time and construct a live migration time cost model based on KVM. The evaluation of time cost model shows that the average prediction accuracy is above 90% in comparison with measured time. Based on time cost model, we propose 2 optimized live migration strategies for different application scenarios, one for load balance and fault tolerance, the other for server consolidation. The evaluation shows our optimized migration strategies can save 35%~50% of cost compared to the random migration strategy. We believe this should be the first comprehensive study of optimizing live migration strategy with migration time cost as a key factor.

General Terms

Algorithms, Measurement, Performance, Design, Experimentation.

Keywords

Live Migration; Migration Strategy; Time Cost Model

1. INTRODUCTION

Virtual machine (VM) [1] is widely used in data centers. It provides reliable isolation and greatly increases the utilization of physical resources.

Live migration of VM across physical machines is useful for administrators of data centers. It allows power management [11], fault tolerance [9], load balancing [15], server consolidation [2] and low-level system maintenance.

Live migration of VM is the process of cloning VM OS from source machine to destination machine while the OS keeps running. The Pre-Copy algorithm is the most widely used algorithm to sync up OS memory during live migration. Currently, many Virtual Machine Monitors (such as Xen[17], KVM[16] and VMware[18]) support live migration of VM based on Pre-Copy algorithm, which performs iterative transference of dirty pages to finish live migration. VM live migration technology has attracted considerable interest from data center management and cluster computing in recent years. And research in the area of live migration has followed several avenues [6], [7], [8], [10], [32]. There are also many other studies on the migration strategy for a variety of application cases, concerning the issues of where and when a VM should be migrated [12], [13], [14], [15] and migration cost testing framework [33].

Live migration cost model is a valuable research topic because the model can help data center administrators to decide which VM to migrate in different application scenarios. For example, to reach the goal of load balancing in a cluster, all VMs running on an overloaded physical machine would be potential candidates to migrate. But different migration choices may lead to significant difference in migration time. So some papers[3],[4],[5] talked about the cost model of VM live migration based on Xen. These studies demonstrated that migration time will vary significantly among different workloads and VM configurations (including VM memory amount, network bandwidth, etc). The main effort of these studies is to enable memory dirtying rate tracking in VM to calculate dirty memory amount during migration. But according to the principle of working set [21], [22], programs will tend to access a specific region of memory. So besides tracking memory dirtying rate, to summarize a general memory access pattern is also very important to calculate dirty memory amount. This issue will be addressed in this paper thoroughly.

After constructing the migration time cost model, we also look into the problem of building migration strategies concerning different application scenarios by taking migration time cost into account.

The contributions of this paper are summarized as follows:

- We analyze key parameters that affect VM live migration time. Such as VM memory size, VM memory dirtying rate, network bandwidth, memory zero page amount and memory access pattern. We then modify qemu-kvm[19] source code to enable dirty memory rate tracking.

- We investigate the general memory access pattern of live migration workloads(including several typical workloads in data center) to calculate dirty page amount generated in each Pre-Copy iterations.

- We design a detailed analytical model to estimate the migration time by scrutinizing KVM's live migration algorithm. Then we conduct several live migration tests with different workloads to test the accuracy of our model.

ANCS'16, March 17–18, 2016, Santa Clara, California, USA.

© 2016 ACM. ISBN 978-1-4503-4183-7/16/03...$15.00.

DOI: http://dx.doi.org/10.1145/2881025.2881035

- We propose 2 live migration strategies based on the time cost model. One strategy is for load balance and fault tolerance (LB-FT-Strategy), which is mainly based on optimization approach. The other strategy is for server consolidation (SC-Strategy), which is mainly based on heuristic algorithm. The evaluation shows these 2 strategies perform better than previous strategy mentioned in [2] and [31].

The rest of the paper is organized as follows. Section 2 introduces the detail of Pre-Copy algorithm. Section 3 describes the design of live migration time cost model. Section 4 describes model based migration strategies. Section 5 introduces system implementation. Section 6 presents the evaluation of time cost model. Section 7 gives the evaluation of optimized migration strategy. Section 8 introduces the related work. At last, we conclude our work in Section 9.

2. Pre-Copy algorithm of KVM

KVM is a Linux subsystem which leverages virtualization extensions to add a virtual machine monitor capability to Linux. Using KVM, one can create and run multiple virtual machines. These virtual machines appear as normal Linux processes and integrate seamlessly with the rest of the system. To employ KVM conveniently and perform live migration, we should utilize qemu-kvm. The live migration algorithm qemu-kvm realizes is Pre-Copy.

In Pre-Copy memory migration, KVM copies all the memory pages from source to destination while the VM is still running on the source. Pages dirtied during the migration must be iteratively resent to ensure memory consistency. By iterative it means that Pre-Copy occurs in several rounds and the data to be transmitted during a round are the dirty pages generated in the previous round. The Pre-Copy phase terminates if transference time of the remaining dirty memory is shorter than a pre-set time period. The whole migration procedure of KVM includes the following stages: *iterative Pre-Copy, stop and copy, commitment and activation*, which is depicted in Figure 1.

The stages *stop and copy* and *commitment* contribute to the downtime of VM migration, while total migration time includes downtime and the duration of the stage *iterative Pre-Copy*.

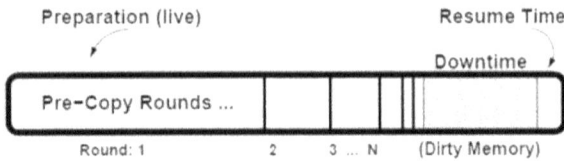

Figure 1. Pre–Copy Timeline [29]

3. TIME COST MODELING
3.1 Define Model Parameters

Time cost of KVM live migration is affected by three main factors. First of all, the size of VM memory has a main effect on the total migration time. And there is a mechanism called zero page copy in KVM live migration. At the beginning of migration, not all memory pages need to be transferred to destination host. Zero pages will be sync to the destination host and won't be transferred. So we will minus zero page amount from total memory amount.

Secondly, the memory dirtying rate, which indicates how fast memory become dirty will impact the number of Pre-Copy iterations and dirty pages generated in each Pre-Copy iteration, hence affects the migration time. Thirdly, the network transmission rate is also crucial to migration time.

In Table 1, we define a number of key parameters and their notations for our time cost model.

Table 1. Parameters for time cost model of live migration

Symbol	Quantity
M	Total amount of VM memory
V	Network bandwidth
D	Zero page amount
R	Instantaneous Memory dirtying rate
$\bar{R}$	EWMA* Memory dirtying rate
T_{mig}	Total migration time
N_{mig}	Total transferred dirty memory amount
T_i	Migration time of ith iteration
N_i	Dirty memory amount generated in i^{th} iteration
T_{down}	Migration down time
T_{MAX}	Pre-set threshold time
B	Speed of sending dirty memory to buffer

*EWMA: exponentially weighted moving average

Note that T_{MAX} is defined in Table 1. In KVM live migration, there is an asynchronous mechanism to transfer dirty memory. As showed in Figure 2, dirty memories are first sent to a buffer, then contents of the buffer are transferred to destination host with socket. The speed of sending dirty memory to buffer is denoted as B in Table 1. If time of remaining dirty memory that is transferred to buffer is shorter than T_{MAX} (T_{MAX} is a pre-set value in qemu-kvm source code), the migration process should reach the *stop and copy* phase.

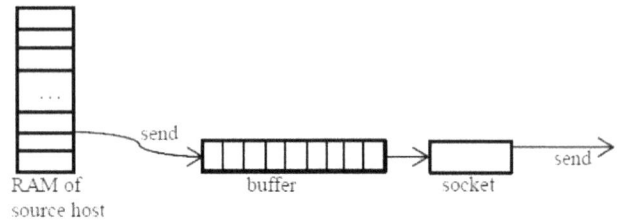

Figure 2. Asynchronous transfer of dirty memory

3.2 Model Total migration time

Suppose there are n Pre-Copy iterations during the live migration, the *total migration time* (T_{mig}) can be calculated as follows:

$$T_{mig} = \sum_1^n T_i + T_{down} \tag{1}$$

In qemu-kvm, T_{MAX} is set to be 30ms. We know from qemu-kvm source code that the condition to reach the *stop and copy* phase is

$$N_i / B < T_{MAX} \tag{2}$$

After the above condition is satisfied, suppose now the migration is in i^{th} iteration, we can calculate T_{down} in (3)

$$T_{down} = N_i \ / \ V \qquad (3)$$

To model the migration time of ith iteration (T_i) is the most challenge part in this paper. Assume the Pre-Copy algorithm proceeds in n iterations. In iteration i($2 \leq i \leq n$), dirty memory generated during iteration i-1 will be transferred through the network. So the elapsed time of each iteration can be calculated as:

$$T_i = \begin{cases} \dfrac{M-D}{V} & i = 1 \\ N_{i-1} \ / \ V & i = 2,...,n \end{cases} \qquad (4)$$

The data transmitted in iteration i can be calculated as:

$$N_i = F(\overline{R}, \ T_i), \qquad i = 2,...,n \qquad (5)$$

Note that in (5) we use the function $F(\overline{R}, \ T_i)$ to calculate N_i. The rest part of this section will discuss why we choose such a function in detail.

Together with (1) (3) (4), we find a way to model T.

3.3 Smooth Instantaneous Memory dirtying rate

Note that in (5) we use $\overline{R}$(EWMA Memory dirtying rate) instead of R(Instantaneous Memory dirtying rate) in the function, but we can only measure R in qemu-kvm (section 5 will introduce how to track R in detail). So we will introduce how EWMA works in our model.

EWMA(exponentially weighted moving average) is a function that smooths a series of data based on a moving average with weights which decay exponentially. It can reduce the effect of odd data points. In our method, EWMA equation is as the form:

$$\overline{R} \ (t) = \lambda * R(t) + (1-\lambda) \ \overline{R} \ (t-1) \qquad (6)$$

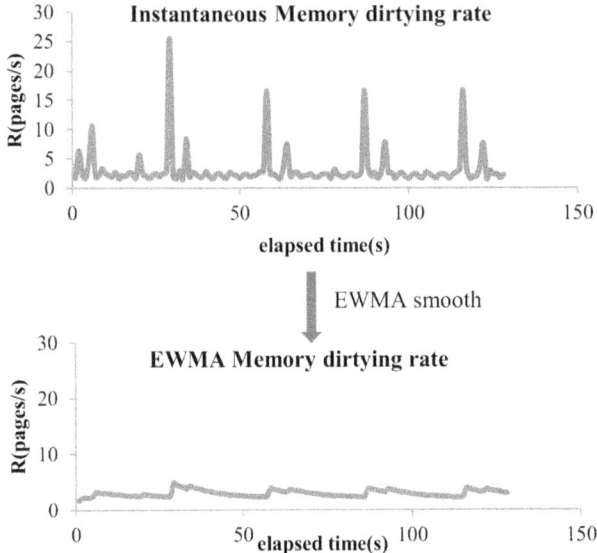

Figure 3. EWMA smooth for Memory dirtying rate

In (6), $\overline{R}(t)$ represents the EWMA Memory dirtying rate at time t. R(t) represents Instantaneous Memory dirtying rate at time t. With EWMA equation, we can smooth memory dirtying rate curve and avoid odd rate point. Montgomery, Douglas[20]

recommended $0.05 \leq \lambda \leq 0.25$. After trying several values of λ, we find that when $\lambda = 0.1$ the curve is well smoothed. So in our case, we set $\lambda = 0.1$, which is shown in Figure 3.

3.4 Model general memory access pattern

From qemu-kvm source code, R is measured by first clean up all dirty pages in the dirty bitmap(a user space data structure, tracking dirty memory status of kernel), then we calculate dirty page amount generated in 1 second. This amount can represent R.

But from the experiment conducted, we find that many migration iterations period are longer than 1 second. According to the principle of working set [21], [22], programs will tend to access a specific region of memory. If a migration iteration period is longer than 1 second, many dirty pages generated after the first second will locate in the memory region that is already dirty. So in (5) we use a function $F(\overline{R}, \ T_i)$ to calculate N_i.

In this paper, we define memory access pattern as the similarity between dirty bitmaps of two periods of time. To model the general memory access pattern, firstly we consider the time period T_i (Migration time of ith iteration) and assume $T_i > 1$, then define

$$Sim(k) \qquad k = 1,....,[T_i]$$

As depicted in Figure 4, Sim(k) is the similarity between dirty bitmaps of first k-1 seconds and the kth second(the shadow time slot). Here, we define Ham(k, k-1) as Hamming Distance of dirty bitmaps between first k-1 seconds and the kth second. Then Sim(k) is calculated with:

$$Sim(k) = 1 - \frac{Ham(k,k-1)}{total\ size\ of\ dirty\ bitmap} \qquad (7)$$

There are several different workloads in our test, such as Linux idle, Jmeter, TPC-C, SPECint and so on. These workloads are typical workloads in datacenter. Memory access patterns of these workloads are somewhat different with each other. But if memory dirtying rate of workload is lower than network bandwidth, we observed that Sim(k)of these workloads are very similar in 2 aspects:

- Sim(k) of these workloads can all be fitted with exponential curve.
- Sim(k) curves of these workloads are so close to each other that we can choose one to represent the others.

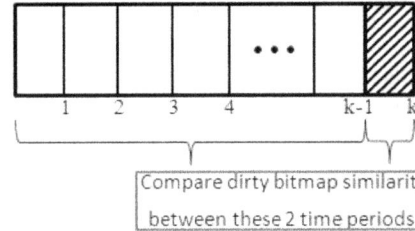

Figure 4. Timeline notation of Sim(k)

From the experiments conducted in section 5, we find that when $k \leq 6$, Sim(k)follows an exponential function. And when k > 6, Sim(k) can be treated as a constant value. Non-linear curve fitting of five workloads is shown in Figure 5. In Figure 5, Sim(k)curves of these workloads are very close to each other. We choose Sim(k) curve of JmeterTest to represent the others because this curve leads to minimum prediction error.

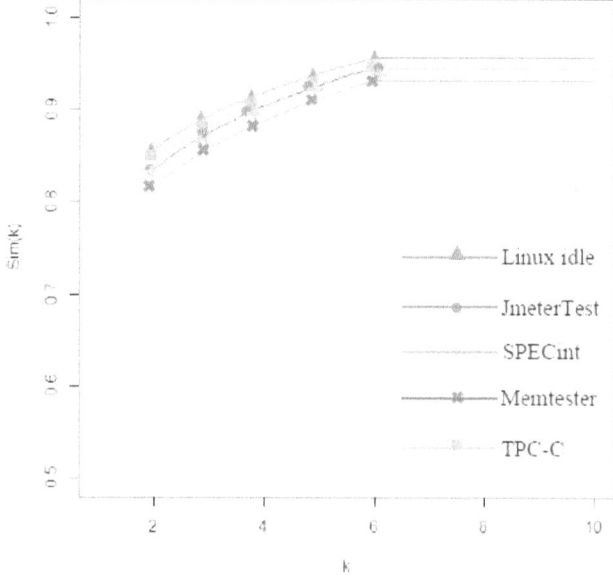

Figure 5. Curve fitting for Sim(k)of five workloads

Sim(k) curve fitting result of JmeterTest is shown in Table 2:

Table 2. Curve Fitting Result

	Estimate	Std. Error	t value	Pr(>|t|)
intercept	-0.228714	0.008820	-25.93	0.000126
power	0.089916	0.005607	16.04	0.000527

We can express Sim(k)as:

$$Sim(k) = \begin{cases} k^{0.089916} - 0.228714, & \text{if } 2 \le k <= 6; \\ 0.93, & \text{if } k > 6. \end{cases} \quad (8)$$

3.5 Model dirty memory amount generated in i^{th} iteration(N_i)

In (4), $N_i = F(\bar{R}, T_i), i = 1, \ldots 2, n$.

With Sim(k), N_i can be calculated. Firstly, If $T_i > 1$, suppose

$$n = [T_i] \quad (9)$$

Then we can define the amount of dirty memory generated in the first k^{th} seconds as S_k. Thus

$$N_i = \begin{cases} \bar{R} * T_i, & 0 < T_i < 1 \\ S_n + \bar{R}(1 - Sim(n + 1) * (T_i - n)), & T_i > 1 \end{cases} \quad (10)$$

When $0 < T_i < 1$, the total memory region just begins to get dirty. So the probability of one certain page getting dirty more than once during this period is much lower compare to $T_i > 1$. Thus, for simplicity, we approximate N_i as a linear function of T_i when $0 < T_i < 1$.

We can calculate S_k in the following equations

$$\begin{aligned} S_1 &= \bar{R} * 1 \\ S_2 &= S_1 + \bar{R}(1 - Sim(2)) * 1 \\ S_3 &= S_2 + \bar{R}(1 - Sim(3)) * 1 \\ &\ldots\ldots \\ S_k &= S_{k-1} + \bar{R}(1 - Sim(k)) * 1 \end{aligned} \quad (11)$$

With some mathematical calculation, we get S_n as:

$$S_k = \bar{R}(n - \sum_{j=2}^{k} Sim(j)) \quad (12)$$

Finally, we can compute N_i in the following equation

$$N_i = F(\bar{R}, T_i) =$$

$$\begin{cases} \bar{R} * T_i, & 0 < T_i < 1 \\ \bar{R}\left([T_i] + 1 - \sum_{j=2}^{|T_i|} Sim(j) - Sim([T_i] + 1) * (T_i - N)\right), & T_i > 1 \end{cases}$$

$$(13)$$

3.6 Model Construction

Based on the above analysis, our migration time cost model can be shown in Algorithm 1.

All input variables can be measured from practical workloads. The size of VM memory M can be got from configuration. T_{MAX} is determined by the configuration of migration algorithm. The memory dirtying rate $\bar{R}$ can be measured before VM migration decision. V is also an EWMA value. B is treated as a constant value. The detailed measurement of $\bar{R}$ and $F(\bar{R}, T_i)$ is described in Section 5.

To follow qemu-kvm Pre-Copy algorithm and simulate real memory transference process more accurately, we don't use (3) directly in our model. Instead, a unit data block (U) of 4096K is used to simulate the iterative memory transference process, which is reflected in line 7, 8 in Algorithm 1. In fact, according to qemu-kvm source code, data block of 4096K is the actual amount of data unit that is transferred .

Algorithm 1: Time Cost Model of VM Migration

---

1. **Input**: M, T_{MAX}, D, $\bar{R}$, V, U, B   **Output**: T_{mig}

2. $N_0 = M - D$

3. $T_{mig} = 0$

4. $i = 0$

5. **while** true **do**

6.   **if** $N_i > 0$ **then**

7. $N_i = N_i - U$

8. $T_{mig} = T_{mig} + U / V$

9.   **else**

10. $i = i + 1$

11. $N_i = F(\bar{R}, T_i)$

12.   **if** $N_i / B < T_{MAX}$ **then**

13.   **break**

14.   **end if**

15.   **end if**

16. **end while**

17. $T_{down} = N_i / V$

18. $T_{mig} = T_{mig} + T_{down}$

Note that in line 18 of Algorithm 1, migration down time T_{down} is included in T_{mig}. In many studies, migration down time is also an important metric when modeling migration cost. In our previous analysis, we can know that T_{down} is positively correlated with T_{mig}, which means high T_{mig} will lead to high T_{down}. So in the rest of this paper, we will not discuss migration down time separately.

4. MIGRATION STRATEGIES

There are several types of goal of VM live migration, such as load balance, server consolidation and fault tolerance. When VMs need to be migrated, we should choose the best candidate to minimize the migration cost while achieving the specific goal of migration. Because conditions may vary among different types of goal, we will discuss them separately.

4.1 Load balance and fault tolerance

[9] and [31] introduce the idea of performing load balance and fault tolerance with VM live migration. These two papers share the same idea: set threshold for key parameters (mainly CPU and RAM) and continuously monitor these parameters. If one or more parameters exceed the threshold, trigger live migration to achieve load balance and fault tolerance.

In a cluster of physical machines, if CPU or RAM utilization ratio of a physical machine, which is denoted as PM_S, exceeds the threshold, we should migrate VM from this machine to a destination machine. For each other physical machine (PM) in the cluster, we calculate total utilization (TU) as bellow:

TU = 0.5 * PM's CPU utilization ratio +

0.5 * PM's RAM utilization ratio

The coefficients 0.5 mean the effect of CPU and RAM utilization ratio are equal. The coefficients can be changed in different situations. We choose the PM with the smallest TU as destination machine, which is denoted as PM_d.

Suppose there are n VMs running on the PM_S and we set the CPU threshold as C_T and RAM threshold as M_T. CPU and RAM utilization ratio of PM_S are C_s and M_s. CPU and RAM utilization ratio of PM_d are C_d and M_d. Now C_s or M_s exceeds the threshold, so we should perform live migration. Suppose CPU and RAM utilization ratio of VM_i (i=1,...,n) on PM_S are C_i and M_i respectively. T_i is the predicted migration time of VM_i. After iterating the n VMs, we can choose the VM which leads to maximum value of function F_i as bellow while satisfying the 5 conditions.

$$\max F_i = \alpha \frac{8}{T_i} + \beta C_i + \gamma M_i$$

$$\begin{cases} \alpha + \beta + \gamma = 1 \\ C_s - C_i < C_T \\ M_s - M_i < M_T \qquad i = 1,...,n \quad (14) \\ C_d + C_i < C_T \\ M_d + M_i < M_T \end{cases}$$

We use βC_i to model the effect of CPU utilization, γM_i to model the effect of RAM utilization and $\alpha \frac{8}{T_i}$ to model the effect of migration cost. Because our goal is to minimize T_i but F_i should be maximized, so we put T_i on the denominator. The value 8 is a normalized factor for T_i, which will scale the effect of T_i to be close to C_i and M_i. The value 8 is an empirical value.

Note that in the function $F_i = \alpha \frac{e}{T_i} + \beta C_i + \gamma M_i$, there is a tradeoff between T_i and C_i, M_i. To make CPU and RAM

utilization ratio far from the threshold, it's better to choose the VM that consumes as much CPU and RAM as possible, which may lead to too high migration cost. So we take T_i into consideration. In the same idea, T_i also can't be too small. Because if so, migration may not achieve the migration goal. So this model will choose the most "profitable" VM from the n VMs to migrate. Here "profitable" means achieving the goal of live migration while minimizing migration cost.

Algorithm 2 shows the detail process of this migration strategy. We call this strategy as LB-FT-Strategy.

The complexity of Algorithm 2 is O(n), n is the number of VMs.

Algorithm 2: LB-FT-Strategy
1. **Input**: $VM_1, VM_2, ..., VM_n, e, \alpha, \beta, \gamma, C_s, M_s, C_d, M_d, C_T, M_T$
2. **Output**: VM_{mig}
3. VM_SET = { $VM_1, VM_2, ..., VM_n$ }
4. F = 0
5. MAX_INDEX = 0
6. **foreach** VM_i **in** VM_SET
7.   **if** $C_s - C_i < C_T$ **and** $M_s - M_i < M_T$ **and** $C_d + C_i < C_T$ **and** $M_d + M_i < M_T$ **then**
8. T_i = VM_i's predicted migration time cost
9. $F_i = \alpha \frac{e}{T_i} + \beta C_i + \gamma M_i$
10.   **if** $F_i > F$ **then**
11.   MAX_INDEX = i
12.   **end if**
13.   **end if**
14. **end foreach**
15. VM_{mig} ← VM_SET[MAX_INDEX]

4.2 Server Consolidation

According to [2], the problem of server consolidation can be treated as a 2-dimission bin packing problem. Virtual machine (VM) can be treated as a rectangular item with CPU and RAM utilization ratio as width and height. Physical machine (PM) can be treated as square bin. The problem is to map each rectangular into square bins and minimize the number of square bins. To solve the bin packing problem, we can use integer programming or heuristics. In this paper we choose to use heuristics. Although heuristics do not guarantee an optimal solution, the required time to obtain a feasible solution is much shorter than integer programming. Besides, the process of heuristics algorithm is actually a cost-saving way for server consolidation.

Traditional 2-dimission bin packing problem can be solved with BLF (bottom left fill) algorithm [30]. But algorithm we use in this paper, which we denote as TRF (top right fill), is different with BLF.

As shown in Figure 6, when inserting one item into a bin, BLF will place the item bottom-left aligned at the first possible insertion position. The bin is far from being full. But in our case, the item should be placed at the top-right point of the last item to ensure CPU or RAM utilization is not overlapped. The bin is already full.

Figure 6. Comparison of BLF(left) and TRF(right)

Our goal is to achieve server consolidation while minimizing migration cost. Based on the test of migration cost model, PM with high migration cost (PM's migration cost is the sum of VM migration cost in the PM) usually has low remaining capacity (CPU and RAM). So we should migrate VMs from PM with highest remaining capacity to PM with lowest remaining capacity. Let's consider a small cluster with 3 physical machines. First we sort these machines by remaining capacity, as shown in Figure 7. The oblique line area represents the remaining capacity.

Figure 7. Sort PMs by the remaining capacity

Now we should migrate VM_1, VM_2, VM_3 in PM_3 to PM_1 and PM_2. But only one of the 3 VMs can be migrated to PM_1. To choose one VM from the 3 VMs, we follow the Max-utilization Principle, which is described in Figure 8

Figure 8. Max-utilization Principle

In left side of Figure 8, the big rectangle is the remaining capacity of a PM before migration, with RAM=a and CPU=b. The rectangle at bottom-left is the VM should be migrated, with RAM=x and CPU=y. Max-utilization Principle chooses the VM which minimize the following function:

$$f(x,y) = |\frac{x}{y} - \frac{a}{b}| \qquad (13)$$

Following the Max-utilization Principle, we can avoid choosing VM that requires too much of one resource compared to the other resource, which is shown in right side of Figure 8.

Based on Max-utilization Principle, we choose VM_2 to migrate to PM_1. After that, PM_1 has no capacity to hold VM_1 and VM_3, so the 2 VMs are migrated to PM_2. The migration process is shown in Figure 9.

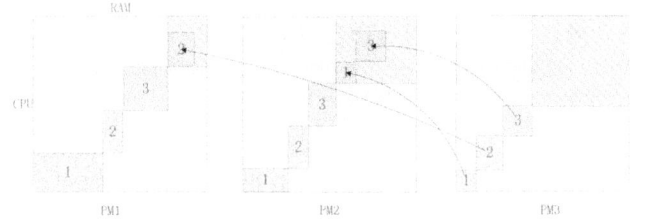

Figure 9. Migration process

Suppose there are P physical machines in the cluster. Algorithm 3 illustrates the migraiton strategy for server consolidation. We call this strategy as SC-Strategy. The complexity of Algorithm 3 is O(P*log(P)).

Algorithm 3: SC-Strategy
1. **Input**:PM_1, PM_2,..., PM_P **Output**: RESULT_SET{}
2. PM_SET = { PM_1, PM_2,..., PM_P }
3. CAPACITY_SET = {0, 0, ..., 0}
4. RESULT_SET = {}
5. **set** head = 1, tail = p
6. **while** tail > head **do**
7. **set** head = 1
8. **foreach** PM_i **in** PM_SET
9. CAPACITY_SET[i] = remaining capacity of PM_i
10. **end foreach**
11. sort CAPACITY_SET
12. re-order PM_SET to match CAPACITY_SET
13. **while** PM_SET[tail] is not empty **and** tail > head **do**
14. migrate VM from PM_SET[tail] to PM_SET[head] based on Max-utilization Principle
15. **if** PM_SET[head] can't hold more VM
16. head = head + 1
17. **end if**
18. **end while**
19. **if** PM_SET[tail] is empty
20. remove PM_SET[tail] from PM_SET
21. **set** tail=tail-1
22. **end if**
23. **end while**
24. RESULT_SET= PM_SET

5. Implementation

To demonstrate the validity of our model, we have designed and implemented a prototype based on qemu-kvm platform. The model is also applicable for other virtualization platforms that have similar Pre-Copy algorithm for live migration.

We modified qemu-kvm source code to achieve following functions:

- Track memory dirtying rate and calculate general memory access pattern.

- Add qemu shell commands 'dirtyspeed', 'stopdirtyspeed', and 'ramsize' to provide interfaces for monitoring.

The source code of our modification can be accessed from [36]. In 5.1 and 5.2 we will illustrate the implementation in detail.

5.1 Memory dirtying rate track

There is a data structure called dirty_bitmap(one page per bit) in KVM user space to record which memory pages are dirty at current time. And each call to the system call *kvm_vm_ioctl(s, KVM_GET_DIRTY_LOG, &d)* in *kvm-all.c* will sync the dirty memory status in kernel space to dirty_bitmap since the last call to *kvm_vm_ioctl(s, KVM_GET_DIRTY_LOG, &d)*. With the dirty_bitmap data structure, we can calculate how many pages get dirtied during this time period. Thus, we can call *kvm_vm_ioctl(s, KVM_GET_DIRTY_LOG, &d)* every 1 second to measure memory dirtying rate.

5.2 Calculating memory access pattern (Sim(k))

To calculate Sim(k), we firstly need to compare dirty_bitmap similarity between 2 time periods. We modified qemu-kvm source code to achieve this. In *exec-obsolete.h*, several lines of code are added to export dirty_bitmap to a file. Then we can compare the dirty_bitmap in the file to calculate Sim(k), which is the memory access pattern as mentioned before.

5.3 Migration strategy module implementation

Block diagram of system framework is shown in Figure 10.

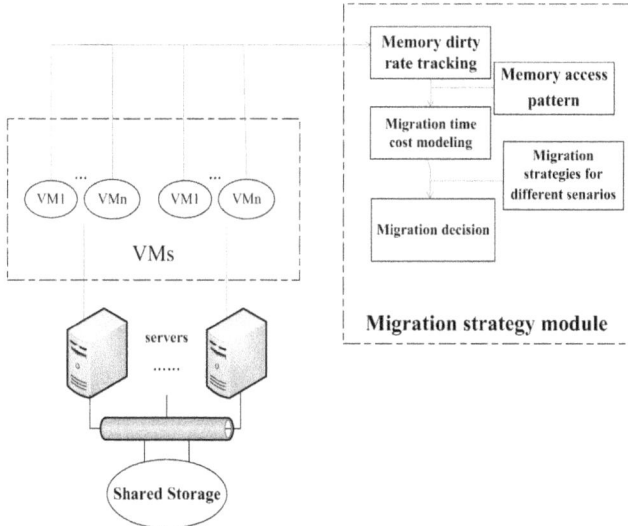

Figure 10.　Block diagram of system framework

In Figure 10, there is a migration strategy module. The block diagram of this module is shown in Figure 11.

As shown in Figure 11, qemu-kvm export QMP interface which allows other applications to communicate with VMs and send control command via telnet protocol.

The control scripts block is the core of this module. The scripts communicate with VMs to be migrated to retrieve VM status data (including memory dirtying rate, RAM size and duplicate page amount) via QMP interface and calculate time cost of each VM. Then the control scripts use specific migration strategies to make migration decision. Finally the control scripts send migration command to finish the migration.

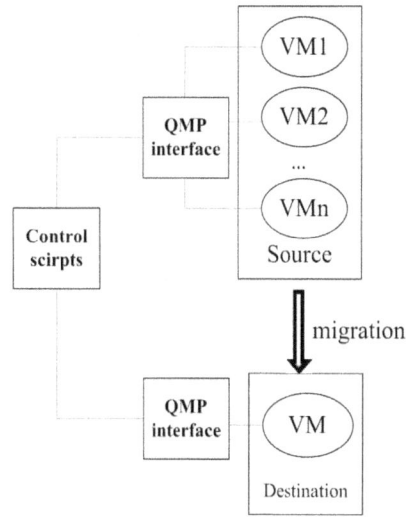

Figure 11.　Migration strategy module

It is necessary to consider the RAM and CPU cost of this module because an efficient management module for live migration should cost as less resource as possible. We measure RAM and CPU cost of the control scripts and result shows that these scripts just consume around 20M RAM and 0.01% of CPU. This is a rather low cost and proves the migration decision module is efficient.

6. EVALUATION OF TIME COST MODEL

In this section, we first introduce the experiment environment. Then we validate the model by comparing the model estimated migration time with measured migration time.

6.1 Experiment Setup

We conduct the experiments on a cluster of 10 physical machines, each with 4 core Intel i5 3.2 GHz processor, 16GB RAM, 500GB SATA hard disk. The physical machines are running Ubuntu 14.04 with Linux 3.5.0 kernel and the VMM is qemu-kvm. The guest OSes are running Ubuntu 10.04 with Linux 2.6.18.8 kernel. For live migration, all of the VM images can be accessed with shared storage. In order to simplify the migration problem, all VMs are configured to use 1 VCPU and 4GB RAM. The experiments used six workloads

1) *Linux idle:* an idle Linux OS for daily use. This workload is used as a frame of reference for comparison.
2) Apache Jmeter[24]: Apache JMeter may be used to test performance both on static and dynamic resources. We configured 500 threads to test Apache HTTP service in our experiment.
3) Memtester[25]: a user space utility for testing the memory subsystem. We use this tool to apply 10M memory in each iteration. The number of iterations is no limit. This will generate constant pressure to memory.
4) TPC-C[27]: TPC-C simulates a complete environment where a population of terminal operators executes transactions against a database. We configure 500 terminals threads and 500 database connections in our experiments.
5) Make Linux kernel: this is the process of compile Linux kernel in VM, which will generate highly intensive read and write load to memory.
6) SPECint[30]: a computer benchmark specification for CPU's integer processing power. In our evaluation we choose 401.bzip2 benchmark.

6.2 Memory dirtying rate tracking

With the method introduced in 5.2, memory dirtying rate can be tracked before migration starts. A set of tests are conducted to measure memory dirtying rate for a variety of workloads within 100 seconds. Figure 12 shows EWMA memory dirtying rate of each representative workloads in a VM with 4GB RAM. From these curves we can see that the EWMA memory dirtying rate varies significantly between different workloads. For VMs that runs Jmeter and idle Linux, the memory dirtying rate remains at a relative low level and hence are excellent candidates for migration.

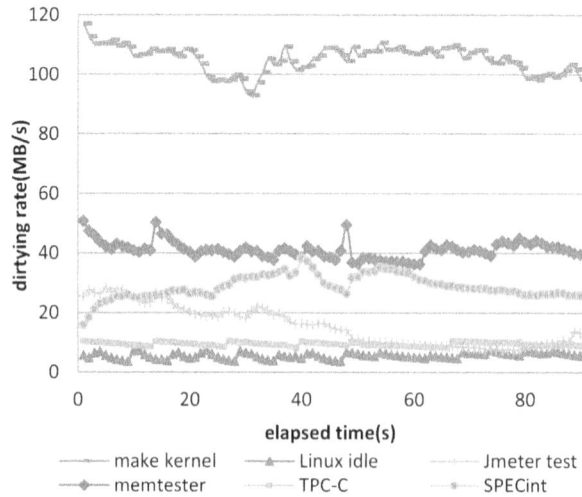

Figure 12. EWMA memory dirtying rate tracking

6.3 Network bandwidth and buffer write speed measuring

We use the tool Iperf[23] to measure network bandwidth in testing environment. The network bandwidth measured is around 500Mbps.

Buffer write speed, which is B in Table 1, is the value of b_width in function ram_save_iterate() of arch_init.c in qemu-kvm source code. We measure this value by taking the average value of historical series of b_width. Finally we get the value of B as 2500M/s.

Table 3 shows the value of constants used in the experiment.

Table 3.   Value of Constants for experiment

Symbol	Quantity
V	500Mbps
T_{MAX}	0.03s
M	4GB
B	2500M/s

6.4 Model Accuracy Validation

We conduct experiments by migrating 6 types of VMs between two physical machines. Each VM runs Linux idle, TPC-C, Jmeter test, Memtester, SPECint, Make kernel respectively. For each type of VM, migration is tested for 10 times, and we calculate the average migration time as measured time. Then we collect parameters before migration and use Algorithm 1 to calculate predicted time. Predicted time is also an average value.

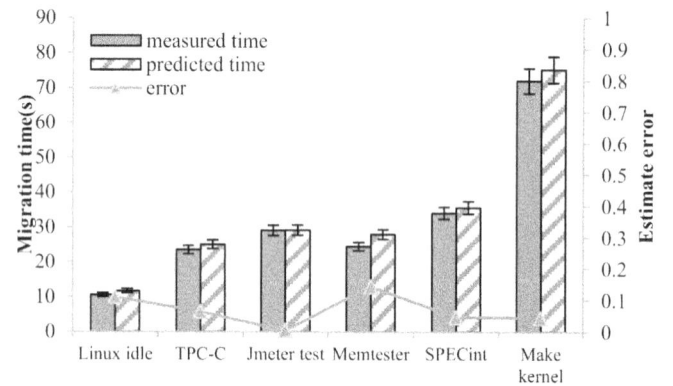

Figure 13.   Model Accuracy Validation

Figure 13 shows measured time, predicted time of each workload and the prediction error of our model. The average estimated error of these 6 workloads is less than 10%, which means our model achieves satisfying accuracy for practical use.

7. EVALUATION OF OPTIMIZED MIGRATION STRATEGY

We now show our model is useful for cost reduction in live migration. Here cost reduction means reduction of migration time and network traffic (total amount of data transferred during migration). These two metrics can be got directly from qemu-kvm source code.

7.1 Load balance and fault tolerance

In this evaluation, there are 6 physical machines in the cluster. One physical machine is set as the "hot-spot", which means there are many VMs running on the machine and CPU or memory utilization ratio exceeds the threshold. We run 4 VMs on the "hot-spot". Apache Web Server, TPC-C, Memtester, and SPECint are running on each of the VM, one VM with one application. The other 5 physical machines are initially set to hold only one VM, each VM running only one workload. Table 4 shows the averaged workload details of the four workloads.

Table 4.   Averaged Workload Details

Work load	CPU usage	Memory usage
Apache Web Server	27.3%	13.2%-17.8%
TPC-C	14.5%	13.7%
Memtester	15.2%	12.3%
SPECint	25.1%	27.4%

Before migration, when either CPU or RAM utilization of the "hot-spot" exceeds threshold, we use LB-FT-Strategy to perform migration. Migration is tested for 20 times, the total cost is summed up for each migration metric. The strategy for comparison is the strategy mentioned in [31], this strategy doesn't specify which VM should be migrated when performing load balance. However, with LB-FT-Strategy, we choose the VM which will achieve the migration goal and minimize migration cost. The result of using LB-FT-Strategy for migration cost reduction is shown in Figure 14. Figure 14 shows that migration cost can be significantly reduced with LB-FT-Strategy. Migration time cost and network traffic are reduced by 35.1% and 34.9%.

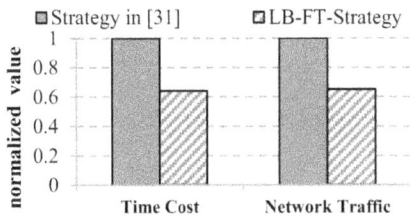

Figure 14.   Migration Cost Saving

7.2 Server consolidation

In this evaluation, we conduct 10 rounds of test. Each round we randomly assign X VMs to 10 physical machines. Each VM runs one type of workloads of the following types: Apache Web Server, TPC-C, Memtester, and SPECint.

In each round of test, we consolidate X VMs from 6 physical machines to Y physical machines with SC-Strategy. SC-Strategy will always choose the machine with high resource utilization as migration destination. However a random method will randomly choose migration destination regardless of migration cost. Figure 15 shows that migration time cost, network traffic are reduced by 50.2%, 49.1%.

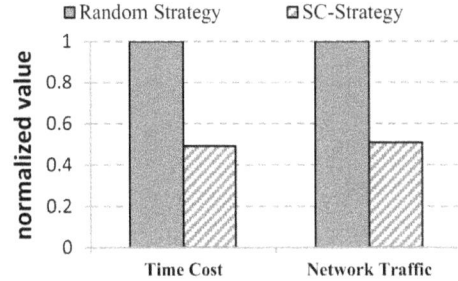

Figure 15.   Migration Cost Saving

Besides, we also conduct experiments to compare SC-Strategy and heuristic method mentioned in [2]. By following the Max-utilization Principle in SC-Strategy, we can get a mapping result closer to the optimal result than the heuristic method mentioned in [2], which is shown in Table 5. This means that SC-Strategy is better than heuristic method mentioned in [2].

Table 5.   Server Consolidation Test

X	Optimal(results of integer programming)	Y₁(results of SC-Strategy)	Y₂(results of heuristic in [2])
24	5	6	6
32	7	7	7
40	8	8	9
48	9	9	10

8. RELATED WORKS

The performance of live VM migration has been studied on a variety of workloads in [6]. This technique had proven to be a very effective tool to enable service relocation in a non-disruptive manner. W.Voorsluys [14] evaluated the performance degradation of Web2.0 applications running inside VMs while they were being migrated. The main objective they concerned is the service level agreement (SLA) violation rather than the migration performance. None of these works provided a methodology to estimate the VM migration performance.

An automatic and transparent mechanism for proactive fault tolerance for arbitrary MPI applications has been studied and implemented using Xen live migration [28]. In their research, the authors give a general overview on total migration time and possible parameters affecting it, specifically the amount of memory allocated to a guest VM

Sherif Akoush and Ripduman Sohan addressed the issue of live migration performance in [3]. They mainly model migration performance in terms of migration time. Liu H then address this issue again in [4], The effect of Writable Working Set is considered in this paper but their migration strategy is purely based on migration cost, not considering the impact of migration goal. Our migration strategy is the first which chooses the best migration VM to minimize the cost while achieving the specific goal of migration.

[9], [21] and [35] introduce the idea of performing load balance and fault tolerance with VM live migration. But they didn't construct a precise mathematical model to quantify the effect of

migration cost. [2] illustrates how to conduct server consolidation with VM live migration. But the heuristic algorithm was not discussed in [2] in detail. We discussed heuristic algorithm thoroughly in section 4.2 and construct a strategy which performs better.

9. CONCLUSION

In this paper, we designed a migration time cost model to estimate VM migration performance. Our theoretical analysis and experimental results indicates that the parameters such as VM memory size, network bandwidth, memory dirtying rate and zero page amount are the major factors impacting migration time cost. We validated the model by comparing the estimate migration time cost with experimentally measured results. The experimental results showed that the prediction accuracy is higher than 90%. We also propose 2 live migration strategies based on the time cost model. The evaluation shows our optimized migration strategies can save 35%~50% of cost compared to the random migration strategy. Thus we can lower service performance vibration during migration and reduce network traffic at the maximum extent. In addition, the model can also introspectively guide the design of KVM migration algorithm for different tradeoffs among the migration performance metrics, such as the tradeoff between migration time cost and migration down time, which will be investigated in our future work.

10. ACKNOWLEDGMENT

This work is supported by National Natural Science Foundation of China(NSFC 61472241). And we'd like to give special thanks to Dr. Eddie Dong at Intel Corp, for his valuable comments and sharing of his knowledge.

11. REFRENCES

[1] R. Goldberg, "Survey of virtual machine research," IEEE Computer, 1974, pp. 34–45.

[2] Ferreto T C, Netto M A S, Calheiros R N, et al. Server consolidation with migration control for virtualized data centers[J]. Future Generation Computer Systems, 2011, 27(8): 1027-1034.

[3] Akoush S, Sohan R, Rice A, et al. Predicting the performance of virtual machine migration[C]//Modeling, Analysis & Simulation of Computer and Telecommunication Systems (MASCOTS), 2010 IEEE International Symposium on. IEEE, 2010: 37-46.

[4] Liu H, Xu C Z, Jin H, et al. Performance and energy modeling for live migration of virtual machines[C]//Proceedings of the 20th international symposium on High performance distributed computing. ACM, 2011: 171-182.

[5] Wu Y, Zhao M. Performance modeling of virtual machine live migration[C]//Cloud Computing (CLOUD), 2011 IEEE International Conference on. IEEE, 2011: 492-499.

[6] C. Clark, K. Fraser, S. Hand, J. G. Hansen, E. Jul, C. Limpach, I. Pratt, and A. Warfield. Live Migration of Virtual Machines. In Proceedings of Second Symposium Networked Systems Design and Implementation (NSDI'05), May 2-4, 2005, pp. 273-286

[7] M. Hines and K. Gopalan. Post-Copy Based Live Virtual Machine Migration Using Adaptive Pre-Paging And Dynamic Self-Ballooning. In International Conference on Virtual Execution Environments (VEE'09), Washington DC, USA, March 11-13, 2009, pp.51-60.

[8] H. Liu, H. Jin, X. Liao, L. Hu and C. Yu. Live Migration of Virtual Machine Based on Full System Trace and Replay. In Proceedings of the 18th International Symposium on High Performance Distributed Computing (HPDC'09), June 11-13, 2009, Munich, Germany, pp.101-110.

[9] A. B. Nagarajan, F. Mueller, C. Engelmann, and S. L. Scott. Proactive Fault Tolerance for HPC with Xen Virtualization. In Proceedings of ACM Annual International Conference on Supercomputing (ICS'07), Seattle, Washington, USA, June 17-21, 2007, pp. 23-32.

[10] M. Nelson, B. H. Lim, and G. Hutchins. Fast Transparent Migration for Virtual Machines. In Proceedings of USENIX Annual Technical Conference (USENIX'05), Anaheim, California, USA, April 10-15, 2005, pp.391-394.

[11] R. Nathuji and K. Schwan. Virtual Power: Coordinated Power Management in Virtualized Enterprise Systems. In Proceedings of ACM Symposium on Operating Systems Principles (SOSP'07), Stevenson, WA, USA, October 14-17, 2007.

[12] K. Sato, H. Sato, S. Matsuoka. Model-based Optimization for Data-intensive Application on Virtual Cluster. In The 9th IEEE/ACM International Conference on Grid Computing (Grid'08), Tsukuba, Japan, pp.367-368

[13] A. Verma, P. Ahuja, and A. Neogi. pMapper: Power and Migration Cost Awae Application Placement in Virtualized Systems. In Proceedings of the 9th ACM/IFIP/USENIX International Conference on Middleware (Middleware'08), Springer-Verlag, Leuven, Belgium, December 1-5, 2008, pp.243-264.

[14] W. Voorsluys, J. Broberg, S. Venugopal, and R. Buyya. Cost of Virtual Machine Live Migration in Clouds: A Performance Evaluation. In Proceedings of the 1st International Conference on Cloud Computing, Lecture Notes In Computer Science, Beijing, China, December, 2009, pp.254-265.

[15] T. Wood, P. Shenoy, A. Venkataramani and M. Yousif. Blackbox and Gray-box Strategies for Virtual Machine Migration. In Proceedings of 4th USENIX Symposium on Networked Systems Design and Implementation (NSDI'07), Cambridge, MA, USA, April 11-13, 2007, pp. 229-242.

[16] Kivity A, Kamay Y, Laor D, et al. kvm: the Linux virtual machine monitor[C]//Proceedings of the Linux Symposium. 2007, 1: 225-230.

[17] Barham P, Dragovic B, Fraser K, et al. Xen and the art of virtualization[J]. ACM SIGOPS Operating Systems Review, 2003, 37(5): 164-177.

[18] Vmware virtualization, http://www.vmware.com/

[19] qemu-kvm source project, http://sourceforge.net/projects/kvm/files/qemu-kvm/

[20] MONTGOMERY J M. Introduction to statistical quality control (3rd ed'96)[J]. 1996.

[21] Denning P J. The working set model for program behavior[J]. Communications of the ACM, 1968, 11(5): 323-333.

[22] Denning P J, Schwartz S C. Properties of the working-set model[J]. Communications of the ACM, 1972, 15(3): 191-198.

[23] Iperf. The National Laboratory for Applied Network Research. Available: http://sourceforge.net/projects/iperf/

[24] Apache JMeter, http://jmeter.apache.org/

[25] memtester, userspace utility for testing the memory subsystem, http://pyropus.ca/software/memtester/

[26] stress, workload generator for POSIX systems. http://weather.ou.edu/~apw/projects/stress/

[27] TPC-C, http://www.tpc.org/tpcc.

[28] Nagarajan A B, Mueller F, Engelmann C, et al. Proactive fault tolerance for HPC with Xen virtualization[C]//Proceedings of

the 21st annual international conference on Supercomputing. ACM, 2007: 23-32.

[29] Hines M R, Deshpande U, Gopalan K. Post-copy live migration of virtual machines[J]. ACM SIGOPS operating systems review, 2009, 43(3): 14-26.

[30] SPEC CINT2006 , http://www.spec.org/cpu2006/CINT2006/

[31] Lu P, Barbalace A, Palmieri R, et al. Adaptive live migration to improve load balancing in virtual machine environment[C]//Euro-Par 2013: Parallel Processing Workshops. Springer Berlin Heidelberg, 2014: 116

[32] Shribman A, Hudzia B. Pre-Copy and post-copy VM live migration for memory intensive applications[C]//Euro-Par 2012: Parallel Processing Workshops. Springer Berlin Heidelberg, 2013: 539-547.

[33] Hu W, Hicks A, Zhang L, et al. A quantitative study of virtual machine live migration[C]//Proceedings of the 2013 ACM Cloud and Autonomic Computing Conference. ACM, 2013

[34] Pintea C M, Pascan C, Hajdu-Măcelaru M. Comparing several heuristics for a packing problem[J]. International Journal of Advanced Intelligence Paradigms, 2012, 4(3-4): 268-277.

[35] Li X, He Q, Chen J, et al. Informed live migration strategies of virtual machines for cluster load balancing[M]//Network and Parallel Computing. Springer Berlin Heidelberg, 2011: 111-122.

[36] Qemu-kvm,   https://github.com/shadowwill/qemu-kvm

Forwarding Strategies for Applications in Named Data Networking

Hila Ben Abraham and Patrick Crowley
Computer Science and Engineering
Washington University in St. Louis
{hila, pcrowley}@wustl.edu

ABSTRACT

Named Data Networking (NDN), an information-centric Internet architecture, introduces a new forwarding model, in which the forwarding plane can choose between multiple interfaces when forwarding a packet. While the forwarding module brings new opportunities it also introduces challenges when the application's performance or correctness is affected by a conflict between the application design and the assigned forwarding strategy. In this paper we demonstrate the impact of the forwarding strategy decision on the performance and correctness of NDN applications.

1. INTRODUCTION

Named Data Networking (NDN) [1] is a consumer-driven architecture that focuses on retrieving a content according to its name. To request a content item, a consumer expresses an Interest packet, which is forwarded in the network until it can be satisfied by a router's Content Store (CS), or by an application that serves as the content producer. The content is returned to the consumer in a Data packet that follows the reverse path of the Interest packet.

As in IP, the Forwarding Information Base (FIB) table is used to determine the packet's next hop. An entry in the NDN FIB consists of a namespace and one or more possible faces. Each face represents an interface to a possible next hop. When the faces list consists of multiple faces, the forwarding plane needs to decide on which face(s) to forward the interest. The forwarding decision is determined by the selected *forwarding strategy* of the requested namespace.

Two Information-centric network (ICN) prototypes, the NDN forwarder (NFD) [2] and the CCNx project [3] provide an API for NDN or CCN applications. These prototypes allow pairing a forwarding strategy with an application namespace, and therefore affect the way the application packets are forwarded in the network. A developer can choose an existing forwarding strategy, or, alternatively, develop a new one to satisfy application-specific needs. While this brings new opportunities and advantages, it can pose challenges.

ANCS '16 March 17-18, 2016, Santa Clara, CA, USA

© 2016 Copyright held by the owner/author(s).

ACM ISBN 978-1-4503-4183-7/16/03.

DOI: http://dx.doi.org/10.1145/2881025.2889475

2. FORWARDING AND APPLICATIONS

Existing forwarding strategies have different design approaches. First, if the FIB entry consists of multiple faces, the forwarding strategy must decide on which faces an Interest should be sent. The strategy may choose the best performing face, a subset of possible faces or all available faces. The decision can be made according to the face *cost*, which is determined by the routing protocol, or according to the face *rank*, which is determined by previous measurements of the forwarding strategy. Second, the forwarding strategy must decide how to react when a Data packet is not received on time: 1) **Drop** the Interest packet. 2) **Retransmit** the packet on the same or a different face(s). 3) Reply with a special **NACK packet** to the previous hop. The application developer must be aware of the approach taken by the forwarding strategy to better decide whether an application retransmission is required. Third, in NDN, Interest and data packets are forwarded on the same path (but in reverse direction). Therefore, the forwarding strategy knows which downstream faces work, and how well they work. An **Adaptive Forwarding** strategy records the performance of the faces to improve future decisions. A **Static Forwarding** strategy relies exclusively on the decisions made by the routing protocol. Hence, to stop using a face, a static forwarding strategy requires the routing protocol to remove the face from the FIB or to find a lower cost face.

We describe two use cases to demonstrate the impact of different design approaches and the selected strategy on the application's correctness and performance.

Use Case 1 - Multiple Producers.

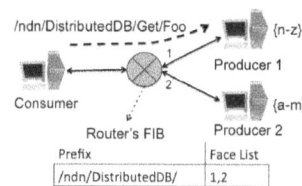

Figure 1: Multiple Producers with Disjoint Content

Figure 1 illustrates a distributed application consisting of multiple producers with disjoint content. Here the namespace is crucial and the strategy selection can play a critical role. When both producers publish the same namespace ndn/DistributedDB, the namespace entry in the router's FIB consists of both faces. If the namespace ndn/DistributedDB is paired with a static strategy, such as *best-route* [2], and face 1 is selected as the best face, then requests for *Foo* will be forwarded to producer 1 even though it cannot satisfy them. A static strategy will change its preferences in case of a link failure, but in our case, the link to 1 stays alive, and therefore face 2 will never get selected as the new best face. To solve this, the developer should design the application to use producer-specific namespaces instead of a general one. Alternatively, the developer must pair the application namespace with a strategy that guarantees a different behavior. One choice could be the *broadcast* [2] strategy. However, such a strategy will flood the network, and therefore is not advised. In this case, an *adaptive* strategy such as the default CCNx [2]strategy, or the *Green-Yellow-Red* [4] strategy will be the preferable choice.

Use Case 2 - Notification Services.

Notification service applications are distributed applications, in which the application's parties do not have clear consumer-producer relations and the distributed parties make requests to inform one another regarding their status.

We describe an example of a synchronization application that sends requests to synchronize the contents of a directory. Whenever a change is made to the synced directory, a participant sends a notification in the form of an Interest packet to inform the others of the change. Here, there are two possible approaches to designing the Interest namespace. The first approach is to make the participant identification part of the routable prefix. In this case, each participant has to learn about the existence of the others, so that he or she can send a dedicated interest packet, consisting of the participant identification, to each party.

In the second approach, the application uses the same namespace to send notice of a change to all the participants. Here, the selection of the forwarding strategy has a great impact on the application performance. A forwarding strategy that chooses a single face, such as *best-route*, forwards the Interest to only one participant, and therefore other participants are out-of-date. Alternatively, the *broadcast* strategy forwards the Interest to all the available faces of the namespace, and thereby guarantees that the notification message is forwarded to all the participants.

The CCNx Sync protocol [3] suggests an interesting design approach to a similar problem. The protocol uses the *default CCNx* strategy to notify all the participants by sending a single Interest packet. The strategy selects one face when forwarding an Interest, but retransmits the Interest on additional faces if the Interest timer expired before the Data packet was received. In the CCNx Sync protocol, the participants do not reply to the notification Interest with a Data packet, and therefore the Interest always expires and is retransmitted to the next available face by the strategy.

3. EMPIRICAL RESULTS

We used four hosts in the Open Network Lab (ONL) [5] and NFD version 0.3 to experiment with the topology described in Figure 1. We set the consumer to request 100 chunks of content, with approximately 50% of the requests for content held by producer 1, and the rest held by producer 2. We repeated the experiment using three strategies implemented in NFD 0.3 (ncc, best-route and broadcast), and reported the average number of Interests sent as shown in Figure 2a.

The *broadcast* strategy sent each Interest on both faces,

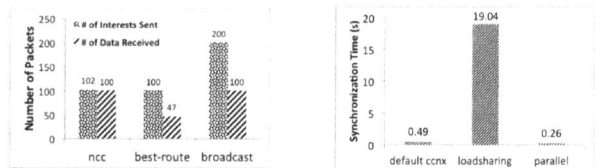

(a) Number of Interests Sent   (b) Average Synchronization Time

Figure 2: Use Cases Empirical Results

and therefore sent twice the number of requests. The results show that *best-route* retrieved only 47% of the content items while *broadcast* and *ncc* successfully retrieved all the content items. Here, the results demonstrate how the application's correctness is affected by the forwarding strategy.

To demonstrate the second use case, we used 16 ONL hosts, each running CCNx version 0.8.2, to measure the performance of CCNx Sync when using different forwarding strategies as shown in Figure 2b. We inserted a content item into the repository of one of the 16 hosts and measured the average synchronization time using different forwarding strategies over a fully connected mesh topology. As expected, the *parallel* strategy achieved the shortest synchronization times, since the notification was multicasted to all the distributed parties simultaneously. The *default CCNx strategy* was 1.8 times slower, and the *loadsharing* strategy was 73.1 times slower. Clearly the selected forwarding strategy significantly impacts the application's performance.

4. CONCLUSION AND FUTURE WORK

In this paper, we discussed the impact of the application triangle (the namespace design, the forwarding strategy and the application workflow) on the application's correctness and performance. We demonstrated that while different applications have different needs, and therefore use different design approaches, the application developer must consider the outcomes of selecting one way over another.

In future work, we would like to investigate real-world applications built on top of NDN. While a developer can select the strategies used in a closed environment, the network operator determines the forwarding strategies in the core network. Therefore, we would like to explore the relationship of forwarding strategies in different locations of the network. Another interesting question is whether one strategy outperforms others for a wide range of applications, and so can be used as the default forwarding strategy for NDN.

5. REFERENCES

[1] Lixia Zhang et al. Named data networking. *ACM SIGCOMM Computer Communication Review*, 2014.
[2] Alexander Afanasyev et al. Nfd developer's guide. Technical report, NDN-0021, NDN, 2014.
[3] Project CCNx. http://www.ccnx.org/.
[4] Cheng Yi et al. A case for stateful forwarding plane. *Computer Communications*, 2013.
[5] Charlie Wiseman et al. A remotely accessible network processor-based router for network experimentation. In *Proceedings of the 4th ACM/IEEE Symposium on Architectures for Networking and Communications Systems*. ACM, 2008.

ParaRegex: Towards Fast Regular Expression Matching in Parallel

Zhe Fu[*†], Zhi Liu[*†], and Jun Li[†‡]

[*]Department of Automation, Tsinghua University, China
[†]Research Institute of Information Technology, Tsinghua University, China
[‡]Tsinghua National Lab for Information Science and Technology, China
{fu-z13, zhi-liu12}@mails.tsinghua.edu.cn, junl@tsinghua.edu.cn

ABSTRACT

In this paper, we propose ParaRegex, a novel approach for fast parallel regular expression matching. ParaRegex is a framework that implements data-parallel regular expression matching for deterministic finite automaton based methods. Experimental evaluation shows that ParaRegex produces a fast matching engine with speeds of up to 6 times compared to sequential implementations on a commodity 8-thread workstation.

Keywords

Deep inspection, Regular expression matching, DFA, Parallelism

1. INTRODUCTION AND MOTIVATION

Regular expression (regex) matching has been widely used in today's network security systems, where the payloads of network packets are matched against a set of rules specified by regular expressions. To perform regex matching, regexes are constructed to Nondeterministic Finite Automaton (NFA) or Deterministic Finite Automaton (DFA). DFA becomes the prior choice for practical time-sensitive applications because it requires only one state transition lookup per input character and is hence fast. However, due to the increasing number of rules and the complicated semantics of regular expressions, state-of-the-art regex matching techniques hardly meet the demands of network speed.

Parallelism is becoming more and more popular and important, which produces new ideas to solve the performance bottlenecks of regex matching. In order to parallelize the regex matching, the input data can be partitioned into several segments and assigned to each thread. For all but the first input segment, the DFA state at the beginning is uncertain. For example, the initial state of the DFA for the second input data segment is determined by the final state of the DFA for the first segment. The basic idea of existing parallel implementations is that starting from the set of all

ANCS '16 March 17-18, 2016, Santa Clara, CA, USA

ACM ISBN 978-1-4503-4183-7/16/03.

DOI: http://dx.doi.org/10.1145/2881025.2889478

Table 1: Average number of *active* states of four different rulesets after any 1 and 2 input

Ruleset	bro50	bro217	snort24	snort34
Number of regexes	50	217	24	34
DFA states	667	8094	8630	10212
after any 1 input	4.60	37.63	62.42	78.70
after any 2 input	1.02	5.17	19.19	31.69

initial states, each thread computes the sub-result based on the input of each segment independently, and then the sub-results of all the threads can be reduced by joining them in sequential order [1, 2, 3].

Obviously, the huge overhead of this speculative implementation introduces significant computation load. Given a DFA with $|Q|$ states, input data with size m, and n processing threads, the time complexity of mapping and matching procedure is $O(|Q|m/n)$ and reducing procedure is $O(|Q|n)$. This reveals that these parallel implementations based on enumeration fail to obtain higher matching speed than the sequential implementation when the DFA is large.

However, the scenario will be quite different when considering with the input data. In this paper, the states that need to be traversed from are defined as *active* states. In a real-world situation, the simultaneously *active* states tend to move to very few states after reading any character, which means that the number of concurrent *active* states is likely to decrease sharply under several arbitrary input characters. As shown in Table 1, the average number of *active* states after one arbitrary input character is less than one percent of the total states number of the DFA. We define the reduction of the number of *active* states as states *convergence*, which brings hope for efficient parallelization of regex matching.

2. DESIGN AND IMPLEMENTATION

ParaRegex is proposed to implement fast parallel regex matching with low overhead, with MSU (Middle State Unit) as its key structure. MSU consists of two parts: a state and a mapping vector. The state denotes the ID of an *active* state, and the mapping vector is a bit vector that associates the original initial states to the state of this MSU.

Figure 1(a) and 1(b) explain how ParaRegex works in practice. As shown in Fig.1(a), there are two input segments S_k and S_{k+1}. Initially, each original state corresponds to an MSU, and the mapping vector of the MSU indicates which state has been traversed from. The first bit of the first MSU's mapping vector is set to 1 while others are set to 0,

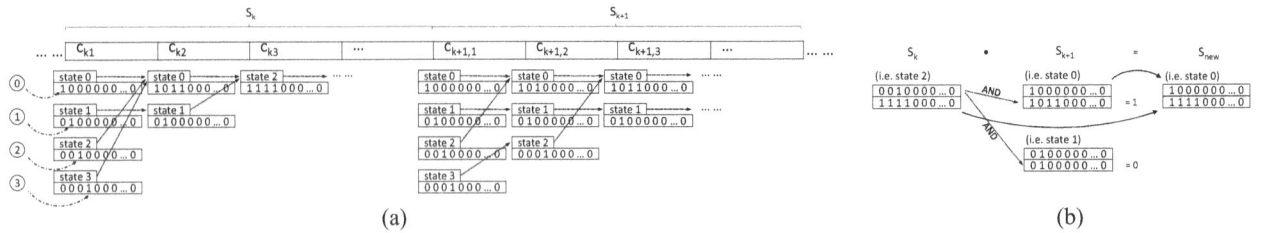

Figure 1: (a) Mapping, matching and (b) reduction procedure of ParaRegex using MSUs

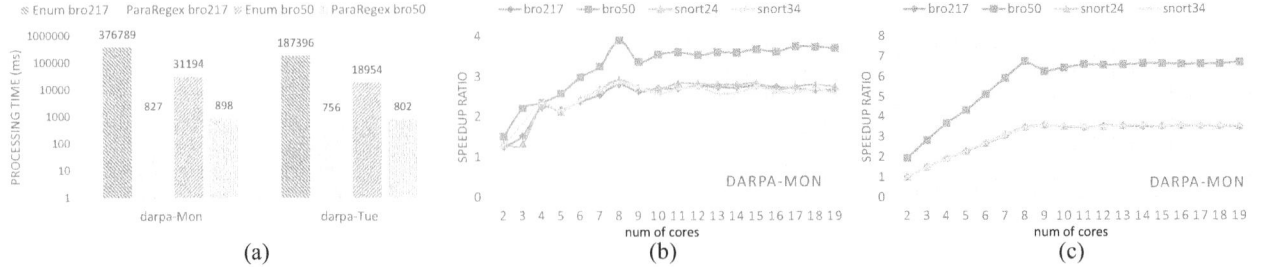

Figure 2: Comparison of ParaRegex and enumeration approach (a) overhead (b) vs. DFA (c) vs. D^2FA

denoting that this MSU derives from state 0. After reading the input character C_{k1} from the input segment S_k, state 0, state 2 and state 3 all jump to state 0, so the first, third and fourth MSUs are merged into one MSU whose state is state 0 and mapping vector is the union of MSU 0's, MSU 2's and MSU 3's mapping vectors.

Once all threads have completed their tasks, the set of MSUs corresponding to each segment would be reduced. The state in each MSU is encoded to a bit vector named state vector, and then the previous MSU's state vector performs an AND operation with the latter MSU's mapping vector. If the result of AND operation is 1, the two MSUs are supposed to be reduced into one which is composed of the previous MSU's mapping vector and the latter MSU's state.

Benefiting from the fast OR and AND operations of bit vectors, the processing of multiple MSUs can be very efficient. It must be noted that ParaRegex does not modify or create new DFAs, but just provides a general mechanism that is orthogonal to other work. In other words, state-of-the-art work on regex matching can be easily parallelized using ParaRegex by replacing original states with MSUs or just attaching a mapping vector to the original state.

3. EVALUATION

We carry out the preliminary evaluation with an Intel Core i7-4790 CPU (4 cores with 8 threads), and use the Regular Expression Processor [4] as the basic implementation of regex matching and pthread for the thread library. Four rulesets picked from Bro and Snort are tested (Table 1), while the Darpa network traffic is treated as the input data.

We compare ParaRegex to a general enumeration approach [1, 2, 3]. Figure 2(a) shows the matching time on different rulesets and traffic. By introducing the MSU structure, the processing speed of ParaRegex is at least one to two orders of magnitudes faster than that of enumeration approach. Figure 2(b) shows the speed improvement of ParaRegex on

different rulesets, treating [4] as a baseline. As the number of threads in use increases, the matching speed of ParaRegex grows and maximum speed is obtained when 8 threads process simultaneously in parallel. We also apply ParaRegex to D^2FA [5] and gain up to 6 times speedup (Fig. 2(c)). More experiments on other rulesets and traffic, which are omitted from this paper, draw the similar conclusion.

4. CONCLUSIONS AND FUTURE WORK

This paper introduces ParaRegex, a framework orthogonal to state-of-art DFA-based regular expression matching methods. ParaRegex employs MSUs to implement low-overhead and high-efficiency parallel matching engine with nearly linear speed improvement. Our future work will focus on conducting experiments on other distributed processing platforms like Hadoop or Spark, and further parallelize multiple *active* MSUs by specific hardware. We hope all these platforms and algorithms can effectively work together to achieve high performance regular expression matching in parallel.

5. REFERENCES

[1] J. Holub and S. Štekr. On parallel implementations of deterministic finite automata. In *Implementation and Application of Automata*, pages 54–64, 2009.

[2] Y. Ko, M. Jung, Y.-S. Han, and B. Burgstaller. A speculative parallel dfa membership test for multicore, simd and cloud computing environments. *International Journal of Parallel Programming*, 42(3):456–489, 2014.

[3] R. E. Ladner and M. J. Fischer. Parallel prefix computation. *Journal of the ACM (JACM)*, 27(4):831–838, 1980.

[4] Regular expression processor. http://regex.wustl.edu/.

[5] M. Becchi and P. Crowley. An improved algorithm to accelerate regular expression evaluation. In *Proceedings of the 3rd ACM/IEEE Symposium on Architectures for Networking and Communications Systems (ANCS)*, pages 145–154, 2007.

Minflate: Combining Rule Set Minimization with Jump-based Expansion for Fast Packet Classification

Sven Hager[†]   Patrik John[†]   Andreas Fiessler[‡]   Björn Scheuermann[†]

[†]Humboldt University of Berlin, Germany
{hagersve,john,scheuermann}@informatik.hu-berlin.de

[‡]genua mbH, Germany
andreas_fiessler@genua.de

ABSTRACT

Network packet classification is a key functionality for packet filters and firewalls, and its performance is crucial for such systems to maintain a high packet throughput under heavy load situations. However, many existing packet filters employ slow classification algorithms which cannot provide the required lookup performance due to slow rule set traversal. In this work, we address this problem by providing a novel rule set transformation strategy called *Minflate* which combines the advantages of existing orthogonal transformation schemes by first minimizing a source rule set and then encoding decision trees into the minimized rule set. Our results show that the Minflate-generated rule sets are both small and can in many cases be traversed faster than rule sets transformed by existing techniques in isolation.

1. INTRODUCTION

Network packet classification is a key building block for packet filters and firewalls, such as the widely deployed Linux' `iptables` and FreeBSD's `ipfw`. The primary task of these services is to discriminate incoming network packets based on certain header fields with respect to a predefined *rule set* in order to establish a security policy, enable traffic rate limiting, or implement QoS routing. However, if the size of the implemented rule set grows, these systems can easily be brought to their knees in terms of packet throughput, as the classification performance does not meet the line speed requirement. The reason for this behavior is twofold: first, many widely used systems, such as `iptables` and `ipfw`, still employ a basic linear search algorithm to traverse the rule set for every single packet—although there are significantly faster algorithms at hand [4]. Second, these systems often do not properly optimize the installed rule set at load time to reduce the number of processed rules during the packet classification process.

In this work, we propose a novel rule set transformation approach called *Minflate* that significantly increases the classification performance of existing packet filtering systems *without* the need to adapt their current implementation. By composing existing orthogonal rule set transformation techniques, which either minimize [2] or inflate a specified source rule set in a controlled way [1], we gen-

ANCS '16 March 17-18, 2016, Santa Clara, CA, USA

© 2016 Copyright held by the owner/author(s).

ACM ISBN 978-1-4503-4183-7/16/03.

DOI: http://dx.doi.org/10.1145/2881025.2889485

erate an optimized rule set which is semantically equivalent to the source rules, but can be traversed significantly faster than rule sets generated by existing transformation techniques in isolation. Our evaluation indicates that the Minflate approach requires sub-second preprocessing time for rule sets of up to 5,000 rules. Furthermore, our throughput experiments with `iptables` and `ipfw` show that the Minflate-generated rule sets can be traversed over 13 times faster than an original source rule set, and over 1.2 times faster than a rule set generated by existing optimization techniques.

2. PROBLEM STATEMENT

We assume that a *rule set* $\mathscr{R}$ with N rules R_i is an ordered collection $\mathscr{R} = \langle R_1, \ldots, R_N \rangle$. Each rule R_i consists of an *action* A_i and one or more checks C_j which are executed on specific header fields of an incoming packet P, e.g., $\texttt{dst\_port}(P) = 80$ or $\texttt{src\_addr}(P) \in 101.20.0.0/16$. The goal of the packet classification problem is to find the smallest index i^* for a packet P where all checks in rule R_{i^*} match the corresponding header fields in P. Then, the associated action A_{i^*} (e. g., DROP or ACCEPT) is executed.

3. THE MINFLATE APPROACH

The proposed Minflate technique is a source-to-source rule set optimization approach that transforms an input rule set $\mathscr{R}$ into a semantically equivalent output rule set $\mathscr{R}'$, which can be traversed faster by the underlying packet filter. To this end, Minflate combines the existing rule set optimization strategies *Firewall Compressor* [2] and *HiTables* [1], which implement orthogonal optimization strategies in order to achieve the goal that fewer rules have to be processed by the packet filter at run time. The Minflate transformation flow is sketched in Figure 1.

Firewall Compressor, on the one hand, aims to minimize the overall number of rules in the source rule set by decomposing and merging selected rules. The resulting output rule set typically has fewer total rules and thus can often be traversed faster. HiTables, on the other hand, exploits the fact that many existing packet filters, such as `iptables` and `ipfw`, provide the ability to conditionally redirect the packet classification control flow by so called *jump rules* [1]. These jump rules are used by HiTables in order to integrate decision tree search structures [3] into the given source rule set. During the rule set traversal, the jump rules dispatch on the packet's header fields to quickly reach the highest prioritized

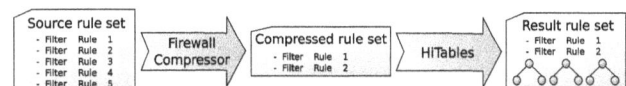

Figure 1: The Minflate approach.

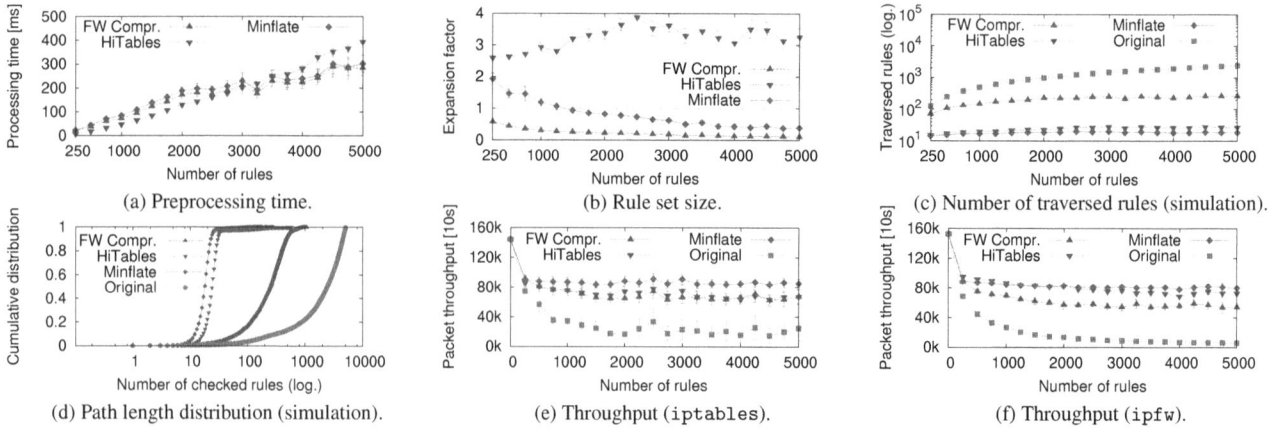

(a) Preprocessing time.

(b) Rule set size.

(c) Number of traversed rules (simulation).

(d) Path length distribution (simulation).

(e) Throughput (`iptables`).

(f) Throughput (`ipfw`).

Figure 2: Evaluation results.

matching rule. Although this process increases the rule set size, it can be traversed faster because many rules that would have been tested in a linear search are skipped.

The key idea behind Minflate is a functional composition of Firewall Compressor and HiTables in order to combine the advantages of both approaches: a small size of the output rule set as well as decision trees for fast traversal. To this end, Minflate computes the output rule set $\mathcal{R}'$ by chaining the Firewall Compressor and HiTables techniques, i. e., $\mathcal{R}' = \text{hitables}(\text{fw\_compressor}(\mathcal{R}))$. Thus, the input rule set $\mathcal{R}$ is first transformed to a compressed rule set $\mathcal{R}_C$, and subsequently translated to the output rule set $\mathcal{R}'$ which contains decision trees for fast traversal.

4. EVALUATION

We evaluated the efficiency of Minflate in terms of preprocessing time, the number of rules in the output rule set, and matching performance both in a simulated environment as well as with generated network traffic on the `iptables` and `ipfw` packet filters. To this end, we used the ClassBench benchmark tool [5] in order to generate rule sets with sizes ranging from 250 up to 5,000 rules, in steps of 250. For each rule set size, we generated 20 different rule sets. Also, for each rule set we generated a corresponding trace of 100,000 packet headers uniformly distributed over the rule set. Our measurement results are shown in Figure 2. All values are averaged over the 20 test runs for each rule set size, and the error bars represent 95% confidence intervals.

Figure 2a shows the preprocessing times for C++ implementations of the Minflate, Firewall Compressor, and HiTables techniques on an Intel Xeon E7 2.5 GHz machine running Linux. It can be seen that Minflate has the highest preprocessing times for rule set sizes up to 3,000. For larger rule sets, Minflate executes faster than HiTables, as the rule set compression in the first step enables a faster decision tree generation in the second step.

Next, Figure 2b depicts the size of the transformed rule sets in terms of a factor to the size of the source rule set. While Firewall Compressor reduces the overall size, the HiTables-generated rule set is enlarged, which is due to the decision trees encoded in the generated rule set. We also see that Minflate enlarges the compressed rule set, but still generates rule sets smaller than the source rule set for more than 1,500 rules.

Figures 2c shows the mean number of traversed rules in the rule sets. Furthermore, Figure 2d exhibits the distribution of the number of traversed rules, for rule sets of 5,000 rules. These results were obtained by matching the generated headers against the corresponding rule sets in a simulated environment. The plots reveal that the Minflate-generated rule sets classify the given headers by traversing the least amount of rules.

Finally, Figures 2e and 2f show our throughput results using `iptables` and `ipfw`. Here, we used `tcpreplay` to loop over the generated traces for 10 seconds and send minimal-sized packets to Raspberry Pi 1 machines, which ran Linux with `iptables` and FreeBSD with `ipfw`, respectively. The number of processed packets after 10 seconds were counted with `netstat`. In both figures, we observe a sharp throughput drop between 0 and 250 rules, which demonstrates the large overhead induced by the packet classification system. However, the figures also show that, while the throughput for the original rule sets continues to drop with increasing rule set sizes, the optimization techniques are able to significantly improve the classification performance. In case of `iptables`, Minflate performs always best for each evaluated rule set size, outperforming HiTables by a factor of over 1.2. For `ipfw`, HiTables gives better results for small rule set sizes up to 2,000. However, for larger rule sets, Minflate outperforms HiTables by a factor of up to 1.1. The reason for the slightly worse results for small rule sets is an inefficient representation of IP ranges in `ipfw`.

5. CONCLUSION

We presented Minflate, a novel rule set optimization technique which combines the benefits of existing transformation schemes through functional composition. Minflate first minimizes a source rule set with Firewall Compressor and subsequently augments it with decision trees using HiTables to generate output rule sets which can be quickly searched by the underlying packet filter. Our simulation- and traffic-based experiments confirm that the Minflate-generated rule sets can in most cases be traversed faster than rule sets generated by the above-mentioned techniques in isolation.

6. REFERENCES

[1] S. Hager, S. Selent, and B. Scheuermann. Trees in the list: Accelerating list-based packet classification through controlled rule set expansion. In *CoNEXT '14*, pages 101–107, Dec. 2014.

[2] A. Liu, E. Torng, and C. Meiners. Firewall compressor: An algorithm for minimizing firewall policies. In *INFOCOM '08*, pages 691–699, Apr. 2008.

[3] Y. Qi, L. Xu, B. Yang, Y. Xue, and J. Li. Packet classification algorithms: From theory to practice. In *INFOCOM '09*, pages 648–656, Apr. 2009.

[4] D. Taylor. Survey and taxonomy of packet classification techniques. *ACM Comput. Surv.*, 37(3):238–275, Sept. 2005.

[5] D. Taylor and J. Turner. ClassBench: a packet classification benchmark. *IEEE/ACM Transactions on Networking*, 15(3):499–511, June 2007.

Toward Fabric: A Middleware Implementing High-level Description Languages on a Fabric-like Network *

Sayed Hadi Hashemi, Shadi A. Noghabi, John Bellessa, Roy H. Campbell
University of Illinois at Urbana-Champaign

ABSTRACT

Many in the networking community believe that Software-Defined Networking, in which entire networks are managed centrally, has the potential to revolutionize the field. However, SDN faces several challenges that have prevented its wide-spread adoption. Current SDN technologies, such as OpenFlow, provide powerful and flexible APIs, but can be unreasonably complex for implementing nontrivial network control logic. The generality offered by these low-level abstractions impose no structure on the network, requiring programmers to herd switches themselves, with little guidance. Many researchers argue that SDNs must adopt more structured models, such as Fabric, with an intelligent edge and a fast but simple label-switched core. Our work draws heavily from these ideas.

To that end, we propose ToF, a middleware architecture for implementing policies and behaviors from high-level network descriptions on top of a Fabric-like network. We have implemented a prototype using a combination of widely used technologies, such as MPLS, and our own proposed technologies. Based on our results, we reach near linear scalability with respect to the number of addresses routed over the network, all while introducing minimal performance overhead and requiring no changes to packet structure.

1. INTRODUCTION AND DESIGN

In this paper, we present ToF, a middleware architecture for implementing policies and behaviors from high-level network descriptions on a Fabric-like network [2]. ToF takes abstract high-level rules as an input, and makes the rules concrete at runtime by observing the topology and traffic from a running network. Then, ToF compiles these rules into "Network Control Commands" understandable by the underlying system. These network control commands are

*The material in this paper is based upon work supported in part by the Air Force Research Laboratory and the Air Force Office of Scientific Research, under agreement number FA8750-11-2-0084.

ANCS '16 March 17-18, 2016, Santa Clara, CA, USA
© 2016 Copyright held by the owner/author(s).
ACM ISBN 978-1-4503-4183-7/16/03.
DOI: http://dx.doi.org/10.1145/2881025.2889487

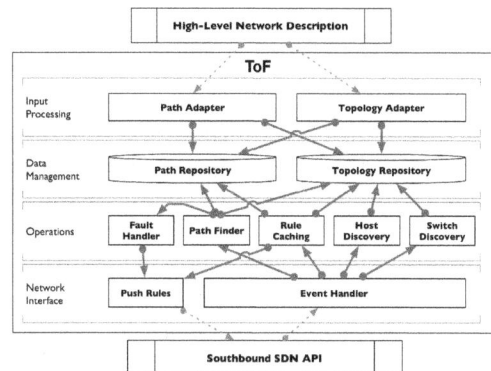

Figure 1: This figure shows the layered architecture of the system, and how ToF acts as a middleware. It also shows the layers and components inside ToF.

installed throughout the network in such a way that they implement the network descriptions provided as input.

To reach a decoupled core network from the edge network, the core network uses "Layer 2 Labeling" in which the destination MAC address acts as a placeholder for storing the label assigned to the packet.

The overall architecture of the system and the internal layered architecture of ToF is shown in Figure 1:

High-level Network Description: ToF inputs a high-level network description in a path- or topology-based format provided by the user, application, or even a configuration file from other existing systems such as MPLS. This input is converted to an internal representation, and installed in the underlying network.

Southbound SDN API: This is the channel through which a ToF system would connect to individual switches. OpenFlow as an example of a Southbound API has been used in this project. Another, future example might be a Fabric controller, or a vendor-specific control API.

Input Processing: The main goal of this layer is to convert a variety of input descriptions to internal representations. This internal representation has two formats: Topology (a graph of switches and links) and Path (routes in the networks).

Data Management: Stores, Retrieves, and updates internal representations in repositories.

Network Interface and Operations: The Network Interface communicates with the underlying network, and acts as the communication channel between higher layers of ToF and the network. This interface has two main respon-

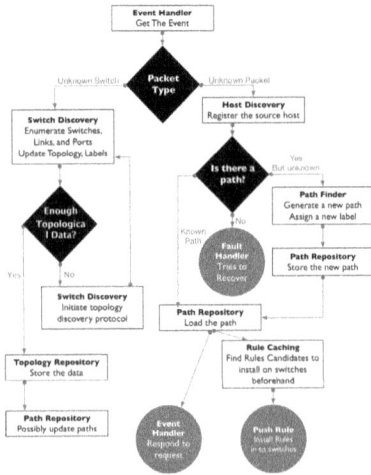

Figure 2: Event Handling process in ToF: Edge switches notify the controller of unrecognized packets. The controller determines the flow's path, generates a label, and installs rules to send packets with matching label along the path.

sibilities: Routing control events received from the network to operations layer (via event handler), translating internal rules to platform specific network commands, and deploying these rules in the network through the Southbound SDN API. Figure 2 shows the details of event handling logic.

2. EVALUATION

We have designed a few experiments to evaluate the proposed middleware. Our main concentrations are performance of switching and scalability of the system with respect to number of end nodes. In all of these experiments we used a set of packet traces made available by Benson, et al., from their study of network traffic characteristics in production data centers [1] [1]. This real-world datacenter packet capture has traffic among 500 servers, as well as several thousand external hosts. We have done a number of preprocessing on the dataset to become usable for these experiments.

We use two evaluation approaches to test the system:

Network Emulator: We generated a Mininet [3] version of the dataset network which is connected to a RYU SDN controller with an implementation of our system.

Rule Caching Simulator: To test the effect of a large variety of parameters such as rule memory sizes in switches or caching algorithms in a reasonable time we implemented a custom Java-based simulator of caching behaviors of switches in our system.

2.1 Results

Performance refers to the delays imposed by ToF on transmitting packets, i.e. the packet latency. There are a few major delay sources. When a label rule is not cached on the switch, it takes significant time to fetch it from the SDN controllers. Based on [4], this time is $11.54\,ms$ on average up to $1268.58\,ms$ in worst case. In our experiment the simulator is fed with real-world traces of a network with over 5000 addresses. Figure 3 shows the result of this experiment. According to this figure, Edge and Gateway switches have a high hit rate even with a small memory size. A hit rate

[1] http://pages.cs.wisc.edu/t̃benson/IMC10_Data.html

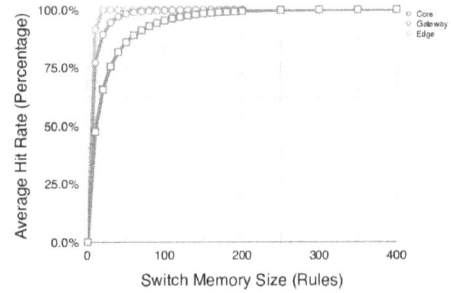

Figure 3: Average hit rate per switch type for different memory sizes when Random Replacement caching algorithm is used.

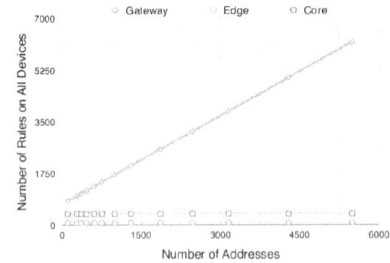

Figure 4: Total number of required rules per switch to support certain number of addresses when LDP is used for path finding.

of 99.99% can be reached in all switches with less than 200 entries. This suggests that we can achieve extremely low rule churn in switches with even relatively modest hardware.

Scalability: Having more addresses increases the required memory on devices to handle larger number of labels and rules. In this experience the effect of adding addresses on the memory usage using the LDP protocol has been studied. Figure 4 shows the result of this experiment. As shown, the total number of rules for Edge switches increase linearly, while it stays almost constant for Core and Gateway switches. This result shows the core networking is very scalable regard less of number of access networks.

3. REFERENCES

[1] BENSON, T., AKELLA, A., AND MALTZ, D. A. Network traffic characteristics of data centers in the wild. In *Proceedings of the 10th ACM SIGCOMM conference on Internet measurement* (2010), ACM, pp. 267–280.

[2] CASADO, M., KOPONEN, T., SHENKER, S., AND TOOTOONCHIAN, A. Fabric: a retrospective on evolving sdn. In *Proceedings of the first workshop on Hot topics in software defined networks* (2012), ACM, pp. 85–90.

[3] LANTZ, B., HELLER, B., AND MCKEOWN, N. A network in a laptop: rapid prototyping for software-defined networks. In *Proceedings of the 9th ACM SIGCOMM Workshop on Hot Topics in Networks* (2010), ACM, p. 19.

[4] TOOTOONCHIAN, A., GORBUNOV, S., GANJALI, Y., CASADO, M., AND SHERWOOD, R. On controller performance in software-defined networks. In *USENIX Workshop on Hot Topics in Management of Internet, Cloud, and Enterprise Networks and Services (Hot-ICE)* (2012), vol. 54.

Virtual Network Functions Instantiation on SDN Switches for Policy-Aware Traffic Steering

Cheng-Liang Hsieh
Southern Illinois University
Carbondale, Illinois, USA
hsieh@siu.edu

Ning Weng
Southern Illinois University
Carbondale, Illinois, USA
nweng@siu.edu

ABSTRACT

Software-Defined Networking (SDN) provides the capability to steer traffic in a network to lower the management cost. Network Function Virtualization (NFV) gives the chance to implement network functions at the right time and the right place to increase operation flexibility. Together SDN and NFV show the potential to create an agile system with a low operations cost and a high customer satisfaction. However, the combination of SDN with NFV results in the redundant packet forwarding traffic inside SDN in order to forward packets based on the deployed network functions for a service chain. Besides, it also increase the computation requirement of a controller for possible packet header modifications and flow states management. In this paper, we propose to implement network functions on SDN switches to lower the traffic inside of SDN and the computation requirement of a SDN controller. We create network function modules for open virtual switches and make those functions to be managed by a controller with an algorithm to streamline the implemented service chains. Our results show that the proposed system can reduce about 2/3 of current network traffic compared to the current solutions without the modification of forwarding tables and packets.

Keywords

Network Management; Software-Defined Networking

1. INTRODUCTION

Software-Defined Networking (SDN) offers the ability to configure switches forwarding rules to increase the agility of a network with the centralized traffic management at a low cost. Network functions provided by different middleboxes are critical to create service chains in a network. Network Function Virtualization helps to improve the system flexibility without sacrificing network functionalities. Together SDN and NFV enable the potential of dynamical service chain modifications to meet the real time demand.

ANCS '16 March 17-18, 2016, Santa Clara, CA, USA

© 2016 Copyright held by the owner/author(s).

ACM ISBN 978-1-4503-4183-7/16/03.

DOI: http://dx.doi.org/10.1145/2881025.2889486

The middlebox implementations with SDN could generate excessive traffic inside the network when directing packet back and forth between different switches to reach different network functions for a service chain [1][2]. Besides, additional layer and packet modification in SDN controller will be required to ensure packets are directed to the right middleboxes in a service chain.

Network Function Virtualization (NFV) implementations using commercial high volume server [3][4][5] could make a better middlebox placement to lower the traffic in a SDN. It provides system administrators the flexibility to decide where and when to launch a service. However, it still need additional layer at SDN controller for correct traffic steering.

In this paper, we embedded different network functions into the virtual switches and developed a network function placement algorithm for an optimized streamline network system. By integrating NFV concepts at SDN switches, a lean and streamline network system is possible by placing the right network functions at the right places with well-directed network traffic. Our results show about 2/3 of traffic reduction compared to the original setting of the same network. Besides, both packet header and forwarding tables remain unmodified to ensure a low processing overhead.

2. TRAFFIC-AWARE SWITCHES AND CONTROLLER

To construct a specific service chain, a packet is required to traverse a sequence of middleboxes. With SDN, a network administrator can direct the network traffics based on the system policies for a service chain. However, it generates excessive traffic inside the network as shown in Figure 1 and Table 1. For service chain FW1-IDS1-Proxy1, S2, S4, and S5 are visited multiple times for the same packet. This wastes the network bandwidth and increases the transfer latency.

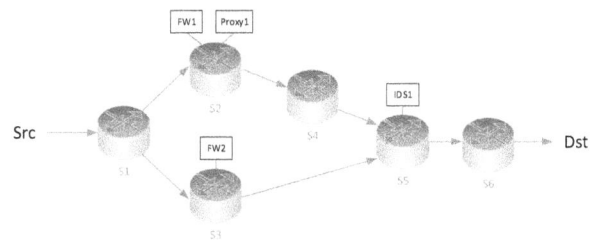

Figure 1: Example to illustrate how middleboxes are deployed in a network.

Service Chain	Physical Sequence
FW1-IDS1-Pxy1	S1 S2 FW1 S2 S4 S5 IDS1 S5 S4 S2 Pxy1 S2 S4 S5 S6
FW2-IDS1-Pxy1	S1 S3 FW2 S3 S5 IDS1 S5 S4 S2 Pxy1 S2 S4 S5 S6
FW1-IDS1	S1 S2 FW1 S2 S4 S5 IDS1 S5 S6
FW2-IDS1	S1 S3 FW2 S3 S5 IDS1 S5 S6

Table 1: Example of the different physical sequences are used to implement different service chains as in Figure 1.

However, a streamline system is possible when network functions are placed at the designed places as shown in Figure 2 and Table 2 where curly bracket means a specific network function is enabled in a switch. NFV allows to terminate and initiate network functions for a service chain. However, it still need additional layer in SDN controller to direct traffic to different middleboxes. Instead of implementing network functions on additional middleboxes, we design virtual switches to be equipped with different network functions to reduce the unnecessary packet forwarding without the need to implement an additional layer in SDN controller.

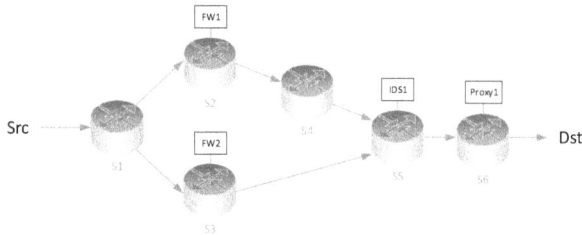

Figure 2: Example to illustrate how virtual switches with the virtualized network functions are deployed in a network to simplify the traffic on a switch.

Service Chain	Physical Sequence
FW1-IDS1-Pxy1	S1 S2(FW1) S4 S5(IDS1) S6(Pxy1)
FW2-IDS1-Pxy1	S1 S3(FW2) S5(IDS1) S6(Pxy1)
FW1-IDS1	S1 S2(FW1) S4 S5(IDS1) S6
FW2-IDS1	S1 S3(FW2) S5(IDS1) S6

Table 2: Example to show the different physical sequences used to implement different service chains when switches are equipped with required network functions.

Besides, an network function placement algorithm is developed to fulfill the requirements of each service chain. This algorithm gives priorities for those network functions in a service chain to avoid the revisit of the same switch and take network topology as a input to generate placement plans. For example, FW1 and FW2 will be given highest priority based on Table 1. With the example topology, we can tell S1, S5, and S6 are on the major trace without branches. S2 and S4 are on the same branch and S3 is on the other branch. Hence, FW1 and FW2 will be placed on S2/S4 and S3 since they share the loading. IDS and Porxy have the second priority and is shared by all services, Hence, they will be placed at S5 and S6 accordingly. Without directing traffic to flow backward as a loop, the place algorithm comes out a streamline system for the same service chains.

3. EXPERIMENTAL RESULTS

Our experimental results show the number of hops inside of a network with different service chains in it. For a more complicated network that is constructed by many network functions, the proposed algorithm and system implementation can reduce the traffic dramatically (about 70%). This is because those redundant packet forwarding has be eliminated by using virtualized network functions. For those simple service chain, the benefit is minor but still significant. Since only few switches are visited, the redundant traffic is less (about 50 %).

Service Chain	Network with SDN only # of hops	Network with SDN and embedded NFs # of hops
FW1-IDS1-Pxy1	15	5
FW2-IDS1-Pxy1	14	4
FW1-IDS1	9	5
FW2-IDS1	8	4

Table 3: Comparison between original SDN network with the proposed network by enabling NFs on the switches.

4. CONCLUSION

Both SDN and NFV represent opportunities to create a network which is transparent to administrator for a low operation cost. In this paper, we try to leverage the benefits provided by SDN and NFV for a better network system by enabling network functions in switches with a network function placement algorithm. However, the flexibility of the proposed system comes at a cost. The performance of the proposed system will be a critical problem with these software-based solutions. Hence, our future works will focus on the improvement of system performance by implementing possible hardware acceleration device for switches.

5. REFERENCES

[1] Z. A. Qazi, C.-C. Tu, L. Chiang, R. Miao, V. Sekar, and M. Yu. Simple-fying middlebox policy enforcement using sdn. In *Proceedings of the ACM SIGCOMM 2013 Conference on SIGCOMM*, pages 27–38, 2013.

[2] S. Vissicchio, O. Tilmans, L. Vanbever, and J. Rexford. Central control over distributed routing. In *Proceedings of the 2015 ACM Conference on Special Interest Group on Data Communication*, pages 43–56, 2015.

[3] A. Bremler-Barr, Y. Harchol, D. Hay, and Y. Koral. Deep packet inspection as a service. In *Proceedings of the 10th ACM International on Conference on Emerging Networking Experiments and Technologies*, pages 271–282, 2014.

[4] R. Gandhi, H. H. Liu, Y. C. Hu, G. Lu, J. Padhye, L. Yuan, and M. Zhang. Duet: Cloud scale load balancing with hardware and software. In *Proceedings of the 2014 ACM Conference on SIGCOMM*, pages 27–38, 2014.

[5] S. Palkar, C. Lan, S. Han, K. Jang, A. Panda, S. Ratnasamy, L. Rizzo, and S. Shenker. E2: A framework for nfv applications. In *Proceedings of the 25th Symposium on Operating Systems Principles*, pages 121–136, 2015.

Node Configuration for the Aho-Corasick Algorithm in Intrusion Detection Systems

Alexsandre B. Lacroix, J.M. Pierre Langlois, François-Raymond Boyer,
Antoine Gosselin and Guy Bois
Computer and Software Engineering Department
Polytechnique Montréal, Canada

{alexsandre.lacroix, pierre.langlois, francois-r.boyer, antoine.gosselin, guy.bois}@polymtl.ca

ABSTRACT
In this paper, we analyze the performance and cost trade-off from selecting two representations of nodes when implementing the Aho-Corasick algorithm. This algorithm can be used for pattern matching in network-based intrusion detection systems such as Snort. Our analysis uses the Snort 2.9.7 rules set, which contains almost 26k patterns. Our methodology consists of code profiling and analysis, followed by the selection of a parameter to maximize a metric that combines clock cycles count and memory usage. The parameter determines which of two types of nodes is selected for each trie node. We show that it is possible to select the parameter to optimize the metric, which results in an improvement by up to 12× compared with the single node-type case.

Categories and Subject Descriptors
• Theory of computation → Pattern matching
• Security and privacy → Intrusion detection systems

General Terms
Algorithms, Performance, Design, Experimentation, Security.

Keywords
Aho-Corasick algorithm; node configuration; pattern matching; string matching; Deep Packet Inspection (DPI); Intrusion Detection System (IDS)

1. Introduction
Network intrusions pose a significant threat to network security. An intrusion detection system (IDS) automates the intrusion detection process by monitoring the packets coming from outside a computer system or network, and analyzes them for signs of a variety of possible attacks or probes. If these problematic packets can be detected in time, it is then possible to stop them from getting inside the network, thus preventing numerous attacks. This detection can be done by inspecting the payload of a network packet and comparing it to a collection of suspicious patterns such as Snort's. Snort is an open source network intrusion detection systems (NIDS) which can perform real-time traffic analysis [1].

The Aho-Corasick (AC) algorithm [2] is used in Snort 2.9.7 [3] and performs multiple keywords pattern matching. It can be di-

vided into two distinct steps. The first step is to build a finite state automaton. For that, a trie or a prefix tree with input words must be constructed. The second step consists of the search of patterns itself. This search involves traveling through the automaton's nodes following transitions according to the values of input character stream. The matches are retrieved from the state of the automaton itself.

While implementing the AC algorithm, there are two key objectives: maximize the throughput, or in other words, minimize the number of clock cycles per character; and minimize the memory requirements of the nodes. In this paper, we propose a way of selecting a node's configuration between two types of nodes in order to achieve a trade-off between these two objectives. Our main contribution is to show that it is possible to select a parameter to obtain an optimal *memory* × *cycle* product.

The rest of the paper is organized as follows. We present the node configuration and our metric in Section 2. The methods used are discussed in Section 3. Section 4 presents the results.

2. Node configuration selection
In this section we present the two types for the node configuration that we propose. We then show how the AC nodes are distributed for Snort 2.9.7, which leads to optimal node type selection. We also present a performance metric.

2.1 Types of nodes
The two types of nodes that we propose are similar to the ones used in Shenoy's hybrid storage [4]. The difference resides in the way to store the pointers to the next nodes. The type 1 node is shown in Figure 1. It is similar to Bremler-Barr's symbol-state pairs array [5]. It consists of an array of r structures which is equal to the number of next nodes. Each structure is composed of two fields. The first field is the character to be matched to reach a next node. The second field is a pointer to the corresponding next node. This type of node is thus compact. A search for a match within the array of characters is linear in the worst case. It can be sped up with a binary search, at the cost of additional computation. In this work, we do not consider this type of search.

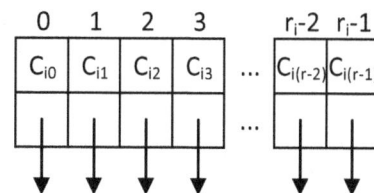

Figure 1 - Type 1 node

The type 2 node is shown in Figure 2. It is similar to Bremler-Barr's lookup tables [5]. It consists of an array of pointers, one for each possible input character. We select an array size of 256, which corresponds to the characters of an extended ASCII table or UTF-8. The character values are used as index to a pointer to the next node if it exists. If there is no corresponding next node, the pointer value is set to NULL. This represents wasted memory. However, a search within the array of pointers can be done in constant time.

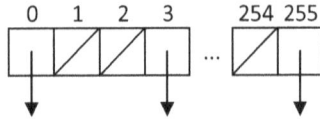

Figure 2 - Type 2 node

2.2 Node distribution and trie construction

Figure 3 shows the distribution of the number of next nodes for a trie built with the Snort 2.9.7 rule set. Almost 92% of the nodes have a single next node. For clarity of presentation, the root node with 254 next nodes is not included in the figure. For numbers of next nodes between 0 and 20, the number of nodes reduces from around a million to ten. Then, the number of nodes stabilizes in between 1 and 10. The first question for the selection of node type thus arises: at what number of next nodes should type 2 be selected instead of type 1? A compromise must be made between overall storage space and time of trie traversal.

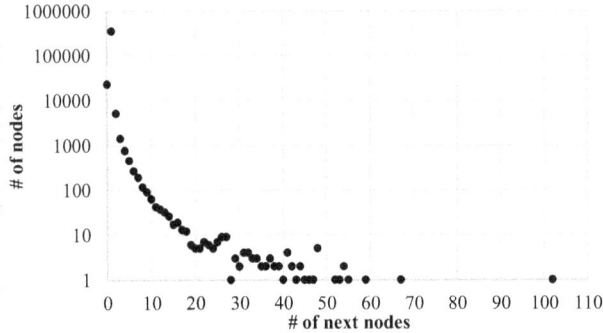

Figure 3 - Number of nodes with a specific number of next nodes

For our experiments, we built an AC trie as follows. The trie is first built with type 2 nodes. Then for each node, the array size required for node type 1 (the number of next nodes r_i) is used to select the final node type according to a defined threshold. For up to n next nodes ($r_i \leq n$), the node will be of type 1, otherwise, it will be of type 2. For example, if we set the threshold at $n = 1$, every node with zero next node will be of type 1 without any structure. The nodes with one possible next node will be of type 1 with a single structure. The nodes with 2 or more possible next nodes will be of type 2. This can lead to significant memory waste for a node. For example, if a node has only six possible next nodes, the type 2 node will have 250 NULL pointers in its array.

In this work, we compare different trie configurations using (1), where P is the performance, C is the number of clock cycles per character and M is the overall memory used. This relation allows to find the best compromise between C and M.

$$P = \frac{10^{10}}{C \times M} \qquad (1)$$

3. Methods

To compare various trie configurations, we used a virtual machine with Xubuntu 14.04 and Valgrind was used as the profiler for the clock cycle count of the AC search.

The tries were constructed with 26328 patterns which are all the unique contents of the 31133 Snort 2.9.7 rules [3], which results in approximately 381k nodes. In order to create and search through a trie, an implementation from Kanani [6] was modified. For test data, many sources were used including real inputs traffics, Internet pages, the Snort rules themselves and some randomly generated character sets. All these inputs have different character counts.

4. Results

A comparison was made between three node combinations with a real traffic test set. In the first case we use only type 1 nodes, which corresponds to a value of $n = 256$. In Figure 4, this is the rightmost point and the metric has a value of 1.48. In the second case, we use only type 2 nodes, which corresponds to a value of $n = -1$. In Figure 4, this is the leftmost point in the curve and the metric has a value of 1.53. In the thirds case, we use a combination of type 1 and type 2 nodes. In Figure 4, this corresponds to all the other points on the curve and various values of n between 0 and 102. The highest value of the metric is achieved for $n = 4$ with a value of 18.51. The performance improvement in this case is approximately 12× compared with the single node-type cases. Thus, it is possible to find a balance between the two node types that trades memory space with search time.

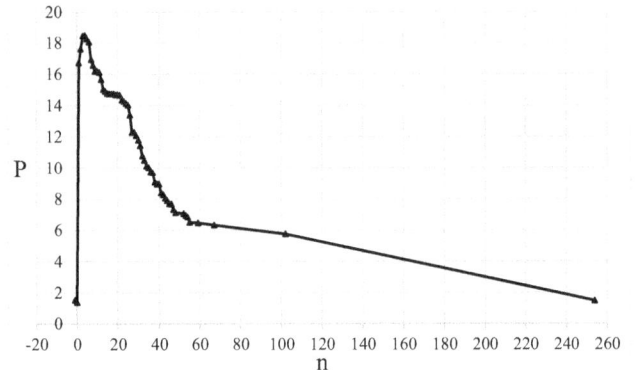

Figure 4 - Performance comparison

5. Acknowledgments

The authors would like to thank Thomas Luinaud for providing support and ideas used in this work.

6. References

[1] M. Roesch, "Snort - Lightweight Intrusion Detection for Networks," in *Proceedings of the 13th USENIX Conference on System Administration*, Berkeley, CA, USA, 1999.

[2] A. V. Aho and M. J. Corasick, "Efficient String Matching: An Aid to Bibliographic Search," *Commun. ACM,* vol. 18, no. 6, pp. 333-340, June 1975.

[3] Snort, "Snort," 2014. [Online]. Available: https://www.snort.org/.

[4] G. Shenoy, J. Tubella and A. Gonzalez, "A Performance and Area Efficient Architecture for Intrusion Detection Systems," in *IEEE International Parallel Distributed Processing Symposium (IPDPS)*, 2011.

[5] A. Bremler-Barr, Y. Harchol and D. Hay, "Space-time tradeoffs in software-based Deep Packet Inspection," in *IEEE 12th International Conference on High Performance Switching and Routing (HPSR)*, 2011.

[6] K. Kanani, "Aho-Corasick implementation (part of multifast)," 2013. [Online]. Available: http://multifast.sourceforge.net/.

A One-Way Proof-of-Work Protocol to Protect Controllers in Software-Defined Networks

Jingrui Li and Tilman Wolf
Department of Electrical and Computer Engineering
University of Massachusetts, Amherst, MA, USA
{jingrui,wolf}@umass.edu

ABSTRACT

Connection setup in software-defined networks (SDN) requires considerable amounts of processing, communication, and memory resources. Attackers can target SDN controllers with simple attacks to cause denial of service. We proposed a defense mechanism based on a proof-of-work protocol. The key characteristics of this protocol, namely its one-way operation, its requirement for freshness in proofs of work, its adjustable difficulty, its ability to work with multiple network providers, and its use of existing TCP/IP header fields, ensure that this approach can be used in practice.

Categories and Subject Descriptors

C.2.0 [**Computer-Communication Networks**]: General—
Security and protection

Keywords

security, denial-of-service, attack, defense, Internet

1. INTRODUCTION

Software-defined networks (SDN) separate data plane operations implemented by simple lookups in network switches, and control plane operations implemented in SDN controllers [1,3]. SDN switches match incoming traffic against a set of flow rules that have been installed by the controller. For new connections that have no matching rules, the switch forwards the flow information to the SDN controller. The controller then makes a routing decision and informs all switches along the path so that they can install a matching rule in their flow tables.

The basic operation of SDN exhibits an imbalance between the small amount of work that is necessary to trigger large amounts of work that is then performed by the SDN controller . An attacker can exploit this imbalance by simply sending traffic with random 5-tuples, triggering a route computation with each packet and effectively overloading the SDN controller and filling flow tables in switches.

ANCS '16 March 17-18, 2016, Santa Clara, CA, USA

© 2016 Copyright held by the owner/author(s).

ACM ISBN 978-1-4503-4183-7/16/03.

DOI: http://dx.doi.org/10.1145/2881025.2889481

To level this imbalance, we introduce the Controller Protection Protocol (CPP), which requires systems wanting to connect through an SDN network to commit resources *before* an SDN controller commits resources for route computation and setup. In our case, the connecting system needs to include a proof-of-work (POW) [2] with the initial packet of a connection. The SDN controller can verify the correctness of the POW easily and thus discard attack traffic with invalid POWs with low overhead. Using this approach, an attacker needs to dedicate a large amount of computational resources in order to send large amounts of attack traffic that triggers route computation on the SDN controller, thus making an attack potentially prohibitively expensive.

2. PROOF-OF-WORK SDN PROTOCOL

The main idea for the Controller Protection Protocol is to use a proof of work during connection setup. This proof of work requires the end-system requesting the connection to commit considerable resources before resources are committed on the side of the SDN controller. When an attacker sends large numbers of connection requests (without committing the resources to include valid proofs of work in each packet), then these packets can be identified and discarded with very little overhead.

The connection setup process based on the Controller Protection Protocol is shown in Figure 1. In CPP, the end-system first computes a proof of work. The result from this computation, i.e., the POW, is included in the first packet sent by the new connection (e.g., the TCP SYN). When the first SDN switch encounters the packet from this new connection, it forwards the connection information, including the POW, to the SDN controller. The controller then checks the validity of POW before performing path computation or any other actions. If the validation fails, the controller discards the packet and the connection is not set up (i.e., no path computation takes place and no forwarding rule is installed in the SDN switches), as shown in Figure 2. If the validation succeeds, the path computation and forwarding rule installation is performed as in conventional SDN. Once the connection has been established, later packets of that connection do not contain a POW, but are forwarded by the SDN switches as in conventional SDN.

3. ONE-WAY OPERATION

Since the proof of work needs to be calculated by the end-system initiating the connection before it is known which path the packet takes through the Internet and which network providers are encountered, we need to design a proof of

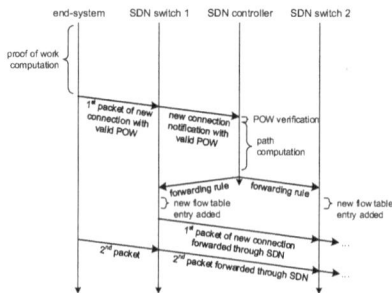

Figure 1: Connection setup in a software-defined network using Controller Protection Protocol.

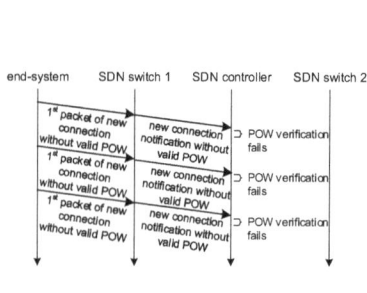

Figure 2: Denial-of-service attack on software-defined network controller using Controller Protection Protocol.

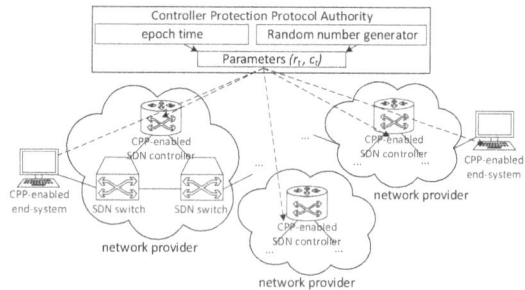

Figure 3: Controller Protection Protocol Authority distributes current CPP parameters to SDN controllers.

work that is acceptable to all network providers. We introduce a Controller Protection Protocol Authority (CPPA), which creates and distributes global CPP parameters. The resulting system architecture for the Controller Protection Protocol is shown in Figure 3. The parameter r is a random number used in the proof-of-work calculation, and the parameter c indicates the difficulty of generating a valid POW. These parameters are distributed to all CPP-enabled components, i.e., end-systems and SDN controllers. The parameter set (r, c) needs to change over time to ensure freshness of proofs and to adapt complexity.

4. PROOF-OF-WORK DESIGN

In CPP, we use the proof of work (e.g., such as in bitcoin mining [4]) that can be verified with a single cryptographic hash computation. We require to find an input to a cryptographic hash computation that generates an output starting with a predetermined number of zeros. Since cryptographic hash functions are one-way functions, the entity generating the proof of work has to try by "brute force" to find a suitable input. This search process is on average time consuming and thus requires dedication of computational resources (i.e., "work"). In contrast, the verifier only needs to do a single computations to see if an input (i.e., "proof") yields an output starting with the required number of zeros.

Figure 4 shows the experimental processing time for generation and verification of a POW. The generation time is significantly larger than the verification time. Thus, the proof of work does cause the necessary commitment of resources on the side of the end-system. Also, incorrect proofs of work can be detected quickly. The ratio between generation and verification time is summarized for some parameter values in Table 1. These results show that, depending on the choice of complexity parameter, the resource commitment on the end-system can be a few hundred times the cost of verifying the proof of work or many million times.

The characteristics of the proof of work discussed above is that it is inherently pseudo-random. Therefore, it is possible to utilize existing header fields, i.e., IP identification field and TCP sequence number, that use randomized values to carry the proof of work. Thus, we believe CPP presents an effective approach to protecting SDN from DoS attacks.

Acknowledgments

This material is based upon work supported by the National Science Foundation under Grant No. 1421448.

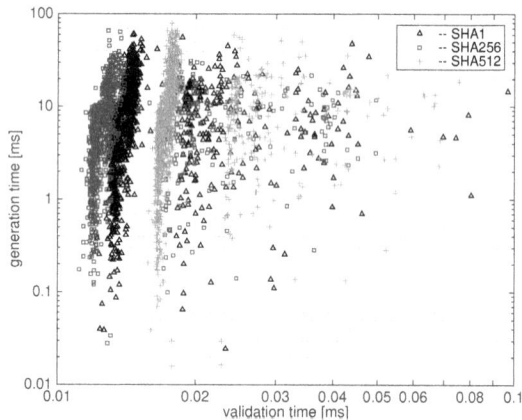

Figure 4: Distribution of generation and verification times for proofs of work in CPP (ten zeroes).

Table 1: Average ratio of generation time and verification time of proofs of work for different cryptographic functions and required number of zeros.

hash	required number of zeros				
function	8	10	12	16	24
SHA-1	134	575	2.23k	35.7k	6.37M
SHA-256	136	581	2.16k	35.7k	7.86M
SHA-512	159	646	2.75k	42.0k	8.64M

5. REFERENCES

[1] M. Casado, M. J. Freedman, J. Pettit, J. Luo, N. McKeown, and S. Shenker. Ethane: taking control of the enterprise. In *SIGCOMM '07: Proceedings of the 2007 conference on Applications, technologies, architectures, and protocols for computer communications*, pages 1–12, Kyoto, Japan, Aug. 2007.

[2] C. Dwork and M. Naor. Pricing via processing or combatting junk mail. In E. F. Brickell, editor, *Proc. of Advances in Cryptology (CRYPTO)*, volume 740 of *Lecture Notes in Computer Science*, pages 139–147. Springer, 1993.

[3] N. McKeown, T. Anderson, H. Balakrishnan, G. Parulkar, L. Peterson, J. Rexford, S. Shenker, and J. Turner. OpenFlow: enabling innovation in campus networks. *SIGCOMM Computer Communication Review*, 38(2):69–74, Apr. 2008.

[4] S. Nakamoto. *Bitcoin: A peer-to-peer electronic cash system*. http://bitcoin.org/bitcoin.pdf, 2008.

P4GPU: Accelerate Packet Processing of a P4 Program with a CPU-GPU Heterogeneous Architecture

Peilong Li   Yan Luo
Department of Electrical and Computer Engineering,
University of Massachusetts Lowell
Peilong_Li@student.uml.edu, Yan_Luo@uml.edu

ABSTRACT

The P4 language is an emerging domain-specific language for describing the data plane processing at a network device. P4 has been mapped to a wide range of forwarding devices including NPUs, programmable NICs and FPGAs, except for General Purpose Graphics Processing Unit (GPGPU) which is a salient parallel architecture for processing network flows. In this work, we design a heterogeneous architecture with both CPU and GPU as a P4 programming target, and present a toolset to map a P4 program onto the proposed architecture. Our evaluation reveals that a P4 program can render promising performance on such architecture by parallelizing its "match+action" engine with the GPGPU accelerator. The experiment results show that the auto-configured GPU kernels achieve scalable lookup and classification speeds: the prototype system can reach up to 580 Gbps for IP lookups (64-byte packets) and 60 million classifications per second for 4k firewall rules, respectively.

Keywords

GPU; Heterogeneous; Packet Processing; P4

1. INTRODUCTION

As a domain specific language for network processing, P4 [1] enhances the programmability of software defined network by providing high-level abstractions and easy-to-use semantics to implement network data plane functions, however, line rate may be compromised if without an efficient hardware target. The whole P4 community is dedicated in extending P4 to a wide range of forwarding devices including CPUs, NPUs, programmable NICs and FPGAs, etc.. GPG-PUs, as an SIMD computing architecture, have shown scalable accelerated performance on network applications [3]. However, no prior work has successfully applied GPGPU as a P4 target due to three major challenges. Firstly, a P4 application assumes "match+action" pipelines as its fundamental architecture, whereas a GPU lacks of dedicated "match+action" hardware. Secondly, as a coprocessor GPU

ANCS '16 March 17-18, 2016, Santa Clara, CA, USA

© 2016 Copyright held by the owner/author(s).

ACM ISBN 978-1-4503-4183-7/16/03.

DOI: http://dx.doi.org/10.1145/2881025.2889480

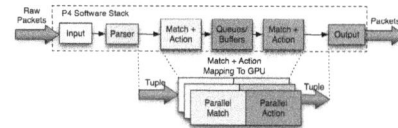

Figure 1: The Software Stack of P4GPU

carries limited memory space and runs at a lower clock frequency comparing with CPUs and NPUs. Thirdly, GPU excels at high parallelism computation such as table lookup and header matching however struggles in branching and dependency as in packet header parsing and state machine transitions.

To overcome these challenges, we propose a tool called P4GPU to map a P4 program to a heterogeneous CPU/GPU architecture. Our contributions in this work are three-fold: 1) to the best of our knowledge, this is the first work to map P4 applications onto a heterogeneous CPU/GPU target. We provide the P4GPU toolset to parse a P4 code and generate the desired GPU kernels, which could be a major step towards implementing a P4-to-GPU compiler; 2) we design a load-balanced heterogeneous framework to accelerate network functions in network data plane; 3) we explore different IP lookup and packet classification kernel designs on GPU for our heterogeneous architecture.

2. SOFTWARE DESIGN

Since table matching and packet classification have become the bottlenecks in packet forwarding nowadays [2, 4], we decide to map the hot spot of the P4 program, namely, the table "match+action" engine, to GPU for acceleration as shown in Figure 1. In particular, we take the P4 community provided "simple router" program as a use case to demonstrate our P4-to-GPU mapping process, and design a generic IP lookup engine and a packet classification engine on GPU that are used in the "match+action" step.

Mapping a P4 program to GPU involves three major steps as depicted in the block diagram in Figure 2: 1) P4 intermediate representation (IR) preparation - this step converts a complete P4 program into P4 IR which is stored in a clean and concrete OrderedDict Python data structure; 2) kernel configuration generation - once obtaining the IR of the P4 program, we apply a IR parser in the second step that reads the IR Python dictionary, finds the region of interest, and extract the target field parameters. We apply regular expression (RegEx) technique on IR to find the correct execution order of all tables; and 3) kernel initialization - in this step, we use the configuration parameters in step 2 to

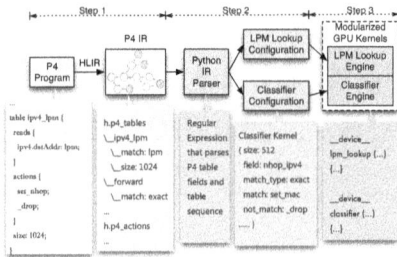

Figure 2: Mapping P4 Program to GPU Kernels

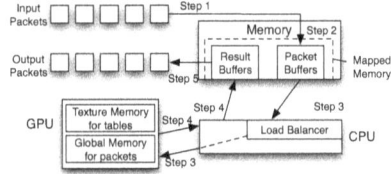

Figure 3: Heterogeneous Packet Processing System Architecture

initialize the pre-defined GPU kernels.

We design two GPU kernel engines for the three tables (ipv4_lpm, forward, send_frame) in "simple router": 1) lookup engine: we implement a generic Longest Prefix Match (LPM) kernel for IPv4 and IPv6 route lookup. Our baseline design is a linear search kernel, and we design two trie-based lookup kernels - binary trie and k-stride multibit trie for comparison; 2) classifier engine: we design a classifier engine with exact/wildcard-match capabilities. Our baseline design is linear search, and we also implement the grid-of-tries algorithm for optimized performance.

3. ARCHITECTURAL DESIGN

We depict the packet processing flow on the proposed architecture in Figure 3 and explain it in the following steps. Step 1: DMA directs the incoming packets that arrive at NIC to the system main memory; Step 2: CPU controls the incoming packets to fill packet buffers that will be fed into the GPU coprocessor by batches; step 3: depending on the behavior of incoming packet workload, load balancer (LB) on CPU will determine the percentage of workload that is offloaded to GPU and CPU. The design of LB is lightweight and responsive. Since GPU is more responsive to high packet rate, we implement a counter-based workload profiler to estimates the packet rate, and use the estimation to decide how many packets are offloaded to coprocessor; step 4: GPU and CPU process their share of workload and send buffered results back to main memory; step 5: CPU programs NIC to either forward or drop the processed packets.

4. PERFORMANCE EVALUATION

With commodity laptop hardware (CPU - Intel Quad Core i7-36100M; GPU - NVIDIA GT 650M with 384 cores), we use realistic publicly available datasets to evaluate our system performance. We apply the largest available prefix dataset CAIDE RouteView (January 2015) IPv4 with about 550,000 entries and IPv6 with about 20,000 entries for evaluating the GPU lookup engines. To test the performance of the classifier engine, we use ClassBench to generate a set of filters, such as FW (firewall) and ACL (Access Control List), in different sizes.

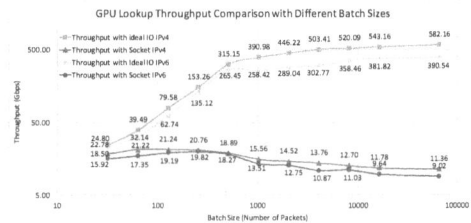

Figure 4: GPU Binary Trie Lookup Throughput Comparison with Different Batch Sizes

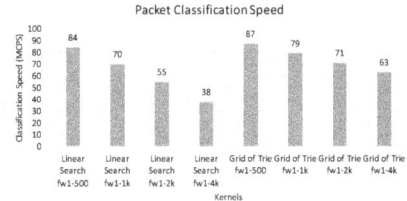

Figure 5: Performance of Different Classifier Kernel Design with Firewall Rules

We design two different network traffic generators for evaluation. The "ideal IO" generator assumes packets are already transmitted to the host memory, therefore no packet transmission overhead is involved. The "socket IO" generator assumes packets are transmitted from Click Modular Router to the host with a socket connection.

The performance metrics include throughput, average latency per packet, million lookups per second (MLPS), and million of classified packets per second (MCPS), etc. As demonstrated in Figure 4, the lookup engine throughput varies with various batch sizes. In the "ideal IO" case, system throughput can reach up to 580 Gbps for IPv4 and 390 Gbps for IPv6; and in the "socket IO" case, we observe that the maximum throughput is around 20 Gbps for both IPv4 and IPv6. With fixed batch size being 512, Figures 5 show the classifier kernel performance with linear search and grid-of-trie algorithm. We can observe that packet classification speed can reach as high as 93 MCPS with linear search algorithm for 500 firewall rules, and classification speed can still keep above 60 MCPS with grid-of-trie algorithm when the number of firewall rules is 4k.

5. REFERENCES

[1] P. Bosshart, D. Daly, G. Gibb, M. Izzard, N. McKeown, J. Rexford, C. Schlesinger, D. Talayco, A. Vahdat, G. Varghese, and D. Walker. P4: Programming protocol-independent packet processors. *SIGCOMM Comput. Commun. Rev.*, 44(3):87–95, July 2014.

[2] P. Bosshart, G. Gibb, H. Kim, G. Varghese, N. McKeown, and M. Horowitz. Forwarding metamorphosis: Fast programmable match-action processing in hardware for sdn. In *ACM SIGCOMM 2013*. ACM, August 2013.

[3] S. Han, K. Jang, K. Park, and S. Moon. Packetshader: A gpu-accelerated software router. *SIGCOMM Comput. Commun. Rev.*, 40(4):195–206, Aug. 2010.

[4] G. Liao, H. Yu, and L. Bhuyan. A new ip lookup cache for high performance ip routers. In *Design Automation Conference (DAC), 2010 47th ACM/IEEE*, pages 338–343, June 2010.

Cache Sharing Using a Bloom Filter in Named Data Networking

Ju Hyoung Mun and Hyesook Lim*
Dept. of Electronics Engineering
Ewha Womans University
Seoul, Korea
jhmun@ewhain.net, *hlim@ewha.ac.kr

ABSTRACT

In Named Data Networking (NDN), routers have caches to store frequently requested contents, and hence cache management scheme becomes a key factor for efficient content delivery. In this paper, we propose the sharing of cache summaries using a Bloom filter among neighboring routers for efficient content delivery and high cache utilization at NDN. When an *Interest* packet is received, a router can forward the *Interest* to a neighboring router which has the high potential of the requested content. The proposed scheme is evaluated by using ndnSIM, which is a NS-3 based named data networking simulator. Simulation results show that the summary sharing using our proposed method is beneficial in content diversity and average content delivery time.

Categories and Subject Descriptors

C.2.6 [**Internetworking**]: Routers

Keywords

Named data networking; Bloom filter; Cache summary; Cache content sharing

1. INTRODUCTION

Internet traffic has increased rapidly, and especially video traffic would be more than 86% of all IP traffic by 2016 [1]. Since the majority of video traffic is caused by few popular contents, network resources are wasted to deliver the same contents repeatedly in the current Internet. In order to cope with today's communication needs, Named Data Networking (NDN) technology has been introduced as a promising candidate for the future Internet [2].

The NDN is characterized by name-based routing and in-network caching. An intermediate node can serve requested contents instead of original servers. Since popular contents are more likely retrieved from an in-network cache, content delivery time is reduced and the bottleneck near content sources is resolved. The utilization of the in-network caches

ANCS '16 March 17-18, 2016, Santa Clara, CA, USA

© 2016 Copyright held by the owner/author(s).

ACM ISBN 978-1-4503-4183-7/16/03.

DOI: http://dx.doi.org/10.1145/2881025.2889477

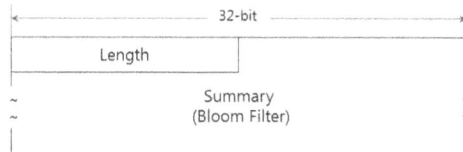

Figure 1: Summary Packet

highly affects the performance of content dissemination in NDN infrastructure. As cache storage is a limited resource, if NDN routers make caching decisions independently, the same content may be stored repeatedly. Achieving maximal benefits by caching the contents effectively becomes a challenge for the realization of NDN [2, 3, 4].

In this paper, we propose the sharing of cache summaries represented with a Bloom filter [5] among neighboring routers to increase the cache diversity within an autonomous system (AS) in order to reduce the inter-AS traffic. On the cache miss for an *Interest* packet, a router examines the summaries and then forwards the *Interest* to a possible hit node.

2. PROPOSED ALGORITHMS

The knowledge of what contents neighbors have in their caches is beneficial to increase the cache diversity. In our proposed architecture, each NDN router broadcasts the summary of its cached contents, which is represented by a Bloom filter, when needed (periodically or when updated). By examining the summaries, a router can avoid storing the duplicate contents that neighboring routers might have.

While the scope of summary sharing can be configurable, the summaries are shared only among its neighboring routers without knowing about the network topology in our proposed architecture. Hence, the traffic overhead for propagating summaries can be the minimum. We define a new type of packet for the summary as shown in Fig. 1 and a repository called Summary Store to store the summary in each incoming face. On receiving a *Data* packet, before adding the content to the content store (CS), the Summary Store is queried first. The data is cached only if the querying result is negative, and then update its summary as well.

The procedure of the *Interest* packet processing is shown in Algorithm 1. On receiving an *Interest* packet, the Summary Store is searched first. If the matching summary is found, the *Interest* is forwarded towards the corresponding face. If the matching summary is the summary of its own cache, it sends the requested data right away. If the incoming face is the same as the face for forwarding, we consider it

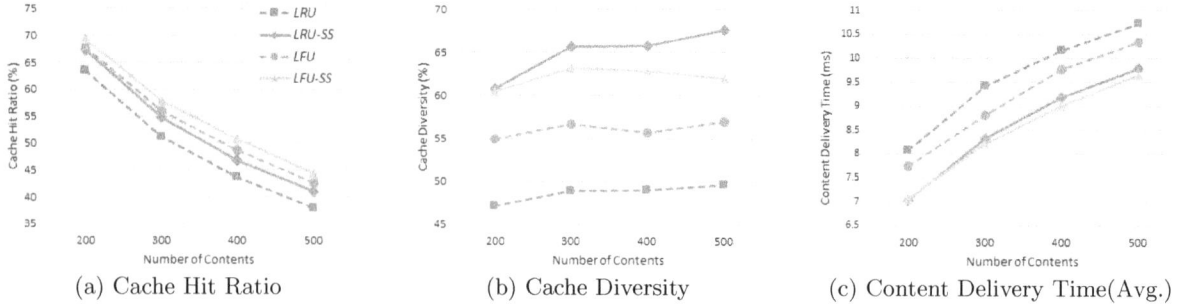

| (a) Cache Hit Ratio | (b) Cache Diversity | (c) Content Delivery Time(Avg.) |

Figure 2: Performance of Proposed Summary Sharing Scheme

Algorithm 1: Procedure of *Interest* packet processing

```
Function OnInterest (interest)
    matchFaceLst = Summary.Query(interest);
    foreach face in matchFaceLst do
        if face is itself then
            cachedData = ContentStore.Find(interest);
            if cachedData then
                Forward( data, incomingFace );
                return;
            else
                // false positive
            end
        else if face ≠ incomingFace then
            Forward( interest, face ); return;
        end
    end
    fibResult = FIB.Find(interest);
    Forward(interest, fibResult);
end
```

---

as a false positive. In this case, the *Interest* is forwarded according to the usual forwarding process using the forwarding information base (FIB).

3. PERFORMANCE EVALUATION

The proposed cache sharing scheme is evaluated by using ndnSIM, which is a NS-3 based NDN simulator [6]. The 6-node Sprint PoP topology [7] is used for the evaluation. Each gateway router is connected to one producer, and each access router is connected to 3 consumers. A CS of a router stores up to 100 contents. All consumers generate *Interest* packets following Zipf-Mandelbrot distribution. For summaries, the 1024-bit Bloom filter is used with 2 indices.

The proposed method is applied to both *least recently used* (*LRU*) and *least frequently used* (*LFU*), which are individual cache replacement schemes. The evaluation is performed with 4 cases: *LRU*, *LFU*, *LRU with summary sharing* (*LRU-SS*), and *LFU with summary sharing* (*LFU-SS*). A set of metrics is used: cache diversity, cache hit ratio, and the average content delivery time.

Fig. 2(a) shows the cache hit ratio as the number of contents grows. The proposed scheme works fine with both *LFU* and *LRU*, regardless of the number of contents. Because the hit ratio is highly related with content popularity, both *LFU* based schemes show better hit ratio than *LRU* schemes.

Fig. 2(b) shows the cache diversity. Because all en-route nodes store the same content, *LRU* shows the worst cache diversity. In contrast, *LRU-SS* have the best cache diversity, because the recently requested items are more diverse than frequently requested items. Therefore, summary sharing is

more effective for *LRU* in terms of the cache diversity.

Fig. 2(c) shows the average content delivery time, which is affected directly by the forwarding route and partly by the cache hit ratio. The *LFU-SS* shows the shortest content delivery time. *LRU-SS* shows better performance than *LFU*, because contents can be cached nearer to consumers. Simulation results show that the summary sharing is beneficial in the content diversity and the average content delivery time.

The traffic overhead for the summary sharing is 128KB. Although the Bloom filter is compact, the traffic caused by the summary may not be negligible. Because the false positive rate depends on the size of a Bloom filter and the number of contents is expected to be huge, a summary cannot be shrinkable over a certain size. To reduce the overhead further, the compressed Bloom filter can be used. Because a summary carries the content location information, it can be also used for building an FIB.

4. ACKNOWLEDGMENTS

This research was supported by the National Research Foundation of Korea (NRF), NRF-2014R1A2A1A11051762 and NRF-2015R1A2A1A15054081. This research was also supported by MSIP, Korea, under the ITRC support program (IITP-2015-H8501-15-1007) supervised by IITP.

5. REFERENCES

[1] Cisco Visual Networking Index: Forecast and Methodology, 2012-2017, May 2013.

[2] V. Jacobson, D. K. Smetters, J. D. Thornton, M. F. Plass, N. H. Briggs, R. L. Braynard, "Networking named content," *ACM CoNEXT*, 2009, pp. 1-12.

[3] H. Wu, J. Li, Y. Wang, and B. Liu, "EMC: The Effective Multi-Path Caching Scheme for Named Data Networking," *IEEE ICCCN*, 2013, pp. 1-7.

[4] H. Choi, J. Yoo, T. Chung, N. Choi, T. Kwon, and Y. Choi, "CoRC: coordinated routing and caching for named data networking," *ACM/IEEE ANCS*, 2014, pp. 161-172.

[5] B. H. Bloom, "Space/time trade-offs in hash coding with allowable errors," *Communications of the ACM*, vol. 13, no. 7, pp. 422-426, 1970.

[6] C. Yi, A. Afanasyev, I. Moiseenko, L. Wang, B. Zhang, and L. Zhang, "A case for stateful forwarding plane," *Computer Communications*, vol. 36, no. 7, pp. 779-791, 2013.

[7] N. Spring, R. Mahajan, and D. Wetherall, "Measuring ISP topologies with rocketfuel," *ACM SIGCOMM*, 2002, pp. 133-145.

Software Defined Networks-on-Chip for Multi/Many-Core Systems: A Performance Evaluation.

R. Sandoval-Arechiga,[*]
R. Parra-Michel
CINVESTAV-IPN, GDL Unit
Zapopan,
Jalisco, Mexico
{rsandoval,rparra}@gdl.cinvestav.mx

J. L. Vazquez-Avila
Univ. Autonoma del Carmen,
Cd. del Carmen,
Campeche, Mexico
jvazquez@pampanio.unacar.mx

J. Flores-Troncoso and
S. Ibarra-Delgado
Univ. Autonoma de Zacatecas
Zacatecas,
Zacatecas, Mexico
{jflorest,sibarra}@uaz.edu.mx

ABSTRACT

By means of a management framework and programmable routing tables, Software Defined Network (SDN) architectures offer network's adaptability to today's computer systems. In Networks-on-Chip (NoC) based systems, management methods have been implemented as specific solutions unable to be reused in further designs. A Software Defined NoC (SDNoC) architecture will permit on-the-fly re / configuration and reduce Non-Recurring Engineering costs. In this paper, performance evaluations of a SDNoC through flit-accurate SystemC models are presented. We measure the average values of the configuration time (CT), global delay and throughput for various routing algorithms and packet injection rates.

1. INTRODUCTION

In recent years, Many-Core systems have proliferated. For example, IBM's Cyclops64, Tilera's Tile-GX100, Intel's Knights landing and Adapteva's Epiphany 64-core, among others. Network-on-Chip's adaptability to communication patterns among cores in Many-Core systems is crucial to improve parallel algorithm's performance. Many-Core system architects must build from the ground the support subsystems for every new application, leading to poor engineering process: low hardware & software reutilization, which contribute to large validation processes and recurrent costs. Software Defined Networking (SDN) concepts [3] have become a revolution in computer networks. Its main feature is the simplification of the network management process to achieve network's adaptability to the applications. Although the SDN concepts have been introduced in NoCs [2, 4, 5], a SDN controller performance and re/configuration overhead

evaluation is missing in the literature. In this paper we evaluate a Software Defined Network-on-Chip (SDNoC) architecture as the interconnection among the Processing Elements (PEs) in a Many-Core system.

2. SYSTEM MODEL & EVALUATION

From the architecture presented in [4], we constructed flit-accurate SystemC models based on Noxim [1]. Although a mesh is used, the architecture is independent from the topology. The model consists of a homogeneous system built by 70 tiles organized in a 7x10 2D mesh. Each tile is composed of a SDN router, Network Interface (NI), memory and a PE (in our model a CPU). The SDN controller was modeled in SystemC as a process running in the PE of tile 34 (at the center of the mesh). It has functions for sending packets for PE and router configuration, stop and start computation in a per flow basis. It is important to mention that every function mentioned has its counterpart in the SDN Client of the respective NI that executes the command in the tile (Router or Processing Element).

We used a simple router architecture with a two stage pipeline: buffering and routing in one clock cycle and arbitration and forwarding in other cycle. Then, the zero load delay for the router architecture modeled is 2 clock cycles. If the output port is unavailable, the flit is buffered until the arbitration process sends a grant signal. A buffer size of 4 flits and no virtual channels were used throughout the evaluations. The router has a flow-based routing and a XY routing for configuration packets that have a zero-valued flow ID. The latter is for backup purposes, notice that a misleading configuration could divide the network in zones that would be unreachable. Then, with a independent setup routing for configuration packets we can guarantee the delivery of packets to every node in the network. The flow-based routing consist of routing tables that are filled by the configuration process in the NI with values given by a specific routing algorithm, e.g. XY, West First, North Last, etc. If the algorithm gives more than one output port a selection process is executed. In our model every output port is selected with the same (uniform) probability. A synthetic scenario was used to measure the Configuration Time (CT). The CT is the time spent by the network forwarding configuration packets, from the SDN controller to every other node in the network. The assumption here is that every node needs configuration data, then, a packet of fixed length is sent: by default a 8 flits packet (32 Bytes). Data packets

[*]Corresponding Author. This work is partially supported by CONACYT's scholarship number 195462 and CONACYT-AEM Sectoral fund with project number 248410.

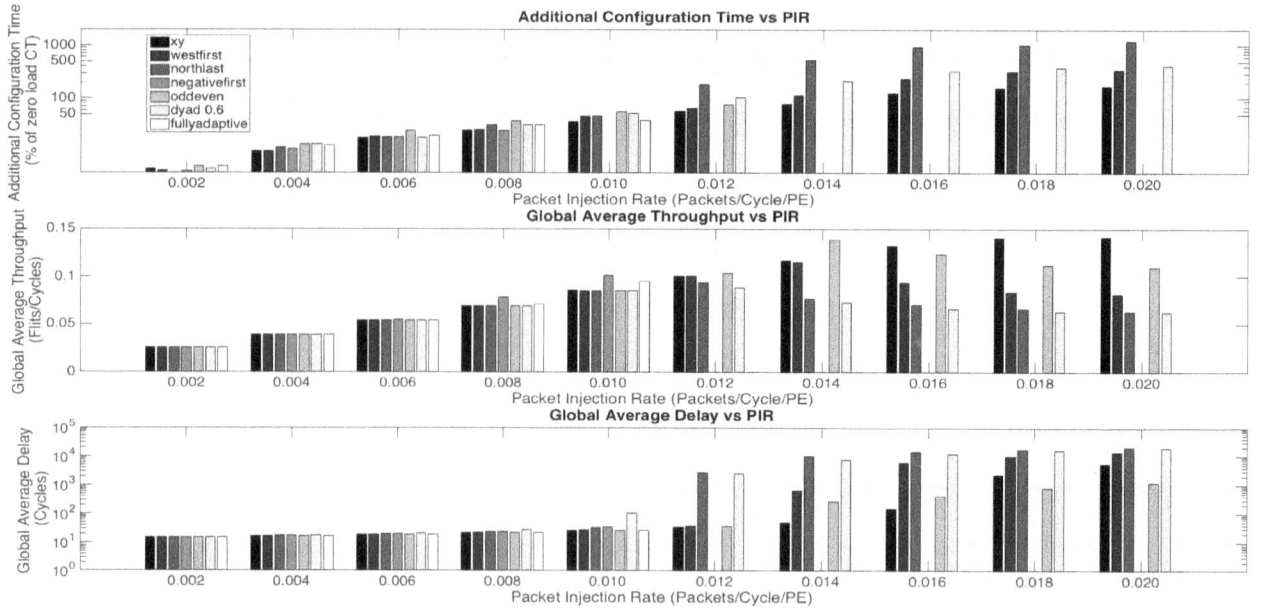

Figure 1: Performance for different routing algorithms: Configuration Time (Up), Global Average Throughput (Middle) and Global Average Delay (Bottom).

have a length of 8 flits. A uniform distributed random traffic pattern is set. Different routings were used for every packet (Data only) and the SDN controller sends a configuration packet to every node in the network. For statistic soundness, 20 repetitions were made with different random seeds. For every synthetic workload the system starts empty, then, traffic starts to flow. A warm up period of 1000 cycles is left to achieve a steady state then packet statistics are collected. Finally, at 5000 clock cycles, the configuration takes place, so we can measure the configuration time. Every scenario was compared with a zero load configuration time, i.e. the time spent by the network sending the configuration to all the nodes in the network in absence of any other traffic. The zero load configuration time is 1138 clock cycles for configuration packets with length of 32 Bytes (8 flits).

3. RESULTS

In this section the results derived from the evaluation of a SDNoC with different scenarios are analyzed. Figure 1 shows a bar plot for the average additional CT, throughput and delay values versus the PIR. This figure shows that the CT (in logarithmic scale for visibility purposes) depends on the routing algorithm used up to 0.008 packets/cycle/PE. Beyond that point the CT is highly sensitive to the Routing Algorithm (RA). In some extreme cases such as Fully Adaptive RA, the system collapses as throughput and delay (in logarithmic scale) plots show. This is due to that high values of PIR in some RAs, e.g. Fully Adaptive, the network presents a live-lock behavior. In other words, the adaptive RA, searches the less congested output port, but in the way, spreads the packets and the congestion to all the network, collapsing the system. So, the packets never arrive at its destination, in such cases the delay and the throughput can not be determined, as Figure 1 shows. It is worth noticing that a deterministic routing, such as XY, achieves a good performance in wide range of PIR.

4. CONCLUSION AND FUTURE WORK

A performance evaluation of a Software Defined Network-on-Chip Architecture for Many-Core systems is presented. The configuration time of several synthetic scenarios were analyzed. The configuration time, delay and throughput were evaluated with respect to different routing algorithms and packet injection rates. Energy and area evaluations are still pending as a future work.

5. REFERENCES

[1] V. Catania, A. Mineo, S. Monteleone, M. Palesi, and D. Patti. Noxim: An open, extensible and cycle-accurate network on chip simulator. In *Application-specific Systems, Architectures and Processors (ASAP), 2015 IEEE 26th International Conference on*, pages 162–163. IEEE, 2015.

[2] L. Cong, W. Wen, and W. Zhiying. A configurable, programmable and software-defined network on chip. In *Advanced Research and Technology in Industry Applications (WARTIA), 2014 IEEE Workshop on*, pages 813–816. IEEE, 2014.

[3] N. McKeown. Software-defined networking. In *INFOCOM 2009 Keynote talk*, volume 17, pages 30–32, 2009.

[4] R. Sandoval-Arechiga, J. L. Vazquez-Avila, R. Parra-Michel, F.-T. J., and I. D. S. Shifting the network-on-chip paradigm towards a software defined network architecture. In *Computational Science and Computational Intelligence, (CSCI), 2015 International Conference on*, pages 869–870. IEEE, 2015.

[5] J. Wang, M. Zhu, C. Peng, L. Zhou, Y. Qian, and W. Dou. Software-defined photonic network-on-chip. In *e-Technologies and Networks for Development (ICeND), 2014 Third International Conference on*, pages 127–130. IEEE, 2014.

NI + Router Microarchitecture
for NoC-based Communication Systems

R. Sandoval-Arechiga, *
R. Parra-Michel
CINVESTAV-IPN, GDL Unit,
Zapopan,
Jalisco, Mexico
{rsandoval,rparra}@gdl.cinvestav.mx

J. L. Vazquez-Avila,
Univ. Autonoma del Carmen,
Cd. del Carmen,
Campeche, Mexico
jvazquez@pampano.unacar.mx

B. I. Gea-Garcia [†]
Intel Guadalajara
Design Center,
Zapopan, Jalisco, Mexico
blanca.isabel.gea.garcia@intel.com

ABSTRACT

Modern communication systems are characterized by intensive computation signal processing algorithms. System-on-Chip implementations of these systems are generally based on Networks-on-Chip (NoC). The router and Network Interface (NI) are the main elements of the NoC, but the router is the architecture most discussed in the literature. Here, a NI + router microarchitecture is presented. Our router implementation outperforms the previous work in operational frequency by a 20%. The NI usually is assumed as a simple wrapper, although results in this work show that the NI can consume almost twice resources than the router. This indicates that further discussions must be carried out for the design of NoC-based communication systems.

1. INTRODUCTION

The complexity of modern communication systems is being increased more and more over recent years. In order to speed up their design process, specialized hardware that execute specific functions, such as coding/decoding, correlation, etcetera, are encapsulated in modules known as Intellectual Property (IP) Cores. To reduce design, testing and manufacturing costs, designers integrate several pre-verified cores in a System-on-Chip (SoC), e.g. IP Cores, DSPs, CPUs, Reconfigurable Cores, etc. Multi/Many-Core Systems-on-Chip (or Multi-Processor SoC, MPSoC) are the weapon of choice for implementing on-Chip communication systems [1, 3]. In order to fully exploit heterogeneity and inherent parallelism from both algorithm and architecture, the Network-on-Chip approach has become the de facto standard for communicate

*Corresponding Author. This work is partially supported by Mexican CONACYT scholarship number 195462.

†B. I. Gea-Garcia was with CINVESTAV-IPN, GDL Unit when the work was done.

cores in MPSoCs. A NoC architecture is composed by Processing Elements (PEs)[1], Network Interfaces (NI), Routers and links. Among these, the router's microarchitecture has been an interesting research topic [5]. However, the NI have not received the same attention than the router by the research community. In this work, a NI + router microarchitecture is presented, with the aim of analyzing the NI complexity and assessing its importance in NoC designs. In addition, a comparison with a router implementation in the state of the art is carried out in terms of hardware resources.

2. NI + ROUTER MICROARCHITECTURE

Router. The principal function of a NoC router is forwarding packets based on the destination address. The proposed router microarchitecture is showing in Figure 1; it was designed to fullfill the main router requirements describe in detail in [2]. Here the packets arrive to the **Input Ports** where the LSB (Least Significant Bit) of the first flit selects the input **Virtual Channel (VC)** where the flits will be stored. In this work, flits have a 32-bit length. Then, the **Input Arbiter** selects the **VC** channel to be served using a round robin scheme. If the input flit is a header the **Routing** module is enabled, and it generates the index of the output port based on a dimension order routing. The **VC Allocator** produces the index of the **VC** channel for the next router based on the **Output Port**'s Xon/Xoff signals. In addition, it counts the flits to know when the **Input Arbiter** must be liberated or the **Output Ports** must to be enabled and synchronized with the **Crossbar Switch**. The **VC allocator** will hold the selected **Input/Output Ports** until the last data flit of the transmitted packet is sent; then a signal is sent to release the **Input Arbiter** and **Crossbar Switch**. The **Output Arbiter** follows a round robin scheme and selects the **Input Port** that will be connected to the **Output Port** through the **Crossbar Switch**. The **Output Arbiter** and the **Routing** will maintain its request and selected crossbar switch inputs until a release signal arrives from the **VC Allocator**. Finally, the **Crossbar Switch** forwards the packet to the corresponding output register, based on the **Output Arbiter** decisions.

Network Interface. The NI has several functions: translate the message from NoC into commands to the PE attached, partition of the messages in packets and the packets

---

[1]Such as CPU or IP Cores.

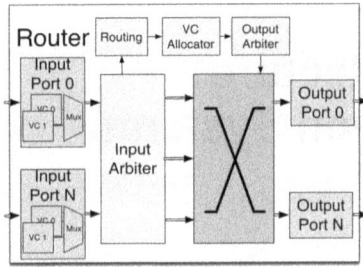

Figure 1: Router microarchitecture for NoC-based Communication Systems.

Table 1: Hardware utilization summary of one NI and one router on Stratix IV EP4SGX230 Altera FPGA.

	NI	Router	
Resource	Proposed	Proposed	2015 [5]
Logic Cells (LCs)	1013 (0.56%)	676 (0.37%)	2722 (1.49%)
Memory bits (Mem)	1320 (0.01%)	792 (0.01%)	46080 (0.32%)
Ports	-	2	4
VC per Port	-	2	4
LCs/Port/VCs	-	169	170.12
Mem/Port/VCs	-	198	2880
Fmax (MHz)	294	221	177
Delay (Clock cycles)	-	4	2

in flits, assembly of the message from packets, and the packets from flits. The proposed NI microarchitecture is shown in Figure 2. The **Input Port** is composed of buffers that storage the flits before being processed. The **Depacketizer** assemblies the packets from the flits and extracts the message. In addition a CRC is calculated to ensure a correct assembly. If the packet is corrupted a NACK is generated, otherwise an ACK is sent. The **PE interface & Control Unit** controls the PE and the communication to and from the PE. It translates the message into commands to be expressed through the generic interface used by the PE. Besides, it generates the response messages, e.g. ACK/NACK, to the source. The **Packetizer** is the counterpart of the **Depacketizer**, it constructs packets from the messages from the PE or **the Control Unit**, and produces the flits to be stored in the **Output Port**. The **Ouput Port** is a buffer that storages the flits before sending them to the NoC. The attached router may be in congestion, so the importance of these buffers. Our NI is more complex than other design in the literature, e.g. [4]. While [4] is only a wrapper for an AMBA AHB interface, our NI can interpret and execute command packets, through a generic interface defined by the PE.

3. RESULTS

Table 1 presents the hardware summary of our NI + router proposal and the state of the art implementation in [5]. The routers and NI have a buffer depth of 4 flit in every VCs. The percentages represents the resources used w.r.t. the total available FPGA resources.

Router discussion. In order to make a fair comparison between the proposed and previous work [5], the used resources are normalized with respect to the number of ports and the number of VCs, provided by the compared design.

From Table 1 (row 7) it can be noticed that both approaches practically spend the same normal. In addition, it is a 20% faster than the compared implementation. The greater delay of the proposed approach is due to the pipelined architecture. This delay may be considered negligible for the targeted communication system design.

NI discussion. From Table 1 it can be observed that a NI requires almost twice the resources than the router. This has a serious impact in the NoC designs, considering that for every core attached to the network a resource quantity equivalent to three routers (router + NI) is consumed. This has not been discussed in depth but suggests that NoC architectures should be reviewed.

4. CONCLUSION

A NI + Router microarchitecture was presented. Implementation results show that the proposed router improves state of the art router design. Nonetheless, our study shows that the NI can consume practically twice the resources required by a router. Therefore, further research devoted to NI microarchitectures should be carried out for leveraging the network design of NoC-based communication systems.

5. REFERENCES

[1] O. Arnold, E. Matus, B. Noethen, M. Winter, T. Limberg, and G. Fettweis. Tomahawk: Parallelism and heterogeneity in communications signal processing mpsocs. *ACM Transactions on Embedded Computing Systems (TECS)*, 13(3s):107, 2014.

[2] W. J. Dally and B. P. Towles. *Principles and practices of interconnection networks*. Elsevier, 2004.

[3] B. I. Gea-Garcia, J. L. Vazquez-Avila, R. Sandoval-Arechiga, J. L. Pizano-Escalante, R. Parra-Michel, and M. Siller. Noc-based hardware function libraries for running multiple dsp algorithms. In *Reconfigurable Computing and FPGAs (ReConFig), 2013 International Conference on*, pages 1–6. IEEE, 2013.

[4] G. Luo-Feng, D. Gao-ming, Z. Duo-Li, G. Ming-Lun, H. Ning, and S. Yu-Kun. Design and performance evaluation of a 2d-mesh network on chip prototype using fpga. In *Circuits and Systems, 2008. APCCAS 2008. IEEE Asia Pacific Conference on*, pages 1264–1267. IEEE, 2008.

[5] A. Monemi, C. Y. Ooi, and M. N. Marsono. Low latency network-on-chip router microarchitecture using request masking technique. *International Journal of Reconfigurable Computing*, 2015:13, 2015.

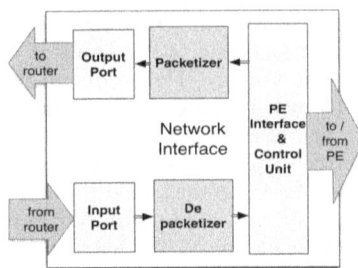

Figure 2: Network Interface microarchitecture for NoC-based Communication Systems.

On Data Plane Latency and *Pseudo*-TCP Congestion in Software-Defined Networking

Dongzhe Tai, Huichen Dai, Ting Zhang and Bin Liu
Department of Computer Science and Technology, Tsinghua University

Keywords

Software-Defined Networking (SDN); Latency; Pseudo-TCP Congestion

1. INTRODUCTION

Software-Defined Networking (SDN) decouples the network control and forwarding functions, enabling the programmability of network control and the abstraction of underlying infrastructure [2].

The packet forwarding delay is governed by 1) the interaction between the switch and the controller (*packet_in* and *flow_mod*) if there is no matching rule, 2) installing the rule, and 3) looking up the flow table on the data plane. The first two issues can be resolved by the *proactive* mode, which installs flow tables ahead of time for all the traffic, so that no *packet_in* will be generated for new flows. In commodity switches, hardware flow tables (typically TCAM) are widely used to achieve fast packet forwarding, but packets may also experience long lookup latencies when TCAM is updating.

Except for updates to hardware tables issued by the controller [1], in this work we find that TCAM insertions can also happen frequently from the switch itself with proactive mode. Because the TCAM size is generally limited, it can only hold a small number of forwarding rules that are used recently, and the rest ones are kept in SRAM. Flows misses in TCAM will insert the matching rules from SRAM into TCAM, or replace some victim entries if TCAM is full. TCAM generally stores high priority rules at low (preferred) memory addresses, if a high-priority rule is going to be inserted into TCAM, all the existing entries will shift by one entry to higher addresses to make room for this rule, keeping the priority order of all the rules. (A replacement will remove a victim entry at first, then repeat the insertion process.) Obviously, this insertion process is time-consuming. Extremely, if each rule is inserted in the *increasing priority* order, we need to shift all prior rules for each single insertion!

Our in-depth experiments indicate that the forwarding delay caused by TCAM insertions could be tremendous, because no lookup can be performed when TCAM is being up-dated. We observe that such long delay can harm the establishing of TCP connections in SDN, as well as the throughput due to long RTTs even after the connection has been established. This makes TCP feel that the network is severely congested while it is actually in good condition, so we refer to this phenomenon as *pseudo*-TCP congestion. This paper presents a thorough exploration of the latency introduced by TCAM insertions and how it affects the performance of TCP connections. Key highlights from our measurements are as follows: (1) When new flows are issued at a rate of 10 per second, and the TCAM has 3.5K rules installed, the packet forwarding latency in the proactive mode can reach 13.56s! (2) The RTT between TCP SYN and SYN-ACK can be incredibly large, making large proportions of TCP connections fail at the first attempt.

2. TCAM INSERTION LATENCY

This section measures the forwarding latency with the proactive mode. The forwarding delay mainly consists of the TCAM lookup delay and queueing delay due to TCAM insertions. Because the lookup delay is quite small, we measure the queueing delay to reflect the forwarding delay.

2.1 Measurement Methodology

Figure 1 shows our measurement setup. The switch in the experiment is PICA8 3297 (using Broadcom switch fabric); the host has two 1Gbps NICs connected to the switch data ports; the switch control port is connected to the controller (floodlight) running on another host. We run *libnet* to generate traffic on NIC and capture packets by *libpcap*. We send packets from NIC A to NIC B through the switch, packet timestamps at both NICs are recorded by libpacp, and the time difference is the forwarding latency that we care about.

Obviously, TCAM insertion delay can be affected by 1) the priority of the to-be-inserted rules and 2) the load the TCAM. Therefore, we assign three patterns of rule priorities to new arriving flows: *increasing priority*, *decreasing priority* and *same priority*. Each pattern inserts rules with *increasing priority*, *decreasing priority* and *same priority* into TCAM. For the *increasing priority* pattern, each rule insertion requires all the rules already in TCAM to shift by one entry to the higher addresses, and this rule is placed at the lowest address. For the *decreasing priority* and *same priority* patterns, new rules can be *appended* to existing rules in TCAM. Meanwhile, the load of TCAM decides the number of entries to be shifted thus also affecting the insertion latency. Consequently, different experiments that cover three rule priority patterns and different TCAM loads are conducted.

2.2 Experimental Results

We issue 100 new flows from NIC A to NIC B (with proactive mode) at the rate of 10 flows per second. Our configuration will lead them to TCAM misses so that corresponding rules will be inserted from SRAM into TCAM.

This work is sponsored by NSFC (61373143, 61432009), 863 project (2013AA013502), the Specialized Research Fund for the Doctoral Program of Higher Education of China (20131019172), China Postdoctoral Science Foundation (No. 2015T80089) and Jiangsu Future Networks Innovation Institute: Prospective Research Projection Future Networks (No. BY2013095-1-03).

ANCS'16 March 17–18, 2016, Santa Clara, CA, USA

© 2016 Copyright held by the owner/author(s).

ACM ISBN 978-1-4503-4183-7/16/03.

DOI: http://dx.doi.org/10.1145/2881025.2889482

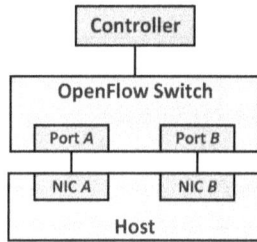

Figure 1: Measurement setup

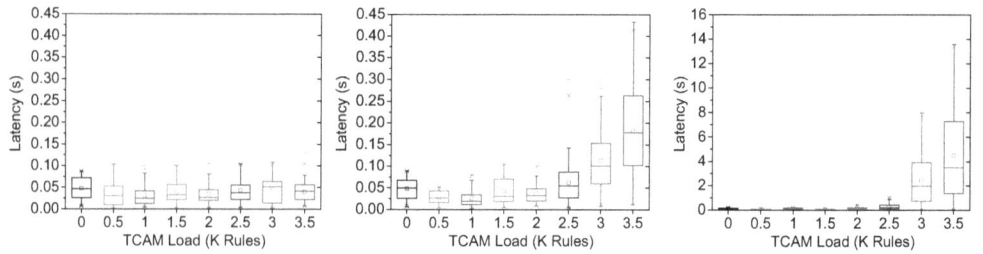

(a) same priority   (b) decreasing priority   (c) increasing priority

Figure 2: The forwarding delay, new flow rate 10/s, 100 flows for each TCAM load.

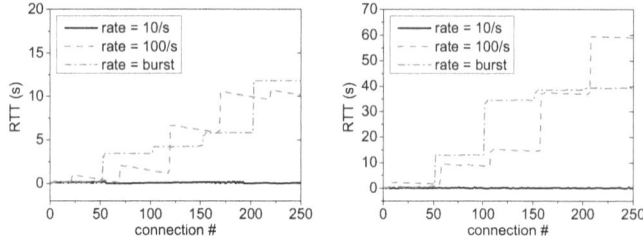

(a) TCAM load = 0.5K rules   (b) TCAM load = 2K rules

Figure 3: RTT between SYN and SYN-ACK.

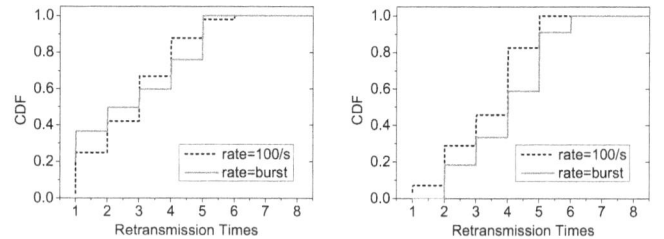

(a) TCAM load = 2K rules   (b) TCAM load = 3.5K rules

Figure 4: CDF of Retransmission Times.

To understand the impact of table load, prior to new flows, we already have R rules installed in the TCAM by background traffic, where R ranges from 0 to 3.5K with a step of 0.5K. Figure 2 presents the measurement results by box chart, where each subfigure corresponds to a priority pattern. Figures 2a and 2b reveal that *same priority* and *decreasing priority* have comparable low forwarding latency, though there is an increase for the *decreasing priority* as TCAM load gets heavier. However, Figure 2c shows that the delay for *increasing priority* are significantly larger, and it augments dramatically as the TCAM load increases. The largest latency reaches 13.56s when TCAM has 3.5K rules!

3. PSEUDO-TCP CONGESTION

The long forwarding latency may lead to timeouts, thus bringing negative impacts on TCP, mainly in two aspects: 1) making TCP connection establishment difficult, 2) low transmission efficiency after connection establishment. Both cases can happen even when the network is in good condition, leading to the *Pseudo*-TCP congestion problem.

3.1 TCP Establishment

After the TCP SYN packet is sent out, the host expects the SYN-ACK packet to return within the RTO (RTT<RTO). (RTO is initialized to 6s in the three-way handshake.) We try to establish TCP connections between NIC A and NIC B in Figure 1, and measure the RTT between the TCP SYN and SYN-ACK messages at different new connection rates and different TCAM loads (with proactive mode). For each configuration, 250 connections are issued in total. Figure 3 presents the RTT with the *increasing priority* pattern[1], revealing that it could be incredibly large with the increase of TCAM load and new connection rate[2]. Such large RTT make 35% TCP connections fail at the first attempt when the TCAM load is 0.5K, and 60% when the load is 2K.

---

[1] Note that a TCP connection consists of two unidirectional flows, all the new flows are assigned rules with *increasing priority*.

[2] Some RTT in Figure 3a degrades a little bit because TCAM insertions are processed in a batch, connections arrive later may have shorter queueing time.

3.2 TCP Transmission

After a TCP connection is established, rules of the two-unidirectional flows have been loaded into TCAM. However, there can still be large RTTs even the matching rules are present in TCAM, because maybe other rules is being inserted into TCAM, so packets can only wait for TCAM to finish the insertion. Another possibility is the matching rule has been evicted from TCAM before the next packet arrives, which needs to insert the rule into TCAM again. Large RTT will cause timeouts and then packet retransmissions, which hinders the cwnd from increasing rapidly, failing to achieve high transmission throughput. In this experiment, we measure how many retransmissions are required before the first data packet (after the TCP connection is established) is successfully acknowledged. Figure 4 presents the CDF of the retransmission times with different new connection rates and TCAM loads, which shows that 5 to 6 retransmissions may be required to successfully deliver a packet! This will definitely lead to poor TCP throughput, meaning that long latency can bring remarkable negative impacts on TCP.

4. CONCLUSION

This paper dissects the source of forwarding latency on the data plane in proactive SDN, and reveals that TCAM insertions with increasing priority can lead to incredibly large forwarding delay. As far as we know, this is the first work that identifies the pseudo-TCP congestion problem caused by long data plane latency. Preliminary experimental results on forwarding delay and TCP performance are presented.

5. REFERENCES

[1] K. He, J. Khalid, A. Gember-Jacobson, S. Das, C. Prakash, A. Akella, L. E. Li, and M. Thottan. Measuring control plane latency in sdn-enabled switches. In *Proceedings of the ACM SOSR'15*, pages 25:1–25:6, 2015.

[2] N. McKeown, T. Anderson, H. Balakrishnan, G. Parulkar, L. Peterson, J. Rexford, S. Shenker, and J. Turner. Openflow: Enabling innovation in campus networks. *SIGCOMM Comput. Commun. Rev.*, 38(2):69–74, Mar. 2008.

Evaluating Information-Centric Networks in Disconnected, Intermittent, and Low-Bandwidth Environments

Thiago Teixeira
University of Massachusetts Amherst
151 Holdsworth Way
Amherst, Massachusetts
tteixeira@umass.edu

Michael Zink
University of Massachusetts Amherst
151 Holdsworth Way
Amherst, Massachusetts
mzink@cas.umass.edu

ABSTRACT

This paper studies information dissemination in wireless ad hoc networks, using standard routing protocols, such as OLSR, as well as Information-Centric Networking. We performed simulations using NS-3 and ndnSIM with different node counts and transport protocols. Our simulations show that TCP performs better in lower hop count scenarios, while NDN performs better in higher hop count scenarios.

Keywords

Information-Centric Networks; Mobile Ad hoc Networks

1. INTRODUCTION

In Mobile Ad hoc Networks (MANETs), nodes frequently experience disruptions and intermittent connectivity due to the inherent nature of the network, as nodes move in and out of communication range. Resource limitation caused by, e.g., battery operated radios with limited transmission power result in nodes transmitting with lower bandwidth to achieve a higher communication range. Mobile networks of such characteristics are called Disconnected, Intermittent, Low-bandwidth (DIL), in which the dissemination of information from sender to destination is quite challenging.

Existing routing protocols, such as Optimized Link-State Routing (OLSR) [1], aim to reduce the flooding of message in MANETs by selecting specific nodes, called multipoint relays (MPRs), to re-broadcast data packets, reducing collisions in the wireless channel. However, when nodes go out of communication range, thus, disrupting the end-to-end paths, intermediate nodes should take a store and forward approach in an attempt to push the content close to the user.

In a new approach, called Information-Centric Networking (ICNs) [4], content is addressed by its name, and not an IP address. The communication is started by the consumer by sending out an Interest packet, indicating the desired name of the content. The Interest packet is relayed until reaching the content source or a router with a cached version of the data. The data chunks then follow the breadcrumbs back

to the consumer, leaving cached copies along the path. This dynamic in-network caching allows other nodes to retrieve the same content even when the source is no longer available.

Because of in-network caching, ICNs are specially interesting in ad hoc scenarios in which the network tends to partition. In this paper, we present a preliminary evaluation of a MANET routing protocol and ICN.

2. METHOD

In this work, we evaluate the performance of TCP and UDP using OLSR as routing protocol for wireless ad hoc networks. The evaluation is done via simulations using NS-3 [6] and the Flow Monitor tool [3].

To simulate ICN, we use the Named-Data Networking simulator ndnSIM [5]. However, the current version of ndnSIM (ver. 2.1) does not support wireless multi-hop communication, as the Interest needs to be re-broadcast on the same face it was received from. Therefore, we use a modified forwarding strategy that allows nodes to re-broadcast Interests [2]. This strategy controls flooding with a timer-based suppression of re-broadcasts, without keeping information about its neighbor nodes. The basic idea is that nodes use a random defer timer to listen to the wireless channel, refraining from re-broadcasting packets if they overhear them. In our simulations, we explore different values of the defer timer.

2.1 Simulation Scenario

For simulating the scenarios, we used a line topology where each node in the network can only communicate with its immediate neighbors (i.e. node 3 sees only nodes 2 and 4). We varied the node count from two up to twelve nodes, with a few exceptions, as shown in Table 1. The consumer and producer are always on opposite ends of the topology. In one case, we deployed two consumers and two producers exchanging information at the same time to increase the channel utilization and analyze bi-directional traffic scenarios.

The random defer timer in NDN is controlled by the defer window size, as described in [2]. Figure 1 shows different window sizes, where in NDN-255 the nodes wait a longer time than NDN-63 before re-broadcasting the packets.

Each node is equipped with an 802.11b interface, configured to 1 Mbps to reflect a low-bandwidth scenario.

3. RESULTS

Figure 1 shows the average delay to retrieve one data packet for different node counts. We can split our analysis into two parts. First, looking at the left part of the

ANCS '16 March 17-18, 2016, Santa Clara, CA, USA

© 2016 Copyright held by the owner/author(s).

ACM ISBN 978-1-4503-4183-7/16/03.

DOI: http://dx.doi.org/10.1145/2881025.2889483

Table 1: Simulation parameters

Category	Parameter	TCP/UDP	ICN
Application layer	Content store size	1000 packets	
	Data payload	1040 bytes	
In-network caching	Content store size	0	100 chunks
Wireless media	Propagation model	Friis	
	Protocol	IEEE 802.11b DSSS	
	Channel capacity	1 Mbps	
	Rx sensitivity	-80 dBm	
	Tx power	5 dBm	
Node layout	Line topology	2,3,4,5,7,9, and 12	
Consumer Application	Constant bit rate	On/Off, Bulk	10 Interest per second
Transport Layer		TCP, UDP	NDN
NDN defer window size		N/A	63, 127, and 255

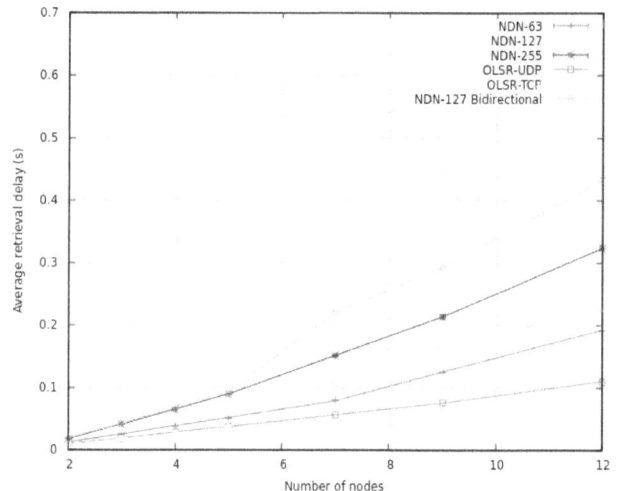

Figure 1: Average data retrieval delay per node for different protocols

graph, we notice that the fewer number of hops between the consumer and the producer, which leads to a fewer number of collisions, is not sufficient to produce a large number of retransmissions. This leads to a linear increase in delay as the node count increases. Thus, NDN does not benefit from caching, performing worse than its counterparts regardless of the defer window size. We attribute this to the fact that, for every data chunk, the consumer has to send an Interest request to the producer, therefore, having a higher overhead than TCP and UDP.

Second, for the right half of the graph (≥ 7 nodes) the higher hop count leads to more traffic and, thus, collisions in the wireless channel, forcing the nodes to re-transmit packets more often. Due to the in-network caching of ICN lost data can potentially be retransmitted from any intermediate node, thus, making retransmissions more efficient, especially if the retransmitted data originate from caches close to the sink.

Since UDP is not a reliable protocol, we observe packet losses in the 7, 9, and 12 node cases, yielding a file completion rate of 75.9%, 82.6%, and 70.4%, respectively. For the TCP case, retransmissions starting to take a toll on the 7-node case, making its performance worse than NDN-63 and NDN-127, and worse than NDN-255 after the 9-node case. This is due to the dynamic caching of the NDN protocol that allows more reliable communication, achieving 100% of file completion in all cases.

Furthermore, we simulated a bidirectional case where the end-point nodes are both consumers and producers, increasing the link utilization. This scenario aims to study the behavior of the aforementioned protocols in situations with higher collisions. As can be seen from NDN-127 Bidirectional, higher link utilization leads to a higher delay.

4. CONCLUSIONS AND FUTURE WORK

In this work, we investigated the use of information-centric networks in MANETs, drawing comparison with different transport and routing protocols. We used a well-known network simulator to evaluate different scenarios, where we observed that TCP performs better than NDN when the hop count is small. NDN, due to dynamic caching, is able to perform better than TCP when the hop count is higher. In future work, we plan to study mobility, different cache sizes, and more scenarios with multiple consumers and producers.

5. ACKNOWLEDGMENTS

The authors would like to thank Marica Amadeo from the Mediterranean University of Reggio Calabria for providing technical support for this work. The first author is supported by National Council for the Improvement of Higher Education (CAPES), Brazil. Partially funded by ONR contract number N00014-15-C-0122. Views presented are those of authors alone.

6. REFERENCES

[1] Optimized link state routing protocol (olsr), 2003.

[2] M. Amadeo, C. Campolo, and A. Molinaro. Forwarding strategies in named data wireless ad hoc networks: Design and evaluation. *Journal of Network and Computer Applications*, 50:148 – 158, 2015.

[3] G. Carneiro, M. Ricardo, and P. Fortuna. Flowmonitor - a network monitoring framework for the network simulator 3 (ns-3). In *Proceedings of ICST NSTools 2009*, Pisa, Italy, October 2009.

[4] V. Jacobson, D. K. Smetters, J. D. Thornton, M. F. Plass, N. H. Briggs, and R. L. Braynard. Networking named content. In *Proceedings of the 5th International Conference on Emerging Networking Experiments and Technologies*, CoNEXT '09, pages 1–12, New York, NY, USA, 2009. ACM.

[5] S. Mastorakis, A. Afanasyev, I. Moiseenko, and L. Zhang. ndnSIM 2.0: A new version of the NDN simulator for NS-3. Technical Report NDN-0028, NDN, January 2015.

[6] NS-3. https://www.nsnam.org. [Online; accessed 17-January-2016].

Enterprise LTE and WiFi Interworking System and A Proposed Network Selection Solution

Lina Xu, Junqing Xie, Xunteng Xu, Shuai Wang
Networking and Mobility Lab, Hewlett Packard Labs
{linax, jun-qing.xie, xunteng.xu, shuai.wang}@hpe.com

ABSTRACT

With a bandwidth reservation mechanism, we propose that LTE can assist existing WiFi networks to improve the Quality of Experience (QoE) of wireless communication in enterprise and meanwhile increase the available spectrum. To address the associated network selection problem between WiFi and LTE, in this paper based on the 3GPP standard Access Network Discovery and Selection Function (ANDSF) framework, a context-aware solution named Extended Dynamic Enterprise ANDSF (EDE-ANDSF) is presented. It can select interfaces according to real time network conditions and cater for specific enterprise requirements.

Keywords

Eenterprise netowrk, LTE, WiFi, context-aware, ANDSF

1. INTRODUCTION

WiFi communication in enterprise encounters the following problems in terms of Quality of Experience (QoE): 1) It takes a long time for UEs to establish connections to a heavily loaded Access Point (AP). 2) Lacking of reservation on network bandwidth, a WiFi connection may be occasionally suspended due to the increasing data traffic. The QoE of bandwidth sensitive applications is hard to be guaranteed. 3) It is difficult to customize users' preference on network usage. In order to improve the current wireless communication quality in enterprise, we propose that the LTE technologies can be applied. However, LTE alone cannot meet the increasing data usage demand. Based on the analysis on the WiFi data collected during the period from May 2014 to Jan 2015 in HP Labs, the total amount of monthly data usage had tripled with the number of monthly users remaining at the same level. Therefore in order to meet the enterprise requirements for both QoE and data throughput, a hybrid infrastructure combining LTE and WiFi is preferred.

In such an integrated network, how to select between the two network interfaces is challenging. 3GPP has introduced the Access Network Discovery and Selection Function

ANCS '16 March 17-18, 2016, Santa Clara, CA, USA

© 2016 Copyright held by the owner/author(s).

ACM ISBN 978-1-4503-4183-7/16/03.

DOI: http://dx.doi.org/10.1145/2881025.2889476

(ANDSF) framework [1], which provides a series of policies and regulations on network accessing that are applicable in different scenarios. Several theoretical alternative approaches based on ANDSF [2] [3] were proposed. In industrial research, various implementations also were developed, for example, CnE by Qualcomm [4], Smart Access Manager (SAM) by InterDigital [5], OpenEPC by FOKUS [6], etc. All the above approaches were conceived from the operators' perspective. A network selection solution specialized for enterprise use is still missing because: 1) Due to the inconstancy of WiFi network conditions, user experience highly depends on the real time information. 2) Owing to the diversity of enterprise requirements, a unified solution can hardly address the dynamic issues, such as employee roles.

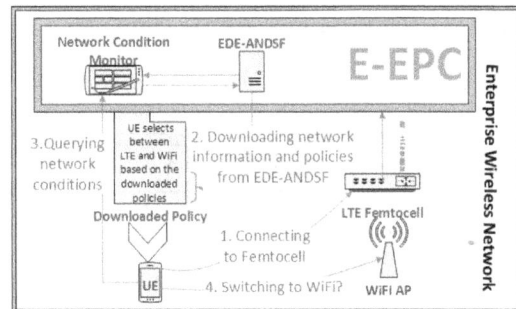

Figure 1: Enterprise LTE and WiFi Network.

2. THE INTERWORKING SYSTEM AND EDE-ANDSF

The enterprise LTE network is composed with enterprise deployed LTE Femtocells and Enterprise Evolved Packet Core (E-EPC) including components like ANDSF, Packet Data Network (PDN) gateway, Serving Gateway, AAA Server, etc. It coexists with the current WiFi network, as shown in Figure 1. All the Femtocells and WiFi Access Points (APs) are connected to the PDN gateway in E-EPC. When a user enters the enterprise campus, firstly the UE will roam from the mobile network to the enterprise LTE. Once being authorized by the E-EPC, it will download the ANDSF policies and then be proceeded to the preferred WiFi network.

In order to solve the network selection problem, based on 3GPP ANDSF Rel.12, our Extended Dynamic Enterprise ANDSF (EDE-ANDSF) is proposed to replace the current ANDSF entity in the E-EPC. Lacking of bandwidth reservation scheme, we have discovered that in WiFi network one

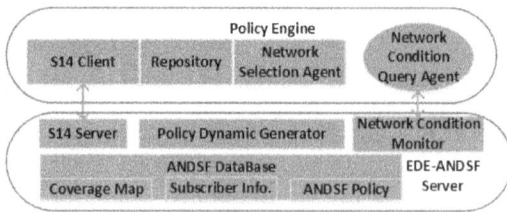

Figure 2: EDE-ANDSF System Architecture.

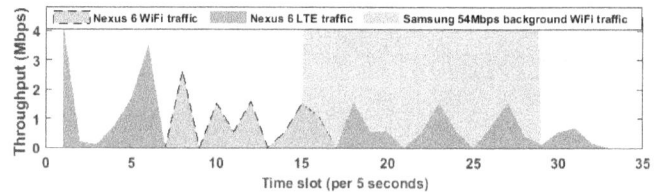

Figure 3: Youtube Traffic Managed by EDE-ANDSF.

user's behaviour may have a significant impact on the others that are connecting to the same AP. The QoE of bandwidth/delay sensitive applications, such as video streaming, varies unpredictably over WiFi connections. With EDE-ANDSF, the UEs can switch between LTE and WiFi in line with the real time network conditions. Also EDE-ANDSF can tailor the network usages to cater for the enterprise requirements. Since WiFi resource is cost efficient and its theoretical maximal download speed can be 10 times faster than LTE, the EDE-ANDSF policies defines that most employees will be prioritized to use WiFi network. As LTE is a highly reliable but relevantly expensive resource, it is used when the WiFi network is congested, serving as a bandwidth backup for WiFi. However, for some specific users, reliable and stable wireless connection is critical. For example, users involved in customer care, QoE for live video conference is highly prioritized in enterprise and should use LTE always. The implementation of EDE-ANDSF is illustrated in Figure 2, including the server part and the client part.

In the server end, the ANDSF database maintains information such as the network coverage map, user subscriptions and ANDSF polices. Policy Dynamic Generator can read data from the database and generate XML formatted policies. The core network is enhanced with a new component called Network Condition Monitor (NetCoM) that can detect the WiFi APs' load. This information regarded as network conditions, can be queried by the UEs directly. At the UE end, a component, referred as Policy Engine can fetch ANDSF policies from the server through the S14 interface. Network Querying Agent periodically queries NetCoM about WiFi conditions. The policies and network information are maintained in Repository. Network Selection Agent can select the best connection among the available ones based on the policies, Radio Signal Strength (RSS) and real time network conditions. It instructs the UE to either remain on the current connection or switch interface.

3. RESULTS

To evaluate the proposed solution, a hybrid network with one ip.access LTE Femtocell, one HP E-MSM 460 Hotspot2.0 AP and a virtual Enterprise Evolved Packet Core (E-EPC) was deployed as presented in Figure 1. The E-EPC network was extended from OpenEPC. EDE-ANDSF defines the following policies in a decreasing order by their rule priorities. Policy No.1: Delay sensitive usages, such as video streaming, are prioritized to use WiFi if its condition is good. Policy No.2: When the WiFi quality is poor, such usages will choose the second preferred network—LTE over WiFi. Policy No.3: The delay sensitive usages from VIP users are maintained on LTE network.

We performed an experiment with Youtube HD video

streaming on a Nexus 6 phone in this network and the results are shown in Figure 3. Since the Nexus 6 was authorized through LTE, its data transmission started over a LTE connection. Then the UE detected that the current WiFi condition was good, it switched the flow from LTE to WiFi according Policy No.1. At time slot 15, the server started to inject heavy WiFi downlink traffic to another phone (Samsung) through iPerf at a data rate of 54 Mbps. The WiFi network immediately became congested. When Nexus 6 detected this change, it realized that Policy No.1 no longer held and Policy No.2 should be applied. Therefore it switched its Youtube streaming flow to LTE, as shown in the shadow area. As mentioned before, for some specific users, having reserved bandwidth is more important than using free and possible high speed WiFi. By Policy No.3, our experimental results shows that the throughput of such users was protected from WiFi congestions. This experiment indicates that a UE can select networks based on the EDE-ANDSF policies and the real time network conditions.

4. CONCLUSION

This paper has stated that the WiFi and LTE interworking system can improve the wireless communication QoE in enterprise and increase the potential bandwidth. The proposed EDE-ANDSF can detect the dynamic changes in WiFi network in order to determine which interface the UEs should select. It can also be tailored for specialized enterprise requirements. Furthermore, the standards-compatible EDE-ANDSF policies are extensible for new features and functionalities.

5. REFERENCES

[1] 3GPP Access Network Discovery and Selection Function (ANDSF) Management Object (MO). http://www.3gpp.org/dynareport/24312.htm.

[2] Young Min Kwon, Jun Suk Kim, Jaheon Gu, and Min Young Chung. Andsf-based congestion control procedure in heterogeneous networks. Jan 2013.

[3] M. Nahas, M. Mjalled, Z. Zohbi, Z. Merhi, and M. Ghantous. Enhancing lte - wifi interoperability using context aware criteria for handover decision. In ICM, Dec 2013.

[4] Qualcomm Connectivity Engine. A 3g/lte wi-fi offload framework: Connectivity engine (cne) to manage inter-system radio connections and applications.

[5] InterDigital Smart Access Manage (SAM). http://www.interdigital.com.

[6] Fraunhofer FOKUS OpenEPC Release 6. http://www.openepc.com.

Author Index